AF573819

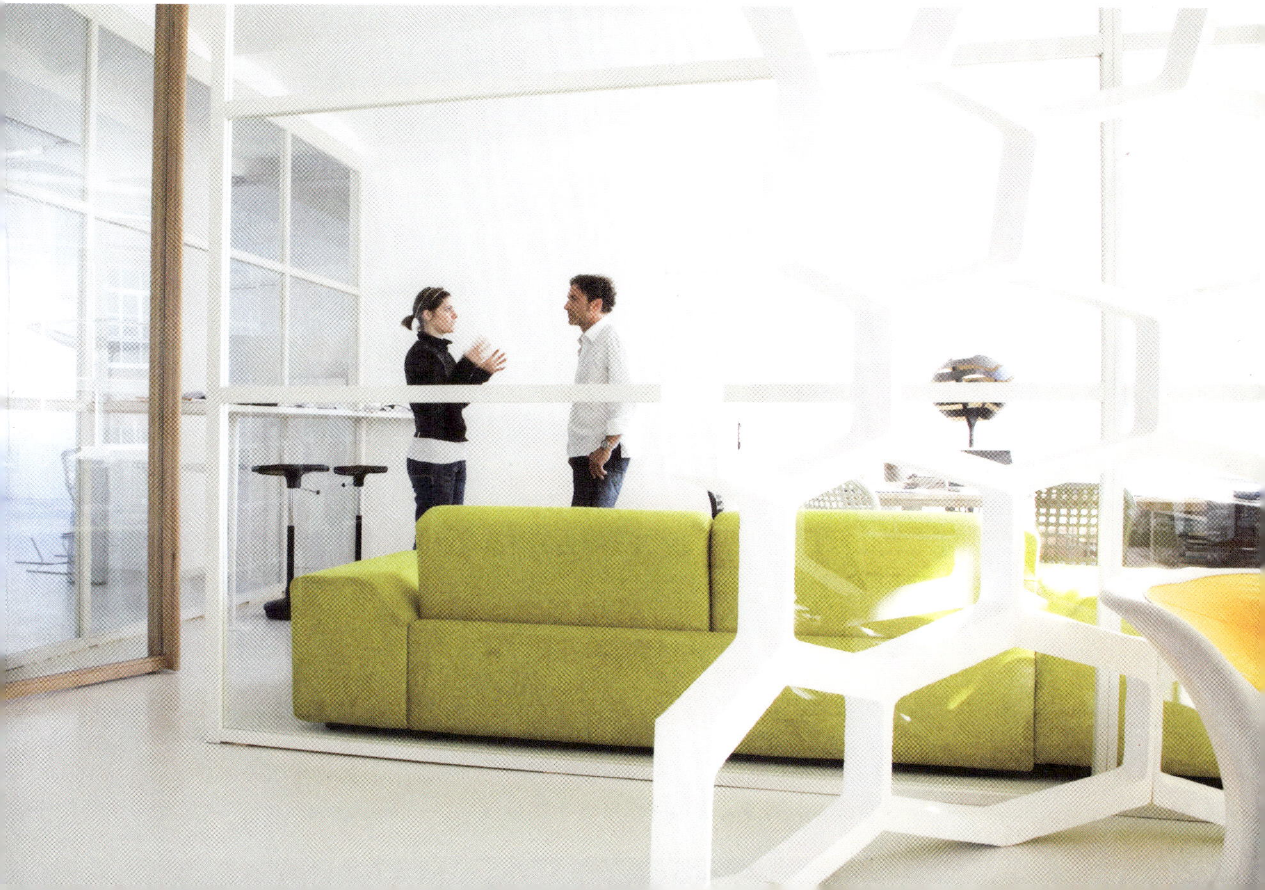

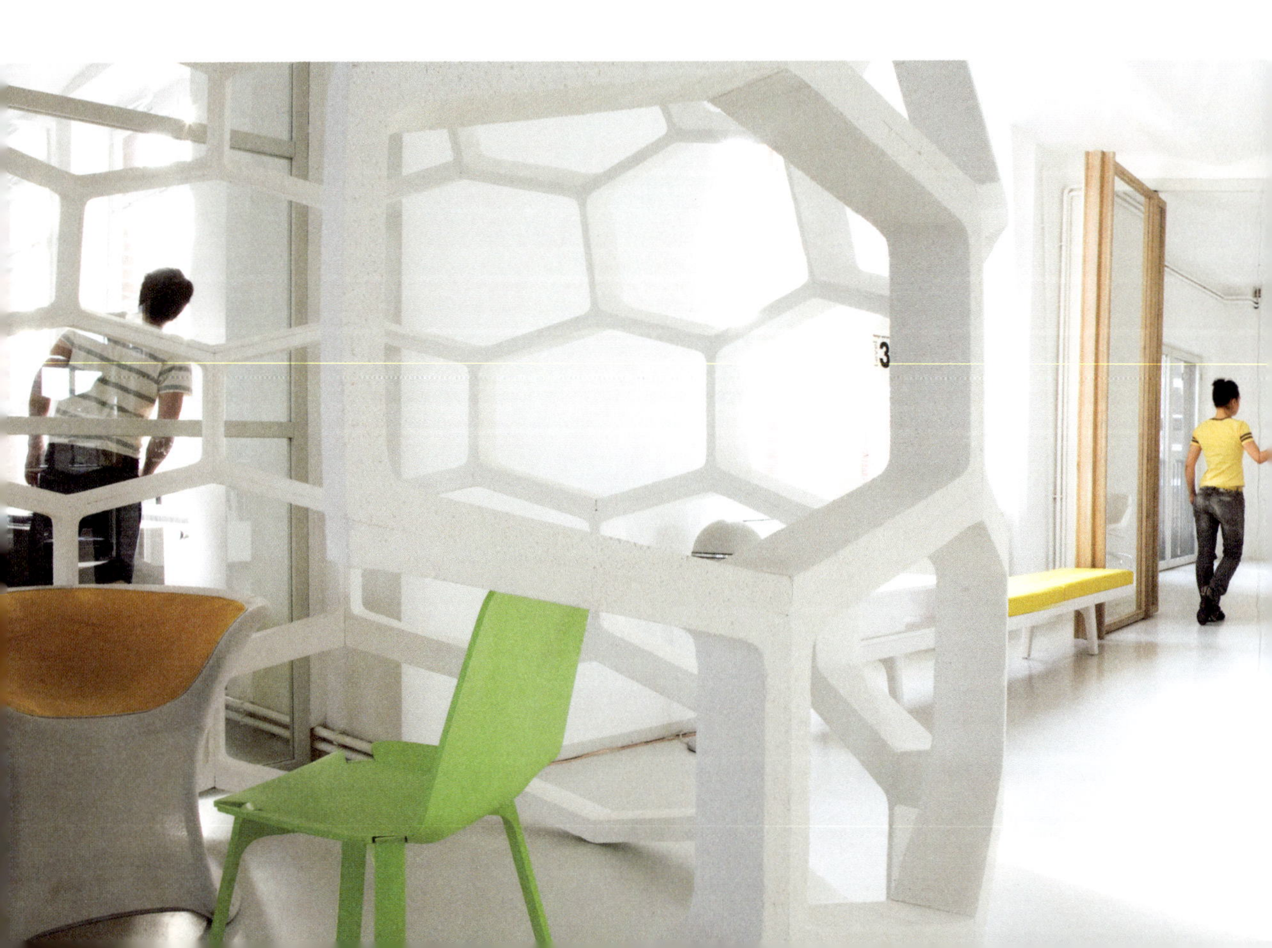

werner aisslinger

⏭ FAST FORWARD

With an introduction by Volker Albus

Mit einer Einführung von Volker Albus

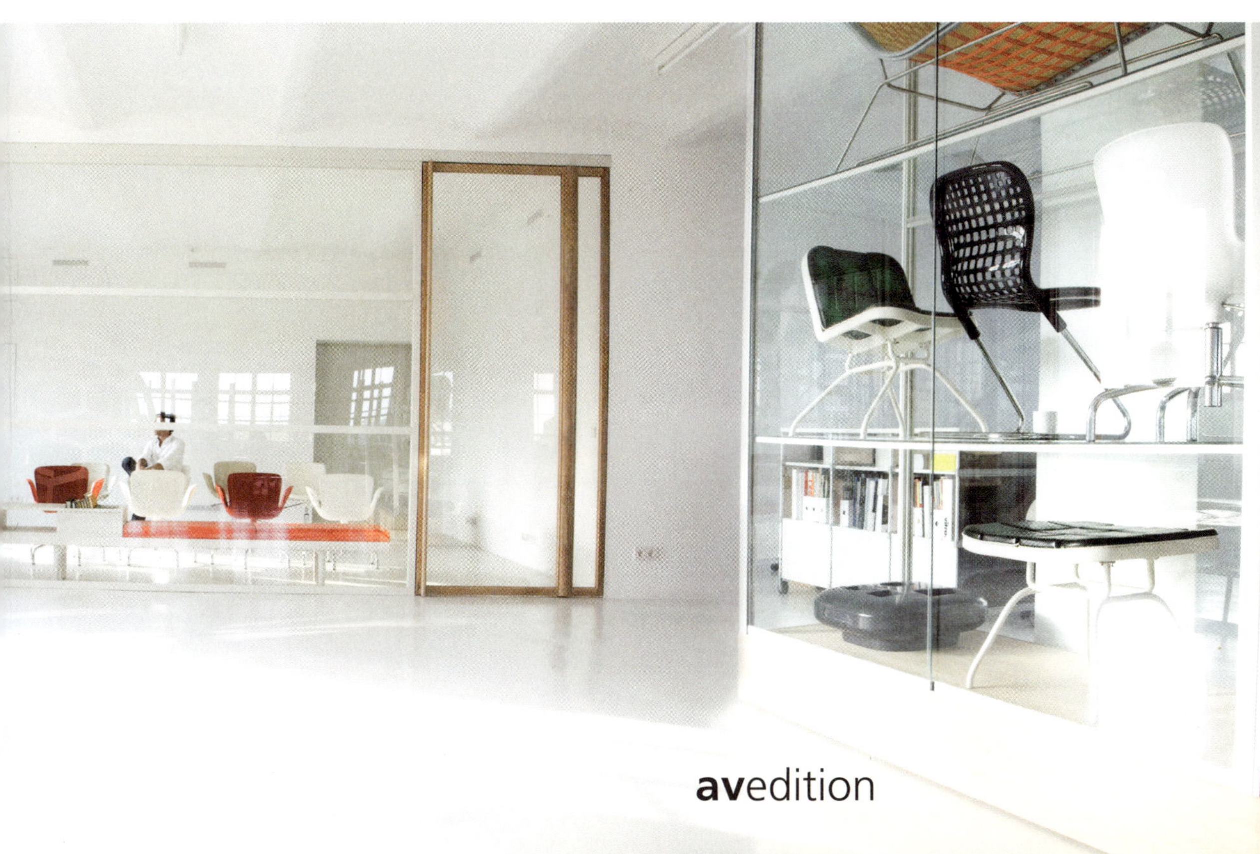

avedition

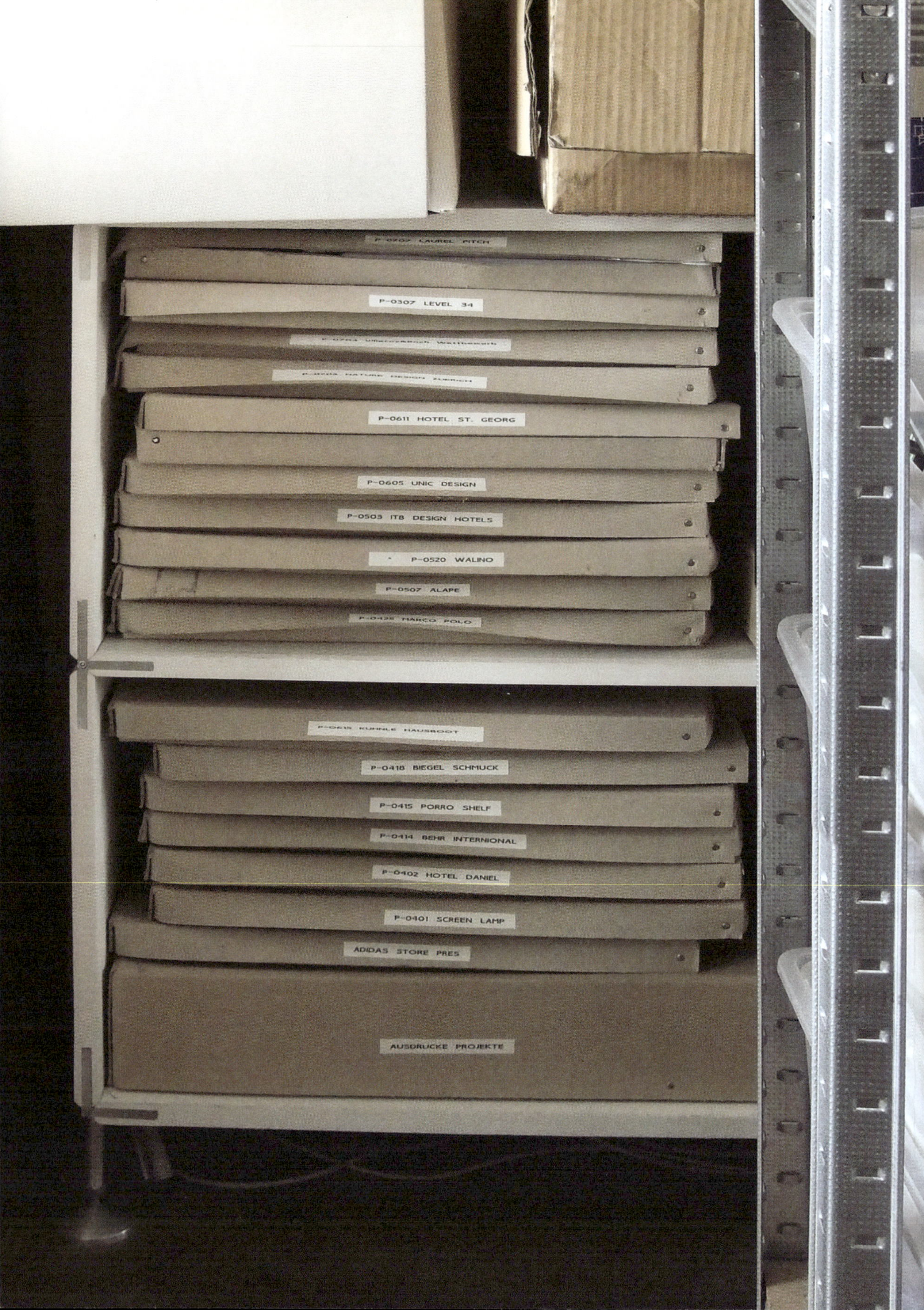
P-0307 LEVEL 34
P-0611 HOTEL ST. GEORG
P-0605 UNIC DESIGN
P-0503 ITB DESIGN HOTELS
P-0520 WALINO
P-0507 ALAPE
P-0418 BIEGEL SCHMUCK
P-0415 PORRO SHELF
P-0414 BEHR INTERNIONAL
P-0402 HOTEL DANIEL
P-0401 SCREEN LAMP
ADIDAS STORE PRES
AUSDRUCKE PROJEKTE

FAST FORWARD!

Introduction by Volker Albus

⏭ When, in the not-too-distant future, the first publications begin to take a retrospective look at design at the end of the 20th century and beginning of the 21st, prophetic capabilities are unnecessary to predict that the work of Werner Aisslinger will be a prime focus of attention. It can be foreseen with even more certainty that not a few chroniclers of the past will give in to the temptation to reduce his work to several very specific formal characteristics. Admittedly, there is a danger of picking out a recurring feature and elevating it to the status of the quintessential Aisslinger constant, for instance a feature extracted from views of the Loft cube, the structure of the Soft lounger or – to take an example from the area of industrial design – the basic geometrical shape of the new rotating switch for Berker. That would, of course, not be completely off the mark and many a "quick course in design at the turn of the century" will highlight precisely this evident attribute before listing the relevant "evidence" and proceeding to the next protagonist in the drama of his work. This would pinpoint a significant aspect of Aisslinger's design but would certainly not identify the real underlying qualities. The latter are not just extremely varied in their scope but can only be explored by looking beyond the supposedly one outstanding feature and considering Aisslinger's creative work from the more down-to-earth points of view of sober industrial design. And these, as is known, tend to be hidden beneath and behind impressions that are absorbed in passing and therefore reflexively abstracted.

In other words, in order to present Werner Aisslinger's work in the worthy manner it deserves, it is absolutely essential to consider the construction and configuration, the material and technical, the typological and conventional potential of his furniture and lamps as well as the systems he developed and his interiors – in short the entire nature of his contributions to contemporary design.

Endless Shelf: Standard shelf However, a chronological approach should be adopted as, at the very beginning of his work as a self-employed designer, Aisslinger's endless shelf demonstrated his exceptional ability not only to deal with the mechanical details independently but also to cleverly incorporate them in a functional holistic concept.

A fundamental and simultaneously modular element of this endless shelf is a square MDF panel approximately 38 x 38 cm in size and around 2 cm thick with 6 cm-deep notches at the corners. Depending on where the panels are positioned in the overall structure, cruciform, T-shaped or

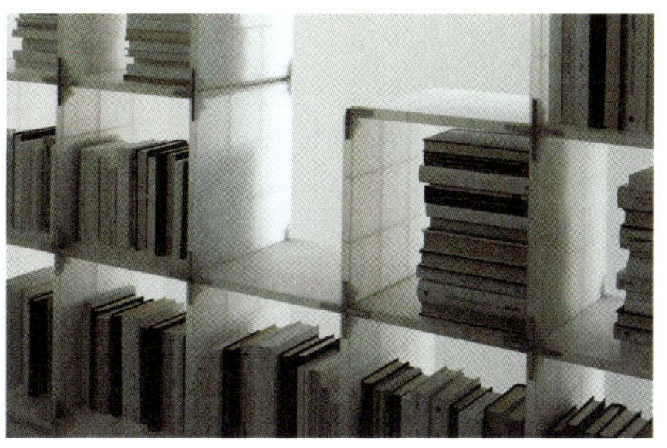

angular aluminium inserts are fitted into these notches and matched with a counterpart on the other side. The final configuration is then entirely up to the user because, apart from this cube, which is made of four panels and is open on two opposite sides, there are no further limitations in respect of the shelf system's actual structure – neither in terms of the number of cubes that can be joined together as desired nor the final shape of the item of furniture in question. Accordingly, the attributive name of the system only partially pinpoints its advantages given that panels can be added to create an endless amorphous row. This means that the user can make the shelf system into a staircase, a kind of standalone chamber or a somehow "abstract" geometrical statement that makes it stand out from its surroundings. Not many systems can do this.

But not only the functional-cum-utilitarian requirements for such furniture are satisfied to perfection; very basic hard criteria such as stability and a renunciation – especially essential for a shelf system – of what is stylistically typical of the time are more than fulfilled. With his endless shelf, Werner Aisslinger achieved a success granted to only a very few designers: the design and complete development of a piece of furniture that can only be adequately described with the attribute "standard".

Juli Chair and Technogel: Material curiosity There are probably not many designers who do not interpret the achievement of such a level as motivation to develop supplementary variations and additions for this system. The reason is that, strictly speaking, this endless shelf is more like a skeleton, a kind of unfinished grid pattern that can be extended and completed without any particular restrictions. And it does not take much imagination to create cupboards and drawers and develop this purely structural element into a veritable combination wall unit – not to mention the possible variability of scale of the final piece of furniture.

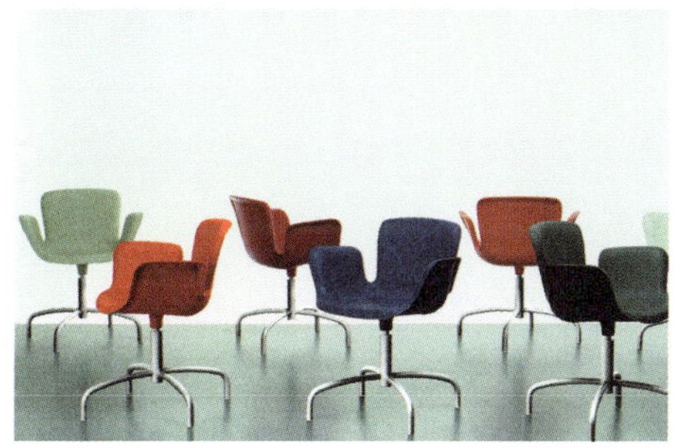

Such supplementary details, however, are not Werner Aisslinger's thing. Not because they don't particularly interest him but simply due to the fact that something else interests him far more. At this time, i.e. from the middle of the 1990s onwards, he focussed intensively on materials that, at least in terms of furniture design, were new, and on the associated methods of manufacture. The first result of his work at the time was the juli chair developed for Cappellini, an integral moulded construction made of polyurethane integral foam.

This manufacturing method had previously been used primarily in the production of components for the interior of cars – e.g. for steering wheels – but, due to the stable yet yielding consistency of the material, was also ideally suited for the organic design of seating furniture.

In this case, it is still possible to note a certain similarity between the original use and the resulting transformation but the gel furniture collection created shortly after the juli chair must be unreservedly accorded the status of a comprehensive innovation. Technogel, the material used, was known solely from of its use in medical devices and sporting equipment but definitely not in product design. Nonetheless, it was not so much this "exotic" relationship – which expressively poled "furniture artists" like to exploit – but the very specific physical qualities that inspired Aisslinger to work with Technogel. Put in simple terms, this synthetic material based on polyurethane behaves very much like a liquid, i.e. the surface which is subjected to a load is not compressed and thus solidified but is merely "displaced" and then "flows" back to its original shape once the load has been removed. The advantage, e.g. for upholstered furniture, is evident: Where approximately 5 cm of conventional upholstery material is needed in order to achieve a certain degree of yield, 1 cm of this material is enough to achieve exactly the same effect. At first glance, this may not sound like much – 4 cm more or less: Who cares? For something such as upholstery which is classically meant to be "thick", however, such a form of compression could set in motion a completely new understanding of design.

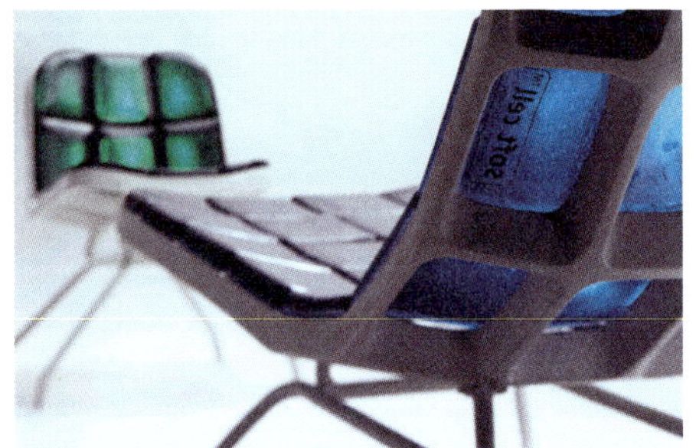

However, we do not want to conceal the fact that, from an economic point of view, the series-produced models for Cappellini and Zanotta resulting from a gel experiment euphorically celebrated by specialists in the field lagged far behind the success in the media. One decisive reason was probably the price or at least the price generally associated with a material such as "plastic" by the public, i.e. a product to be bought on the discount level. In such a case, it is irrelevant whether an article is a work of contemporary design that is made of an exceptional material and, moreover, a highly developed one: plastic is plastic, i.e. practical, cheap and washable!

In any case, the prototype series of the gel furniture as well as its serial development was of decisive importance for Werner Aisslinger in that it impressively demonstrated his ability to create a diametrically opposed species of furniture after such a striking design as the endless shelf. He not only developed a novel independent design but also re-interpreted other basic determinants such as the material nature of the gel in order to use it innovatively and creatively in a new product at that time.

Level 34: Good bye Good Old Office That this multi-facetted competence was not restricted to an unconventional approach to the clearly defined typology of single items of furniture is demonstrated in the example of the level 34 project, a "multifunctional furniture range" for Vitra from the year 2004. This range of furniture is a kit made up of different parts that can be combined in different ways to build an installation-like furniture hybrid, i.e. not the usual selection of single furniture items whose appearance is more or less matching and can be made into a "'set". In this sense, it would be possible to speak of an inversely created range, given that the basic idea is not to distribute the parts necessary for individual needs in different places throughout the room but, on the contrary. to intentionally combine them to form a concentrated unit.

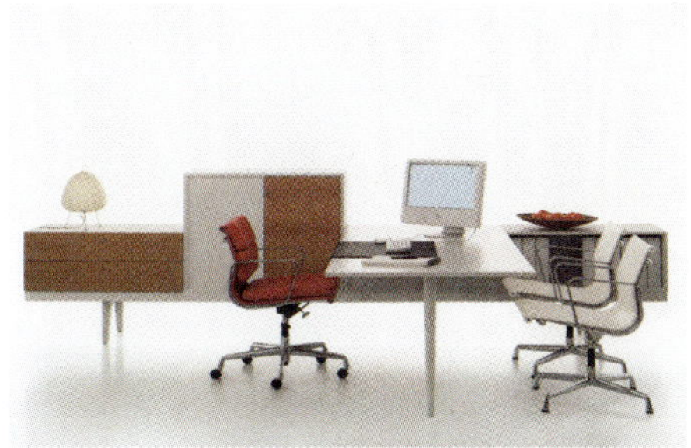

Aisslinger not only permanently invalidated structural ideas about that which we generally understand as the "workplace"; he also expressly distanced himself from the supposedly fixed "mores and habits" of our ageing office culture as regards the diverse elements available for use. Aisslinger simply defined the office in a completely different way; not as an "office", i.e. a place where everything is aligned to the work being done there, but as a place or rather a "zone" in which working is possible but which also facilitates other activities that lead to optimum results: thinking, talking to each other, relaxing.

Loftcube: Cube for the best possible position The interest in socio-cultural changes that he expresses here and the resulting consequences for design had already been clearly demonstrated shortly before in the loftcube project. However, the latter did not concern a facet of classic interior design but was more a kind of concept for the use of space in the "inner borderline zones" of the urban environment, i.e. unused roof surfaces. The starting point was the consideration that, alone due to the cubic architecture typically found in our cities, such spaces are not only abundant but, in their high-up position, are also relatively free from interfering environmental factors such as noise and shade and are only actually used for installation of the necessary technical infrastructure.

Aisslinger's absolutely simple yet totally convincing proposal was to consider these spaces not as structurally contaminated roof surfaces of an existing urban organism but as ubiquitously available building land "in the best possible position" where a specifically designed factory-built house, namely the loftcube, could be placed, with the laws of statics being taken into account in each case. It may, of course, seem reasonable to compare this proposal with the notion of the penthouse and write it off as, at best, a variant of this familiar form of dwelling. But, primarily due to the fact that it is elevated on stilts, this cube allows much greater freedom in respect of where it is finally placed than an added-on rooftop apartment that uses the roof surface as the floor. The simple reason is that all supply and disposal pipes and lines can be connected to the existing infrastructure not directly but independently in the same way as on a piece of land with a completely new building. And right in the middle of the city!

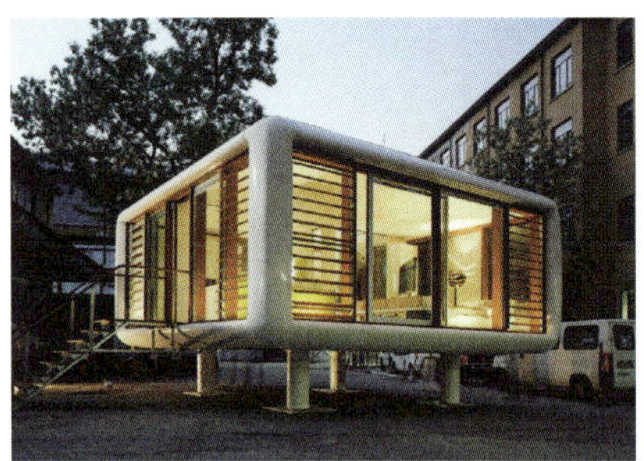

This structural independence, however, would not be of much value if Aisslinger had allowed himself to be carried away and make an exalted architectural gesture, in other words to create a design that not only towers above everything else but, in design terms, also attempts to put all other buildings in the shade. However, it is exactly that which he cleverly did not do. On the contrary, the loftcube is a stringently thought-out and, above all, well-proportioned cube that can be placed practically anywhere: on the concrete brutalism of the 1960s, on the 45° orgies of the 1970s, or on the unnecessary post-modern absurdities of the 1980s. It simply always fits in. But is nevertheless striking and exquisitely unmistakeable.

Fincube: Temporary countryside architecture The same applies to the fincube variant recently developed for hotelier Josef Innerhofer in southern Tyrol. The only difference is that the aesthetic concept was not determined by the urban space but by a landscape generally spared the interventions of the human hand, the Dolomites being one example. But buildings are still being constructed there as well and most of them do not fit seamlessly into the landscape features that exist there. Werner Aisslinger's fincube is a completely different matter: in terms of scale as well as the outer appearance and, last but not least, the overall energy concept, this pavilion takes into account the requirements of all its surroundings.

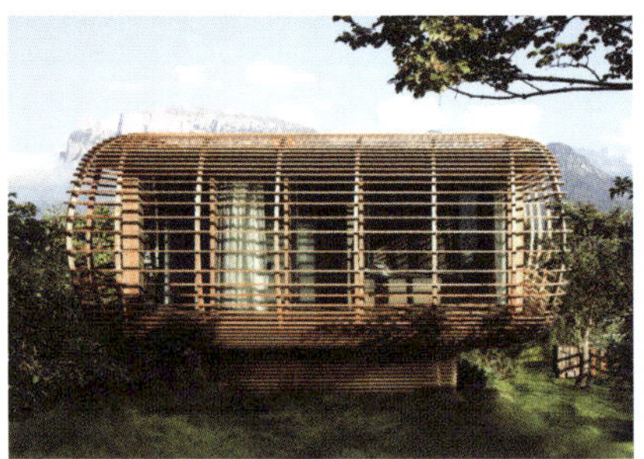

This slightly bulging cube looks almost like an outsized picnic basket that can be placed on a hill or in a clearing as required. And this is exactly what it is all about: a vision of future tourism based on relatively small, temporarily built units that enter into a fitting, even taken-for-granted synthesis with their surroundings during their "service life". This is mainly due to the outer cover, which consists of wooden planking set at a distance from the surface of the structure and passing around it horizontally. Due to its convex shape, it prevents the structure from having any appearance of a rectangular, statically rigid character. This planking, however, is more than just aesthetic ornamentation; its provides privacy and protection against the sun, while acting as camouflage for its occupants and people on the outside. What's more, it is astoundingly simple.

Books, Mesh and NETwork: roomware for tomorrow The list of such different projects as a shelf system, the use of new plastics, an innovative range of furniture and the design of an alternative house concept for the city and the countryside is not intended to give the impression that Werner Aisslinger is a designer who is always "out of breath", hungrily rushing after new, preferably spectacular design achievements only to pounce on a new object of his aesthetic desires once his completed projects have found their echo in the media. Certainly not. The last thing Aisslinger is interested in is seeking attention from the media. His past and present objective is to define the (for him) decisive determinants of contemporary product design and then to permanently update them and make them more precise.

In other words, Werner Aisslinger's aim is to develop his own competence. This results in concrete orders and increases his freedom to choose exactly the jobs he wants. Much more importantly, such jobs are the essential foundation for the innovative series of experiments that Aisslinger has been carrying our regularly for over fifteen years on a more or less regular basis. The fact that nearly all these projects were initiated (and financed) by himself and only went into series production after the creation of 1:1 prototypes or a slightly modified version supports this thesis.

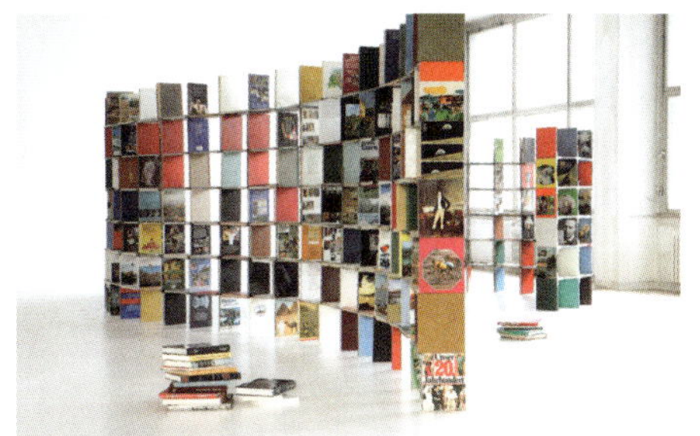

Especially in recent times, he has proven that new insights once gained – irrespective of how successful they may be – are not filed away or routinely revisited but are used as a kind of upwardly displaced starting ramp from which he launches alternatives that attempt to move beyond what has already been attained. In very concrete terms, this is shown by his books shelf installation (première in Cologne, 2007), which is reminiscent of his endless shelf, by his recent mesh composition which shows his curiosity about materials and was created for the Museum für Gestaltung in Zurich (to mark the occasion of the Nature Design exhibition from the same year) and by his latest project NETwork – 3D Stitching.

The references to preceding projects are unmistakeable as are also the fundamental differences, where the innovative impetus is to be found. In principle, the books bookshelf is based on the same components as the endless shelf. In contrast to this, the horizontal and vertical elements do not consist of the same MDF panels but of books, to be precise, books that approximately correspond to the DIN A4 format. Simple cross-shaped metal plates with extremely flat axes approximately 15 cm long and 20 cm deep are inserted into the top and bottom of the books. Each of these "joining" elements has a standardised clamp that holds the book together and enables the metal plates to lie flush with the sides. That is all there is to it!

It is not necessary to point out the superb ingenuity of this ready-made system, in which mechanical, dimensional and economic qualities are set in a new context in such an amazingly logical interlocked formation. On top of this, however, books also possesses a highly critical ironic dimension in that Aisslinger makes use of the prime source of intellectual nourishment and downgrades it by making it a profane component of a piece furniture.

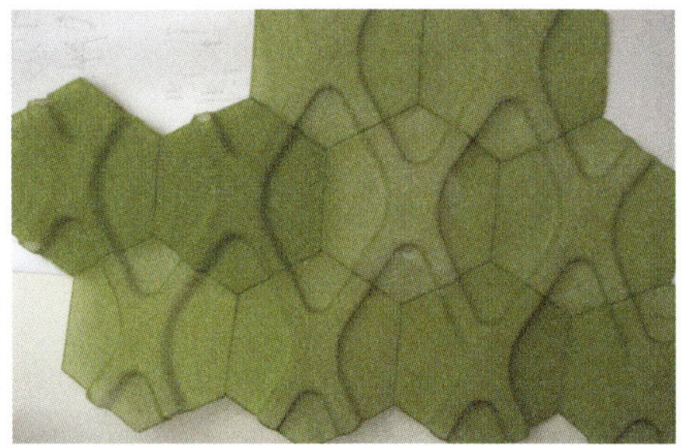

It is far from Werner Aisslinger's intention to recommend that we rush into the nearest bookshop in order to buy a sufficient number of "shelf elements" – such blasphemy towards the book as a cultural asset would hardly occur to him at all. No, Aisslinger's proposal refers to the heaps of unread coffee-table books and others that decoratively bear witness to their owner's supposed familiarity with literature but, in the end, are never taken down from the shelf to be actually read. The books in Aisslinger's design are, of course, dispossessed of their actual function but remain visible to the user; they are just no longer the centre of attention. Nevertheless, there is an effect that can almost be described as a secondary consequence given that the books provide a clear indication of the owner's preferences and personal judgement.

The mesh project, which concerns an exploration of the different ways in which materials that are not usually seen in interiors can be utilised, is completely different and has an entirely technological orientation. In principle, mesh is based on a combination of two different high-tech textiles, whereby one of them has a translucent structure and the other, a hardened melted thread, forms the three-dimensional structure and simultaneously reinforces and stabilises concrete over the long term. It is basically an advanced lightweight material that can be used not only to divide up rooms but also to form enclosed spaces within existing large rooms – the possibilities are practically infinite. It can, of course, be used to make furniture as well, as in the NETwork project, which can be seen as a kind of furniture-oriented specification of the mesh project. However, there is an additional aspect that has not been previously associated with Aisslinger: the use of textile knotting, normally a traditional technique.

What happens exactly? The starting point is a wide-meshed textile that has been designed in such a way that it can be "stretched" into a third dimension, i.e. the thread lengths and the sizes of the empty spaces have so much in reserve that they do not tear when the material expands. This expansion is caused by a negative mould over which the textile is fitted, the textile first having been immersed in a synthetic resin emulsion. As soon as it dries, the negative mould can be removed and the shaped textile is then self-supporting. What is special about this process is that the structure of the textile can be altered again and again by means of an algorithm, i.e. the choice of pattern is individual and infinite. With the help of this technique, the final shape can be matched to any desired volume very exactly and accurately.

In a way similar to books, Aisslinger's mesh and NETwork are two further "tools", a kind of software or, as he called it once with reference to level 34 , roomware for the more or less open space in which basic utilitarian needs can no longer be met solely with introduced configuration notions and manufacturing recipes. Alone because of the altered technical possibilities and the permanent mutation of the socio-cultural micro-climate, such needs require a form of design management that must be continually developed anew and disdains the use of a routinely adopted and minimally changing catalogue of services.

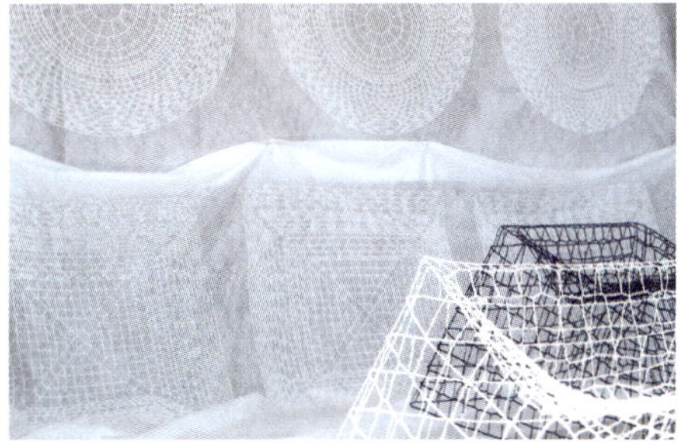

In view of these activities, it is not necessary to mention Werner Aisslinger's innovative potential again – the description alone and the documentation presented in this book demonstrate the exceptional quality both of books and his most recent projects, mesh and NETwork. Only one thing should be pointed out at this particular juncture: the temporal proximity of these relatively different interventions to contemporary design. If the distance between the two similarly pivoted projects is calculated at the beginning of his period of self-employment according to years, there is only a few months between books and mesh. Put another way, an acceleration that has long since deactivated all mechanisms of slowing-down and uncertainty has taken over from a gradual forwards movement in his work. Not "Forward!" is Aisslinger's motto, but a total commitment to the technological and socio-cultural developments of our time. Fast and, above all, fast far forward!

In the near future, intensive consideration will have to be given to Werner Aisslinger not only by the chroniclers of design at the turn of the century but also by those who will some day think back to the essence of design in the 2010s, 2020s and 2030s.

FAST FORWARD!

Einführung von Volker Albus

⏭ *Wenn in nicht allzu ferner Zukunft die ersten Publikationen auf das Design des ausgehenden 20. und des beginnenden 21. Jahrhunderts retrospektiv zurückblicken werden, wird, und dazu gehören gewiss keine prophetischen Gaben, die Arbeit von Werner Aisslinger eine feste Größe darstellen. Und ebenso sicher kann man prognostizieren, dass nicht wenige Chronisten der Versuchung verfallen werden, diese Arbeit auf ganz bestimmte formale Charakteristika zu reduzieren. Zugegeben, die Gefahr ist vorhanden, etwa aus den Ansichten des Loftcube, der Struktur der Liege Soft, und um ein Beispiel aus dem Bereich Industrial Design zu nennen, der geometrischen Grundform des neuen Drehschalters für Berker ein immer wieder auftauchendes Merkmal zu extrahieren, um es dann zu der Aisslingerschen Konstanten schlechthin zu erheben. Ganz falsch wäre das sicher nicht und so mancher „Schnellkurs Design der Jahrtausendwende" wird just auf dieses offensichtliche Attribut abheben und nach Auflistung entsprechender „Beweisstücke" zum nächsten Protagonisten übergehen. Damit würde man zwar ein signifikantes Moment, aber mit Sicherheit nicht die eigentlich tragenden Qualitäten in Aisslingers Design markieren. Denn die sind nicht nur äußerst vielfältig, sie erschließen sich zudem nur dann, wenn man über diese vermeintliche Augenfälligkeit hinwegsieht und Aisslingers Schaffen unter den eher handfesten Aspekten des nüchternen Industrial Designs betrachtet. Und die liegen bekanntermaßen eher unter und hinter den en passant aufgesogenen und dementsprechend reflexartig abgesonderten Impressionen.*

Mit anderen Worten: Um Werner Aisslingers Arbeit gebührend darzustellen, muss man sich mit der Konstruktion und Konfiguration, mit dem materialen und technischen, dem typologischen und konventionellen Potenzial seiner Möbel und Leuchten, seiner System-Entwicklungen und Interieurs, kurzum mit dem gesamten Katalog seiner Einlassungen zum zeitgenössischen Design befassen.

Endless Shelf: Regaler Standard *Man sollte allerdings chronologisch vorgehen, denn bereits zu Beginn seiner selbstständigen Tätigkeit als Designer bewies Aisslinger mit dem Regal-System Endless Shelf seine außergewöhnliche Fähigkeit, mechanische Details nicht nur eigenständig zu entwickeln, sondern sie auch kongenial in ein funktionales Gesamtkonzept einzubringen.*

Grundlegendes und gleichzeitig einziges modulares Element dieses „Endlosregals" ist eine quadratische, ca. 38 x 38 cm große MDF-Platte von ca. 2 cm Stärke, die an den Ecken jeweils mittig

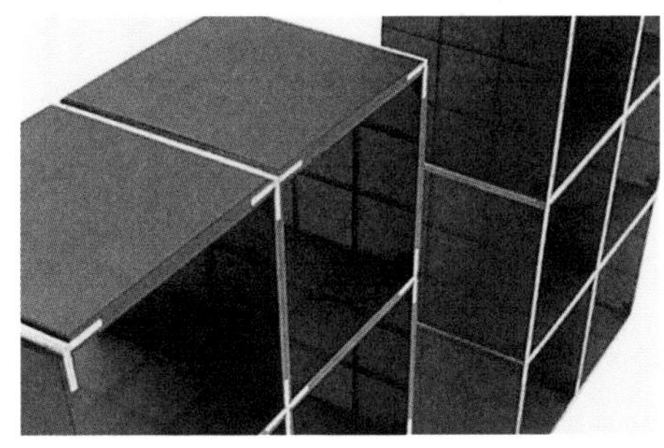

6 cm tief eingekerbt ist. In diese Kerben werden je nach Positionierung der Platten im Gesamtgefüge kreuz-, T- oder winkelförmige Aluminium-Pass-Stücke eingesetzt und mit einem jeweils gegenüberliegenden Pendant gekontert. Die letztendliche Konfiguration liegt dann ausschließlich im Ermessen des Nutzers, denn außer diesem aus vier Platten zusammengesetzten, an zwei gegenüberliegenden Seiten offenen Kubus gibt es keine weiteren Vorgaben bezüglich des regalen Aufbaus – weder hinsichtlich der Anzahl der zusammenzufügenden Kuben noch hinsichtlich der endgültigen Form. Und dementsprechend trifft der attributive Titel die Vorzüge dieses Systems auch nur partiell, denn diese Platten lassen sich auch zu einer endlos formlosen Reihe ausbauen. D.h. der Nutzer kann sein Regal je nach Gusto treppenförmig ansteigen, kammartig verspringen oder irgendwie „abstrakt" geometrisch „aus der Reihe tanzen lassen". Und das können nicht gerade viele Systeme.

Aber nicht nur die funktional-utilitären Ansprüche an solch ein Möbel werden hier bestens bedient, auch die ganz grundsätzlichen Hardcore-Kriterien wie Stabilität und eine gerade für das Regal essentielle Entsagung an eine stilistisch zeittypische Prägnanz werden mehr als erfüllt. Mit dem Endless Shelf gelang Werner Aisslinger etwas, was tatsächlich nur wenigen Designern vergönnt ist: der Entwurf, die komplette Entwicklung eines nur mit dem Attribut „Standard" adäquat zu bezeichnenden Möbels.

Juli Chair und Technogel: Materiale Neugier *Wahrscheinlich gibt es nicht viele Designer, die just das Erreichen einer solchen Ebene nicht als Motivation interpretieren, zusätzliche Variationen und Ergänzungen für dieses System zu entwickeln. Denn genau genommen handelt es sich ja bei diesem Endless Shelf eher um ein Skelett, eine Art offenes Raster, das man ebenso offen und frei bestückt. Und es gehört nicht allzu viel Phantasie dazu, sich hier die entsprechenden „schrankigen" und „schubladigen" Ausstattungen zu denken, mit denen sich dieses reine Strukturelement zu einem veritablen Schrankwandsystem weiterentwickeln ließe – von den denkbar maßstäblichen Varianten gar nicht zu reden.*

Werner Aisslingers Sache sind solche Ausbauprogramme jedoch nicht. Aber nicht, weil sie ihn nicht interessieren, sondern ganz einfach deshalb, weil ihn etwas anderes weitaus mehr interessiert: Zu diesem Zeitpunkt, also ab Mitte der neunziger Jahre, war dies die intensive Auseinandersetzung mit, zumindest für das Möbeldesign, neuartigen Materialien und den damit verbundenen Herstellungsverfahren. Erstes Ergebnis dieser Arbeit war der für Cappellini entwickelte Juli Chair, eine einteilige Schalenkonstruktion aus Polyurethan-Integralschaum, ein Verfahren, das bis dato vornehmlich bei der Herstellung von Komponenten für das Auto-

Interieur – z. B. für Lenkräder angewandt wurde, sich aber aufgrund der stabilen aber dennoch nachgebenden Konsistenz des Materials ebenso ideal für die organische Gestaltung von Sitzmöbeln eignete. Konnte man hier noch von einer gewissen Nähe zwischen der ursprünglichen Anwendung und der daraus resultie-renden Transformation sprechen, so muss man der kurz nach dem Juli Chair entstandenen Gel-Möbel-Kollektion uneingeschränkt den Status einer umfassenden Innovation zubilligen.

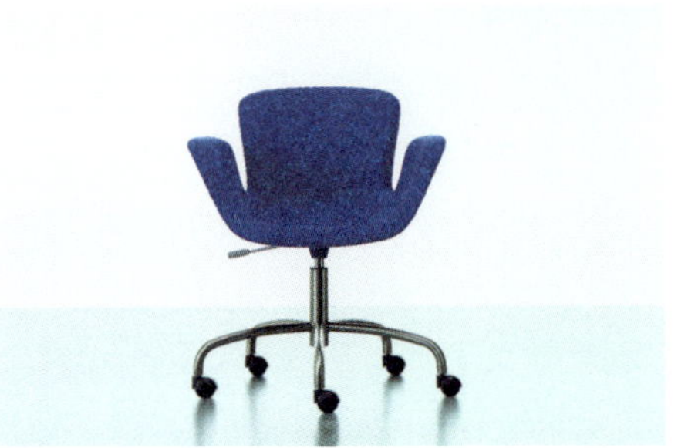

Denn das hier zur Anwendung kommende Material, Technogel, kannte man allenfalls in der Medizin- oder der Sportgerätetechnik, aber bestimmt nicht im Produktdesign. Gleichwohl war es weniger dieser gerade von expressiv gepolten „Möbelkünstlern" gerne ausgespielte „exotische" Bezug als vielmehr die ganz spezifischen physikalischen Qualitäten, die Werner Aisslinger zu der Arbeit mit Technogel inspirierten. Diese bestehen, einfach ausgedrückt, darin, dass sich dieser auf Polyurethan-Basis hergestellte Kunststoff wie eine Flüssigkeit verhält, d.h., die jeweils belastete Fläche wird nicht komprimiert, also verfestigt, sondern sie wird „verdrängt" und „fließt" nach der Belastung wieder in ihre ursprüngliche Form zurück.

Der Vorteil, z. B. für ein Polstermöbel, ist offensichtlich: Wo man gemeinhin ca. 5 cm eines herkömmlichen Polstermaterials benötigt, um einen bestimmten Grad an Nachgiebigkeit zu erreichen, genügen 1 cm dieses Materials, um den gleichen Effekt zu erzielen. Das mag auf den ersten Blick nicht nach allzu viel klingen – 4 cm mehr oder weniger: Was ist das schon? –, für ein klassisch als „dick" geprägtes Element wie dem Polster könnte aber gerade eine derartige Komprimierung ein komplett neues Designverständnis in Gang setzen.

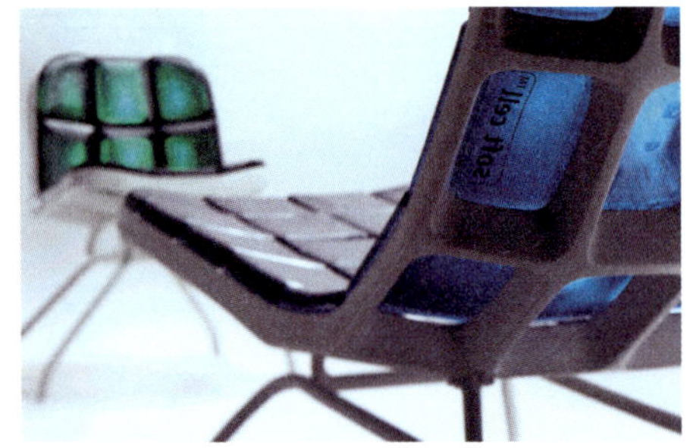

Wir wollen allerdings nicht verhehlen, dass die aus diesem von der Fachwelt euphorisch gefeierten Gel-Experiment resultierenden Serien-Modelle für Cappellini und Zanotta ökonomisch weit hinter dem medialen Erfolg blieben. Ein entscheidender Grund lag wohl vor allem im Preis beziehungsweise in dem vom Publikum mit einem Material wie „Kunststoff" gemeinhin assoziierten Preisniveau – und das liegt bekanntermaßen eher auf Discountlevel. Und da spielt es auch keine Rolle, ob es sich bei einem Produkt um ein exzeptioelles, zudem mit einem hochentwickelten Werkstoff realisiertes Werk zeitgenössischen Designs handelt: Kunststoff bleibt Kunststoff – und das wiederum heißt: praktisch, billig, abwaschbar!

Wie dem auch sei, für Werner Aisslinger, für seine Reputation als Designer war gerade die Prototypenserie der Gel-Möbel als auch deren serielle Weiterentwicklung von entscheidender Bedeutung, belegte sie doch eindrucksvoll seine Fähigkeit, nach einem derart prägnanten Entwurf wie dem Endless Shelf, auch in einem diametral andersartigen Gattungsbereich nicht nur eine wiederum eigenständige Konzeption zu entwickeln, sondern auch andere Basisdeterminanten wie eben die Materialität anwendungstechnisch neu zu interpretieren.

Level 34: Good bye Good Old Office *Dass sich diese vielseitige Kompetenz jedoch nicht nur auf die unkonventionelle Auseinandersetzung mit der klar definierten Typologie von Einzelmöbeln beschränkt, zeigte sich exemplarisch in dem Projekt Level 34, einem „multifunktionalen Möbelprogramm" für Vitra aus dem Jahr 2004. Bei diesem Programm handelt es sich um einen Bausatz verschiedener Teile, die sich, wie auch immer zusammengesetzt, zu einem installationsartigen Möbel-Hybrid formieren, also nicht wie üblich, um ein mehr oder weniger äußerlich aufeinander abgestimmtes und partiell ineinandergreifendes Sortiment von Einzelmöbeln. Insofern könnte man hier auch von einem invers angelegten Programm sprechen, geht es hier im Kern doch darum, die für den individuellen Bedarf notwendigen Teile nicht über den gesamten Raum zu verteilen, sondern sie, im Gegenteil, bewusst zu einer konzentrierten Einheit zusammenzufassen.*

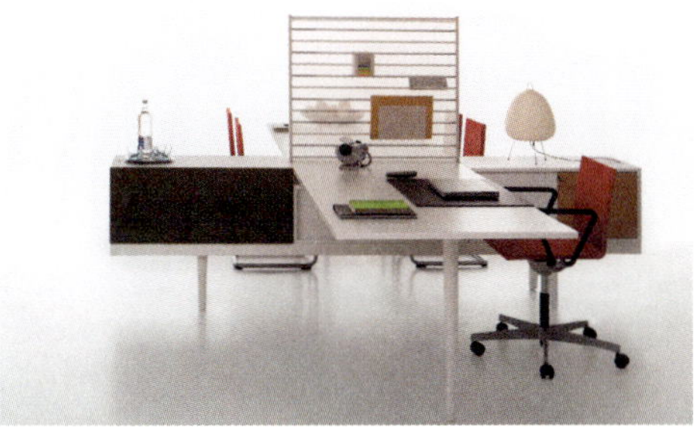

Damit setzte Aisslinger nicht nur die strukturellen Vorstellungen von dem, was wir gemeinhin unter „Arbeitsplatz" verstehen, nachhaltig außer Kraft, auch hinsichtlich der zur Verfügung stehenden Elemente verabschiedete er sich nachdrücklich von den vermeintlich festgelegten „Sitten und Gebräuchen" unserer in die Jahre gekommenen Bürokultur. Aisslinger definiert das Büro hier ganz einfach vollkommen anders, eben nicht als „Büro", als einen Ort also, an dem jedes Teil ausschließlich auf die dort zu verrichtende Tätigkeit ausgerichtet ist, sondern als einen Ort, besser: eine „Zone", in der Arbeiten sehr gut möglich ist, aber ebenso gut genau das, was zu optimalen Arbeitsergebnissen führt: das Denken, das miteinander Reden, das Entspannen.

Loftcube: Cube für die Bestlage *Das hier zum Ausdruck kommende Interesse für soziokulturelle Veränderungen und die daraus resultierenden Konsequenzen für das Design waren bereits kurz zuvor in dem Projekt Loftcube deutlich zum Ausdruck gekommen. Allerdings ging es hier nicht um die Auseinandersetzung mit einer Facette der klassischen Innenarchitektur als vielmehr um eine Art Flächennutzungsskonzept für die „inneren Randzonen" des urbanen Raums: um brachliegende Dachflächen. Ausgangspunkt war die Überlegung, dass, allein schon* *aufgrund der gängigen kubischen Architektur in unseren Städten, solche Flächen nicht nur reichlich vorhanden, sondern dass sie, hoch droben, zudem relativ frei von störenden Umweltfaktoren wie Lärm und Verschattung sind – aber eigentlich nur für die Installation technischer Infrastruktur genutzt werden.*

Aisslingers absolut einfacher wie ebenso überzeugender Vorschlag bestand nun darin, diese Flächen nicht als strukturell kontaminierte Dach-, also Abschlussflächen eines bestehenden Organismus zu betrachten, sondern sozusagen als überall zur Verfügung stehendes Bauland „in Bestlage", auf das man unter Berücksichtigung statischer Gesetzmäßigkeiten, je nach Gusto, ein spezifisch konzipiertes Fertighaus, eben jenen Loftcube, aufstellen kann.

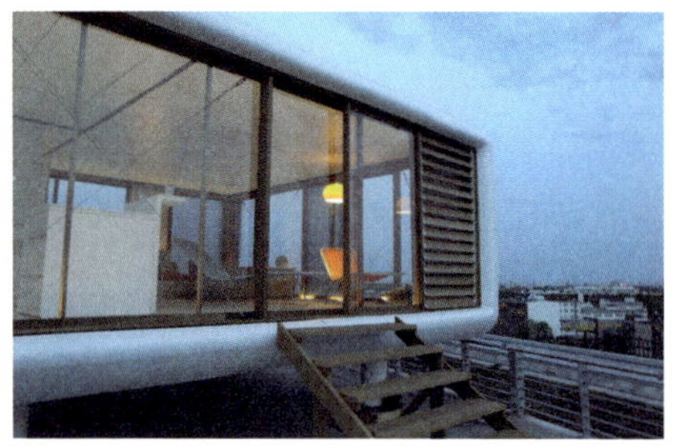

Natürlich liegt es nahe, diesen Vorschlag mit dem bekannten Penthouse abzugleichen und ihn dementsprechend allenfalls als Variante dieses bekannten Bautyps abzuhaken. Aber vor allem aufgrund der Aufständerung erlaubt dieser Kubus eine weit größere Platzierungsfreiheit als ein die Dachfläche als Boden nutzendes zusätzliches Dachgeschoss. Und das ganz einfach schon deshalb, weil sämtliche Ver- und Entsorgungsleitungen nicht unmittelbar, sondern ähnlich wie auf einem neu bebauten Grundstück weitestgehend unabhängig an die existierenden Infrastrukturen herangeführt werden können – und das mitten in der Stadt!

Diese strukturelle Unabhängigkeit wäre allerdings nicht allzu viel wert, hätte Aisslinger sich zu einer exaltierten Architekturgeste hinreißen lassen, zu einem Design also, das nicht nur höhenmäßig über allem thront, sondern zudem auch gestalterisch alles in den Schatten zu stellen versucht. Genau das aber hat er klugerweise nicht getan. Im Gegenteil. Der Loftcube ist ein stringent durchkomponierter und vor allem wohlproportionierter Kubus, der tatsächlich überall hinpasst: auf den Betonbrutalismus der Sechziger ebenso wie auf die 45°-Orgien der Siebziger oder die postmodernen Sperenzien der Achtziger. Er stimmt ganz einfach immer. Und ist dennoch markant und unverwechselbar.

Fincube: Temporäre Landarchitektur *Das gilt auch für die jüngst für den Südtiroler Hotelier Josef Innhofer entwickelte Variante Fincube. Nur dass hier eben nicht der urbane Raum das ästhetische Konzept bestimmte, sondern eine von Bauten, von menschlichen Eingriffen ganz generell verschonte Landschaft – wie z. B. die Dolomiten. Aber auch dort wird gebaut, und zumeist fügt sich das, was gebaut wird, nicht gerade nahtlos in die landschaftlichen Gegebenheiten. Ganz anders sieht das bei Werner Aisslingers Fincube aus: sowohl was die Maßstäblichkeit als auch* *das äußere Erscheinungsbild als auch, last but not least, das energetische Gesamtkonzept anbelangt, vereint dieser Pavillon alle erforderlichen Rücksichten.*

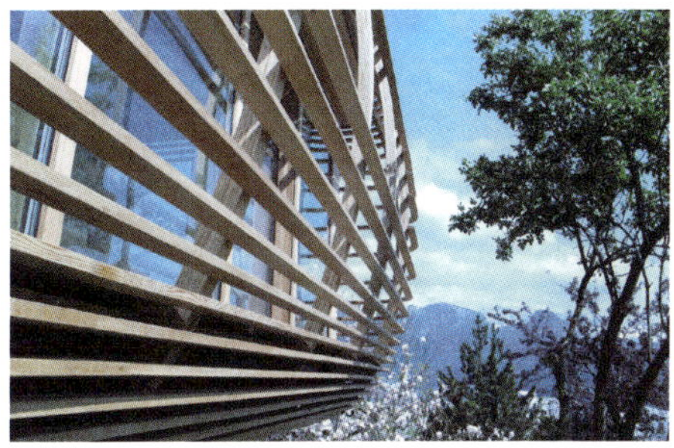

Fast wirkt dieser leicht bombierte Kubus wie ein übergroßer Picknickkorb, den man je nach Bedarf auf eine Anhöhe oder in einer Lichtung platzieren kann. Und genau darum geht es: um die Vision eines zukünftigen Tourismus, der auf relativ kleinen und temporär zu erstellenden Einheiten basiert, die während ihrer „Standzeit" eine stimmige, ja selbstverständliche Synthese mit ihrer Umgebung eingehen. Das liegt vor allem an der Außenverkleidung. Sie besteht aus einer auf Abstand gesetzten und horizontal um den Kubus verlaufenden Holzverschalung, die durch ihre konvexe Anordnung dem Bau jeglichen Anflug einer rektangulären, statisch steifen Anmut nimmt. Diese Verkleidung ist aber eben mehr als nur ein ästhetisches Scharnier: sie ist Sonnen- und Sichtschutz, sie ist Camouflage für die da drinnen – und für die da draußen. Und sie ist von stupender Einfachheit.

Books, Mesh und NETwork: Roomware für Morgen *Nun soll mit der Auflistung solch unterschiedlicher Projekte wie einem Regalsystem, der Anwendung neuartiger Kunststoffe, einem innovativen Möbelprogramm und dem Entwurf eines alternativen Hauskonzepts für Stadt und Land nicht der Eindruck erweckt werden, bei Werner Aisslinger handele es sich um einen Designer, der sozusagen „außer Atem" nach einer immer neuen, möglichst spektakulären Design-Perfomance giert, um sich nach deren Widerhall in der Medienlandschaft gezielt auf ein neues Objekt seiner ästhetischen Begierden zu stürzen. Mit Sicherheit nicht. Denn um die Generierung medialer Aufmerksamkeit geht es Aisslinger zuallerletzt. Vielmehr ging und geht es Aisslinger gerade mit diesen hier aufgeführten Projekten darum, die für ihn entscheidenden Determinanten eines zeitgemäßen Produktdesigns zu definieren und in der Folge permanent zu aktualisieren und zu präzisieren.*

Mit anderen Worten: Werner Aisslinger geht es um die Fortschreibung der eigenen Kompetenz, die zum einen in konkrete Aufträge mündet, die aber andererseits auch die Wahlfreiheit der Annahme solcher Aufträge vergrößert, und, viel entscheidender, die essentielle Grundlage für derartig innovative Versuchsreihen bilden, wie sie von Aisslinger seit nunmehr gut fünfzehn Jahren mehr oder weniger regelmäßig durchgeführt werden. Dass nahezu alle diese Vorhaben ursächlich von ihm selbst initiiert (und finanziert) wurden, und dass sie erst nach der Realisierung von Prototypen 1:1 oder in leicht variierter Version in Serie gingen, unterstützt diese These. Gerade in jüngster Zeit bewies er, dass einmal gewonnene Erkenntnisse – egal, wie erfolgreich sie auch sein mögen –, eben nicht ad acta gelegt oder routinemäßig durchdekliniert werden, sondern eine

Art nach oben verschobener Startrampe markieren, von der aus er neue, weitergehende Alternativen zum jeweiligen Thema konzipiert. Ganz konkret zeigt sich das an seiner an das Endless Shelf erinnernden Regal-Installation Books (Premiere in Köln, 2007), an der neuerlich seine materiale Neugier bezeugenden Gewebekomposition Mesh für das Museum für Gestaltung in Zürich (anlässlich der Ausstellung „Nature Design" aus dem gleichen Jahr) sowie an seinem jüngsten Projekt NETwork – 3D Sticken.

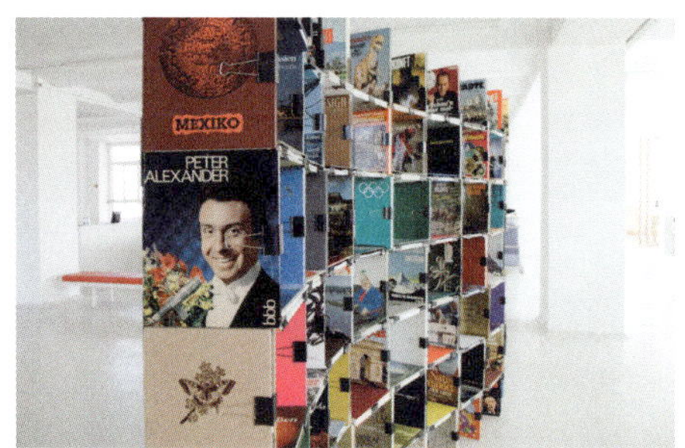

Hier wie dort sind die Bezüge an die Vorläufer unverkennbar - aber ebenso die fundamentalen Unterschiede, sprich der innovative Impetus. So basiert das Regal mooks im Prinzip auf den gleichen Komponenten wie das Endless Shelf. Im Unterschied zu diesem bestehen die waagerechten und senkrechten Elemente allerdings nicht aus der immer gleichen MDF-Platte, sondern aus Büchern, genau genommen aus Büchern, die ungefähr dem Format DIN A4 entsprechen. In diese Bücher wird in einem ersten Schritt jeweils mittig in den Kopf- und den Fußschnitt eine einfache Metallkreuzplatte mit extrem flachen, ca. 15 cm langen und ca. 20 cm tiefen Achsen eingesteckt. Dieses „verbindende" Element wird durch eine standardisierte Klammer ergänzt, die das Buch zusammenhält und so die in die Bücher eingreifenden Metallplatten kraftschlüssig mit den Seiten zusammenklemmt. Fertig!

Dass es sich bei diesem System um ein nicht gerade bravourös ingeniöses Readymade handelt, muss man nicht weiter erläutern, werden hier doch sowohl mechanische, maßliche als auch ökonomische Qualitäten auf frappierend schlüssige Art in einen neuen Kontext gesetzt. Darüber hinaus aber offenbart dieses Books auch eine ungemein kritisch ironische Dimension, als sich Aisslinger hier des intellektuellen Grundnahrungsmittels schlechthin, dem Buch, bedient und es zu einem profanen Bauteil degradiert.

Nun liegt es Werner Aisslinger fern, uns zu empfehlen, in den nächsten Buchladen zu stürmen, um sich dort mit einer ausreichenden Zahl von Regalelementen zu versorgen – eine derartige Lästerung des Kulturguts Buch käme ihm kaum in den Sinn. Nein, Aisslinger verweist mit seinem Vorschlag auf die Halden ungelesener Coffeetable- und sonstiger Bücher, die in unseren Schränken dekorativ von der vermeintlichen Belesenheit ihrer Besitzer künden – aber letztendlich doch nie aus dem Regal genommen werden. Freilich: Auch durch die Umnutzung werden die Bücher ihrer eigentlichen Funktion entzogen, allerdings bleiben die Bücher dem Nutzer sichtbar erhalten; sie rücken allenfalls ins „zweite Glied", geben aber, und das ist ein schon fast als hintergründig zu bezeichnender Effekt, in ihrer mechanischen Einbindung wiederum eindeutig Auskunft über Präferenzen und persönliche Einschätzung des Eigentümers.

Ganz anders, ganz technologisch orientiert ist das Projekt Mesh, bei dem es um die Erkundung der Anwendungsmöglichkeiten eigentlich Interieur-fremder Materialien geht. Im Prinzip basiert Mesh auf einer Kombination zweier unterschiedlicher Hightech-Textilien, in der der eine Stoff die transluzente Struktur bildet, der andere, ein sich aushärtender Schmelzfaden, dazu da ist, die dreidimensionale Struktur zu formen und, gleich der Armierung im Beton, diese dauerhaft zu stabilisieren. Im Grunde handelt es sich also um eine avancierte Leichtbauweise, mit dem sich nicht nur Räume teilen, sondern nahezu unbegrenzt geschlossene Volumen innerhalb bestehender Großräume formen lassen. Und natürlich auch Möbel, wie in dem Projekt NETwork, das man durchaus als eine Art Möbel orientierter Spezifizierung des Mesh Projekts lesen kann. Hinzu kommt allerdings ein Aspekt, den man von Aisslinger bislang nicht kannte: das Aufgreifen einer eher traditionellen Technik, dem textilen Knüpfen.

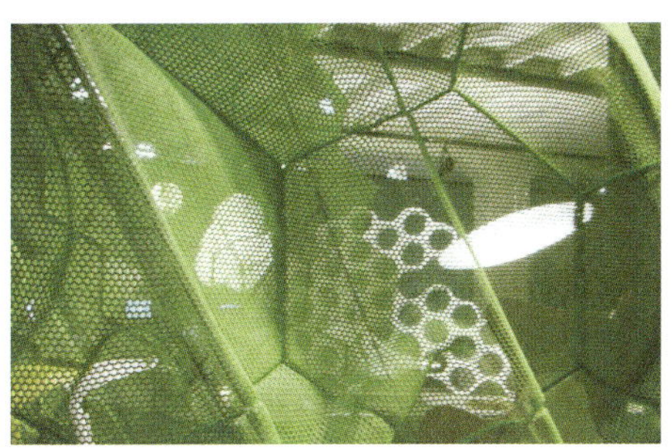

Was passiert genau? Ausgangspunkt ist ein grobmaschiges Textilgewebe, das so angelegt ist, dass es sich in die dritte Dimension „strecken" lässt, d.h. die Fadenlängen und die Größen der Leerräume haben soviel Reserve, dass sie im Zuge der Ausdehnung nicht reißen. Diese Ausdehnung erfolgt mittels einer Negativform, über die das in einer Kunstharzemulsion getauchte Gewebe übergestülpt wird. Sobald der Überwurf ausgehärtet ist, kann die Negativform entfernt werden – der Überwurf trägt sich selbst. Das Besondere an diesem Verfahren besteht darin, dass die Gewebestruktur mittels eines Algorhythmus immer wieder verändert werden kann, d.h. die Wahl des Musters ist individuell und endlos. Und selbst die endgültige Form lässt sich mittels dieser Technik sehr genau auf jedes Volumen abstimmen.

Ähnlich wie bei Books präsentiert Aisslinger mit Mesh und NETwork somit zwei weitere „tools", eine Art Software, oder, wie er es einmal mit Blick auf Level 34 nannte, eine Roomware für den mehr oder weniger offenen Raum, in dem sich die utilitären Grundbedürfnisse eben nicht mehr ausschließlich mit eingeführten Konfigurationsvorstellungen und Herstellungsrezepturen befriedigen lassen, sondern allein schon angesichts veränderter technischer Möglichkeiten und der permanenten Mutationen des soziokulturellen Kleinklimas ein grundsätzlich anderes, ein stets neu zu entwickelndes Designmanagement erfordern als die routinierte Abarbeitung eines sich nur wenig verändernden Leistungskatalogs.

Man muss angesichts dieser Aktivitäten nicht noch einmal auf das innovative Potenzial Werner Aisslingers hinweisen – allein schon die Beschreibung und die in diesem Buch vorgelegte Dokumentation belegen die außergewöhnliche Qualität sowohl des Books als auch der letzten Projekte

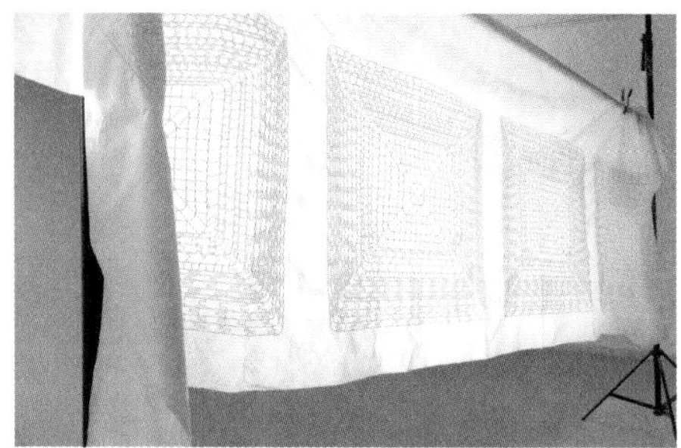

Mesh und NETwork. Nur auf Eines sollte man an dieser Stelle unbedingt hinweisen: die zeitliche Nähe dieser doch relativ unterschiedlichen Interventionen zum zeitgenössischen Design. Bemaß sich der Abstand zwischen den beiden ähnlich gelagerten Projekten zu Beginn seiner Selbstständigkeit noch nach Jahren, so liegen zwischen dem Books und Mesh nur wenige Monate. Anders ausgedrückt: an die Stelle einer kontinuierlichen Vorwärtsbewegung ist längst eine alle Brems- und Bedenkenmechanismen ausschaltende Tempobeschleunigung geworden: Nicht Forward! lautet Aisslingers Devise, sondern, ganz der technologischen und soziokulturellen Entwicklung unserer Zeit verpflichtet: Fast, und vor allem Fast Far Forward!

Und so werden sich in naher Zukunft nicht nur die Chronisten des Designs der Jahrtausendwende intensiv mit Werner Aisslinger beschäftigen müssen, sondern auch diejenigen, die dereinst an die gestalterische Essenz der Zehner-, Zwanziger- und der Dreißigerjahre dieses Jahrhunderts erinnern.

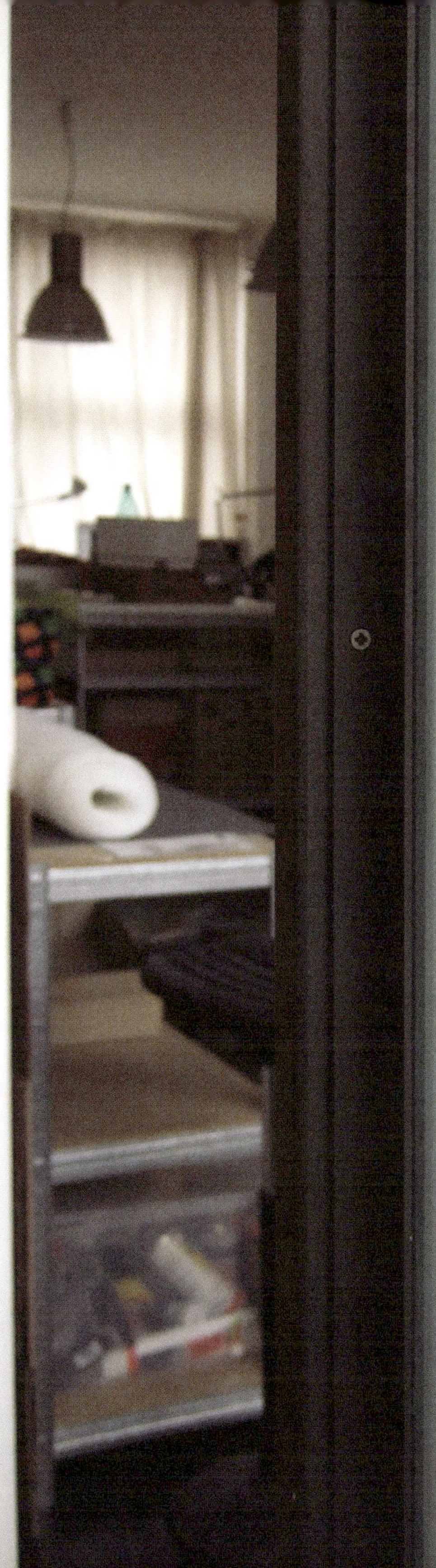

studio aisslinger

FUTURE LIVING

visions and utopia

Since Buckminster Fuller's "dimaxion unit prefab house" in the 1930s, architects, designers and engineers have continuously been exploring the options of mobile houses, transportable living units and nomadic minimal homes. Buckminster Fuller's impact with his geodesic houses also influenced the very first hippy community, "Drop City" in Colorado, with its recycling geodesic self-made domes in 1965. Drop City is still one of the rare examples of a symbiotic development of a new life style combined with experimental homes.

Within their professions, designers and architects are always caught in between serving the real needs of the market and visualising and creating visions or prototype futuristic environments for tomorrow. Designing is a challenge apart from fulfilling daily needs as its one of the professions which can give people a glimpse of the near future of living.

Seit Buckminster Fuller sein „Dymaxion-Haus" in den 1930er-Jahren erfand, haben Architekten, Designer und Ingenieure immer wieder verschiedene Möglichkeiten mobiler Häuser, transportabler Wohneinheiten und nomadenhafter Minimalhäuser erforscht. Die geodätischen Kuppelhäuser Buckminster Fullers beeinflussten auch die erste Hippie-Kommune in Colorado, „Drop City", und deren selbstgefertigte, aus Recyclingmaterial bestehende Domes von 1965. „Drop City" zählt immer noch zu den wenigen Beispielen, bei denen sich ein neuer Lebensstil und experimentelle Häuser symbiotisch ergänzten.

Designer und Architekten laborieren immer im Spannungsfeld zwischen dem real existierenden Markt und dem visionsgetriebenen Anspruch, prototypenhaft futuristische Räume von Morgen zu erschaffen; einerseits müssen sie täglich räumliche und gestalterische Bedürfnisse befriedigen, andererseits wollen sie einen Blick auf das Leben in naher Zukunft ermöglichen.

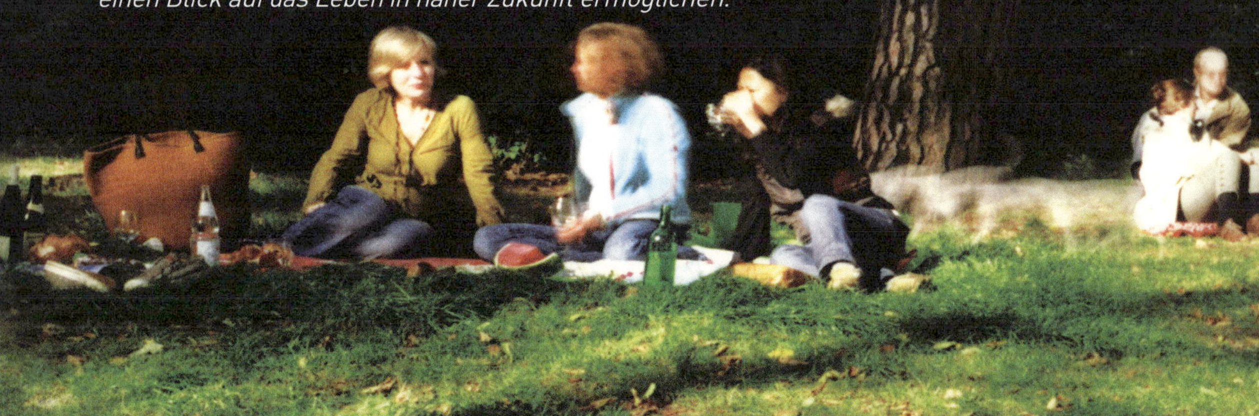

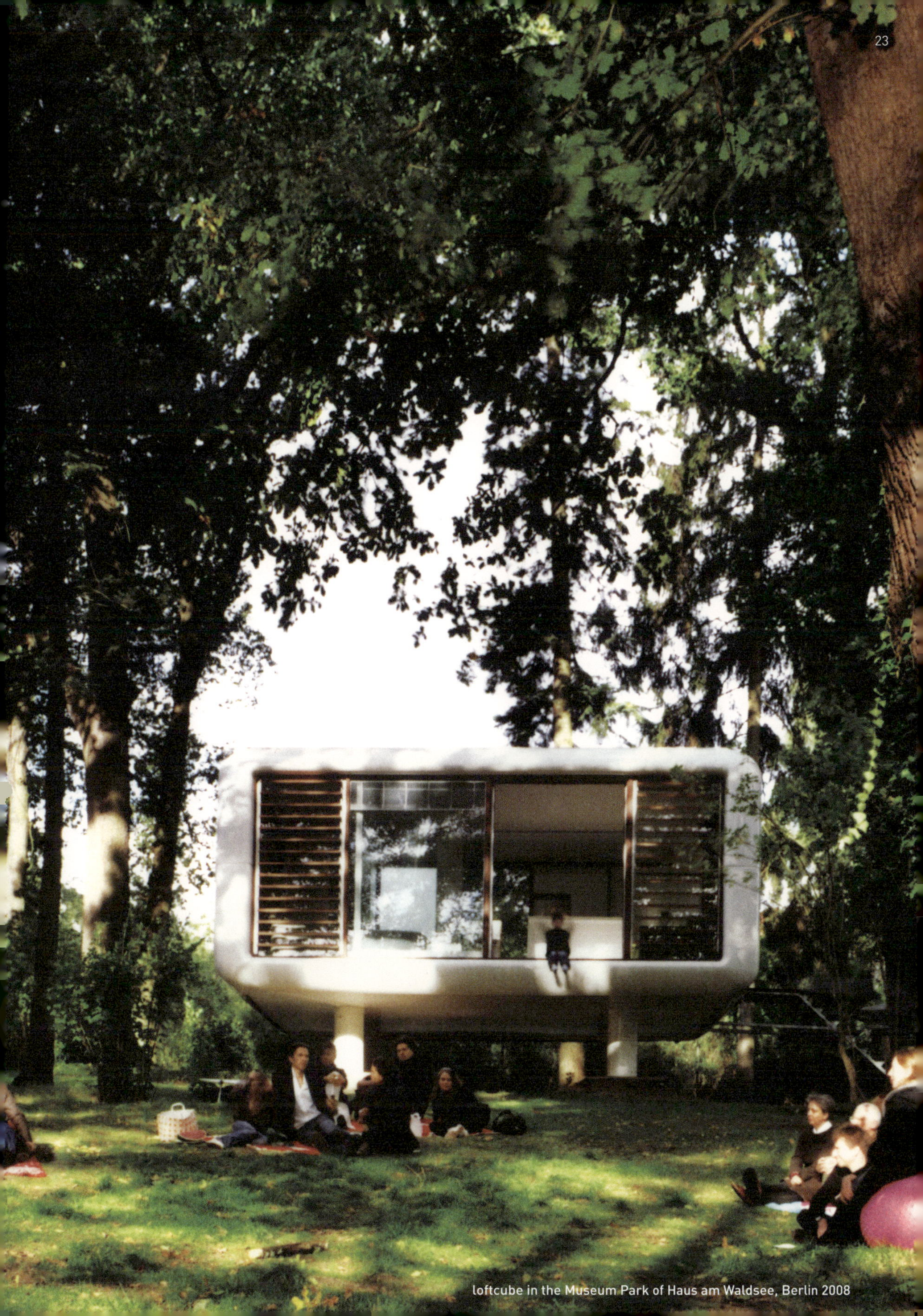

loftcube in the Museum Park of Haus am Waldsee, Berlin 2008

loftcube

nomadic home project 2003/07

The loftcube project was inspired by the vision of rooftop communities inhabited by urban nomads as most flat roofs of high-rise city buildings in urban zones can be used as space for temporary living. The Loftcube is designed to be airlifted to those roofs by helicopter, or it can be dismantled and reassembled atop buildings by a crew of only a few people. The "parasite" structure – using and connecting to the existing housing technology – was initially inspired by the bland, flat roofs of communist-era apartment buildings in East Berlin with square-kilometres of unused sunny city spaces.

Das Loftcube Projekt war von der Vision inspiriert, „communities" auf Dächern anzusiedeln, die von urbanen Nomaden bewohnt werden - urbanististisch ein interessantes Konzept, weil der größte Teil der Flachdächer in städtischen Zonen als temporärer Lebens- und Wohnraum genutzt werden kann. Der Loftcube ist so modular konstruiert, dass er per Hubschrauber auf Flachdächer transportiert werden kann oder von nur wenigen Monteuren auseinander- und oben auf den Gebäuden wieder zusammengesetzt werden kann. Die Idee einer „parasitären" Architektur – bei der der Loftcube an die bestehende Haustechnik angeschlossen wird und diese nutzt – war von den endlosen Ostberliner Flachdächern inspiriert, die auf den WBS 70 Plattenbauten quadratkilometergroße, ungenutzte, sonnige Stadtflächen bieten.

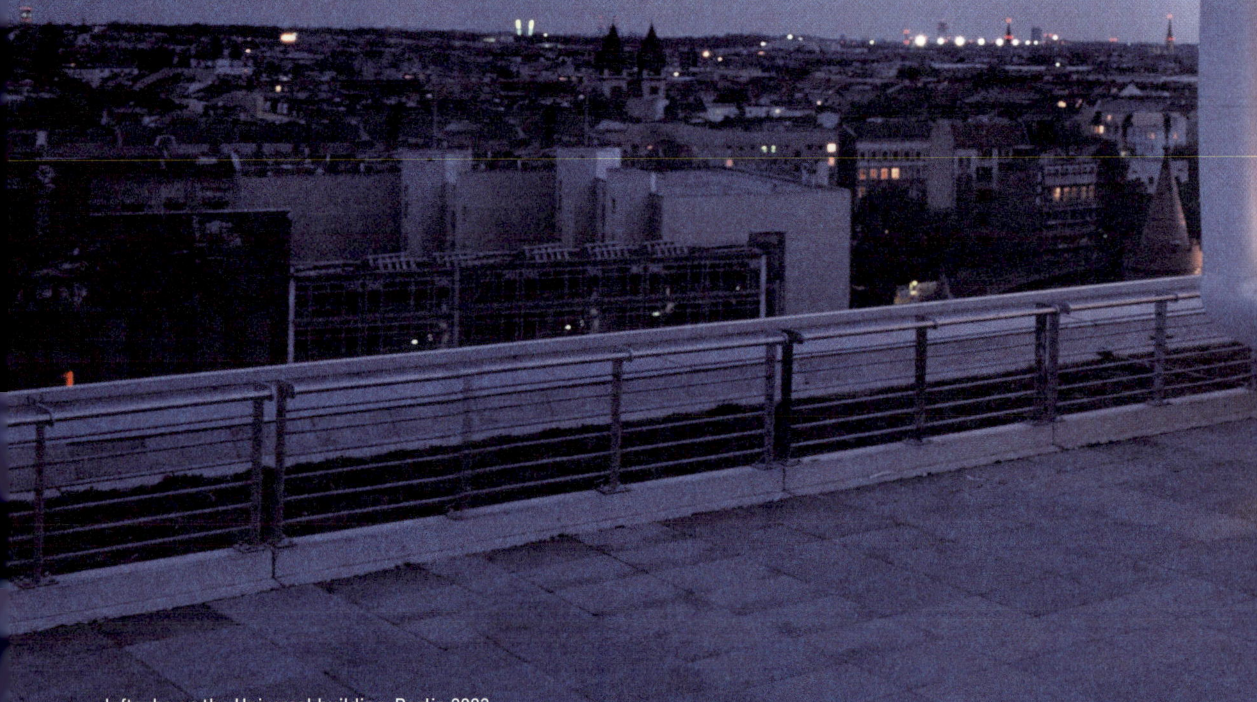

loftcube on the Universal building, Berlin 2003

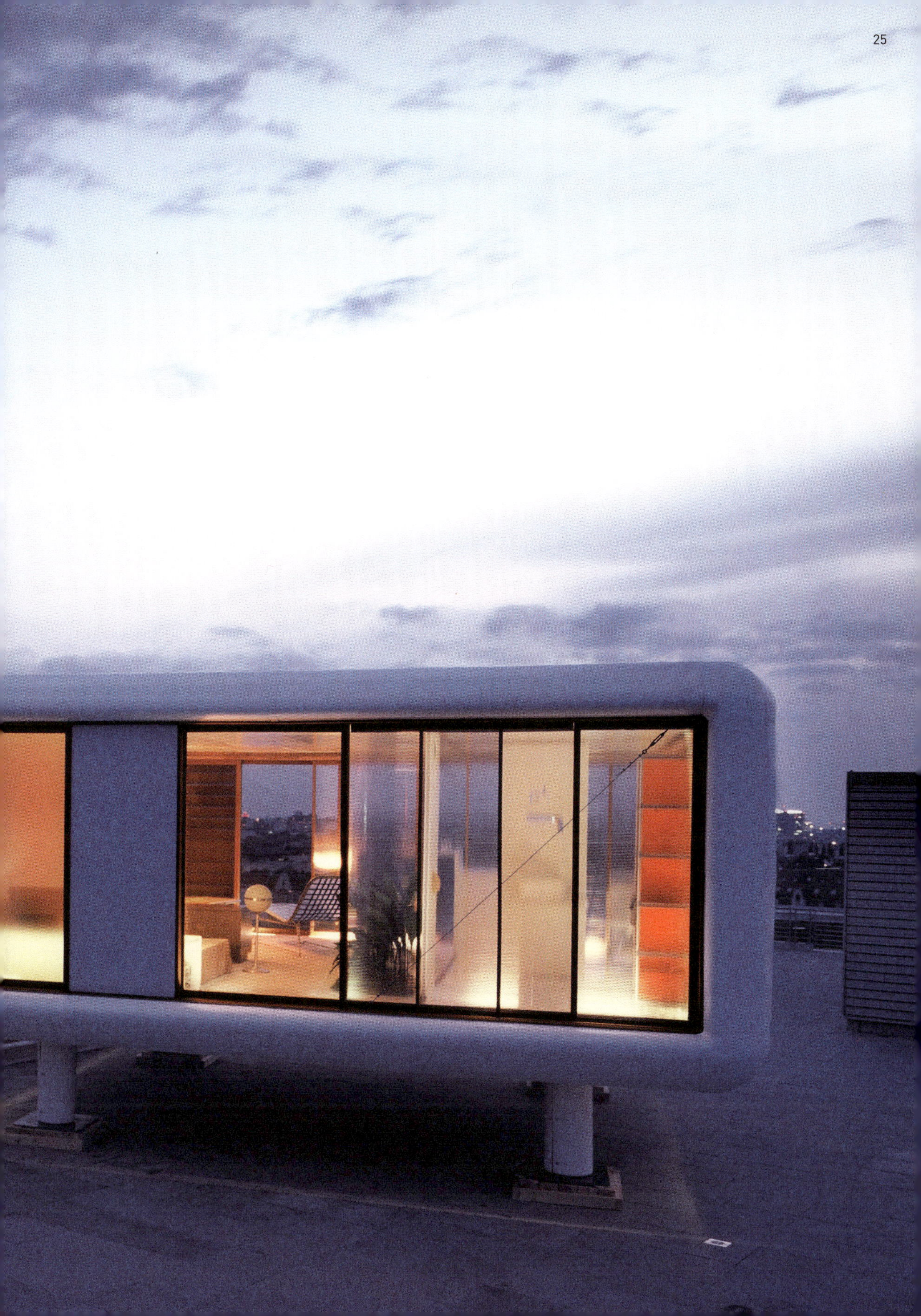

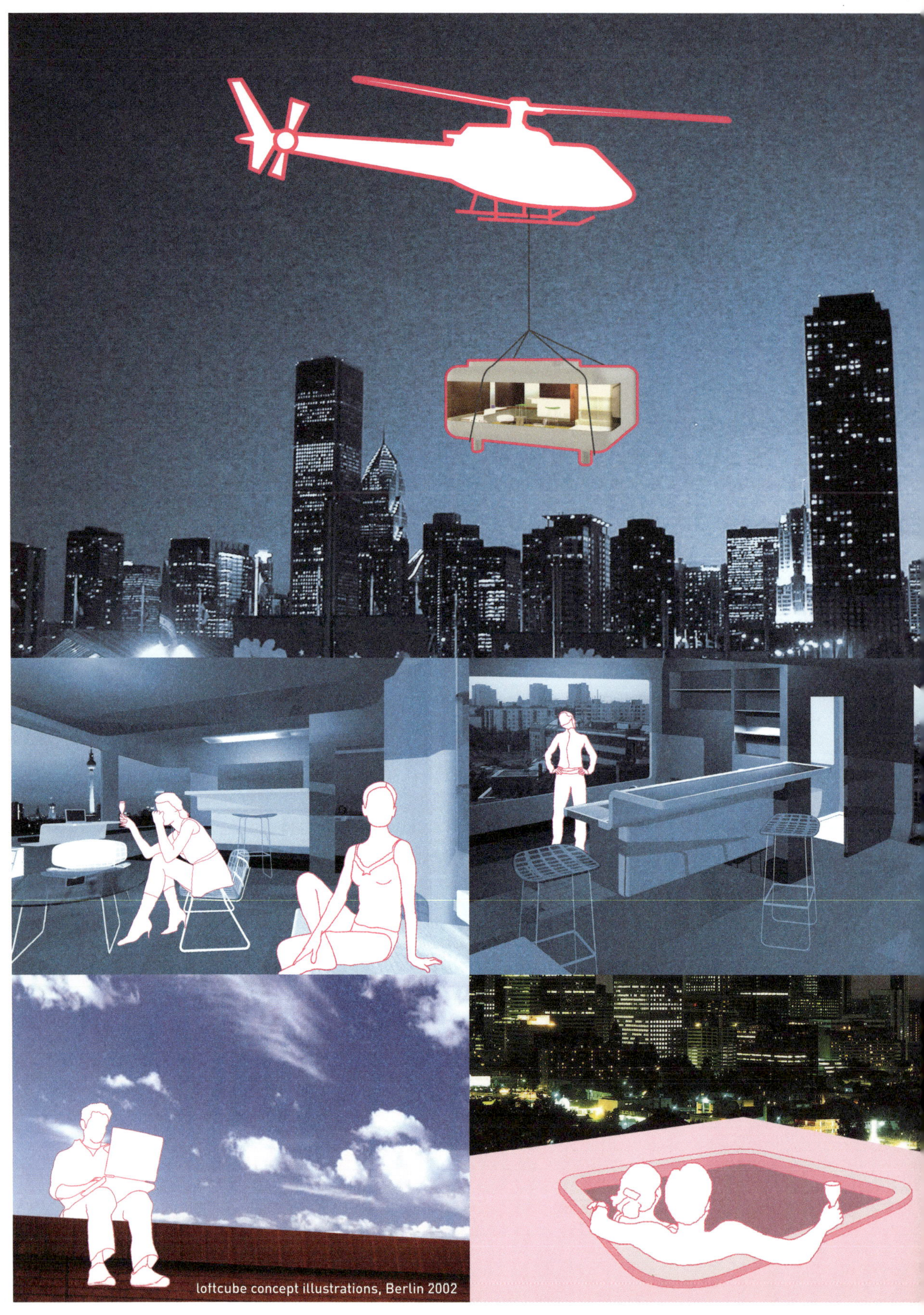

loftcube concept illustrations, Berlin 2002

In a collaborative effort between Christian Friedrich, who founded loftcube GmbH, and architects Achim Aisslinger and Andreas Bracht of and8 in Hamburg, the prototype was transformed from a 1:1 scale model into a high-end low-energy smart house which has been on the market since 2007. Through productive teamwork with diverse involved brand names and suppliers, details were developed and interior components designed: e.g. the central kitchen block is a cooperation with bulthaup and the modular kitchen & bathroom panel system was created with DuPont Corian. Today, the loftcube serves not only as a rooftop living option but also as office space, weekend-home, showroom, hideaway, hotel-suite or info pavilion.

Die Architekten Achim Aisslinger und Andreas Bracht vom Büro and8 in Hamburg verwandelten zusammen mit Christian Friedrich, Gründer der Loftcube GmbH, den hochwertigen Prototyp in ein intelligentes Niedrigenergiehaus, das seit 2007 auf dem Markt ist. Durch die erfolgreiche Zusammenarbeit mit einigen Zulieferern und Markenherstellern konnten Details durchdacht und einzelne Module des Interieurs entwickelt werden. Der zentral angeordnete Küchenblock zum Beispiel ist gemeinschaftlich mit bulthaup entstanden und das modular aufgebaute Paneelsystem für Küche und Bad wurde mit DuPont Corian erarbeitet. Der Loftcube dient heute nicht nur als möglicher Wohnraum auf Dächern, sondern auch als Büro, Wochenendhaus, Showroom, „Hideaway", Hotelsuite oder Infopavillon.

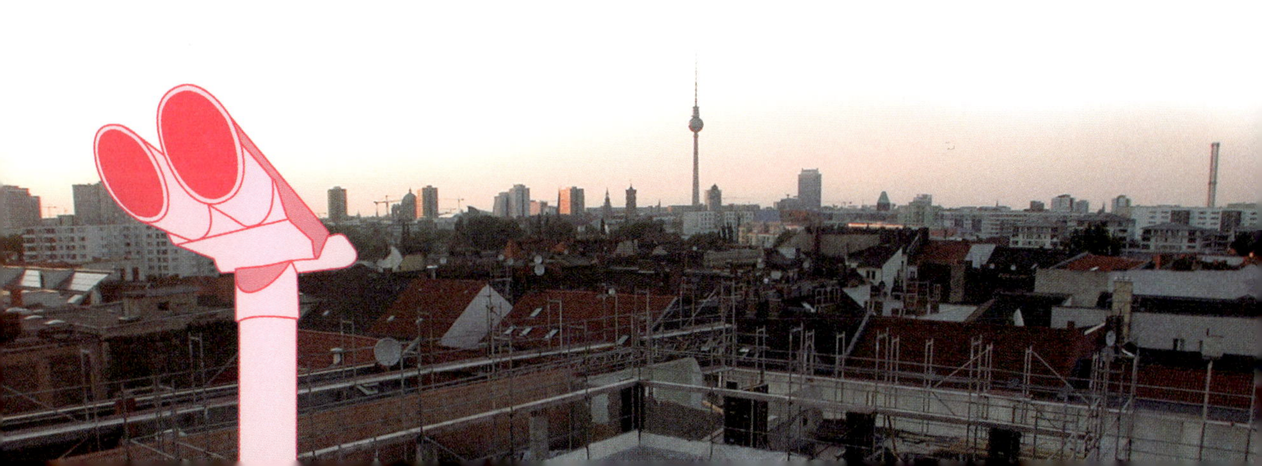

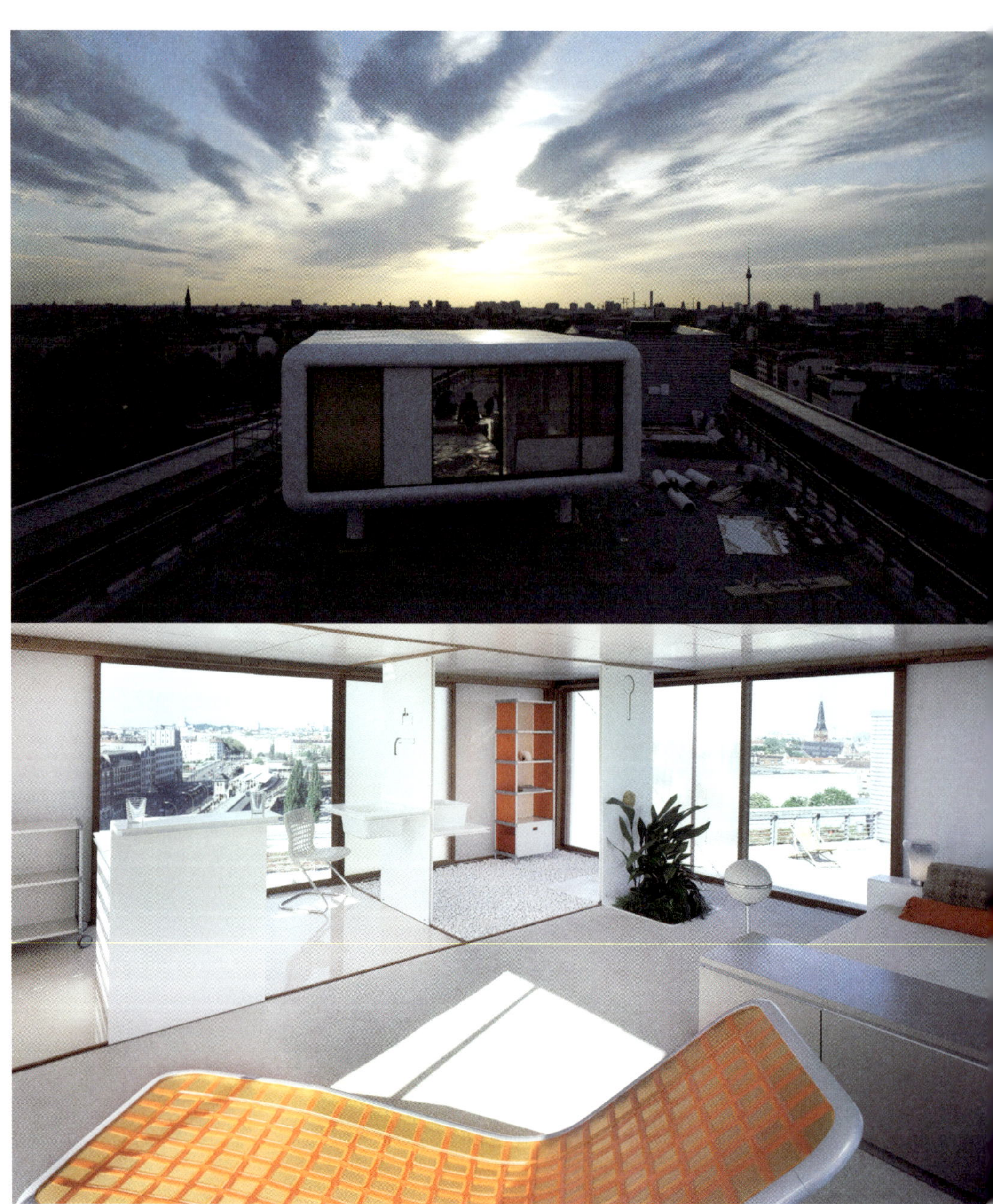

loftcube on the Universal building, Berlin 200

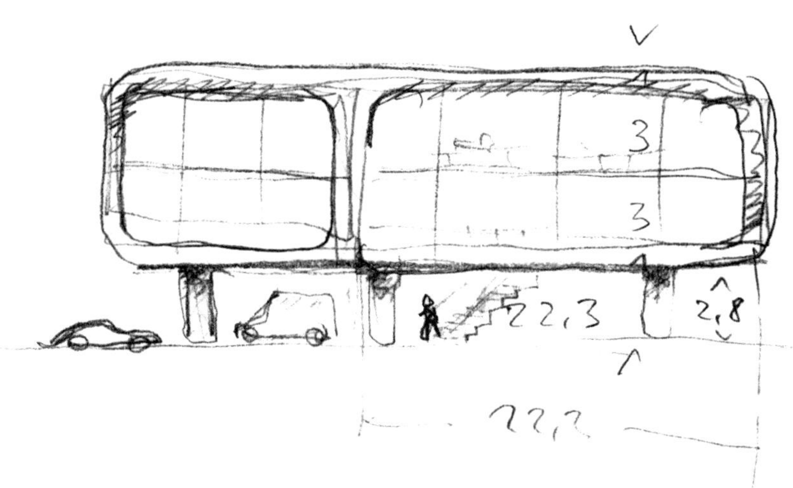

The first prototype designed and made by studio aisslinger was presented in 2003 on top of the Universal Music building at the River Spree in Berlin, whereas the redesigned production version 2007 was displayed during the "salone" design fair in Milan. The mix of a very detailed designed interior and exterior together with a new urban concept generated the interest and success of this future living project.

Das erste vom studio aisslinger entworfene und gefertigte 1:1 Modell wurde 2003 auf dem Dach von Universal Music an der Spree in Berlin vorgestellt, der überarbeitete Produktionstyp später auf dem „salone del mobile" 2007 in Mailand. Die Mischung aus einem sehr detailliert gestalteten Innen- und Außenraum in Verbindung mit einem neuen urbanen Nutzungskonzept legte den Grundstein für den Erfolg dieses Pilotprojektes für zukünftiges nomadisches Wohnen.

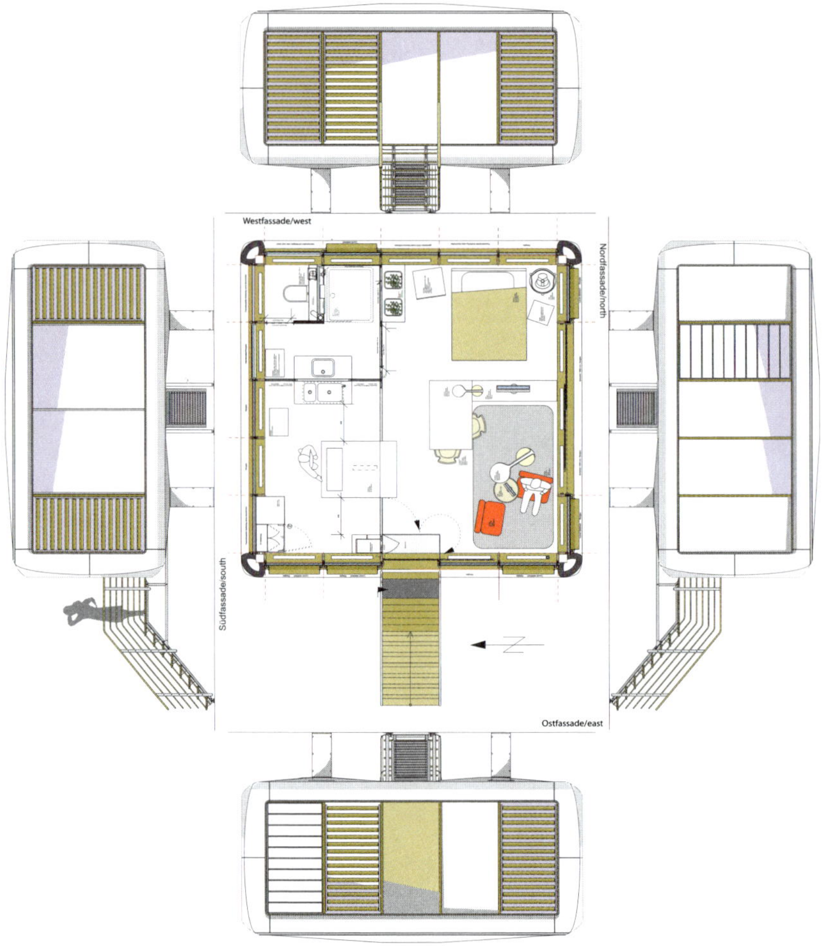

Westfassade/west

Nordfassade/north

Südfassade/south

Ostfassade/east

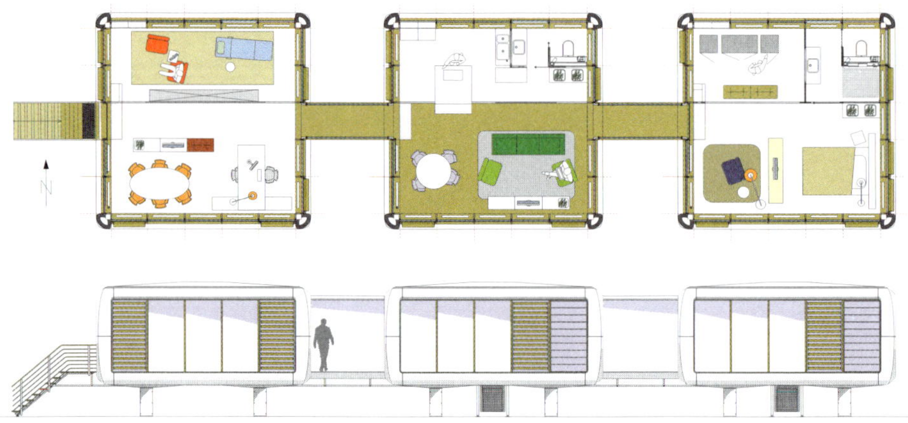

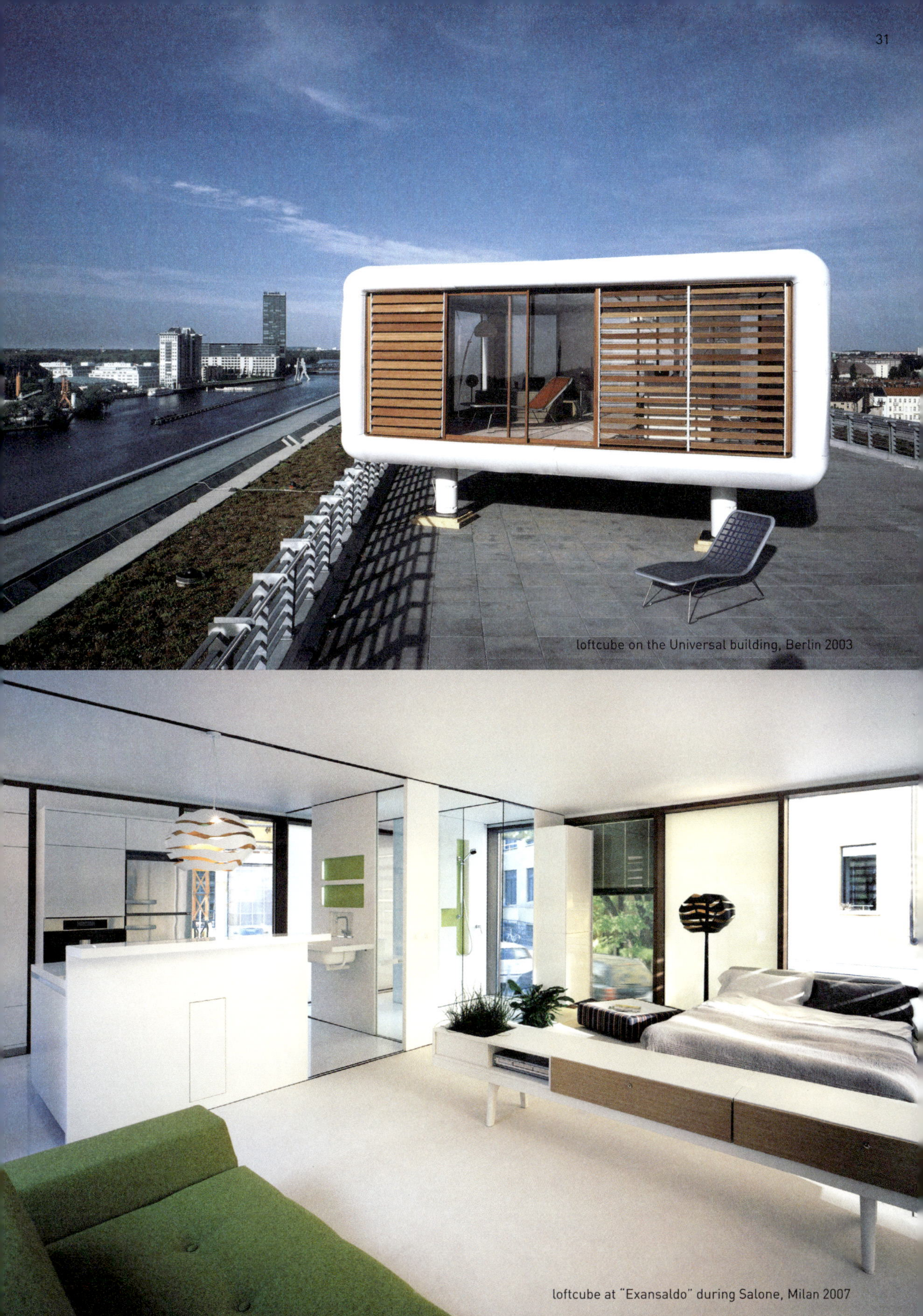

loftcube on the Universal building, Berlin 2003

loftcube at "Exansaldo" during Salone, Milan 2007

Size: Type LC39: 39 m², Type LC55: 55 m²
Net weight: 9 t
Net weight max.: 39,720 t
Frame material: Hot-dip galvanised modular steel frame construction
Facade material: SIPO-timber frame construction
Facade elements: LSG heat protection glass 8 27 2 * 5; 1,1; 36 db, 11 glass panel transparent, 2 Window louvre transparent 6 closed sandwich panels, 1 sliding entrance door, High gloss varnished glass-reinforced plastic-clips (RAL 9010)
Roof-, Bottom membrane: Special architectural membrane, B1 flame proof

Größe: *Typ LC39: 39 m², Typ LC55: 55 m²*
Nettogewicht: *9 t*
Nettogewicht max.: *39,720 t*
Rahmenmaterial: *Feuerverzinkte modulare Stahlrahmenstruktur*
Fassadenmaterial: *Holzrahmenstruktur aus Sipoholz*
Fassadenelemente: *Akustikoptimiertes Sicherheits-Isolierglas, Fassade bestehend aus: 11 Scheibenpaneele transparent, 2 Louvre Lamellenscheiben, 6 Sandwich-Verbundpaneele, 1 Schiebeeingangstür, montiert mit Clipssystem (RAL 9010)*
Dach-, Bodenmembran: *Spezial-Architekturmembran B1 flammhemmend*

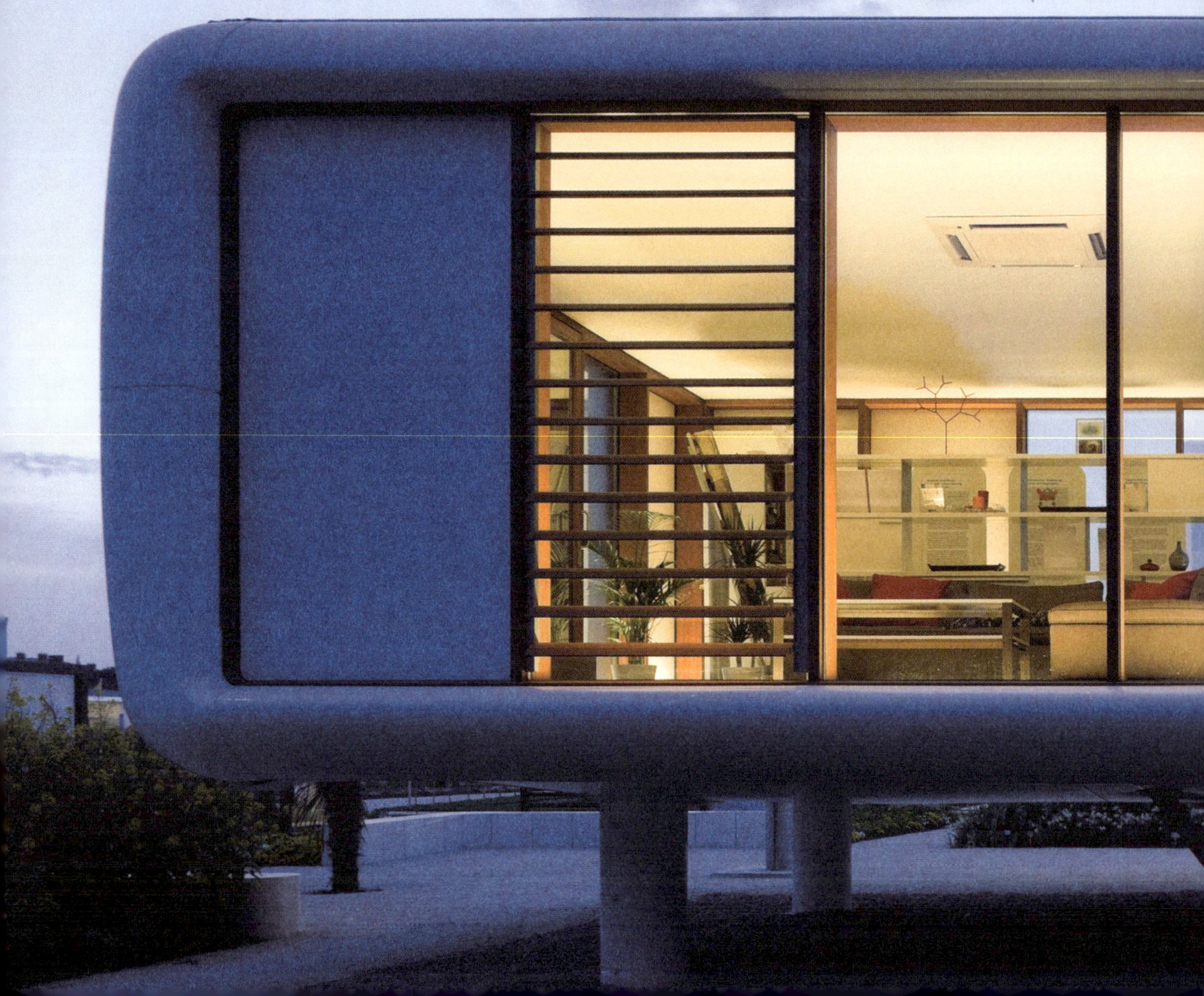

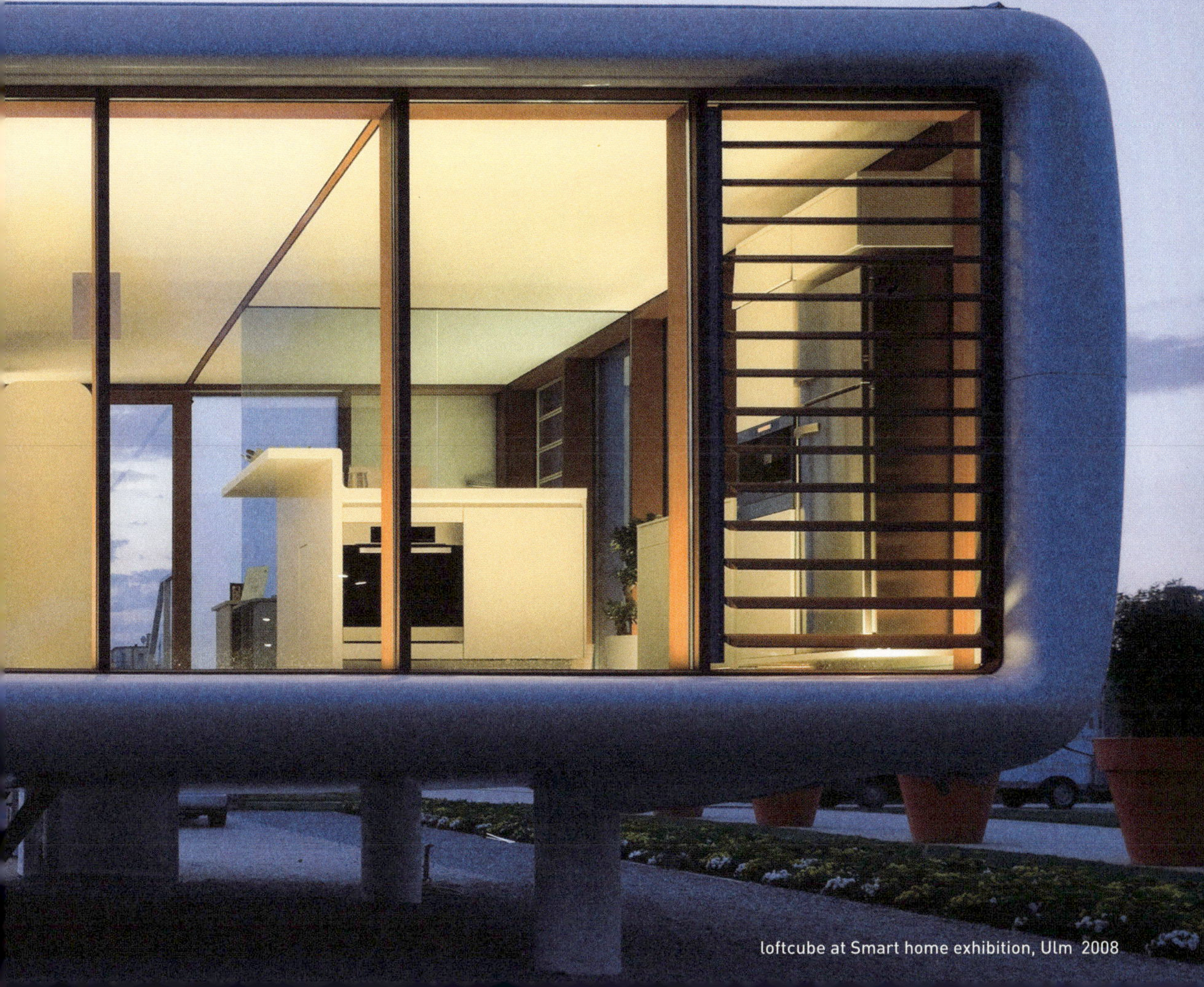

loftcube at Smart home exhibition, Ulm 2008

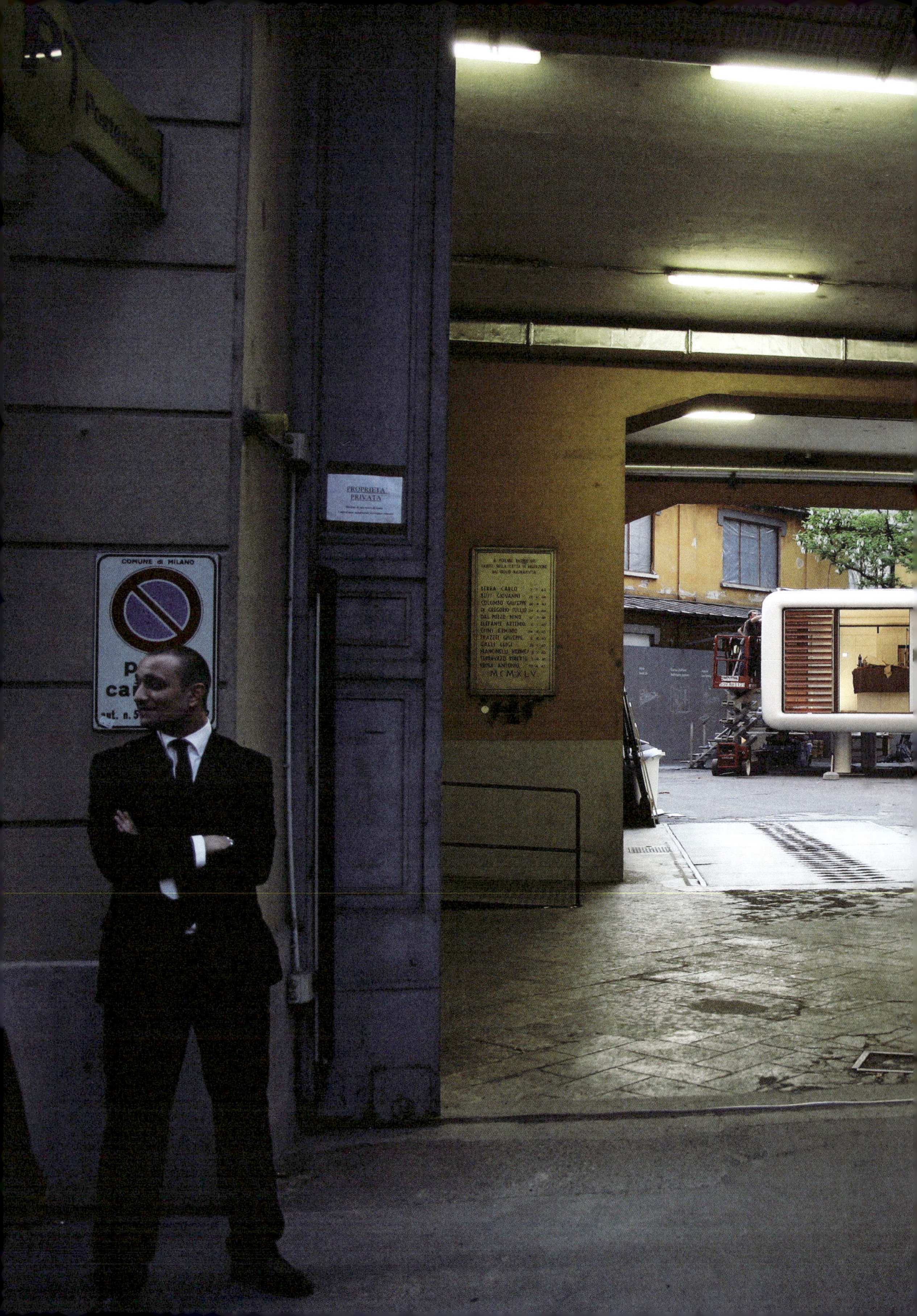

COMUNE di MILANO
PROPRIETA'
PRIVATA
MCMXLV

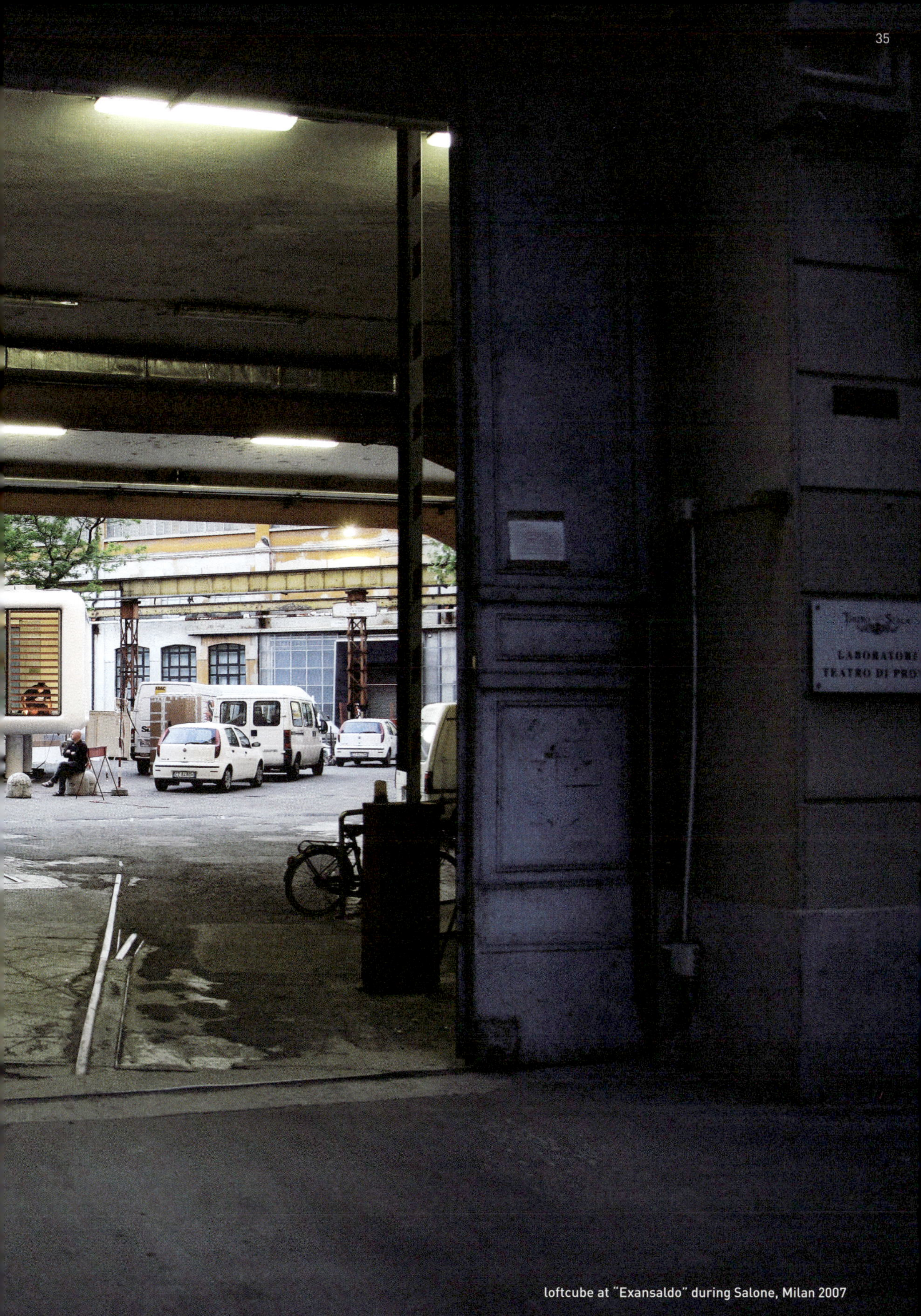

loftcube at "Exansaldo" during Salone, Milan 2007

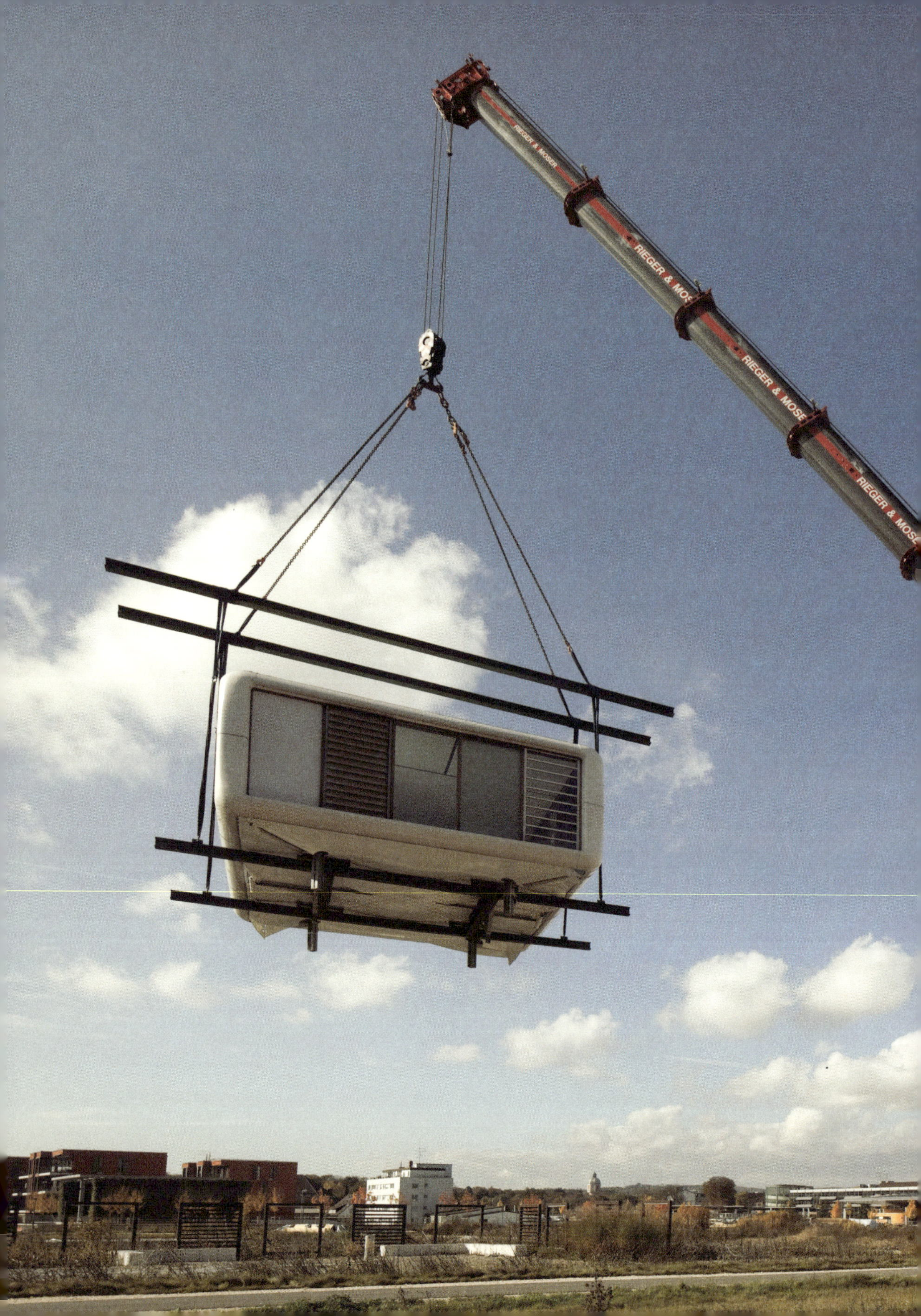
RIEGER & MOSER

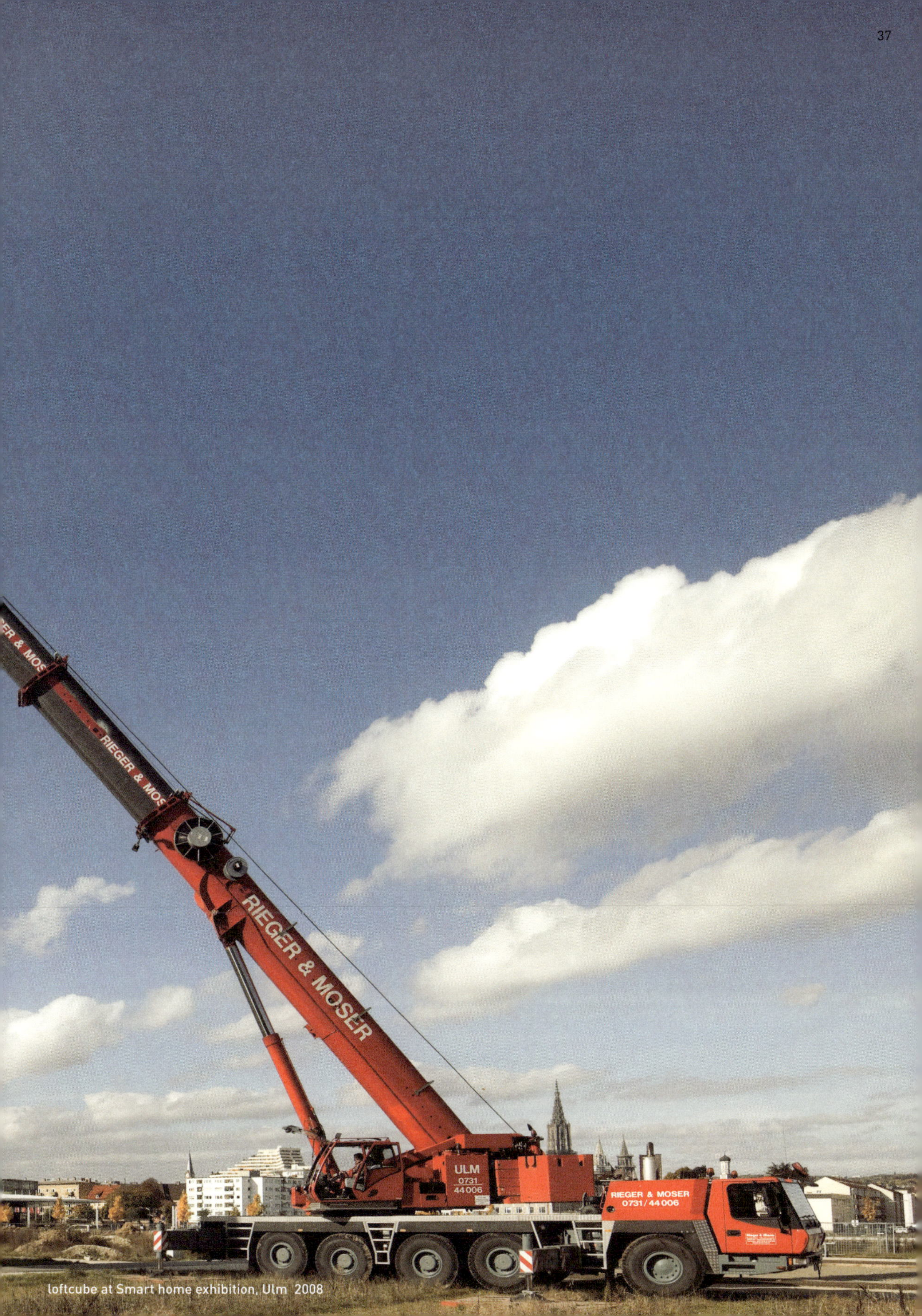

loftcube at Smart home exhibition, Ulm 2008

fincube

prototype 2009

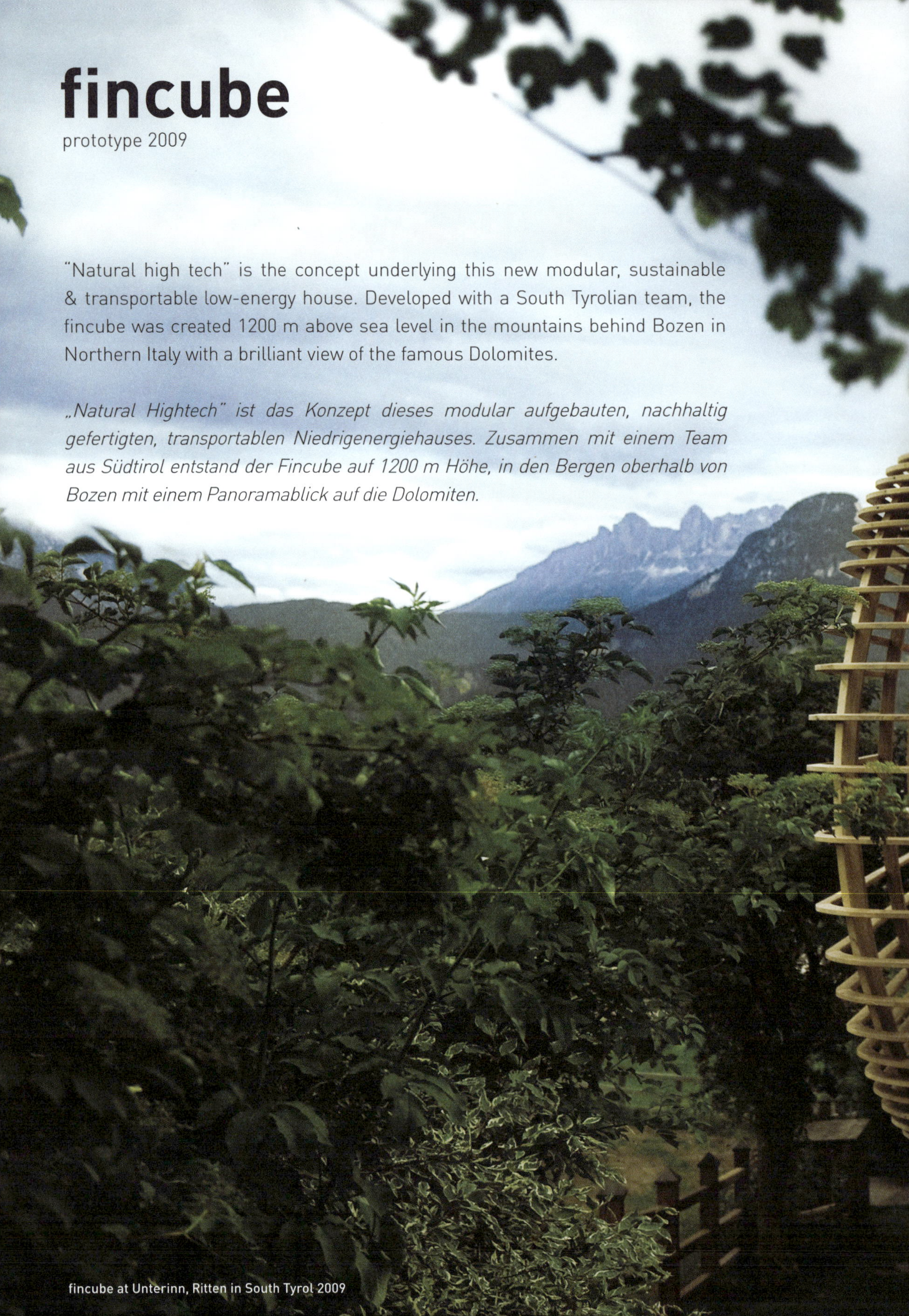

"Natural high tech" is the concept underlying this new modular, sustainable & transportable low-energy house. Developed with a South Tyrolian team, the fincube was created 1200 m above sea level in the mountains behind Bozen in Northern Italy with a brilliant view of the famous Dolomites.

„Natural Hightech" ist das Konzept dieses modular aufgebauten, nachhaltig gefertigten, transportablen Niedrigenergiehauses. Zusammen mit einem Team aus Südtirol entstand der Fincube auf 1200 m Höhe, in den Bergen oberhalb von Bozen mit einem Panoramablick auf die Dolomiten.

fincube at Unterinn, Ritten in South Tyrol 2009

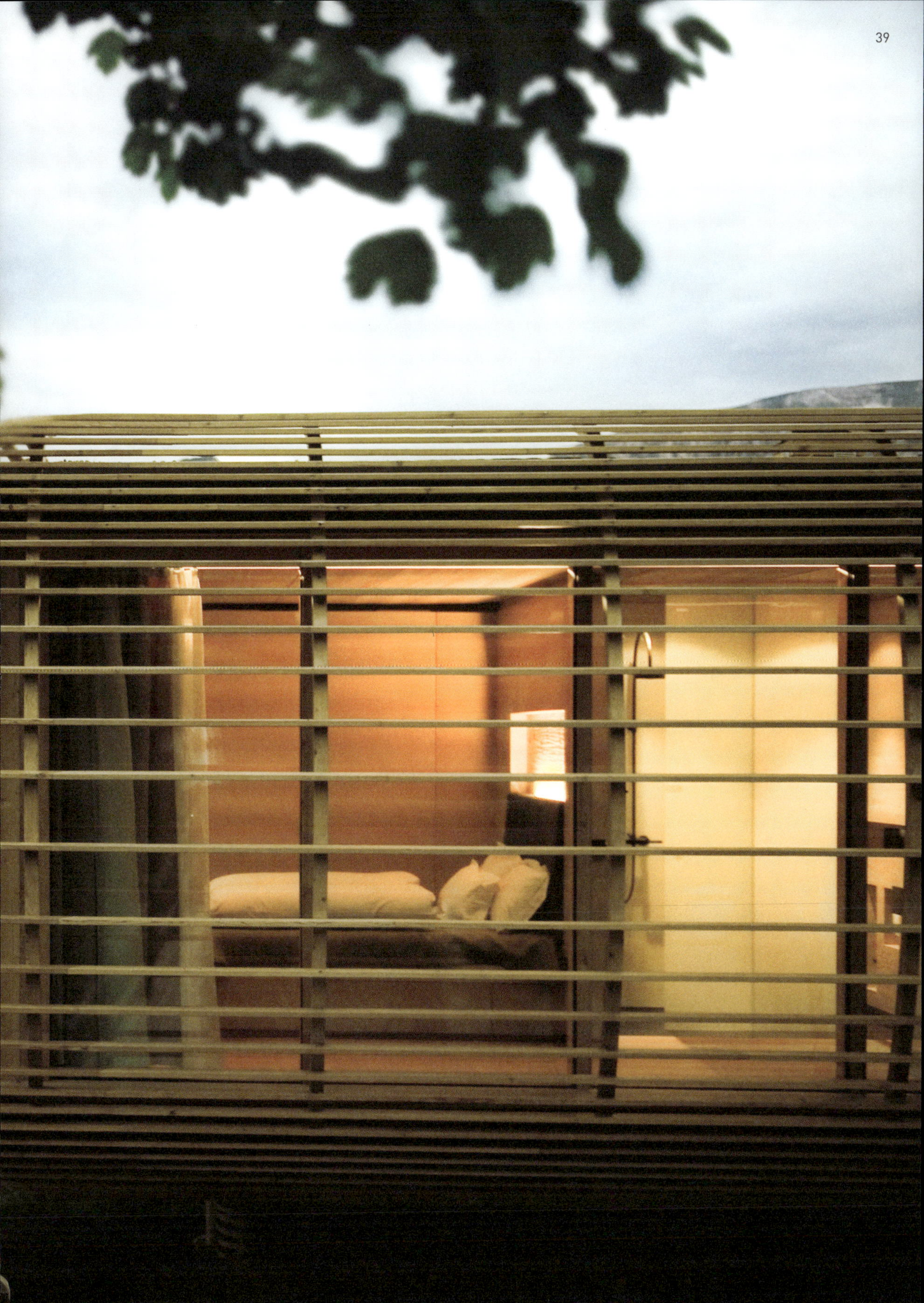

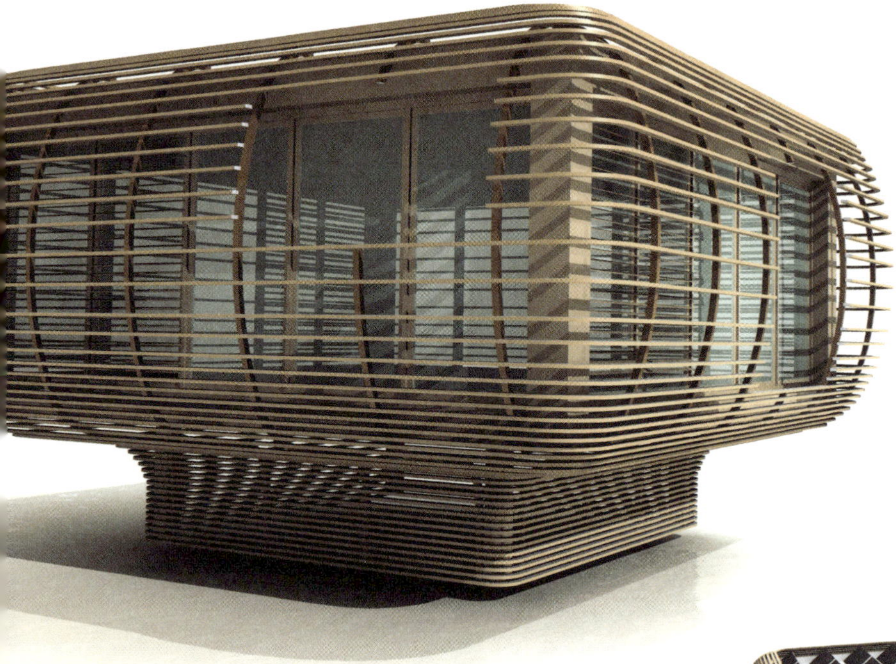

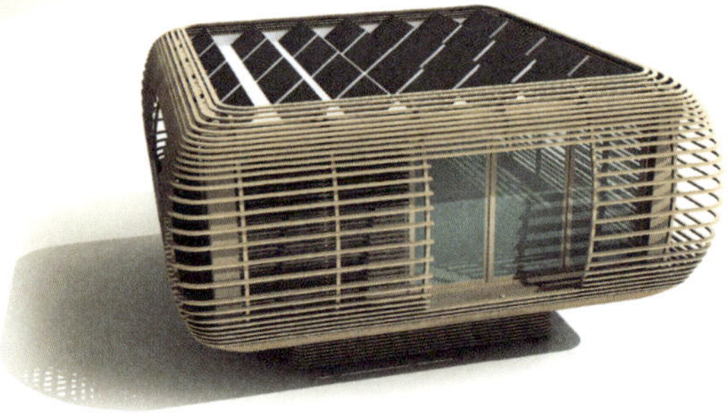

fincube renderings and construction drawings, facade elevation and section from 2008

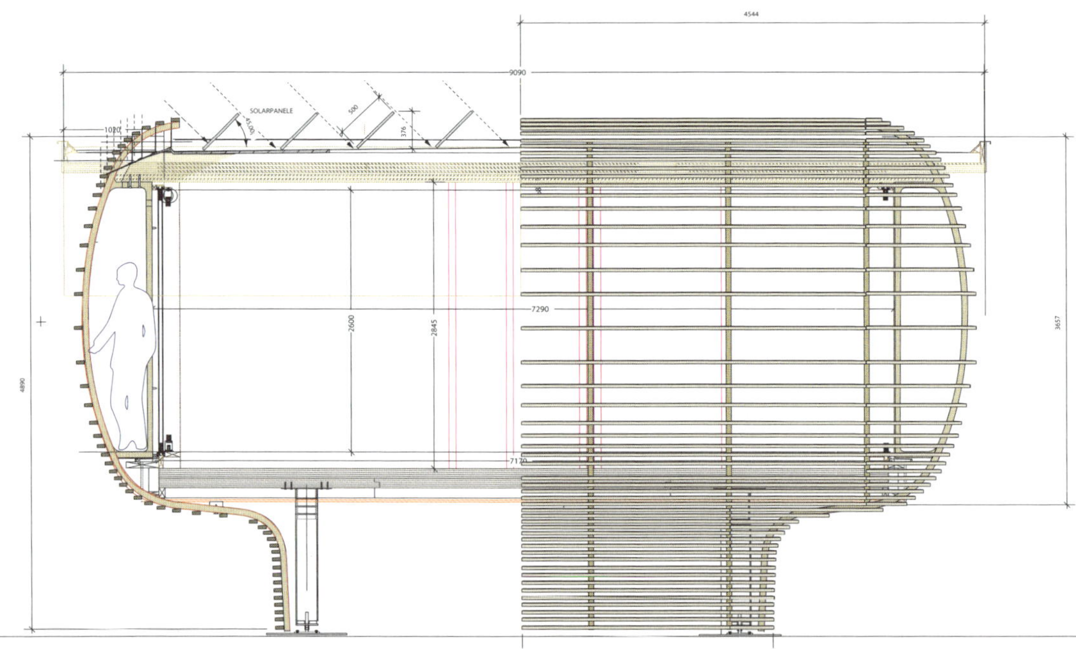

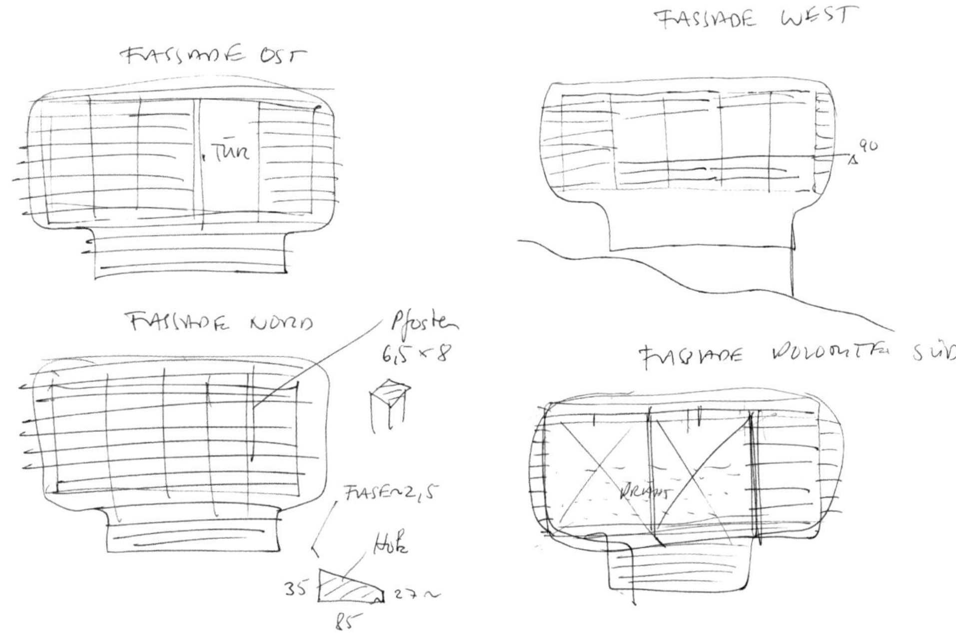

The hideaway-in-nature nomadic housing concept is made entirely of local wood and, with its 47 m² of living space, it creates a minimal CO_2 footprint: local suppliers and local crafts using local durable and recyclable materials manufactured with the precision and care of Tyrolese handwork. The fincube is a materialized vision of a small housing unit with a long lifecycle. It can easily be dismantled and rebuilt on a new site, and, even more important for nature hideaways, it requires minimum soil sealing – just 2 m² that is easily re-natured when the fincube is moved to another location.

Der als mit der Natur synchronisierbare „hideaway" konzipierte, nomadische Fincube besteht vollständig aus heimischem Holz und basiert auf einer minimalen CO_2-Bilanz: Ortsansässige Zulieferer und Handwerker verwendeten langlebige und recycelbare, lokale Ressourcen und Materialien, die handwerklich mit hoher Präzision und Liebe zum Detail von den beteiligten Tiroler Firmen umgesetzt wurden. Der Fincube mit seinen 47 m² Wohnfläche ist eine materialisierte Vision einer minimalen Wohneinheit mit einem maximal langen Lebenszyklus: durch unproblematischen Ab- und Aufbau an unterschiedlichen Standorten wird die Lebensdauer maximiert. Und was für Aufstellorte in der Natur wesentlich ist: Der Boden muss nur gering versiegelt werden – lediglich 2 m² Flächenverbrauch, die ohne Aufwand wieder renaturalisiert werden können, sobald der Fincube an einen neuen Ort wandert.

The design is minimal, material-orientated and in close touch with nature – the wooden space with 360-degree triple glazing is furnished with a second facade layer, producing shade and giving the building a unique overall mushroom-like monoshape. The horizontal ledges provide privacy for the fincube and embed the building in forests, meadows, mountain sides or other natural locations.

Das Design ist reduziert, orientiert sich an Materialbeschaffenheiten und geht konzeptionell von einer Symbiose mit der Natur aus. Der aus Holz bestehende Baukörper ist rundherum mit einer Dreifachverglasung und einem zweiten Fassadenlayer versehen, der dem Innenraum Schatten spendet und ihm seine eigene pilzartige Monoform verleiht. Die horizontal umlaufenden Leisten tragen zur Wahrung der Privatsphäre im Innern des Fincube bei und betten ihn gleichzeitig in Wald, Wiesen, Gebirge oder andere natürliche Umgebungen ein.

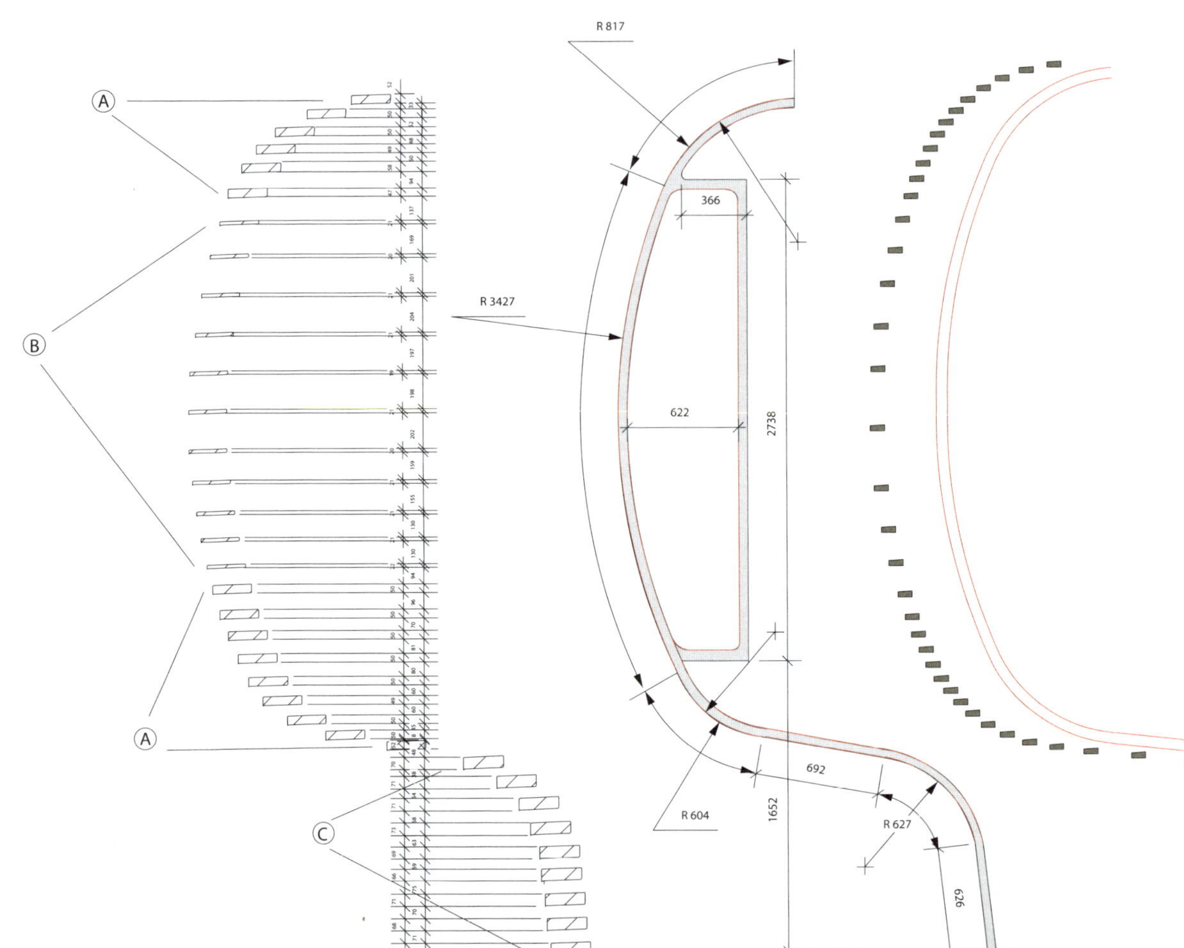

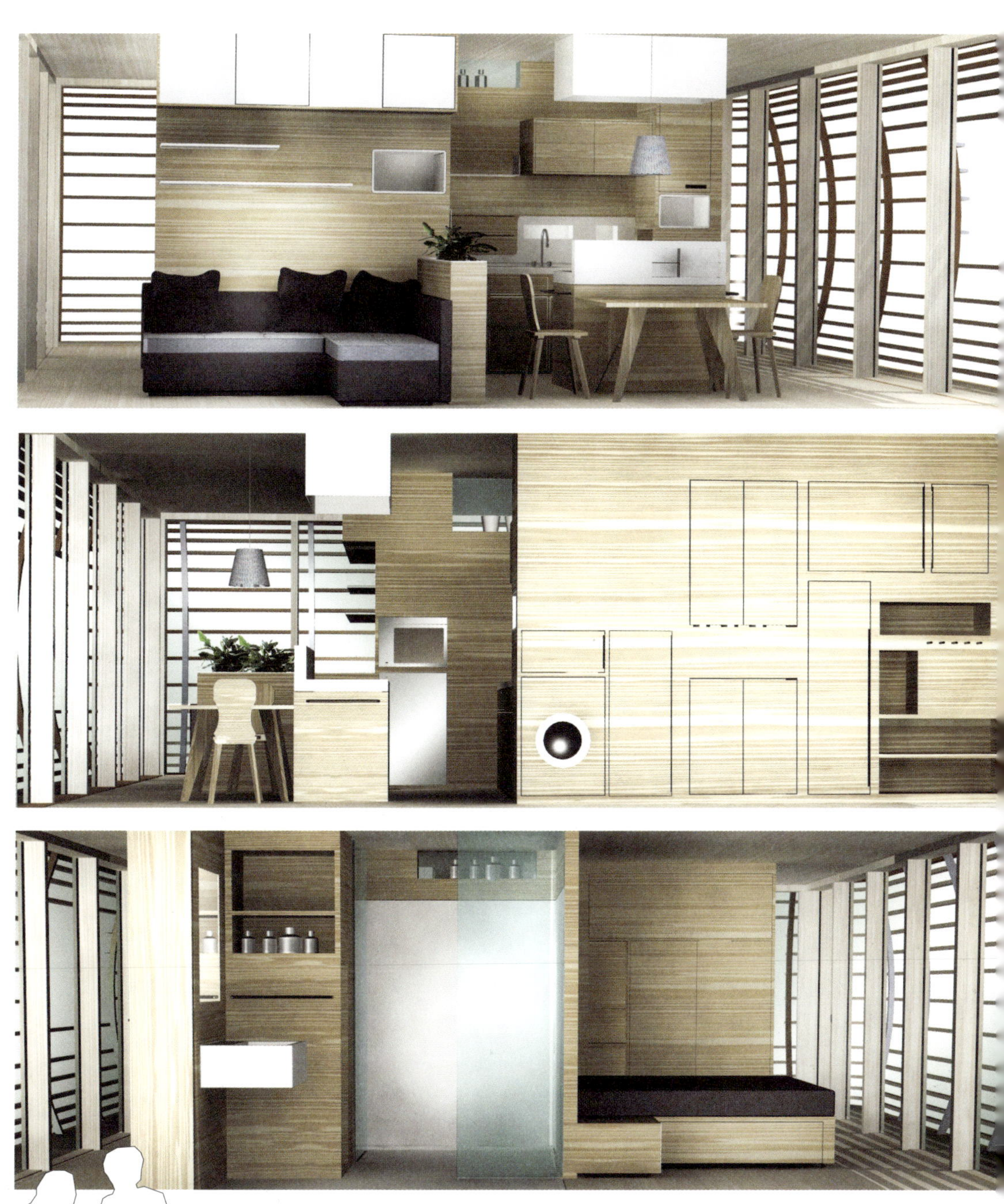

first renderings of fincube interior planning and facade planning 2008

Dimension outside: 8,5 m^2 (with facade)
7 m^2 (without facade)
Size: Total space 49 m^2, usable space 47 m^2
Net weight: 15 t
Frame material: Wood larchframe construction
Facade material: Wood larch, facade elements triple glazing, U-value – 0.70 W/m^2K
Soil sealing: < 2 m^2/4 foundation points à 70 cm^2
Flat roof: Greened roof or PV system for electricity generation
Wood structure: Markus Lobis
Interieur finish: Matthias Prast

Außenmaße: *8,5 m^2 (mit Fassade)*
7 m^2 (ohne Fassade)
Größe: *Gesamtfläche: 49 m^2, Nutzfläche 47 m^2*
Nettogewicht: *15 t*
Rahmenmaterial: *Lärche-Rahmenkonstruktion*
Fassadenmaterial: *Leisten aus Lärchenholz*
Fassadenelemente: *3fach-Verglasung, U-value 0.70 W/m^2K*
Bodenversiegelung: *Unter 2 m^2 auf 4 Fundamentpunkten mit je 70 cm^2*
Flachdach: *Flachdach als Gründach oder mit Solarpaneelbestückung*
Holzstruktur: *Markus Lobis*
Innenausbau: *Matthias Prast*

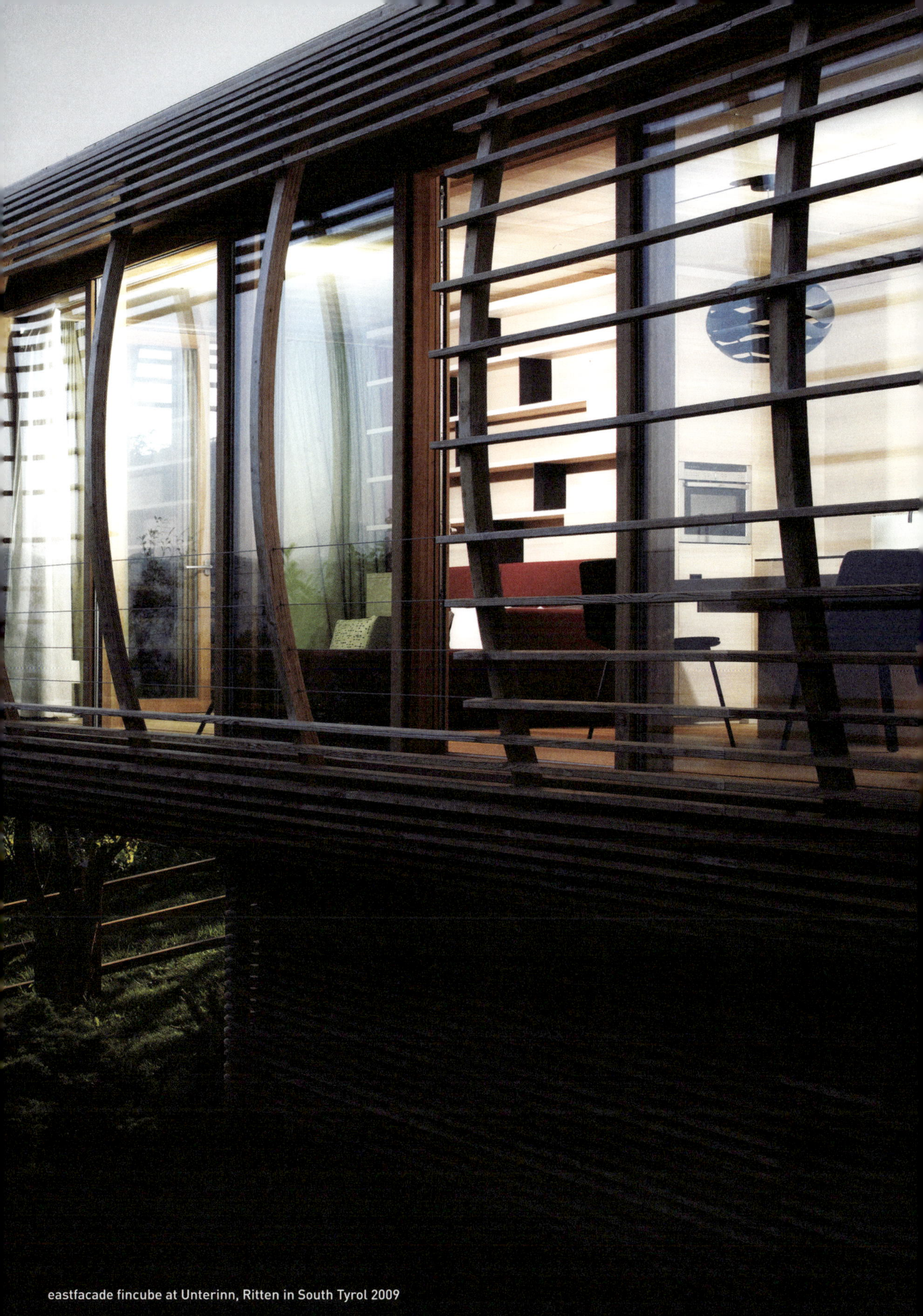

eastfacade fincube at Unterinn, Ritten in South Tyrol 2009

bedroom with bedhead made from stone pine, bath with dark brown corian elements and Dornbracht fittings

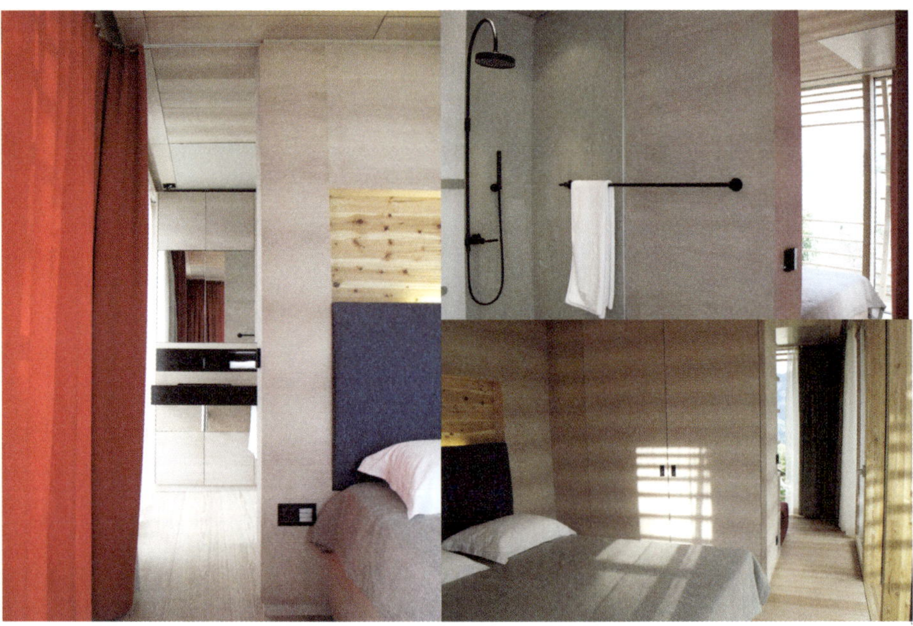

In collaboration with South Tyrolean hotelier Josef Innerhofer, the fincube was also conceptualized as a vision for future hospitality: a temporary fincube village with minimum soil sealing can be placed in the middle of beautiful landscapes without permanently altering them. In contrast to permanent buildings, it can easily be altered, extended, scaled down or removed and the area it is located in is soon re-naturalized back to normal – a possible answer to the future needs of smart tourism.

Der Fincube wurde in Zusammenarbeit mit Josef Innerhofer, einem Hotelier aus Südtirol, auch als Vision zukunftsorientierter „Hospitality" konzipiert. Ein temporäres, aus Fincubes bestehendes Dorf könnte mit geringem Maß an Landschaftsverbrauch und Bodenversiegelung inmitten schönster Naturlandschaften realisiert werden, ohne diese dauerhaft zu verwandeln. Im Gegensatz zu sämtlichen permanenten Gebäuden könnte ein Fincube-Dorf modifiziert oder komplett demontiert und der ursprüngliche Naturzustand wiederhergestellt werden – eine mögliche Antwort auf die zukünftigen Bedürfnisse intelligenten Tourismus.

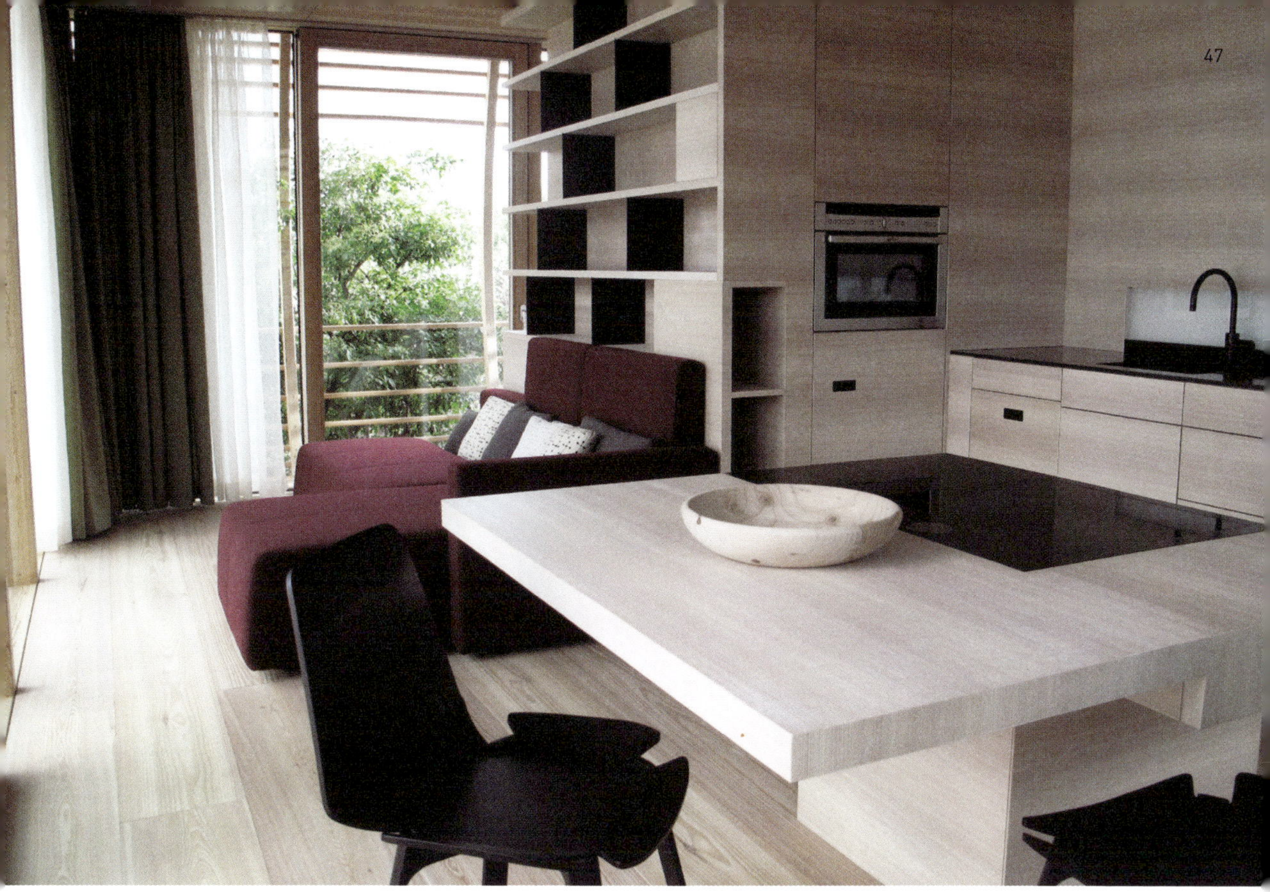

final interior with special designed cooking-table, Gap chair (Fornasarig), custom made sofa corner and smart house control by Berker

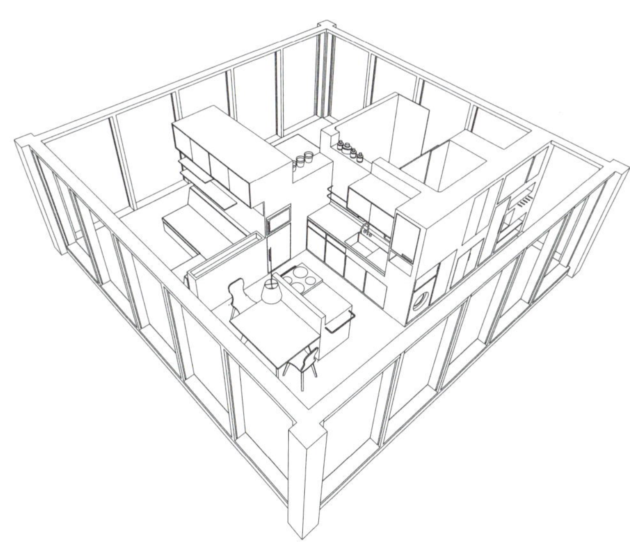

westfacade fincube at Unterinn, Ritten in South Tyrol 2009

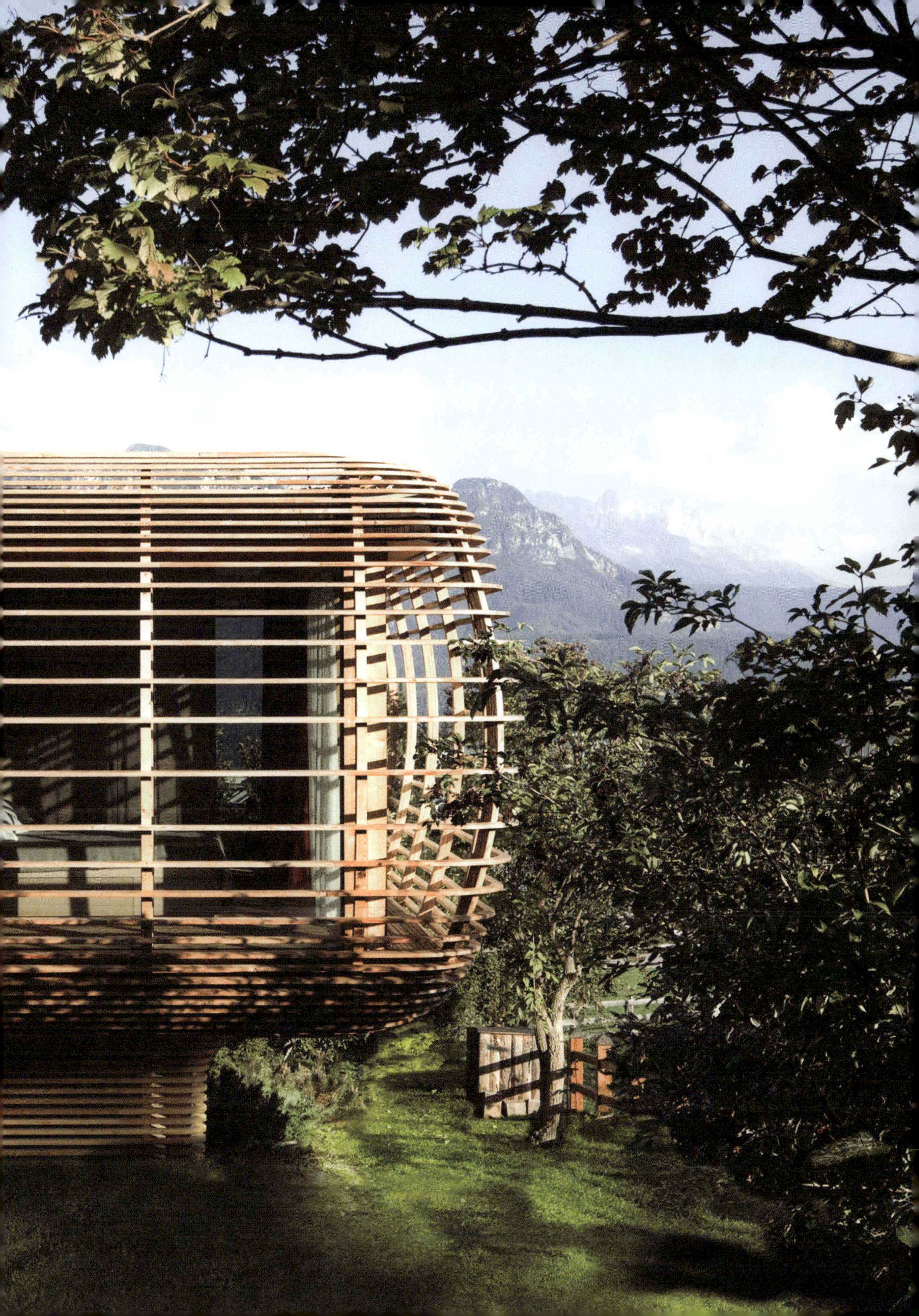

MODULES

modular based furniture systems

Modularity is an enduring constant in industrial construction and in the area of system furniture. Astounding and durable building-block systems are being created again and again but, in their details, are a complicated and difficult challenge for planners, engineers and designers: modular systems must have no disadvantages in terms of design compared to "non-systems", they must conceal their complexity, be no more expensive than "ready—made" objects and must generate considerable advantages in respect of storage, transport and assembly. Designers involved in the world of modularity see themselves as being confronted with a more complex series of tasks than would be entailed by purely formal design projects.

Modular systems not only often display a more complicated geometry; they are also usually "long-runners" in the market and, for modern nomads, are "companions" with a relatively long life-cycle. Modular shelves, for example, can be reconfigured again and again in different offices and living spaces and can also be added to, when necessary, over the years. The flexibility, long life and versatility in terms of the design intentions of the user, who determines his own "personal configuration", make modular systems into one of the most demanding design disciplines.

Modularität ist im industriellen Bauen und im Bereich der Systemmöbel eine dauerhafte Konstante: Es entstehen immer wieder erstaunliche und dauerhafte Baukastensysteme, die im Detail allerdings ein kompliziertes und anspruchsvolles Spielfeld für Planer, Ingenieure und Designer sind. Modulsysteme sollen gegenüber „Nichtsystemen" gestalterisch keine Nachteile haben, Komplexität nicht sichtbar zeigen, kostenseitig nicht aufwändiger als „fertige" Objekte sein und bei Lagerhaltung, Transport und Montage erhebliche Vorteile bringen. Designer, die sich mit dieser Welt auseinandersetzen, sehen sich also einer komplexeren Aufgabenstellung ausgesetzt als es rein formale Designprojekte verlangen würden.

Modulsysteme sind neben ihrer oft komplizierten Geometrie letztendlich meist „longrunner" im Markt und für moderne Nomaden Begleiter mit langen Lebenszyklen: Baukastenregale beispielsweise können in unterschiedlichen Büros oder Wohnräumen immer wieder neu konfiguriert und bei Bedarf über die Jahre erweitert werden. Die Flexibilität, Langlebigkeit und gestalterische Einbeziehung des Nutzers, der letztendlich „seine Konfiguration" bestimmt, machen Modulsysteme zu einer der anspruchsvollsten Designdisziplinen.

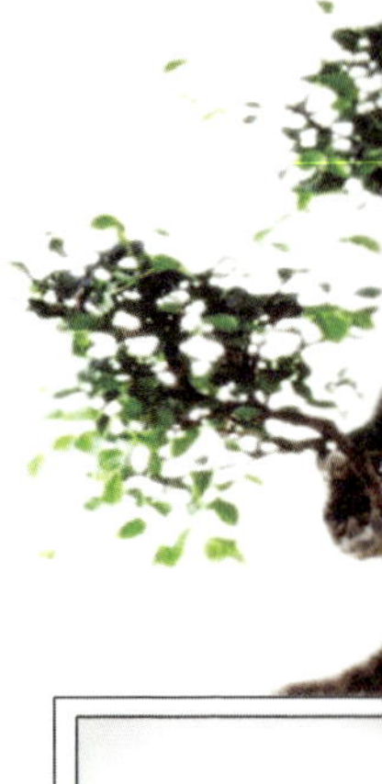

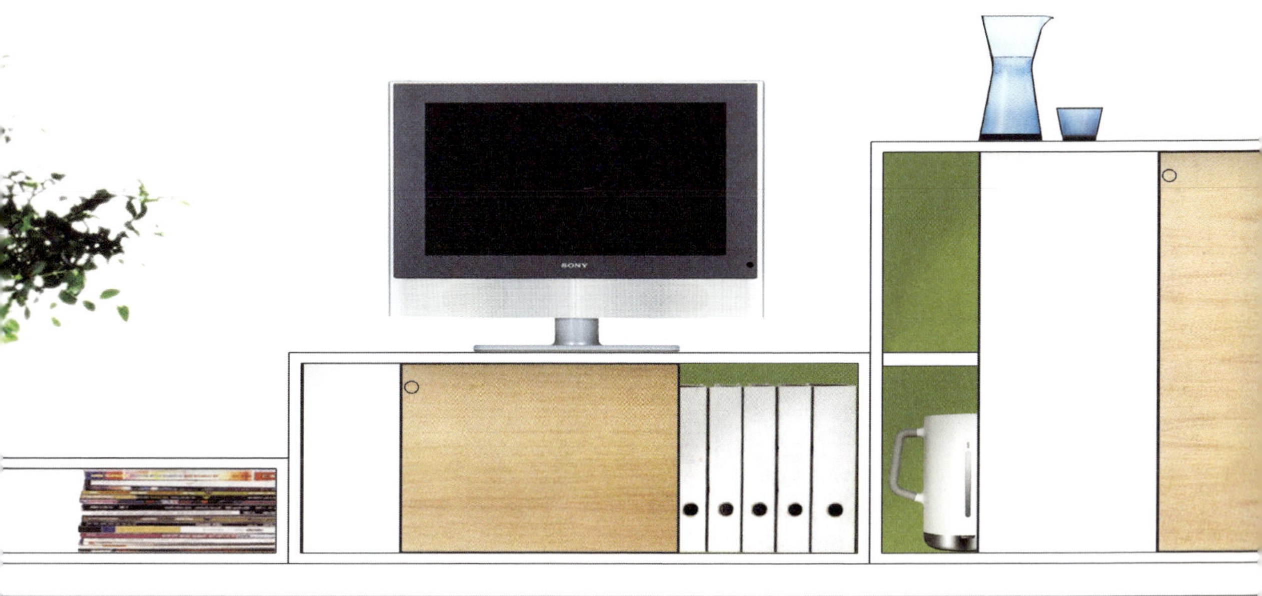
SONY

endless shelf

Porro, Italy 1994

The endless shelf is self explanatory – the cross-shaped die-cast aluminium joints which hold together the horizontal and vertical panels are an archetypal symbol of a connection point. Modularity is visually present but discreet as the joints practically submerge, being flush with the wooden panels. Three types of joint and a single board provide endless possibilities for using bookshelf grids in architecture. The shelf was designed in 1994, first self-produced with local Berlin carpenters and aluminium casting suppliers and distributed to friends and various shops. Werner Aisslinger gave the copyright to Porro, Italy in 1995. Since then, the endless shelf has been on the market and is still a very successful bookshelf typology being sold across the world.

Das Endlosregal ist selbsterklärend – die kreuzförmigen Verbindungselemente aus Aluminiumdruckguss, die die horizontalen und vertikalen Platten zusammenhalten, sind visuell ein archetypisches Zeichen eines Kreuzungspunktes. Die Verbindungselemente schließen bündig mit den Holzplatten ab und verschwinden konstruktiv. Drei verschiedene Verbinder und eine einzige, speziell gefräste Platte ergeben unzählige Möglichkeiten, ein modulares Bücherregal als Raster in Architekturen zu implementieren. Werner Aisslinger übertrug das Copyright des 1994 entworfenen und anfänglich zusammen mit Berliner Schreinern und Aluminiumguss-Lieferanten gefertigten Regals 1995 an die italienische Firma Porro. Seitdem ist das Endlosregal auf dem Markt und stellt immer noch einen der weltweit erfolgreichsten addierbaren Buchregaltypen dar.

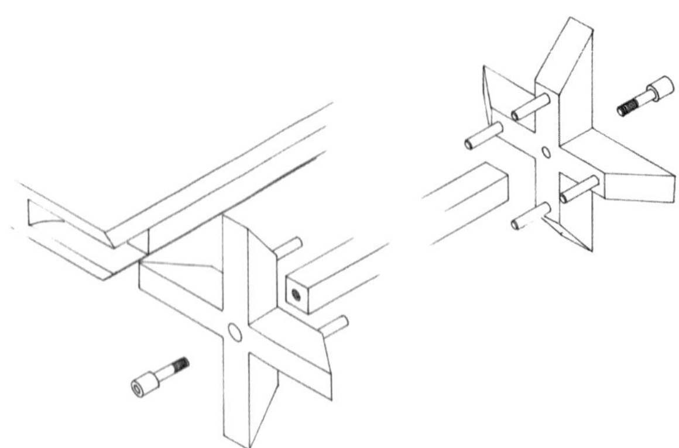

Size: Panels 36 x 37,2 cm
Material: Panels in MDF (in dark mdf or oak veneer) or moulded plastic (PoliMethyl-Metacrilate) in various colours
Joints: Aluminium die cast in matt metal finish or black powder-coated

Größe: *Paneele 36 x 37,2 cm*
Material: *Paneele aus MDF (Schwarz durchgefärbt oder Eichefurnier) oder Kunststoff (PMMA) in verschiedenen Farben*
Verbindungsstücke: *Aluminiumdruckguss-Verbinder, mattiert oder schwarz pulverbeschichtet*

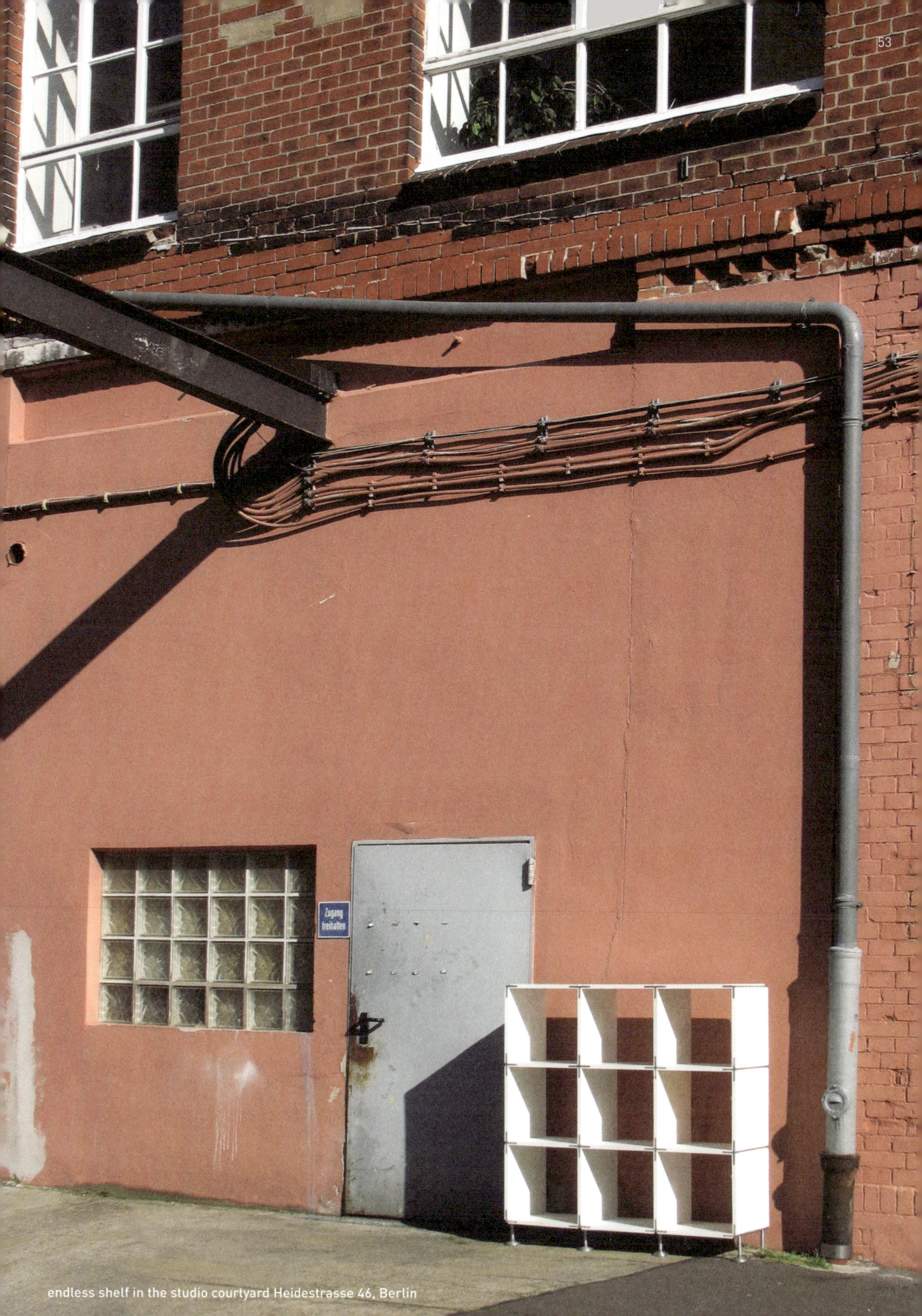

endless shelf in the studio courtyard Heidestrasse 46, Berlin

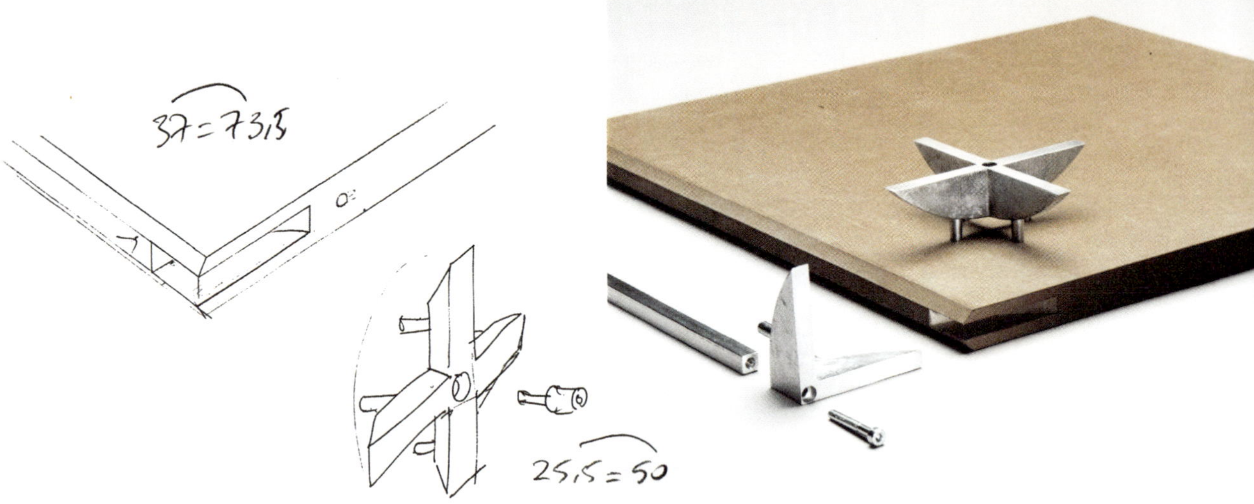

first casted aluminium joints with MDF board

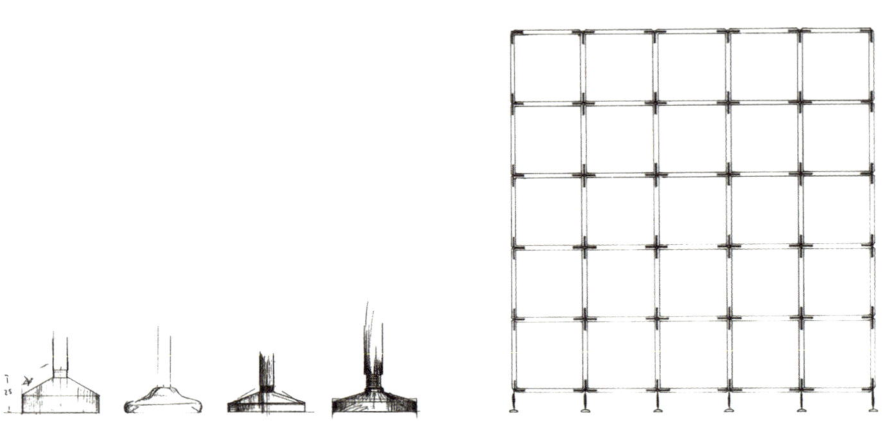

„We remember our first meeting with Werner very well. At that time, he was practically unknown as a young German designer trying to find a manufacturer who would have trust in his first project. Introduced to us by a Porro collaborator in Germany, he came to the first meeting at our factory by car, an old Golf, directly from Berlin. Werner started his presentation and astounded all of us by showing not only professional drawings of his 'creature' but also a wonderful, ready-made prototype made by himself with the help of an artisan in Berlin. Really amazing! We took very little time to arrive at a decision: Endless Shelf was quite immediately handed over to our technical department to be processed for mass production.Only rarely has a a new product undergone such a fast development process at Porro: Endless shelf was, for all of us, a 'coup de foudre' which became suddenly a great success. After 12 years, Endless Shelf is still in production and is one of Porro's more prestige-laden image-products."

Mauro Marelli, Porro

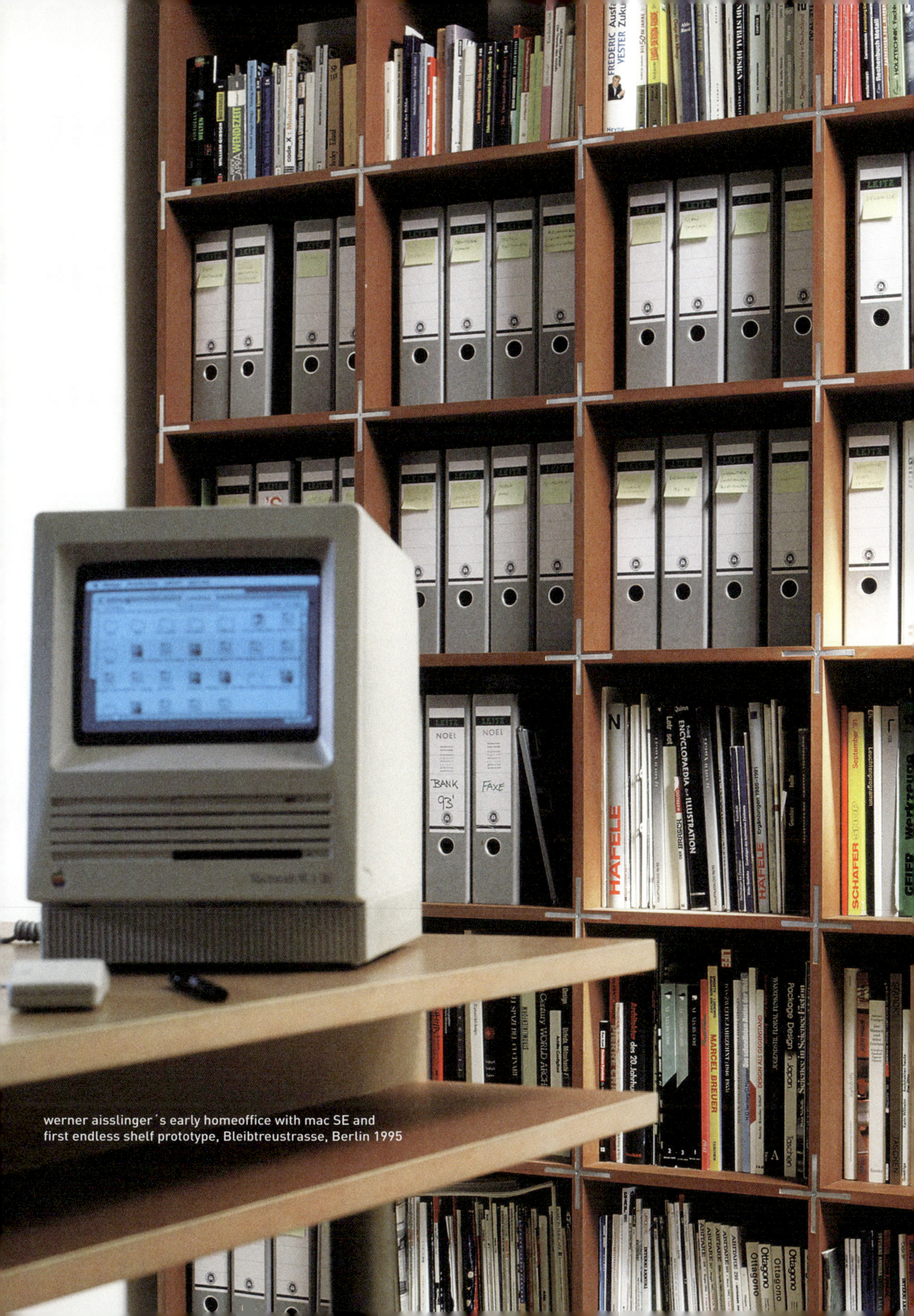

werner aisslinger´s early homeoffice with mac SE and first endless shelf prototype, Bleibtreustrasse, Berlin 1995

books

edition 2007

Books is a modular structure made out of books. In terms of its underlying concept, it is similar to the endless shelf but is more radical and less product-orientated: the content becomes the structural material in that the books are joined by metal connecters to form a supporting wall. Spaces made out of books demonstrate the intense spatial atmosphere that books can generate, a kind of mood best experienced in old libraries and archives. The concept:

Books ist eine modulare Struktur aus Büchern. Sie bewegt sich konzeptionell nahe am Endless Shelf-Projekt, ist aber radikaler und eher Installation als Produkt: der Inhalt wird zum Baumaterial – Bücher werden mit Hilfe von Metallverbindern zu tragenden Wänden. Räumliche Installationen aus Büchern generieren eine intensive atmosphärische Wirkung. Der „spirit" alter Bibliotheken wird hier in einer experimentellen Anordnung puristisch verdichtet und begehbar inszeniert. Das Konzept:

01 Books as a resource: large, used books with outdated titles which are too old to be read are assembled with a specially designed metal connector. The result is an endless modular meta-grid for use on walls, as room dividers or shelves.

Bücher als Rohstoff: Großformatige, gebrauchte oder nicht mehr aktuelle Bücher können zusammen mit den speziell entwickelten Metallverbindern zu einem endlosen modularen Meta-Raster addiert werden und als Wände, Raumteiler oder Regale Verwendung finden.

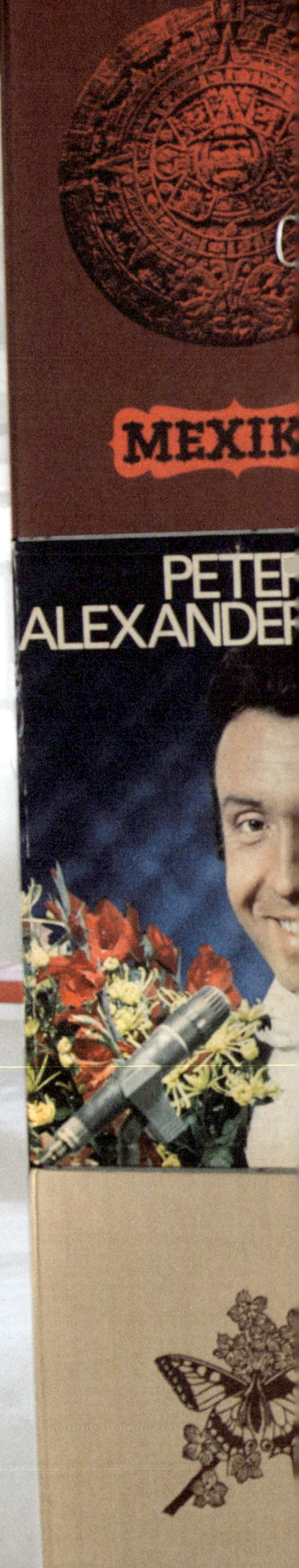

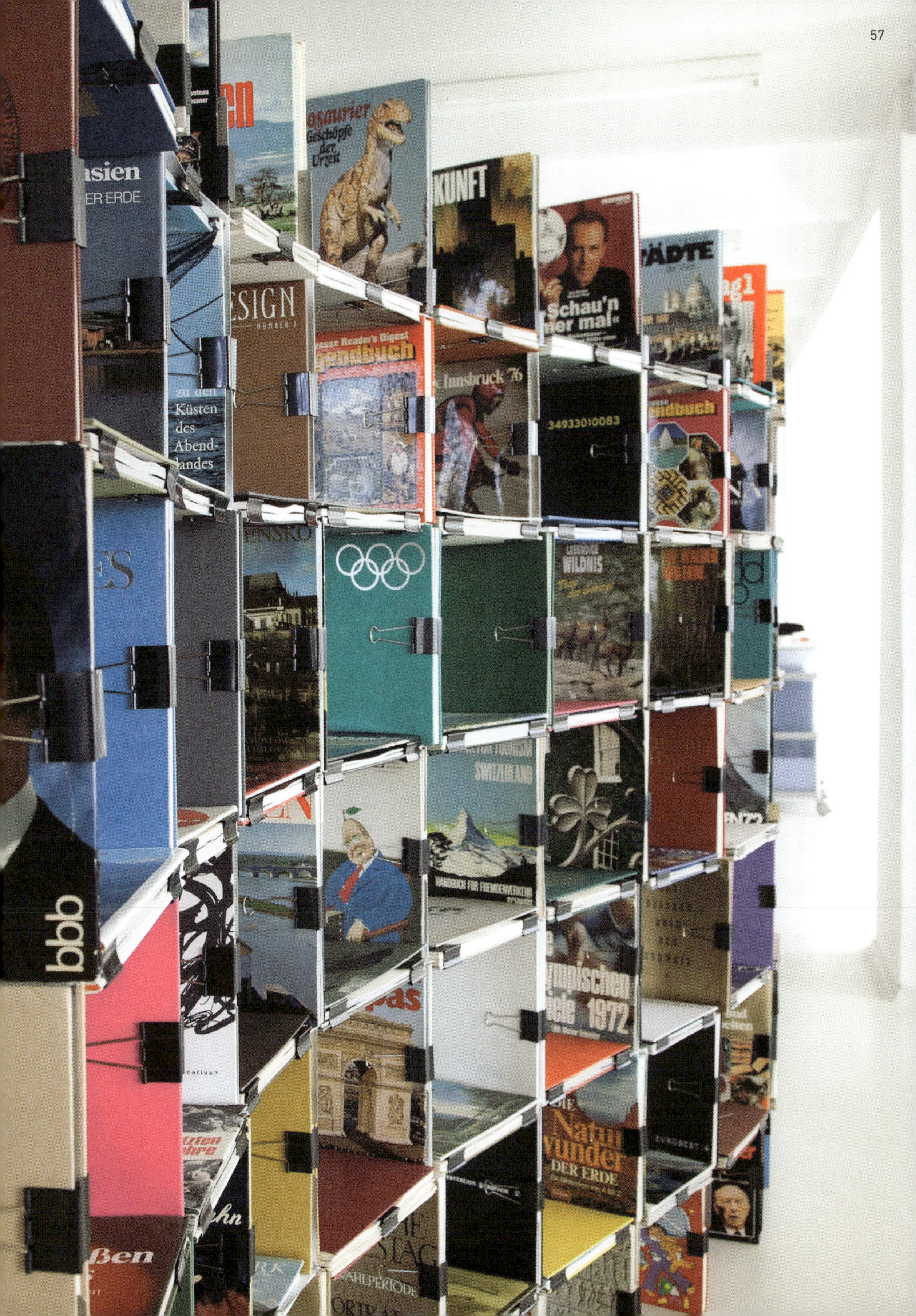
asien
ER ERDE
osaurier
Geschöpfe
der
Urzeit
KUNFT
ESIGN
Reader's Digest
endbuch
Innsbruck 76
Schau'n
mer mal«
ÄDTE
34933010083
endbuch
zu den
Küsten
des
Abend-
landes
LEBENDIGE
WILDNIS
SWITZERLAND
HANDBUCH FÜR FREMDENVERKEHR
ympischen
piele 1972
DIE
Natur
wunder
DER ERDE
bbb
WAHLPERIODE

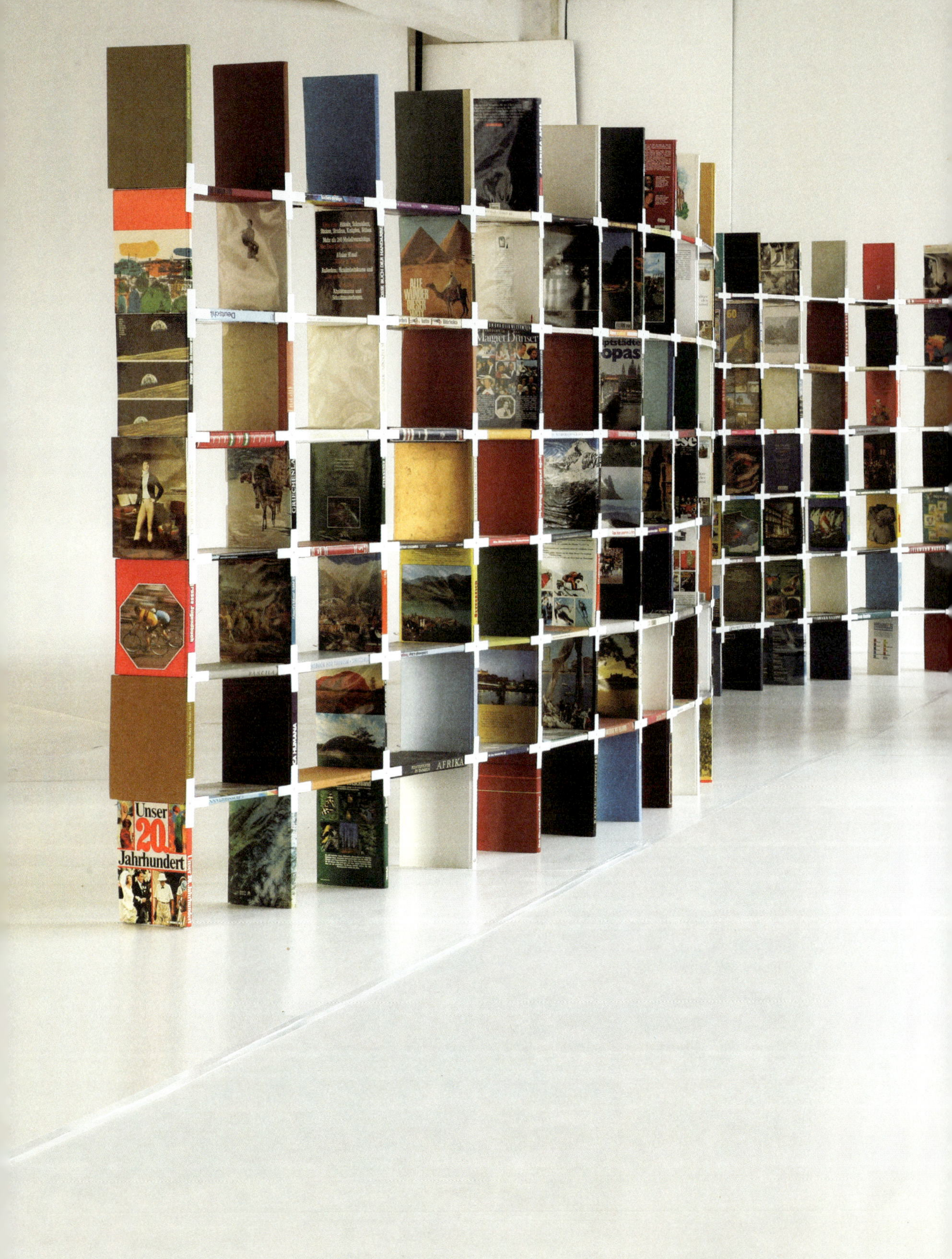

books installation for photoset at studio, Tauthaus, Berlin 2007

02 Global–local: the user is free to collect the basic material locally and in his language from an antique shop, the second-hand shop next door, or online. The metal joints can be ordered from practically anywhere in the world.

Global – local: Der Nutzer kann in seiner Region, mit Literatur seiner Sprache aus eigenen Beständen, vom Antiquariat oder Secondhand-Laden um die Ecke das Basismaterial besorgen und mithilfe der global verfügbaren Verbindungselemente addieren.

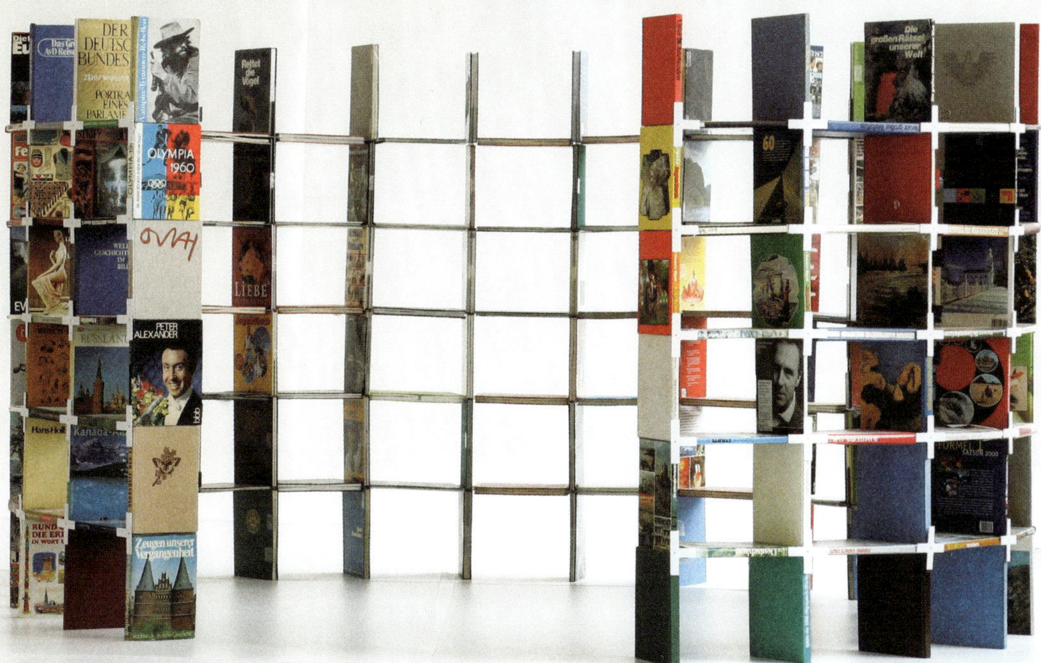

03 Customised product: Ideally, the developed structure is a personalised object. Old books which have been collected over a lifetime are put to new use – the final structure is like no other and a distinctive modular wall can be created!

Customized product: Die entstandene Struktur ist im Idealfall ein persönliches Objekt, da alte Bücher Verwendung finden, die im Lauf eines Lebens gesammelt wurden – keine Struktur wird wie die andere sein. Unverwechselbare Modulwände entstehen.

04 Self-sufficient system: a books installation can grow – any book that has been read is a potential resource for holding new books that are acquired and then, once again, re-used – the system feeds itself.

Selbstreferenzielles System: Eine Books-Installation kann aus sich selbst heraus wachsen. Alle gelesenen alten Bücher sind potenzieller Rohstoff für neue, nachkommende Bücherbestände – das System speist sich selbst.

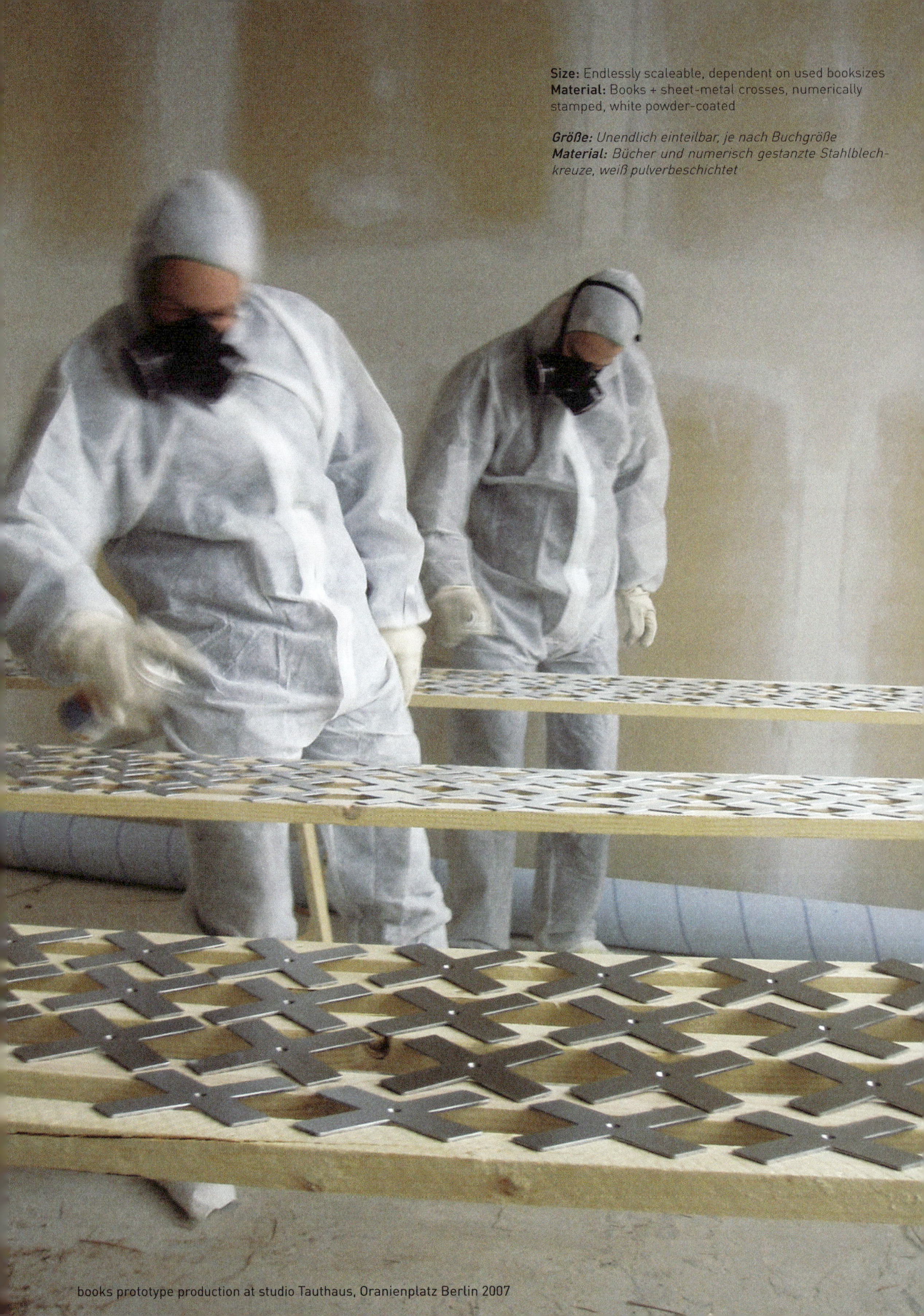

Size: Endlessly scaleable, dependent on used booksizes
Material: Books + sheet-metal crosses, numerically stamped, white powder-coated

Größe: *Unendlich einteilbar, je nach Buchgröße*
Material: *Bücher und numerisch gestanzte Stahlblechkreuze, weiß pulverbeschichtet*

books prototype production at studio Tauthaus, Oranienplatz Berlin 2007

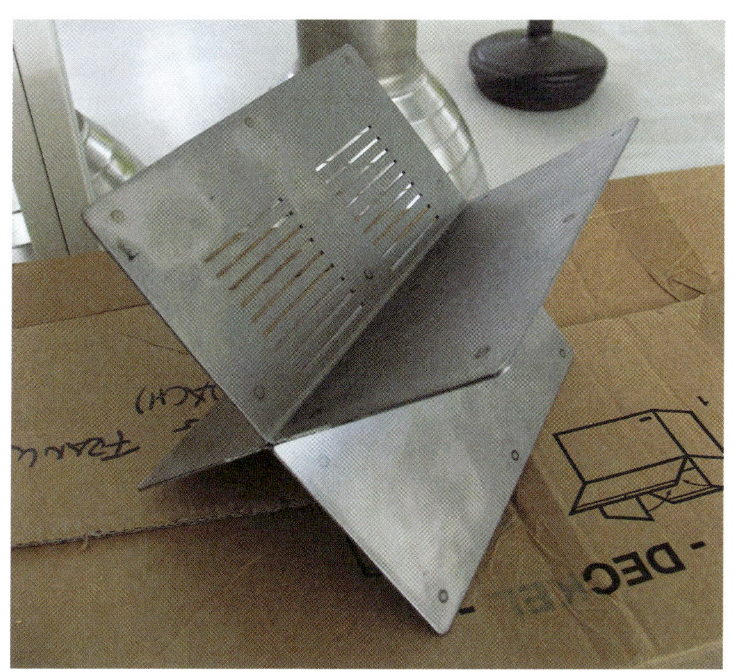

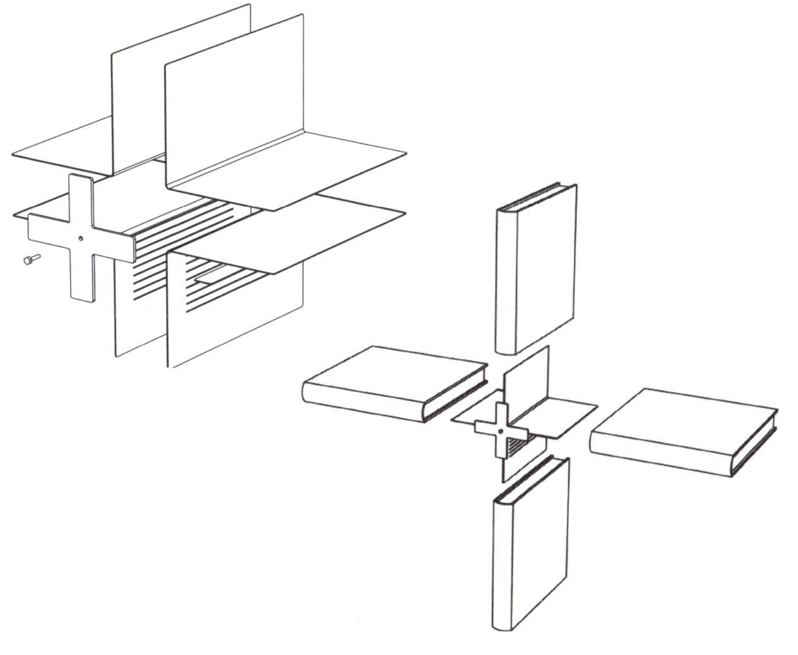

plus unit

Magis, Italy 2001

It took four years to finalise this product with the Magis-RD-Team. Based on a very complicated idea – an endlessly extendable drawer system –, the plus unit is the world's first modular drawer system for stacking and joining together. As each drawer unit is self-loading, endless compositions are possible. The single drawer units in ABS or translucent PMMA are connected by aluminium extrusions with specially developed Teflon sliding mechanisms. Visually, the aluminium "flower-joint" poetically symbolises the interconnection of two or four drawers and illustrates the endless modularity.

Vier Jahre waren nötig, um mit dem Magis-R&D-Team dieses Baukastensystem zu entwickeln. Das Plus Unit Modulsystem basiert auf der sehr komplexen Idee, ein endlos addierbares System von Schubkästen zu erfinden. Es ist das zur Zeit einzige modulare Schubladensystem im Markt, das konstruktiv gestapelt und modular erweitert werden kann. Da jede Schubladeneinheit selbsttragend ist, sind unzählige Konfigurationen möglich. Die einzelnen Schubladeneinheiten aus ABS oder transluzentem PMMA werden mit Strangpressprofilen aus Aluminium und speziell entwickelten teflonbeschichteten Profilen verbunden. Optisch symbolisiert das „Kleeblatt-förmige Verbindungsstück" auf poetische Art die Verbindung von zwei oder vier Schubladen und steht visuell für endlose Modularität.

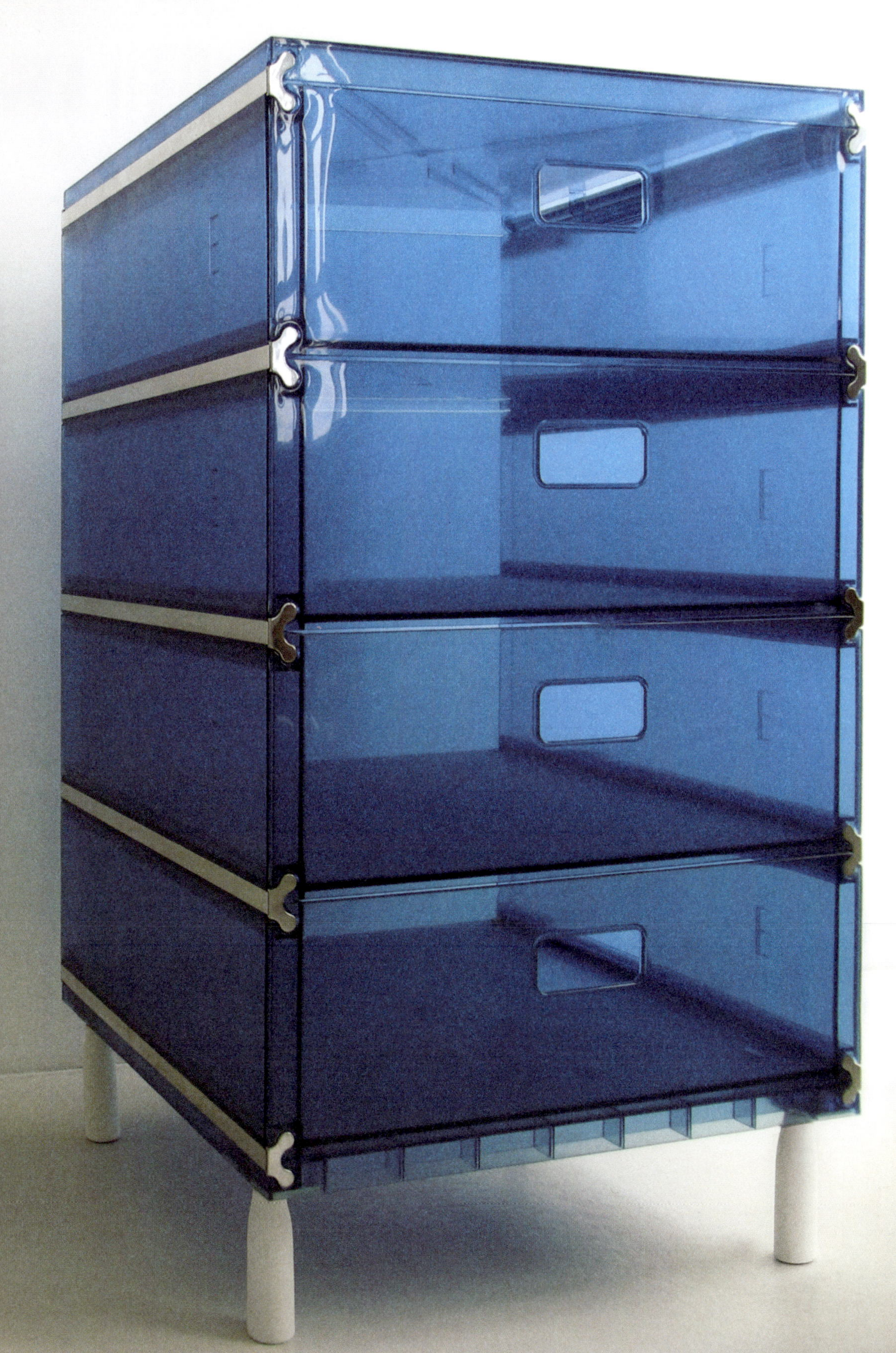

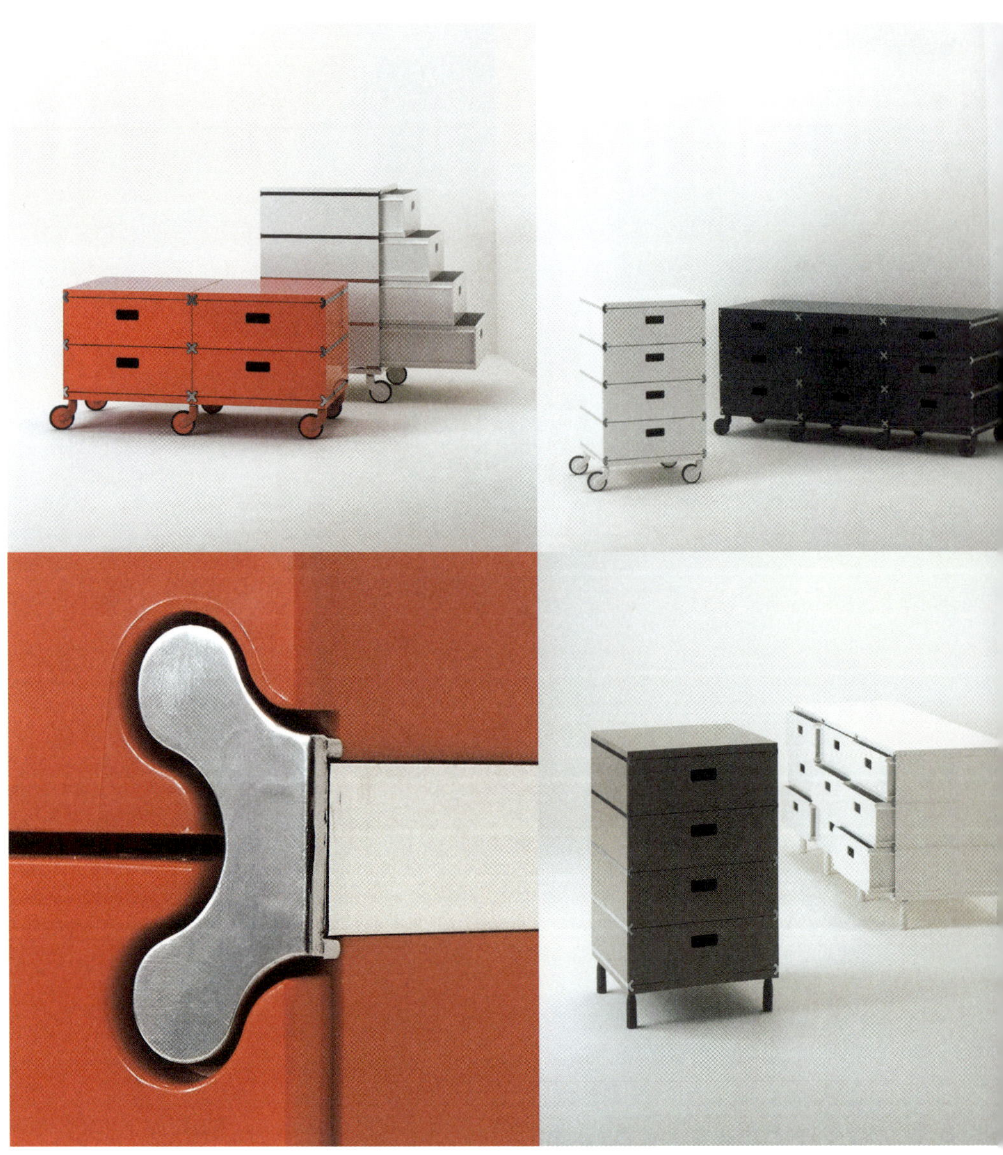

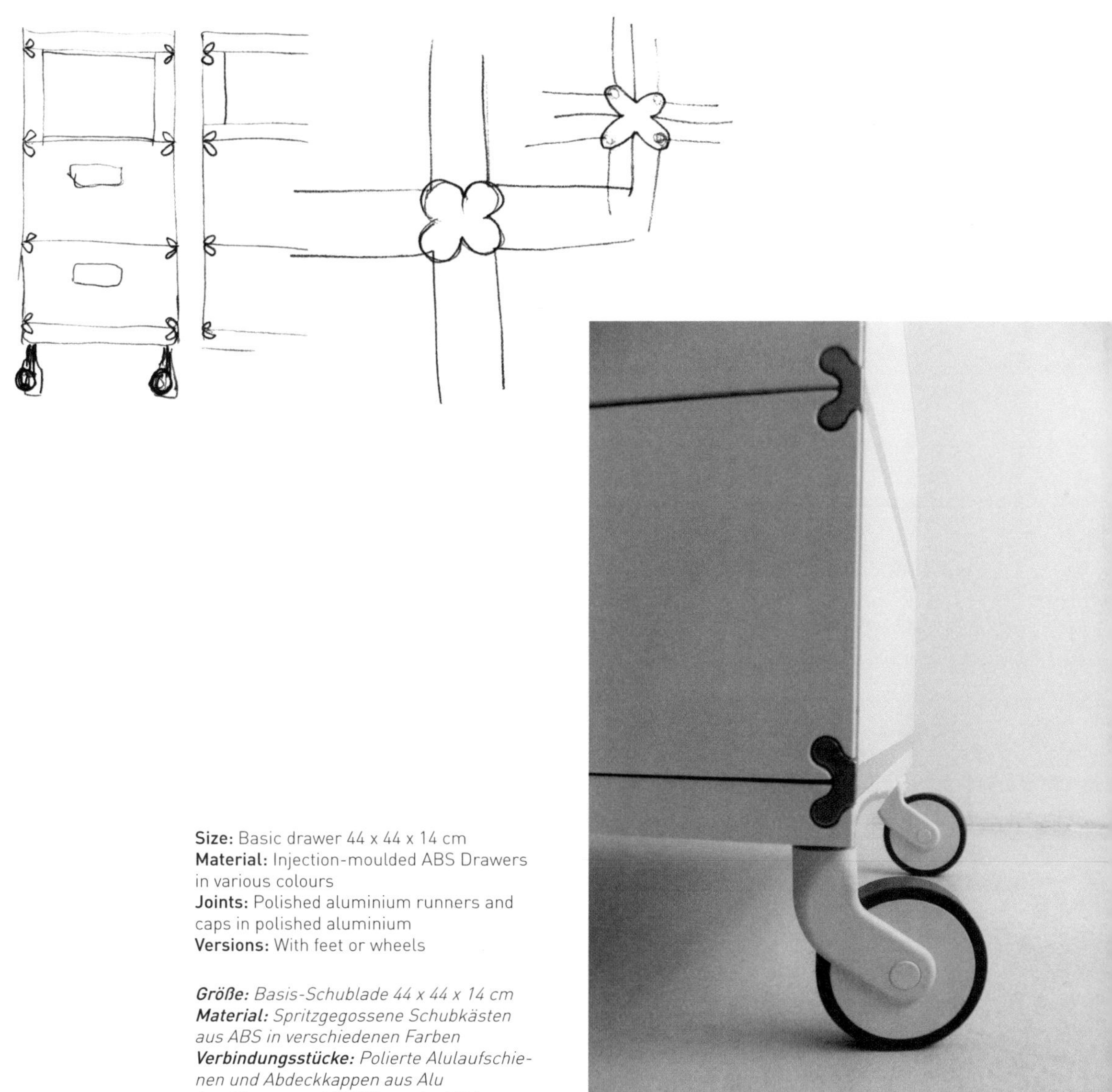

Size: Basic drawer 44 x 44 x 14 cm
Material: Injection-moulded ABS Drawers in various colours
Joints: Polished aluminium runners and caps in polished aluminium
Versions: With feet or wheels

Größe: *Basis-Schublade 44 x 44 x 14 cm*
Material: *Spritzgegossene Schubkästen aus ABS in verschiedenen Farben*
Verbindungsstücke: *Polierte Alulaufschienen und Abdeckkappen aus Alu*
Ausführungen: *Mit Füßen oder Rädern*

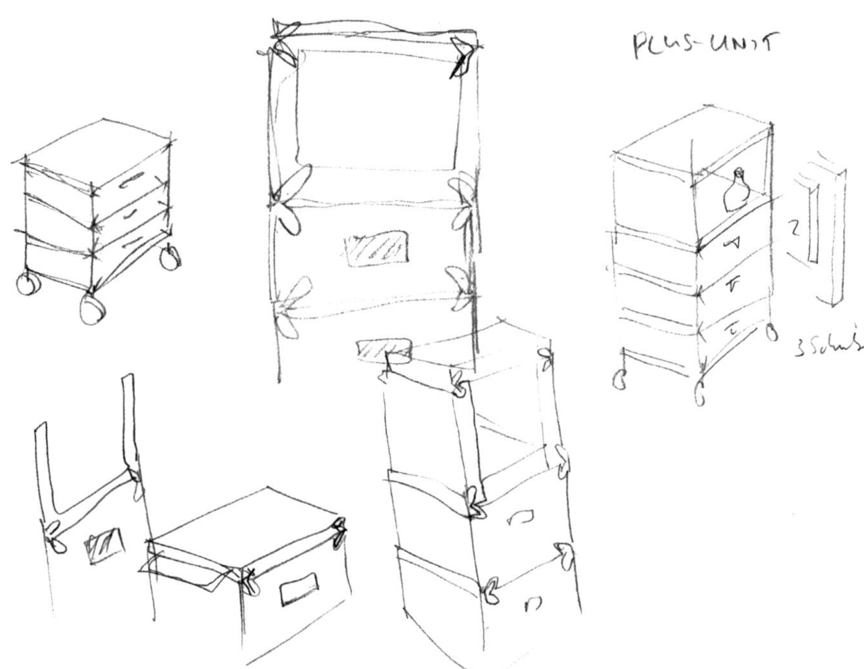
PLUS-UNIT
2

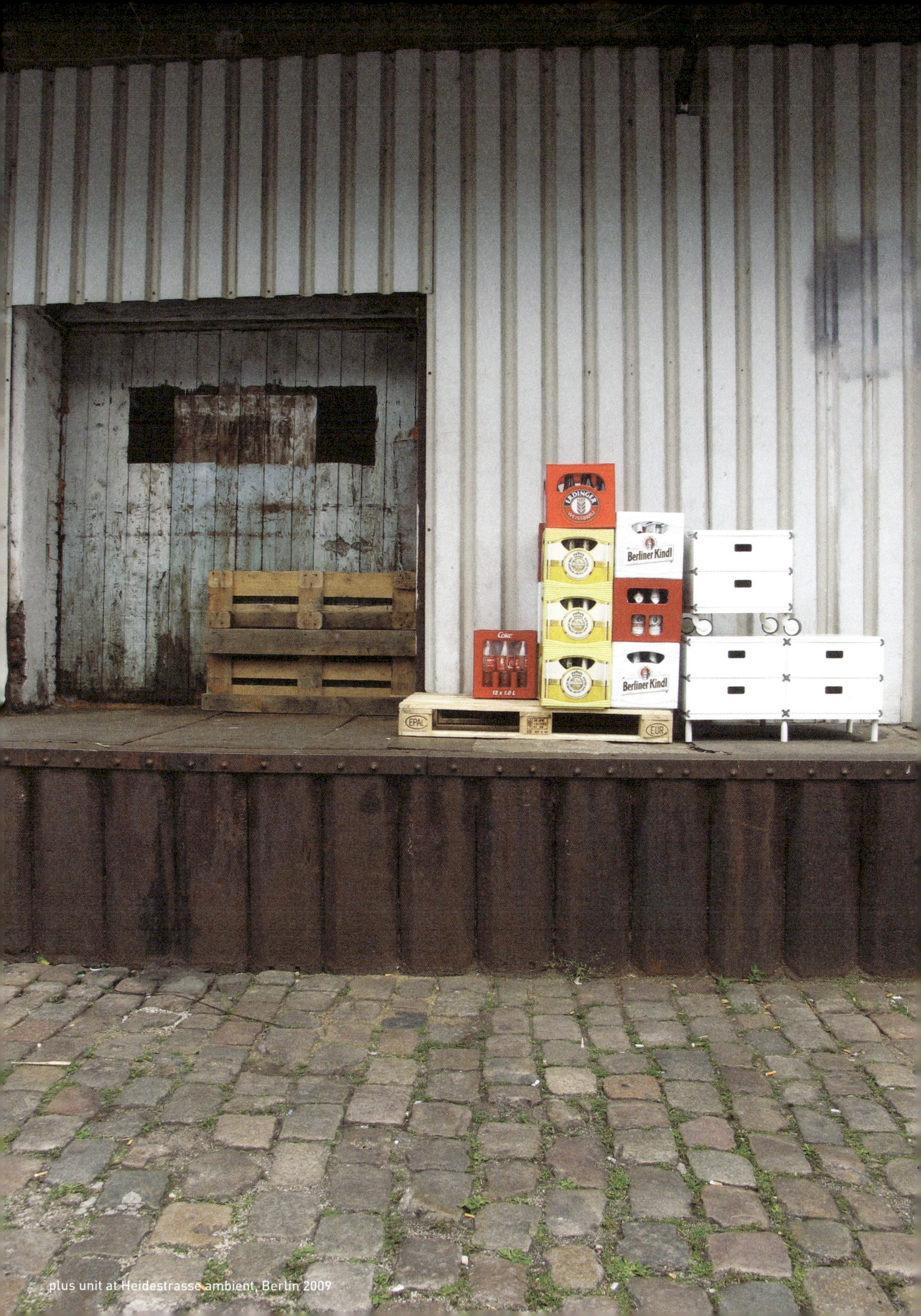

plus unit at Heidestrasse ambient, Berlin 2009

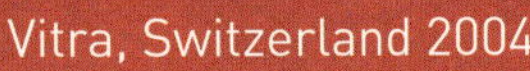

Vitra, Switzerland 2004

Level 34

Designers of office furniture bear a great responsibility. Offices are planned by the employer but the users should feel comfortable working for years with this furniture while remaining physically and mentally healthy. This is a social and humane requirement that has a decisive influence on the design and conception of office worlds. Issues such as mobbing and burn-out are less of a problem in a transparent office in which transparency also exists in the mind, in which a community spirit predominates and where effective teamwork is possible.

Designer von Büromöbeln tragen eine große gestalterische Verantwortung. Büros werden vom Arbeitgeber geplant und die Nutzer sollen jahrelang an diesen Möbeln arbeiten, sich wohlfühlen, mental und körperlich gesund bleiben – ein sozialhumaner Anspruch, der das Design und die Konzeption von Bürowelten wesentlich beeinflusst. Themen wie Mobbing und Burn-out sind in einem transparenten Büro, in dem Gemeinschaftsgeist herrscht und Teamarbeit funktioniert, weniger präsent.

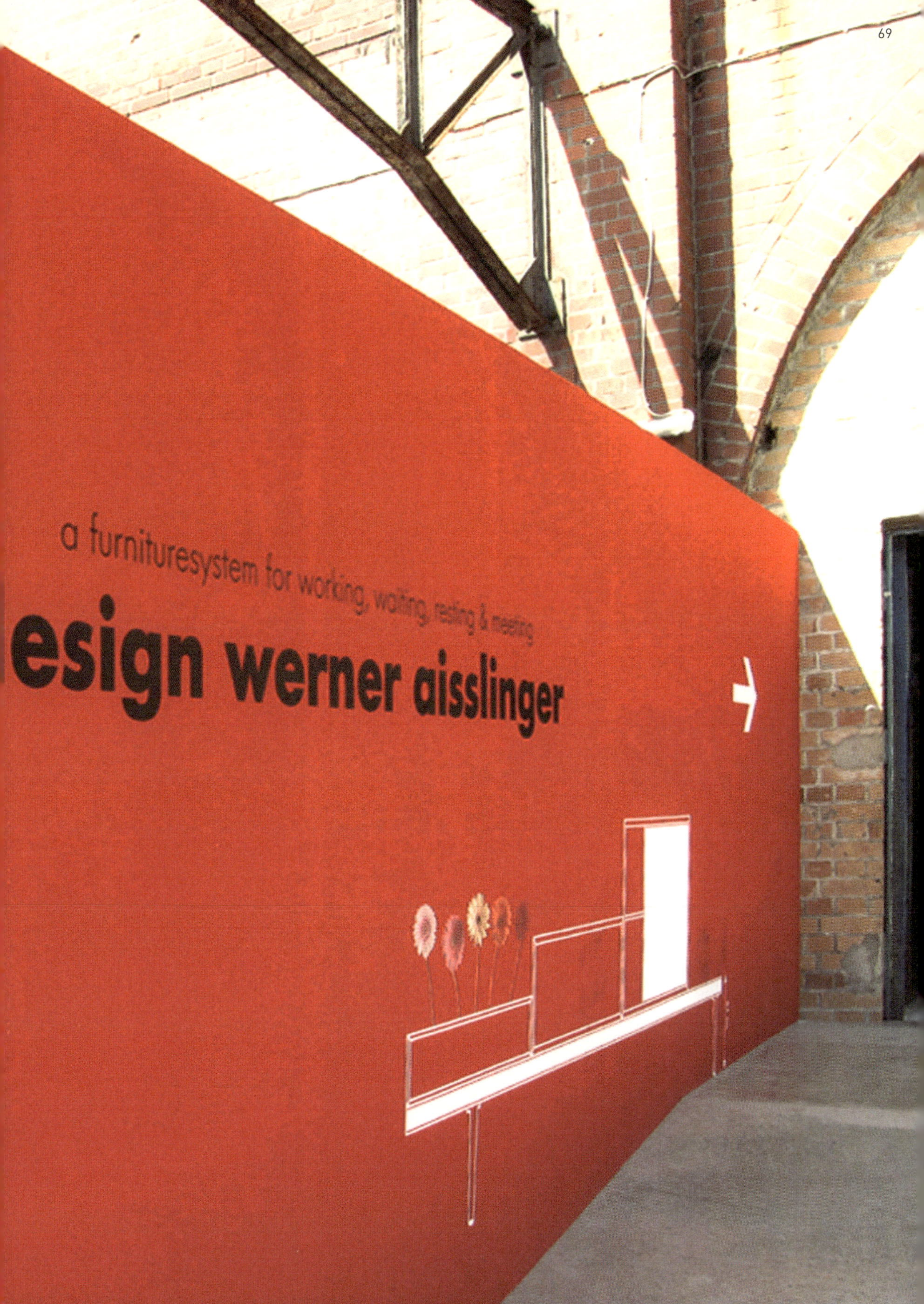
a furnituresystem for working, waiting, resting & meeting
esign werner aisslinger

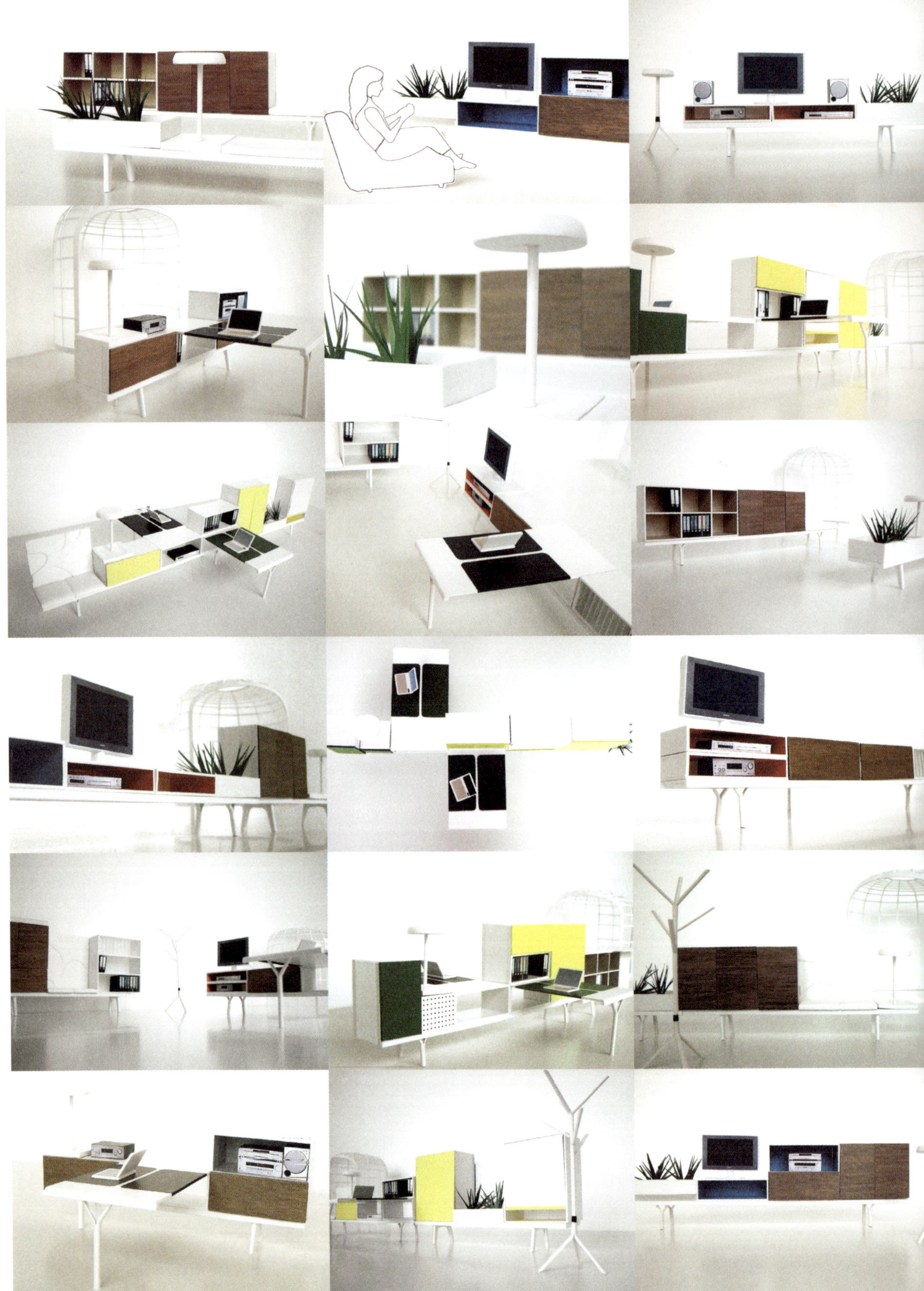

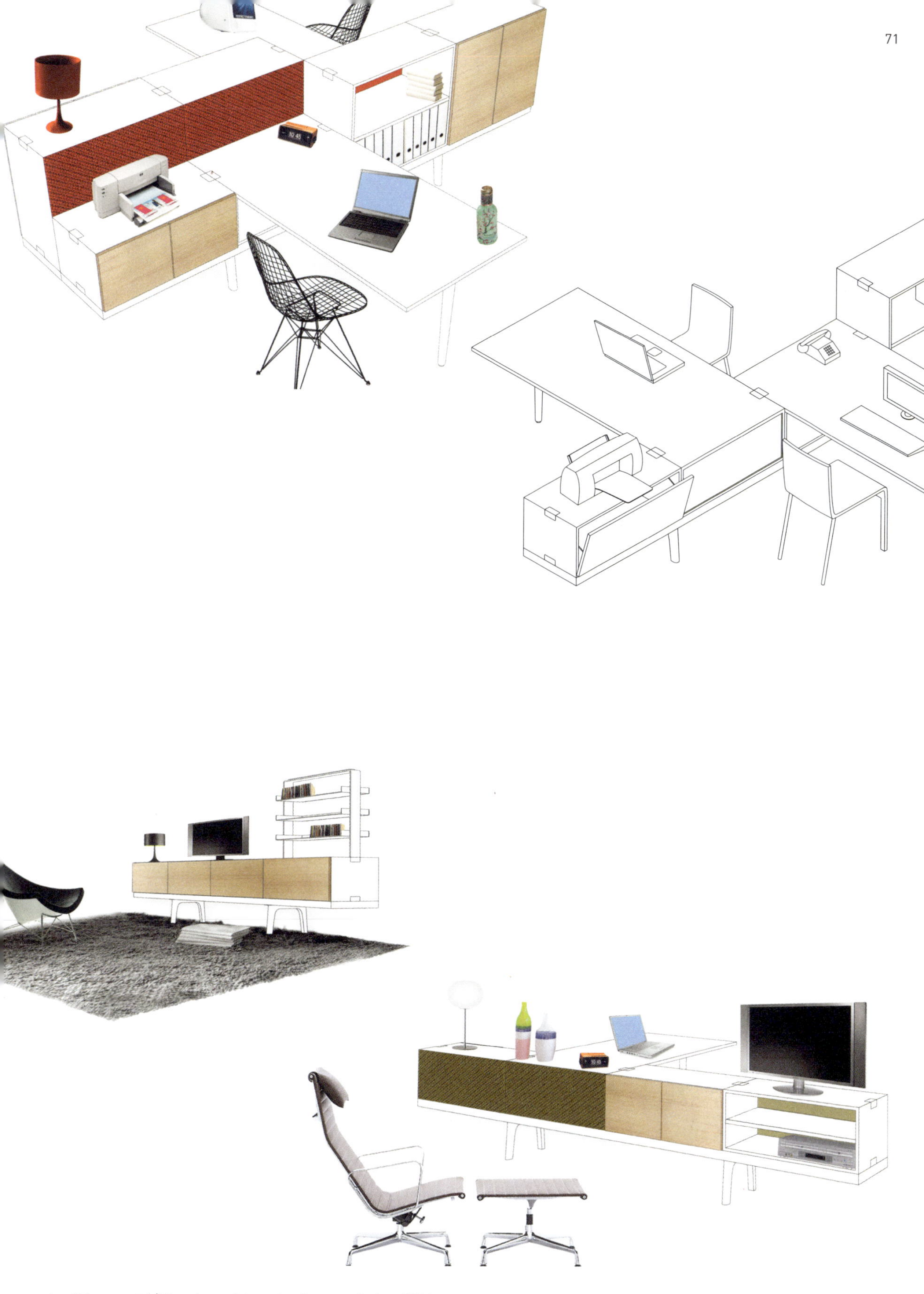

level34 concept 1/10 scale models and collage renderings 2004

Level 34 is a new conceptual approach: working in an open, coloured collage world, in a friendly office landscape that has been conceived for teamwork and integrates homely components into the world of work.

Level 34 ist ein neuer Denkansatz: Arbeiten in einer offenen farbigen Collagewelt, in einem freundlichen „office landscape", das teamorientiert konzipiert ist und wohnliche Komponenten in die Arbeitswelt integriert.

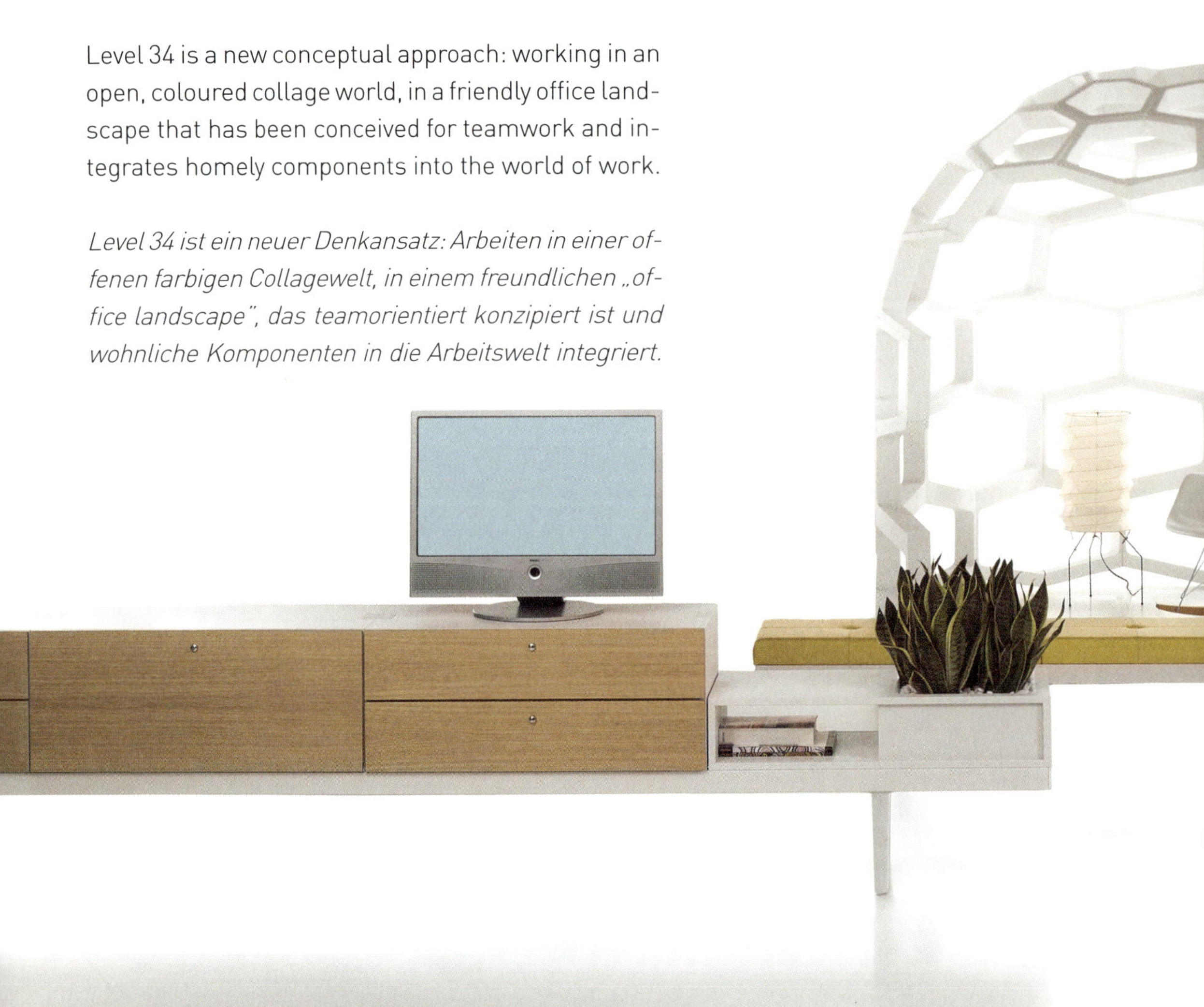

As regards typology, bench systems are not without their historical predecessors such as those by Eames and Nelson, but it was a great challenge to develop a typology that has no analogy in the market and is not based on readily available archetypal products such as tables or chairs. The discussions led to a clear system structure that would be comprehensible and self-explanatory to all its users. The 34 cm-high bench platform is the level on which the use of space can be calculated playfully or rationally and, on the containers, landscape-forming modules or workstations can be configured to produce individual office environments.

Zur Typologie: Bench-Systeme haben zwar historische Vorläufer wie die von Eames und Nelson, dennoch war es eine große Herausforderung, eine Typologie zu entwickeln, die keine Analogie im Markt hat und nicht auf gängige archetypische Produkte wie Tische oder Stühle zurückzuführen ist. Die Überlegungen führten zu einem klaren, für jeden Benutzer verständlichen und selbsterklärenden Systemaufbau. Die 34 cm hohe Bench-Plattform ist das Level, auf dem die Flächenausnutzung spielerisch oder rational kalkuliert werden kann, und auf der Container, landschaftsbildende Module oder Arbeitsplätze individuell konfiguriert werden können.

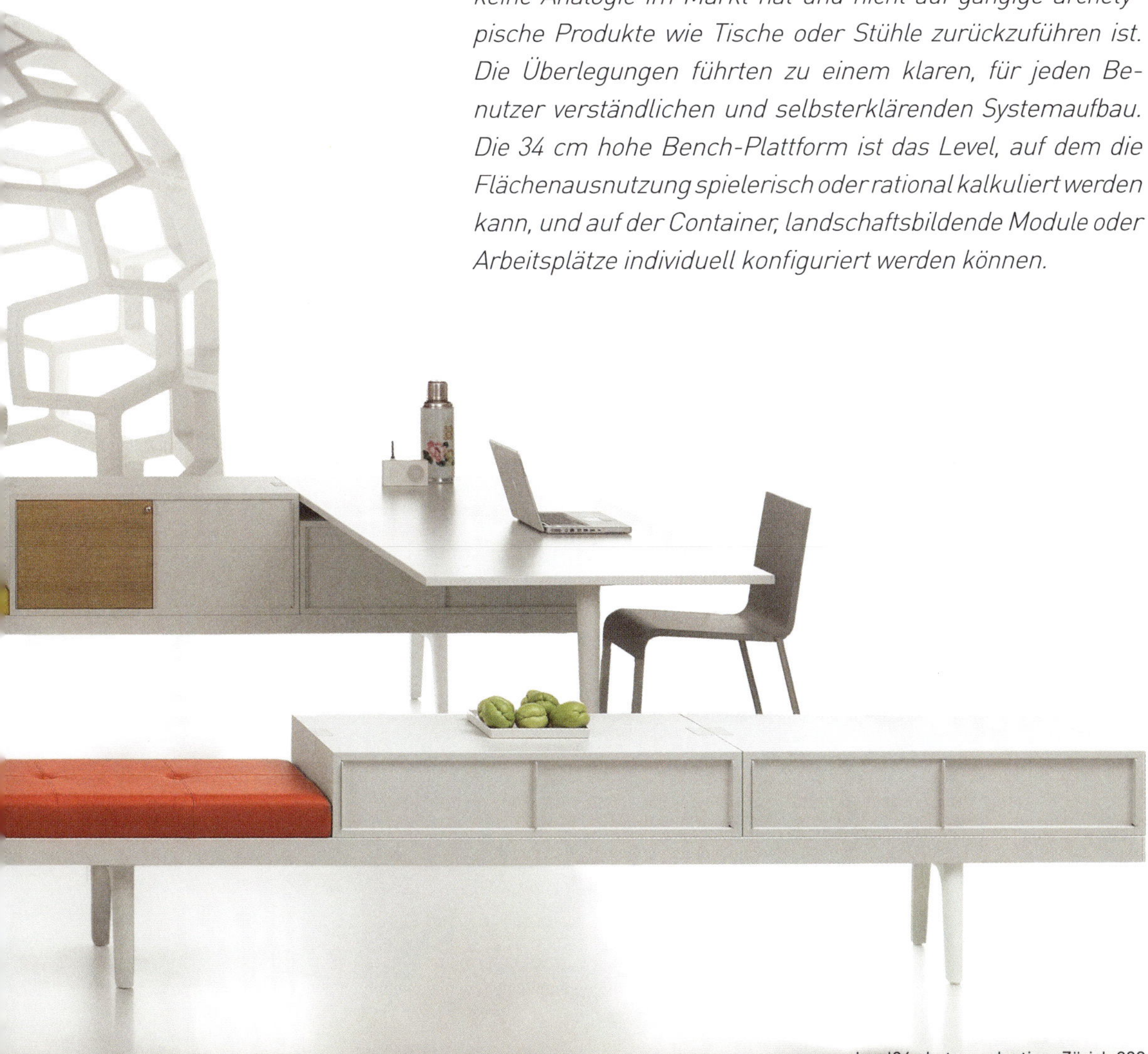

level34 photo production, Zürich 2004

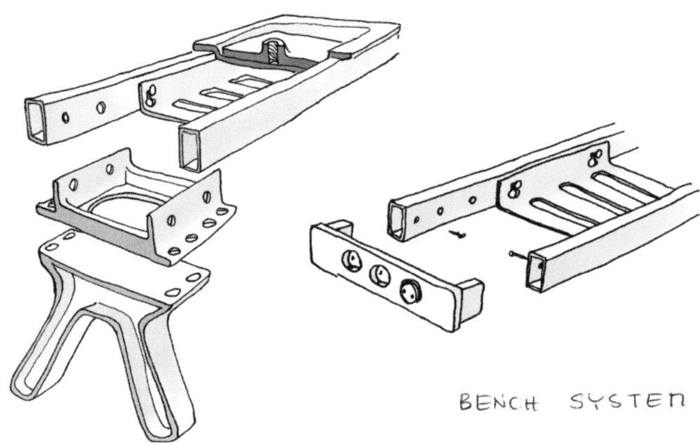

What is new about the concept is the horizontal and vertical cabling in the system modules. The cable-routing bench makes office planning independent of false floors or the architectural arrangement of existing floor tanks. The "cable management" of the horizontal bench is very simple due to cable baskets that can be opened. The vertical cable ducts in the outer walls of the containers enable data lines and supply cables to be routed from the working spaces to the bench and also allow devices to be connected to each other within a unit. Printers with different CPUs as well as monitors or music systems with loudspeaker boxes can be connected, for example. The interconnectable benches are used to supply the room with electricity and data.

Konzeptionell neu ist zum einen die horizontale als auch die vertikale Verkabelung in den Systemmodulen. Die kabelführende Bench macht die Büroplanung unabhängig von Doppelböden oder der architekturseitigen Anordnung vorhandener Bodentanks. Das Kabelmanagement der horizontalen Bench ist durch die herausklappbaren Kabelkörbe sehr einfach. Und die in den Außenwänden der Container verlaufenden vertikalen Kabelkanäle ermöglichen zum einen die Durchleitung von Daten und Versorgungsleitungen von den Arbeitsflächen zur Bench als auch die Verknüpfung von Geräten innerhalb einer Einheit untereinander. So können Drucker mit verschiedenen CPUs (Central processing units) als auch Monitore oder Musikanlagen mit Lautsprecherboxen verbunden werden. Die verkettbaren Benches dienen der Versorgung des Raumes mit Elektrik und Datenleitungen.

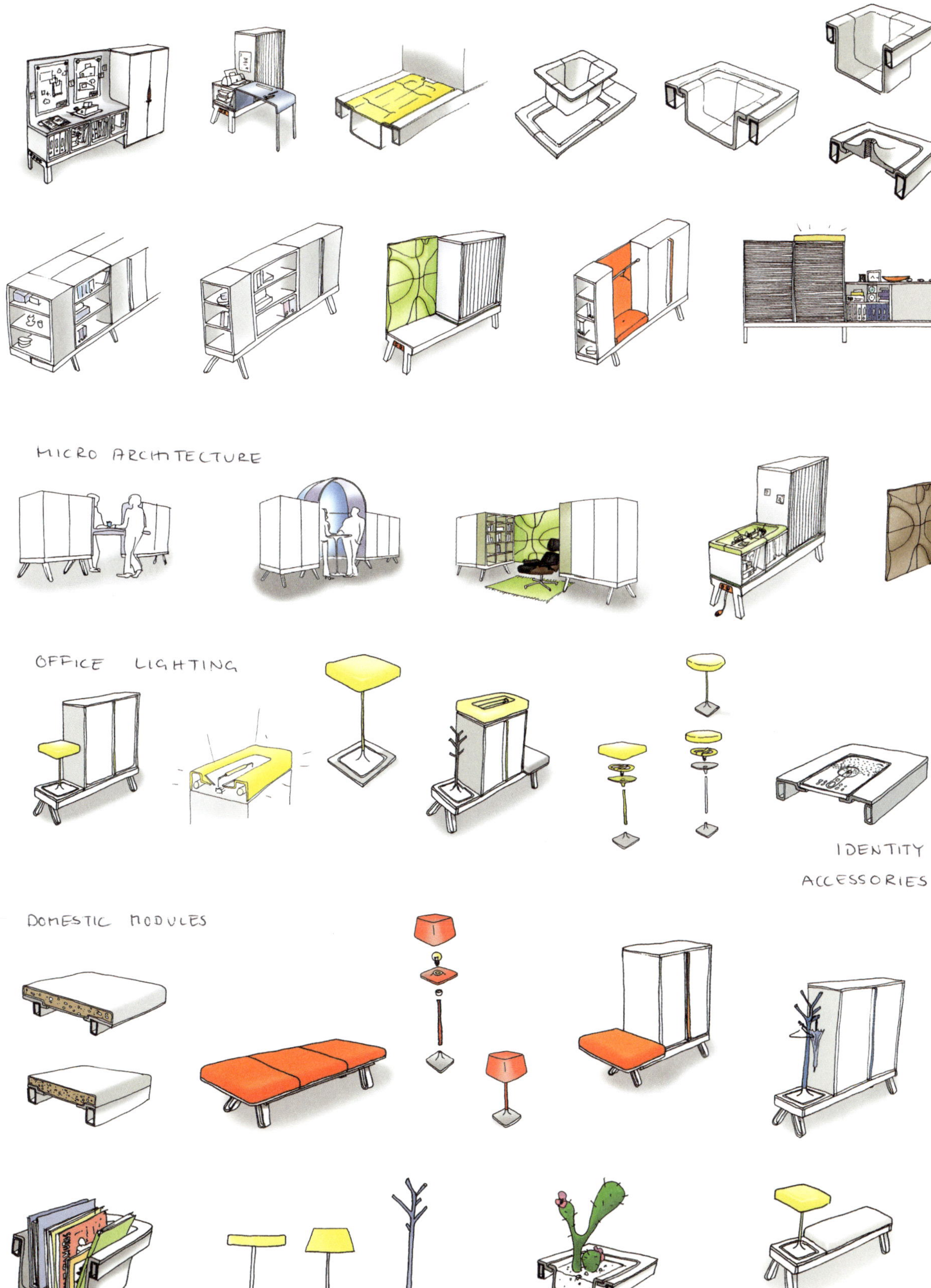

concept - sketches for a level34 product family with various accessories

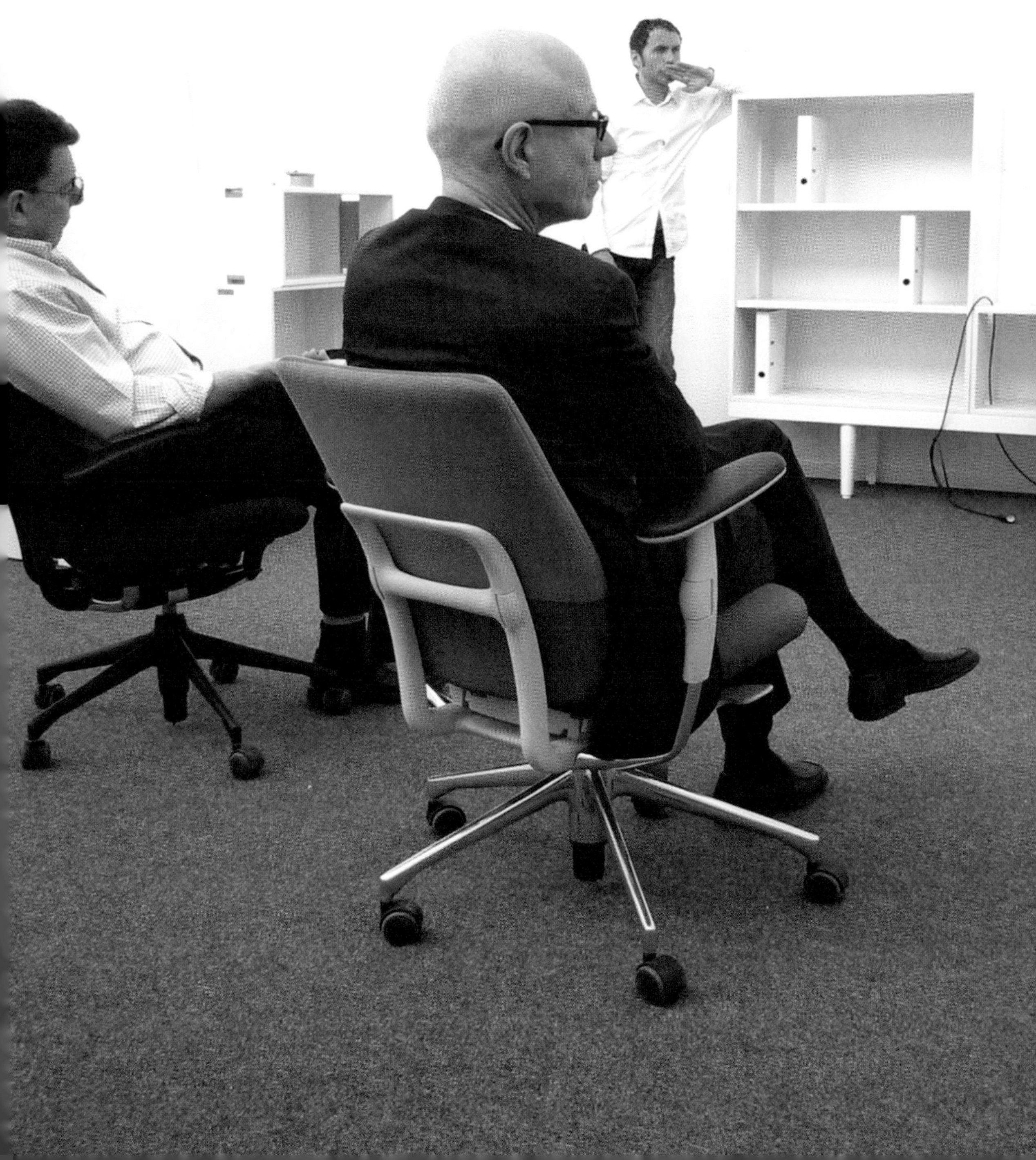

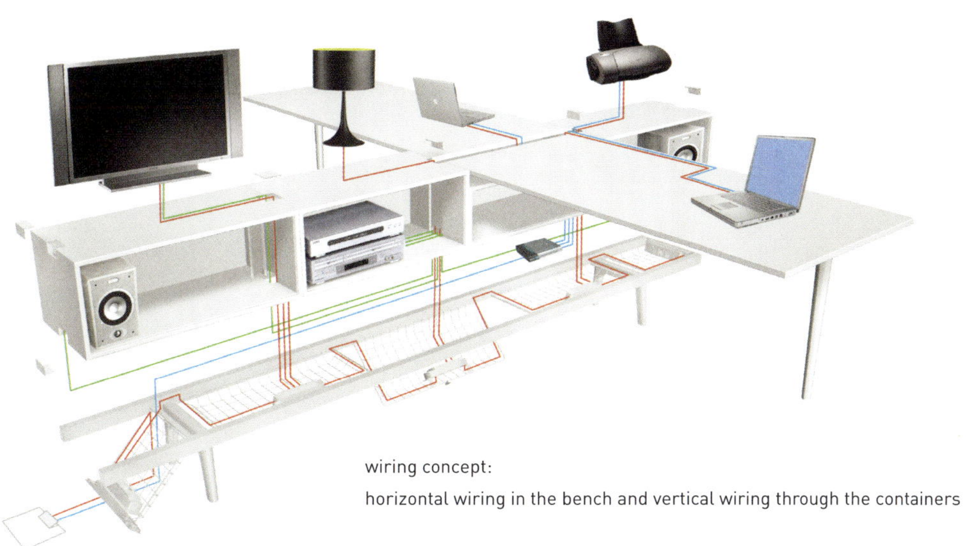

wiring concept:
horizontal wiring in the bench and vertical wiring through the containers

The idea of the bench was developed during a brainstorming session with Rolf Fehlbaum and Egon Bräuning (photo left) in 2002. When the initial theme "intelligent storage" was discussed, scenarios such as pallet systems or spaces equivalent to system floors were considered. They ended in the idea of an intelligent bench with built-on components forming landscapes. In the following months, the bench was developed as an intelligent, cable-routing and interconnectable plateau. At the same time, different scenarios were concocted for modules whose extent and orientation included office applications as well as lobby/lounge situations or home-office worlds. The resulting modular system achieves a minimum in respect of the variety of parts and a maximum in terms of flexibility and viability in architectural environments. The system can be used to create stringent, rational office workstations with adequate storage space or generate spacious, unconventional studio worlds.

Die Idee der Bench entwickelte sich aus einem Brainstorming mit Rolf Fehlbaum und Egon Bräuning (Foto links) im Jahr 2002. Zum Ausgangsthema „intelligentes storage" wurden Szenarien wie Palettensysteme oder mit Systemböden korrespondierende Volumina durchgespielt. Sie mündeten in der Idee einer intelligenten Bench mit landschaftsbildenden Aufbauten. In den folgenden Monaten wurde die Bench als intelligentes kabelführendes und verkettbares Plateau entwickelt, parallel dazu unterschiedliche Szenarien für Aufbaumodule, deren Umfang und Ausrichtung ebenso Office-Anwendungen als auch Lobby/Lounges-Situationen oder Home-Office-Welten beinhalteten. Der entstandene Systembaukasten ist minimal im Bezug auf die Teilevielfalt und maximal in Hinsicht auf Flexibilität und Implementierbarkeit in architektonische Gegebenheiten. Das System kann stringente rationale Büroarbeitsplätze mit entsprechendem Stauraum erzeugen oder großzügige unkonventionelle Studioarbeitswelten generieren.

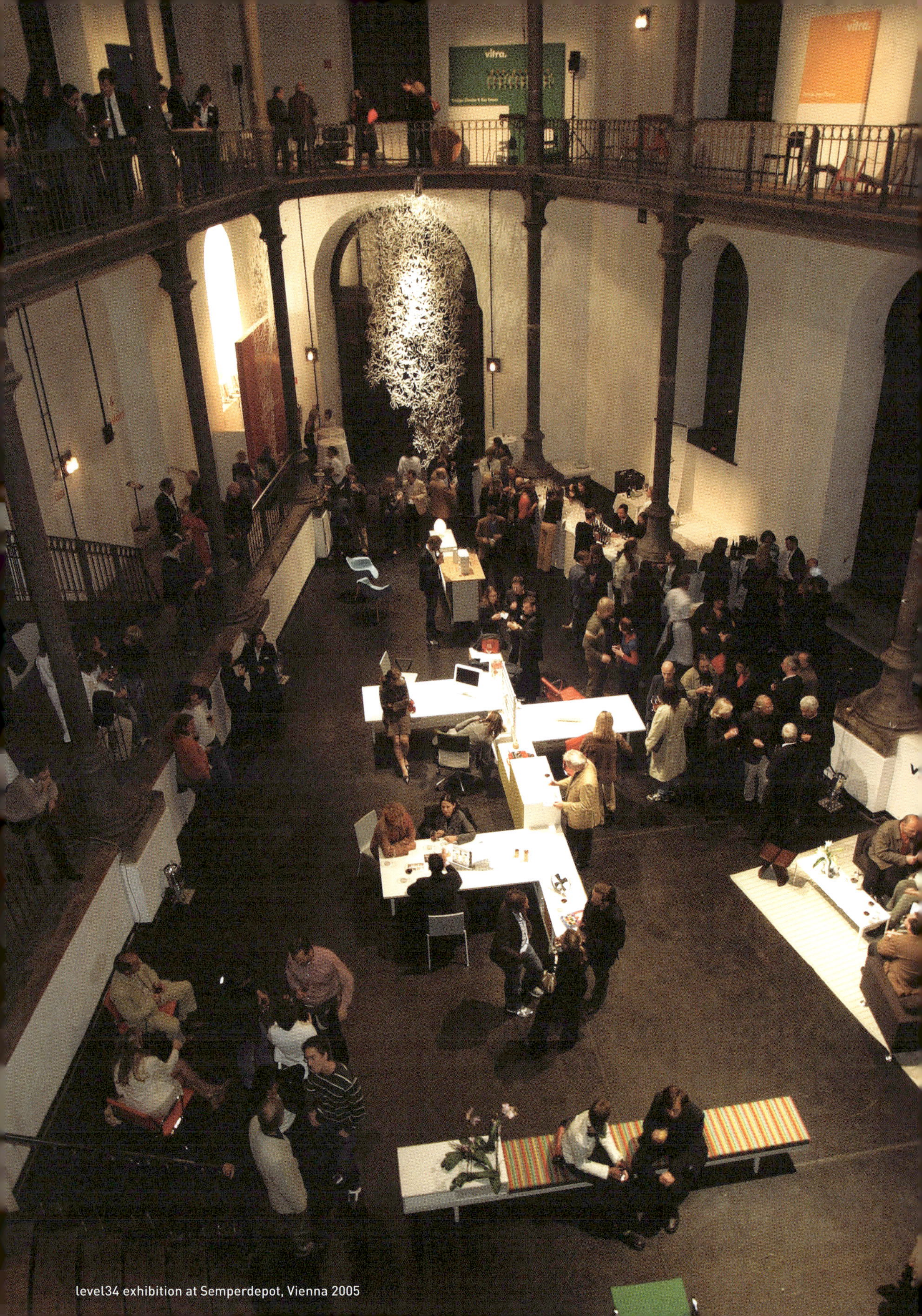

level34 exhibition at Semperdepot, Vienna 2005

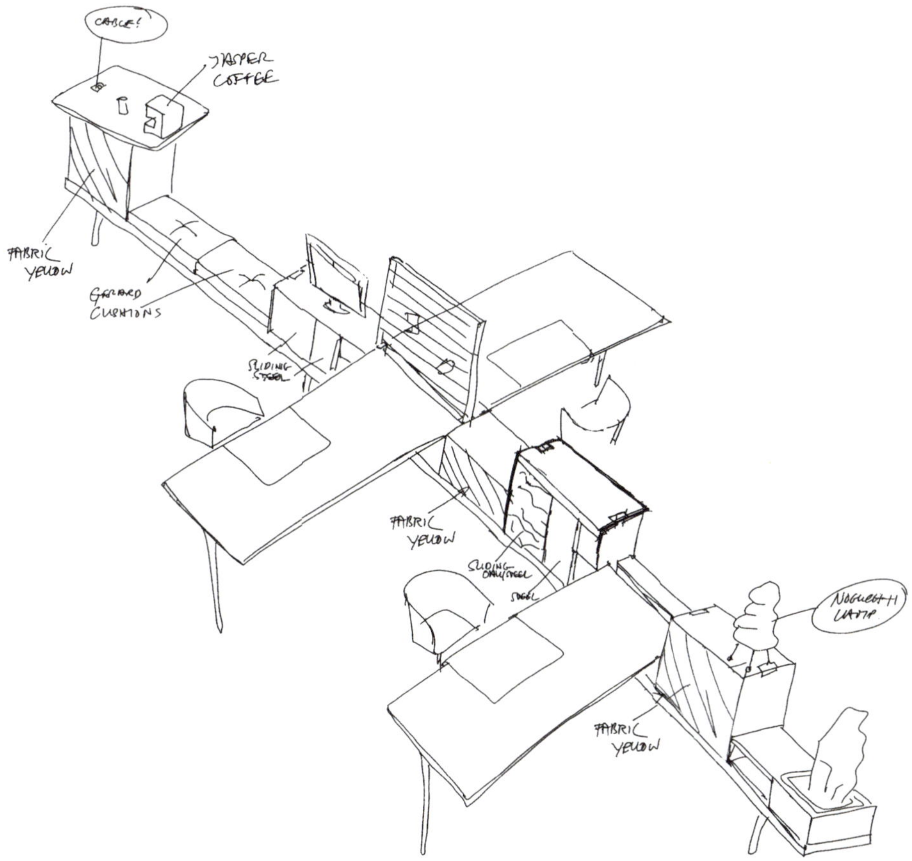

Size: Lengths 180, 270 or 360 cm, height 34 cm
Modules: Various containers, desks and accessories based on 90 cm length and 45 cm depth
Material: Aluminium die-casted legs, framestructure steel powder-coated white, storage boxes foliated and mdf-tabletops powder-coated

Größe: *Längen 180, 270 oder 360 cm, Höhe 34 cm*
Module: *Verschiedene Container, Tische und Accessoires, jeweils in 90 cm Länge und 45 cm Tiefe*
Material: *Füße in Aluminiumdruckguss, tragende Konstruktion aus weiß pulverbeschichtetem Stahl sowie folierte gefaltete Container aus MDF, Tischplatten aus pulverbeschichtetem MDF*

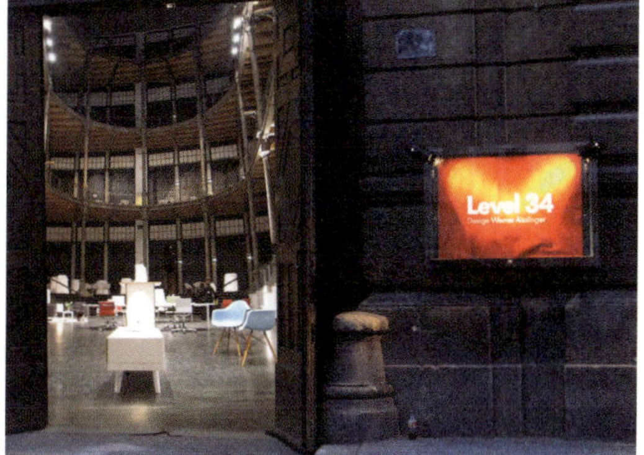

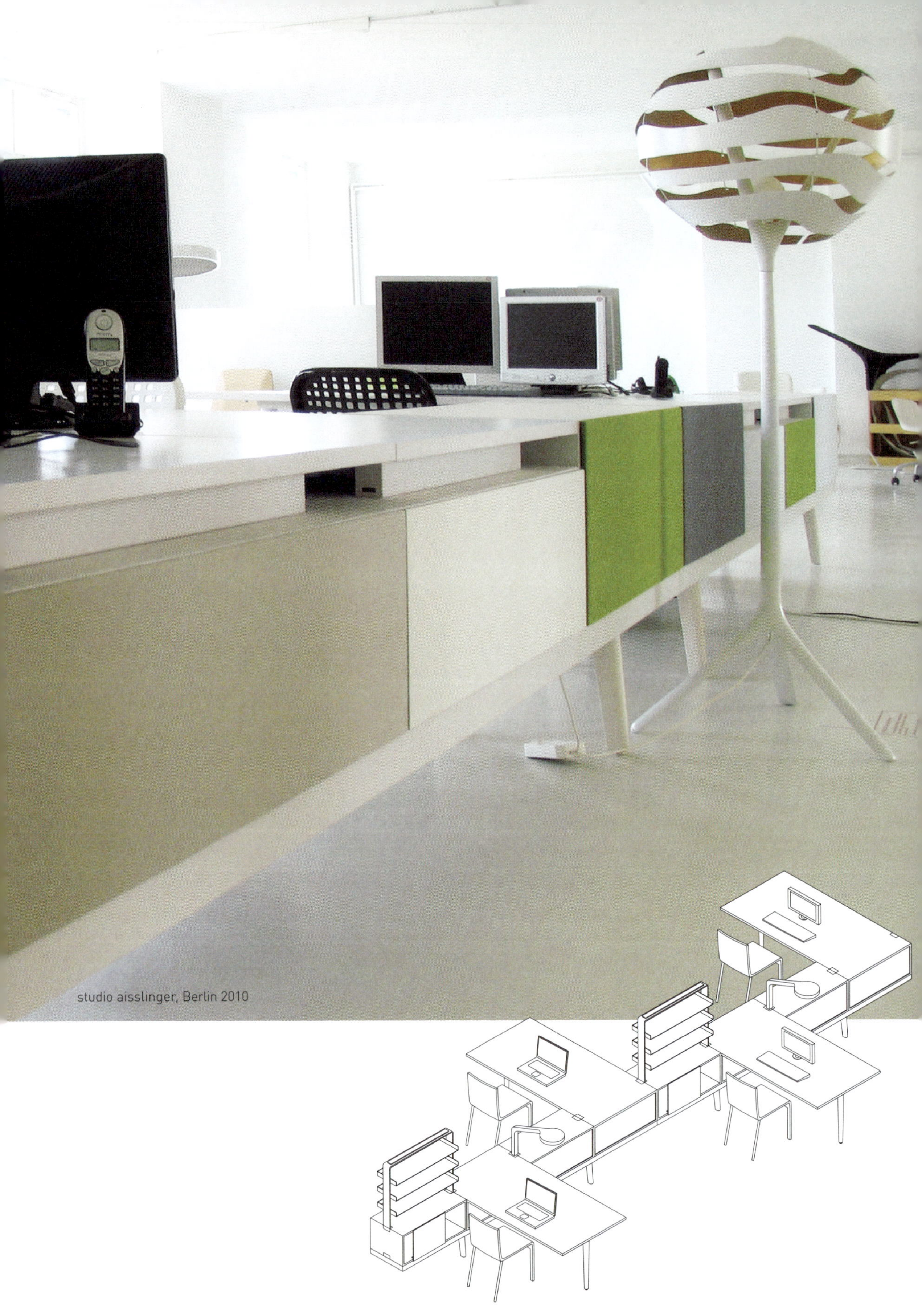

studio aisslinger, Berlin 2010

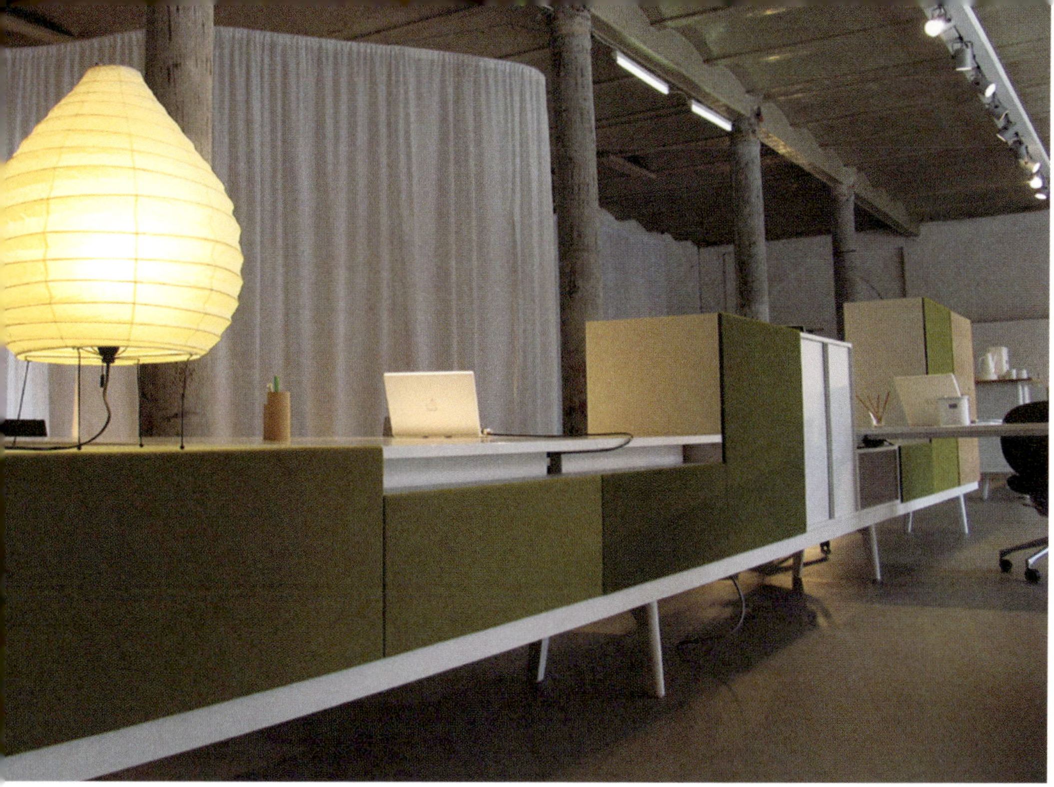

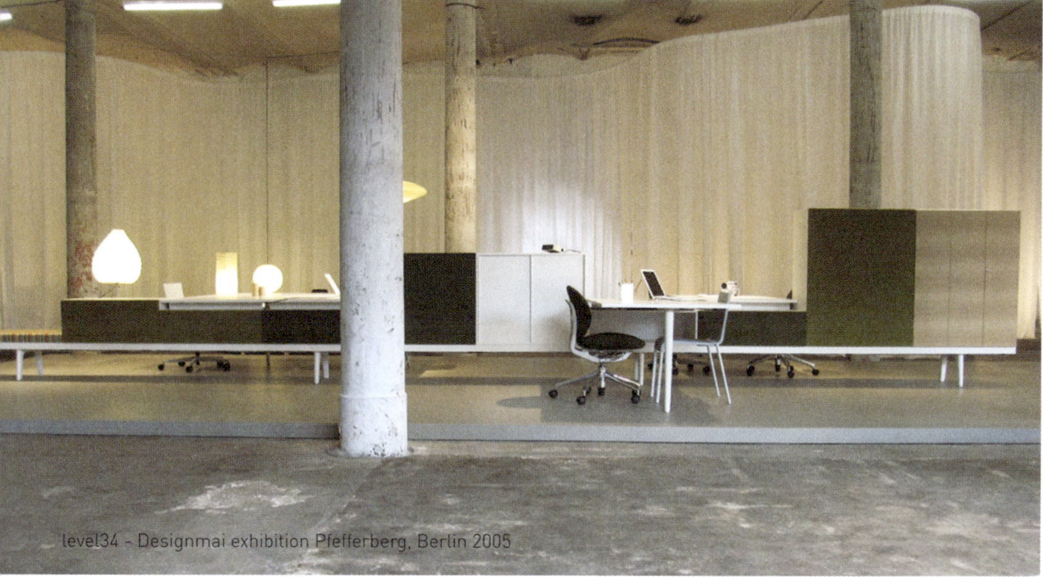

level34 - Designmai exhibition Pfefferberg, Berlin 2005

light wave

installation for Bombay Sapphire 2006

The light wave is a communal lighting object that is made from modules of 50 x 50 cm, combinable in various pixel-type configurations into a bigger "cloudlike" composition: the light wave. One module is designed like sine waves: the special curved outlines create a 3D shape that allows the endless addition of modules – together creating a fluent ongoing movement of convex/concave shapes.

Light Wave ist ein „kommunales" Lichtobjekt aus 50 x 50 cm großen Modulen, die sich pixelartig zu einer größeren wolkenförmigen Komposition addieren lassen. Ein Modul ist aufgebaut wie eine Sinuskurve. Durch die speziell geschwungenen Außenkanten entsteht eine 3D-Wellenform, die additiv endlos erweitert werden kann. Eine durchgängig fließende Bewegung konvexer/konkaver Formen entsteht.

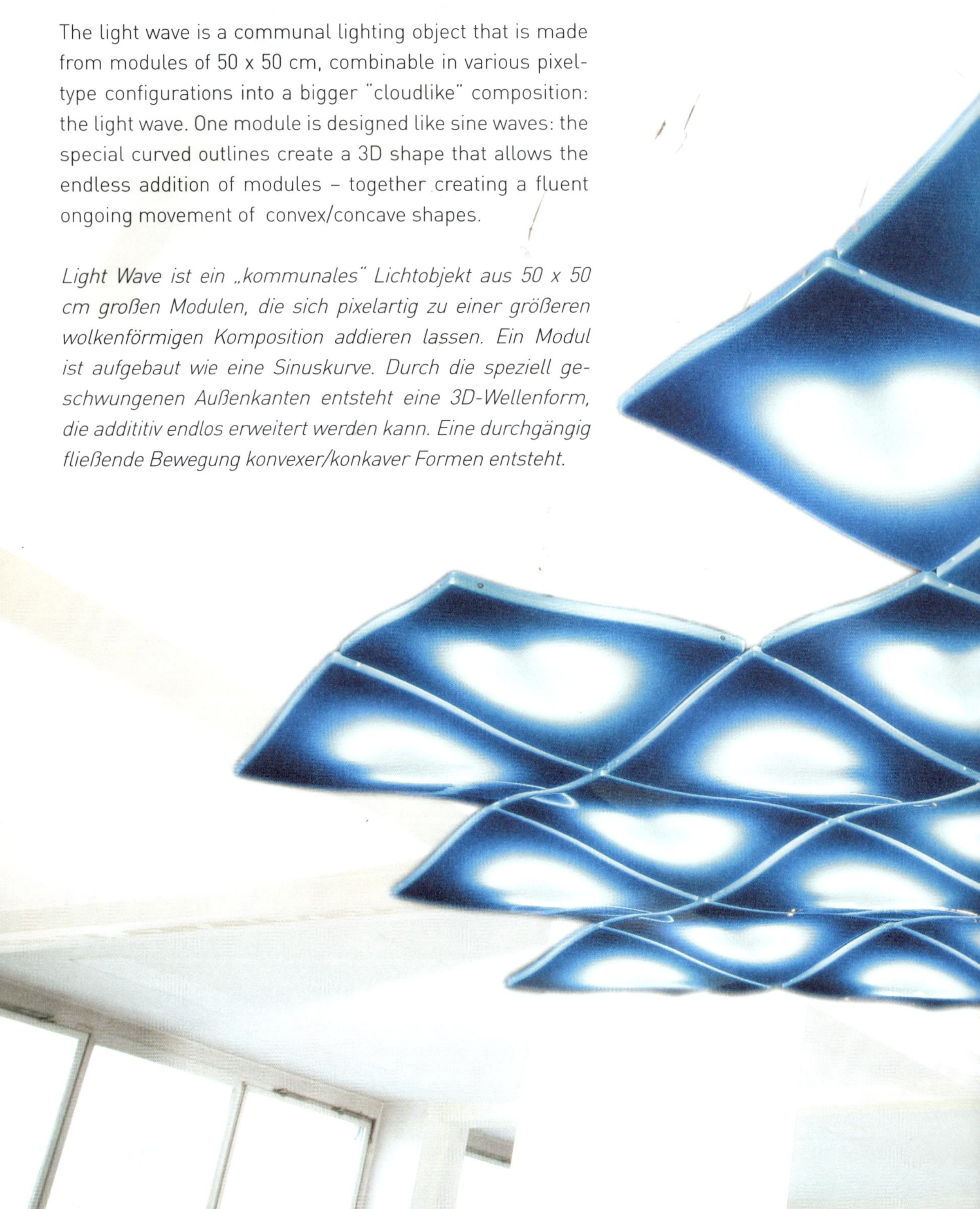

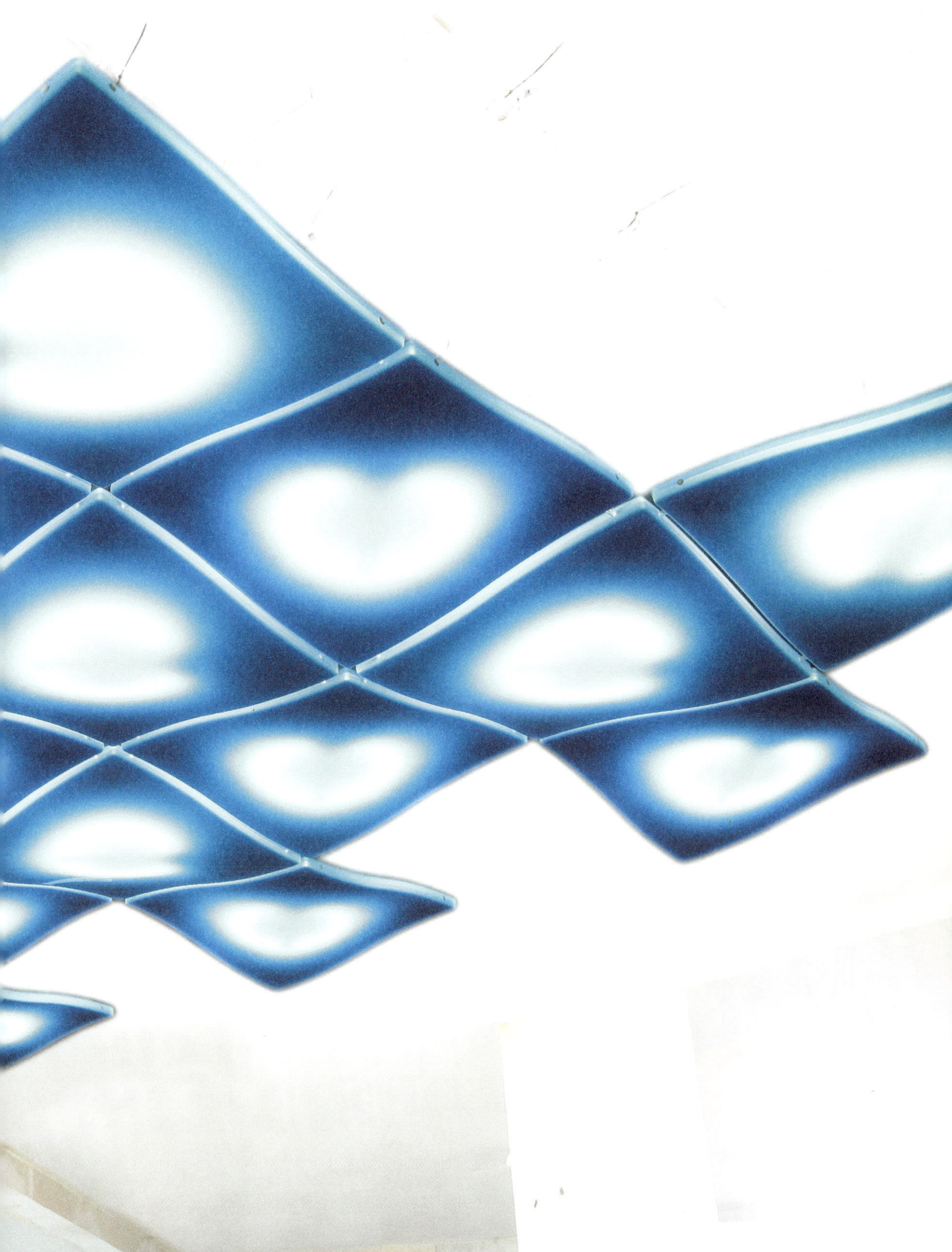

first light wave test installation at Tauthaus, Oranienplatz Berlin 2006

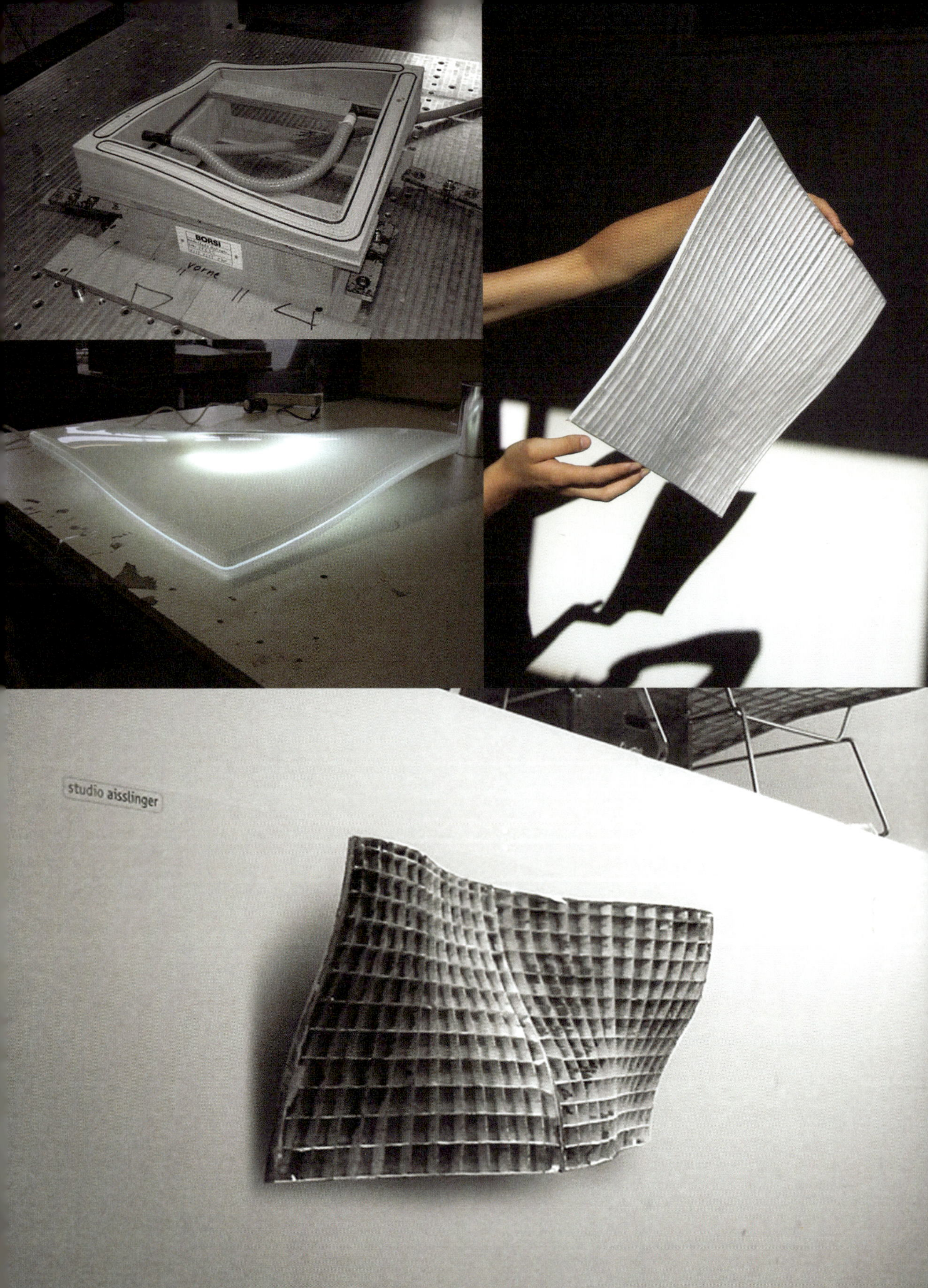

vacuum-moulding, mock-up prototyping and 3D modelling

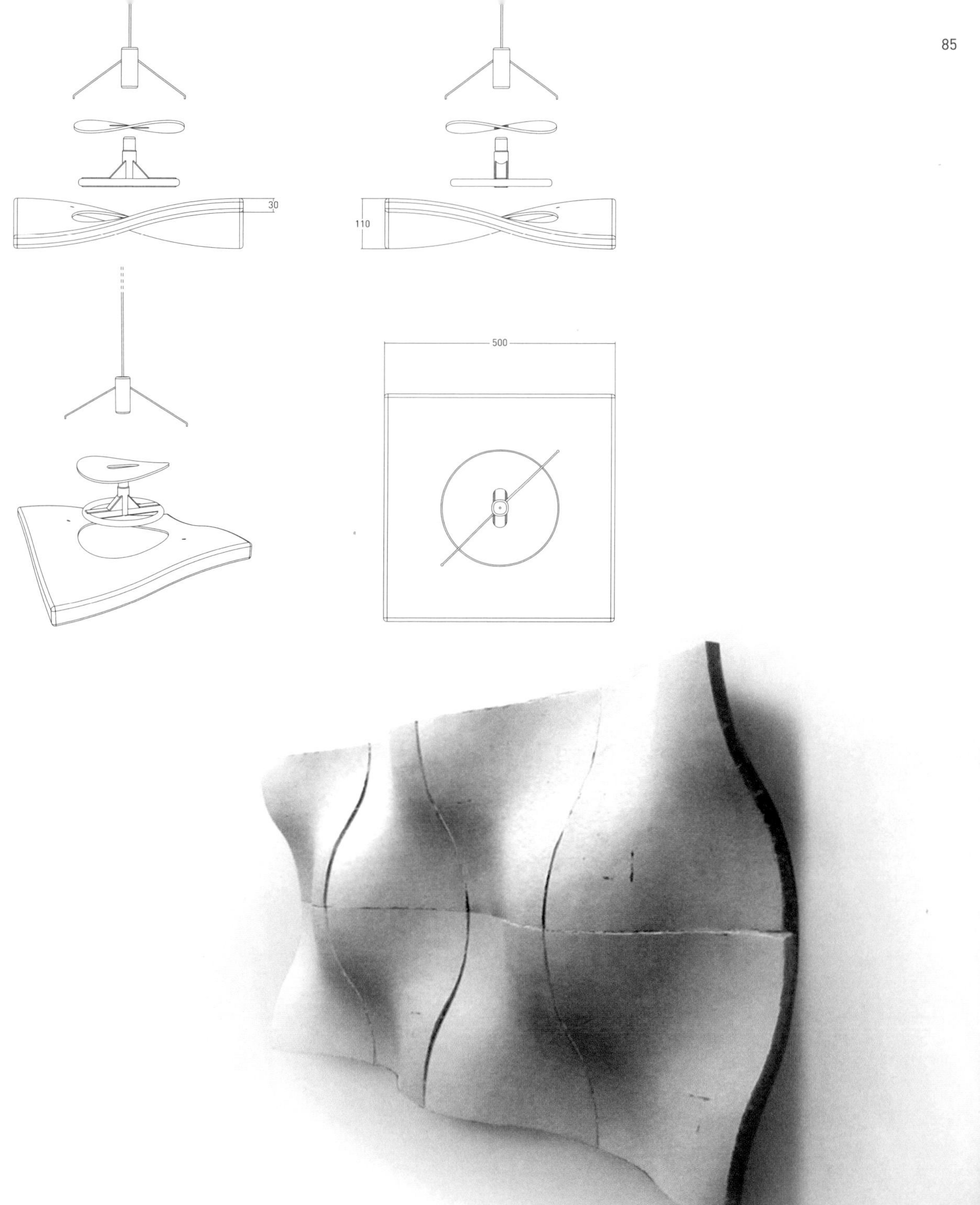

Size: 50 x 50 x 10 cm modules
Material: Blue vacuum-moulded acrylic plastic trays with metal and plastic parts for connection and lighting technology

Größe: *50 x 50 x 10 cm Module*
Material: *Tiefgezogene Schalen aus blauem Acryl, mit Metall- und Kunststoffbauteilen zur Verkettung und Lichttechnik*

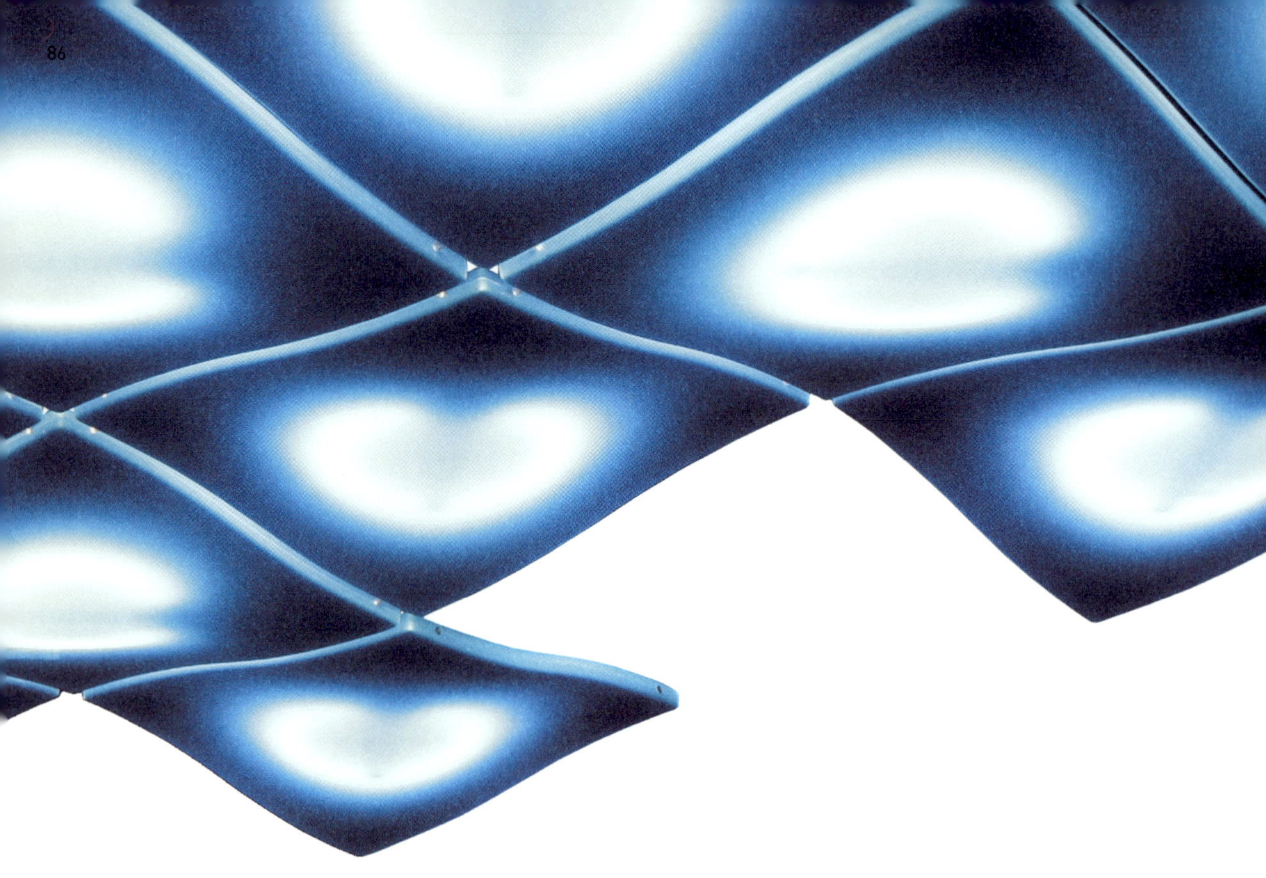

The light of an installation produces an intense light space and below it describes an immaterial area where people can meet each other. The light wave project was a one-off installation with 25 serial modules. Nevertheless it is a modular system that could be mass produced.

Eine Light Wave Lichtinstallation erzeugt einen intensiven Lichtraum, in dessen immaterieller Atmosphäre sich Menschen bei Veranstaltungen treffen können. Das Light Wave Projekt war eine einmalige Installation mit 25 blau leuchtenden Modulen. Dennoch ist es konzeptionell ein Baukastensystem, das auch in Serie produziert werden könnte.

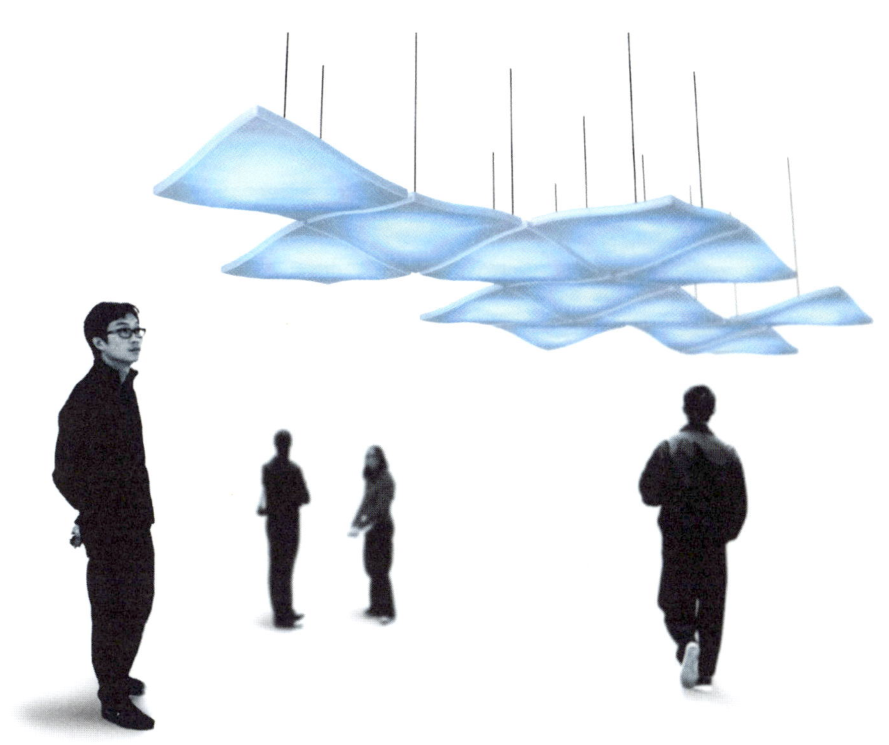

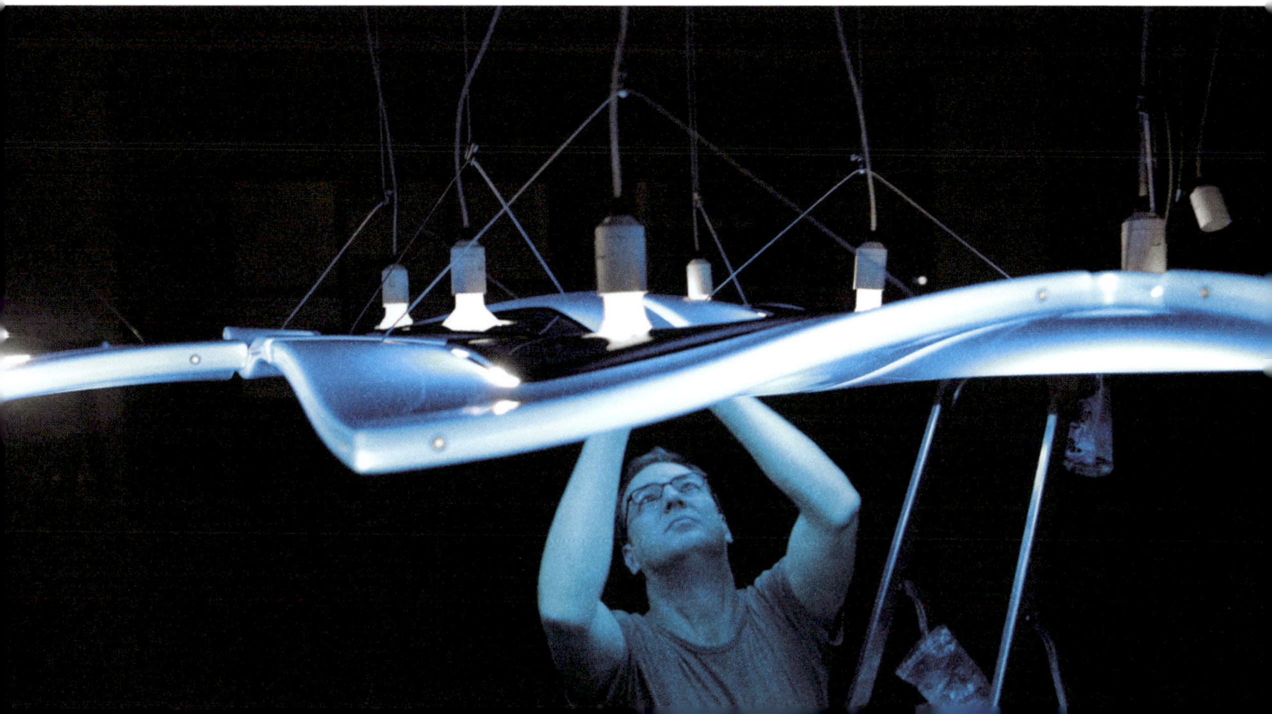

MATERIALS

designing with material innovations and using new production processes

Seen historically, materials are perhaps the most important element in design. A formal idea only develops intensity and the ability to convince if it contains previously unknown materials or a combination of materials. The masterly use of technologies and materials without any loss of the poetry and everyday taken-for-grantedness of an object is the challenge facing designers. In the following projects, material transfers from closely related industries were particularly important. Why should materials that are used successfully in automobile interiors or in medical systems not be used to open up new worlds in the sphere of furniture and furnishings?

Materialien sind im Design, historisch gesehen, die vielleicht wichtigste Einflussgröße. Jede formale Idee entwickelt nur dann Intensität und Überzeugungskraft, wenn sie eine bisher ungekannte Materialwelt oder Materialkombination eröffnet. Der virtuose Umgang mit Technologien und Werkstoffen – ohne dabei die Poetik und alltägliche Selbstverständlichkeit eines Objektes zu vergessen – ist die Herausforderung für den Entwurf schlechthin. Bei den folgenden Projekten waren besonders Materialtransfers aus benachbarten Industrien wichtig. Warum sollen Materialien, die in Automobil-Interieurs oder der Medizintechnik erfolgreich Verwendung finden, nicht auch für Möbel neue Welten eröffnen?

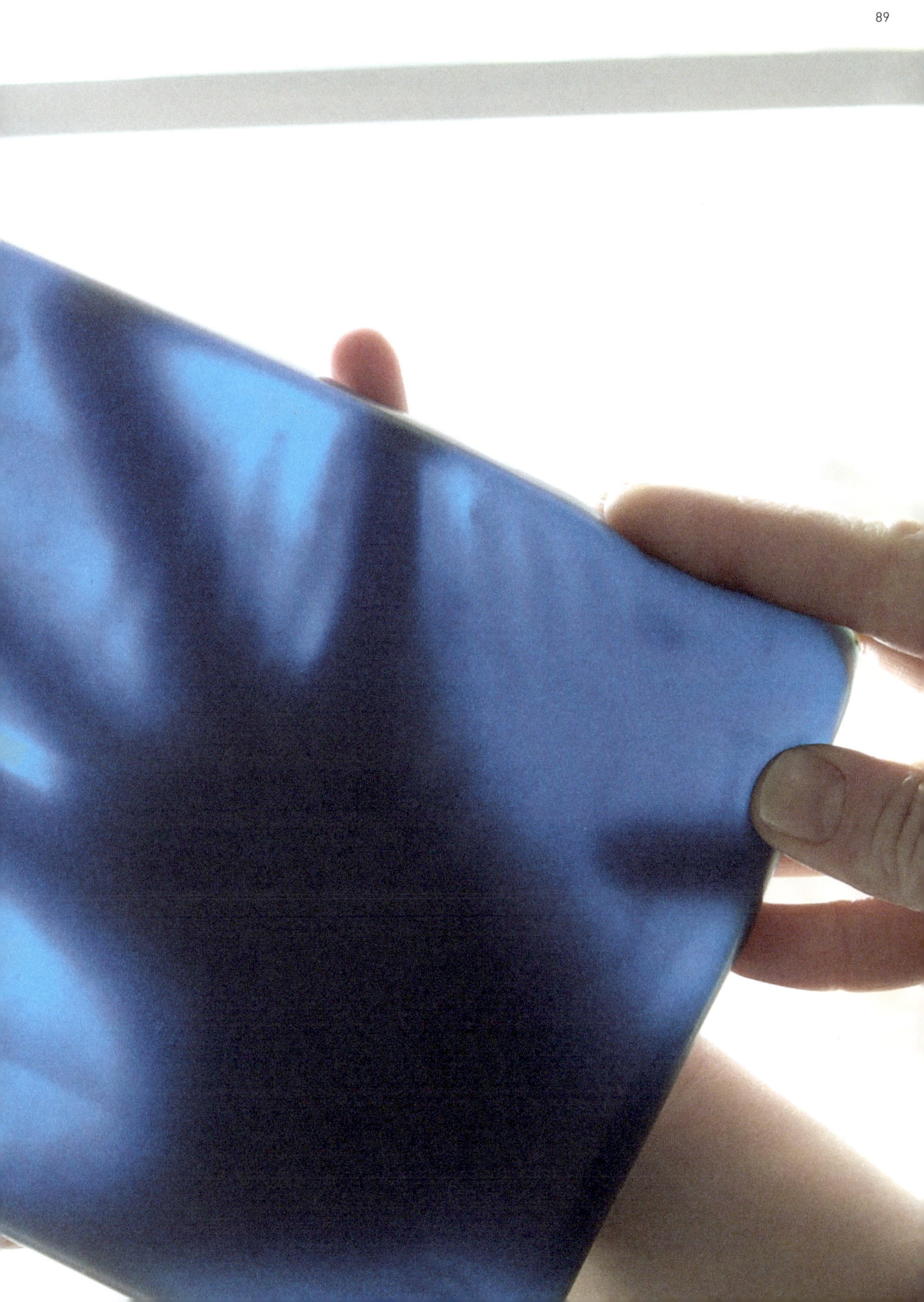

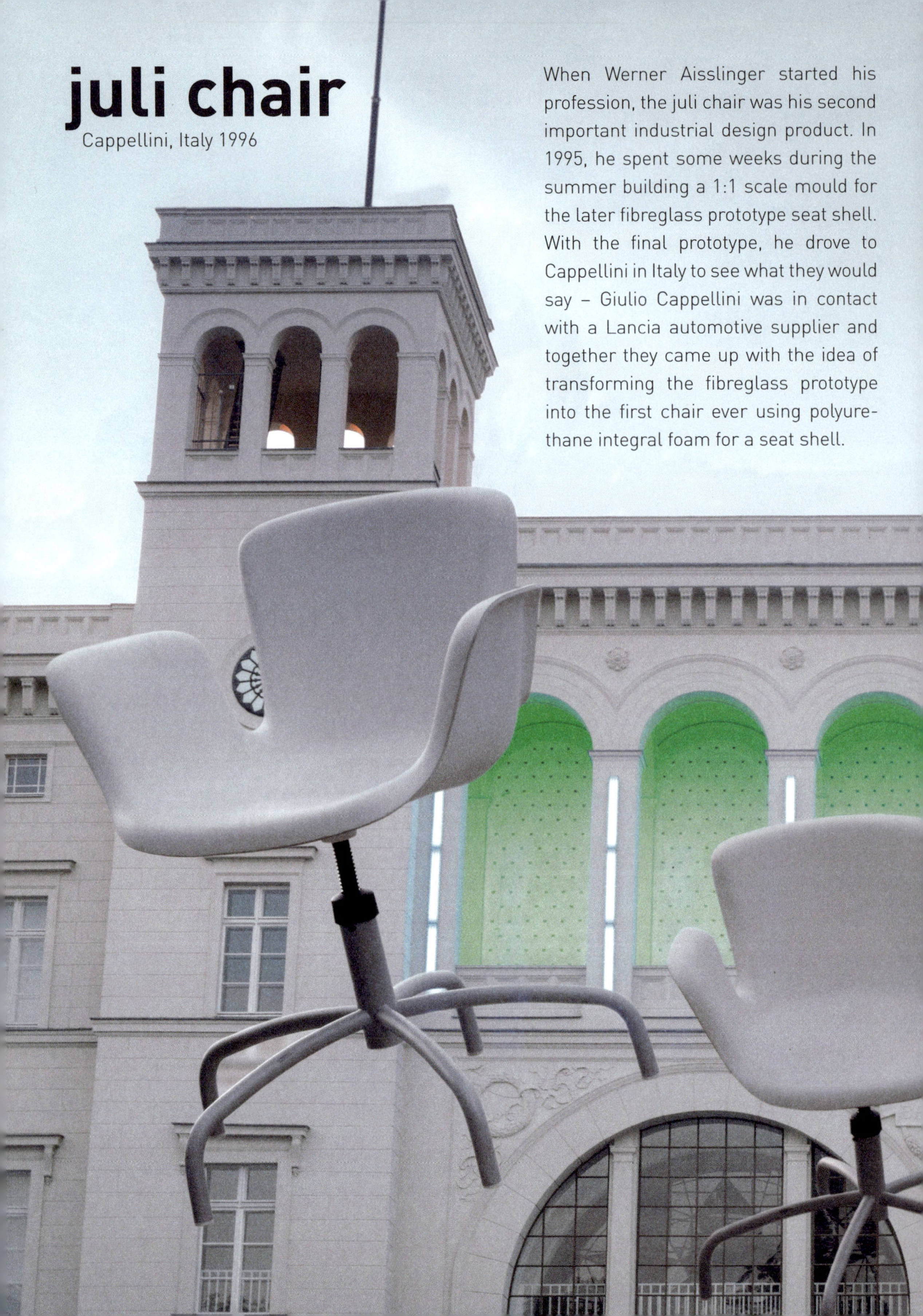

juli chair

Cappellini, Italy 1996

When Werner Aisslinger started his profession, the juli chair was his second important industrial design product. In 1995, he spent some weeks during the summer building a 1:1 scale mould for the later fibreglass prototype seat shell. With the final prototype, he drove to Cappellini in Italy to see what they would say – Giulio Cappellini was in contact with a Lancia automotive supplier and together they came up with the idea of transforming the fibreglass prototype into the first chair ever using polyurethane integral foam for a seat shell.

Der Juli Chair war Werner Aisslingers zweites wichtiges Industriedesign-Produkt. Im Sommer 1995 verbrachte er einige Wochen damit, eine Form im Maßtab 1:1 für den späteren Prototyp der Sitzschale aus Fiberglas herzustellen. Mit dem endgültigen Prototyp im Gepäck fuhr er nach Italien zu Cappellini, um deren Interesse zu testen. Giulio Cappellini war zu der Zeit mit einem Automobilzulieferer von Lancia im Gespräch, und zusammen hatte man die Idee, den Prototyp aus Fiberglas in den ersten Stuhl zu transformieren, dessen Sitzschale aus Polyurethan-Integralschaum bestehen sollte.

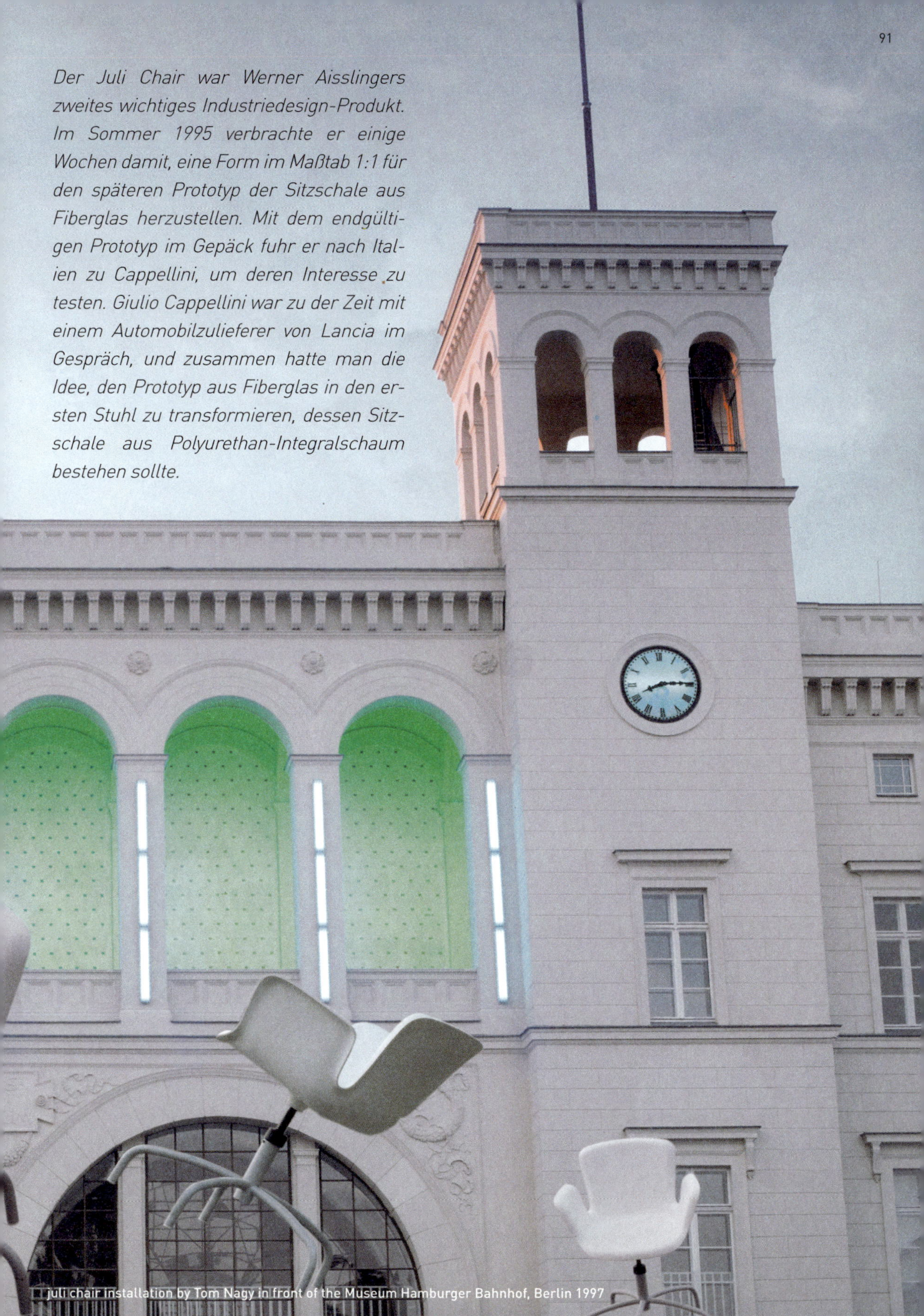

juli chair installation by Tom Nagy in front of the Museum Hamburger Bahnhof, Berlin 1997

This very first soft synthetic shell chair was a sensation at the 1996 salone del mobile and, consequently in 1998, became part of the permanent collection of the Modern Museum of Art in New York, the first German chair design since 1964.

Dieser erste synthetische Softshell Chair war auf dem Salone del Mobile 1996 eine Sensation und wurde dementsprechend 1998 Teil der ständigen Sammlung des Museum of Modern Art (MoMA) in New York. Er war, nach 1964, der erste wieder aus Deutschland stammende Stuhlentwurf im MoMA.

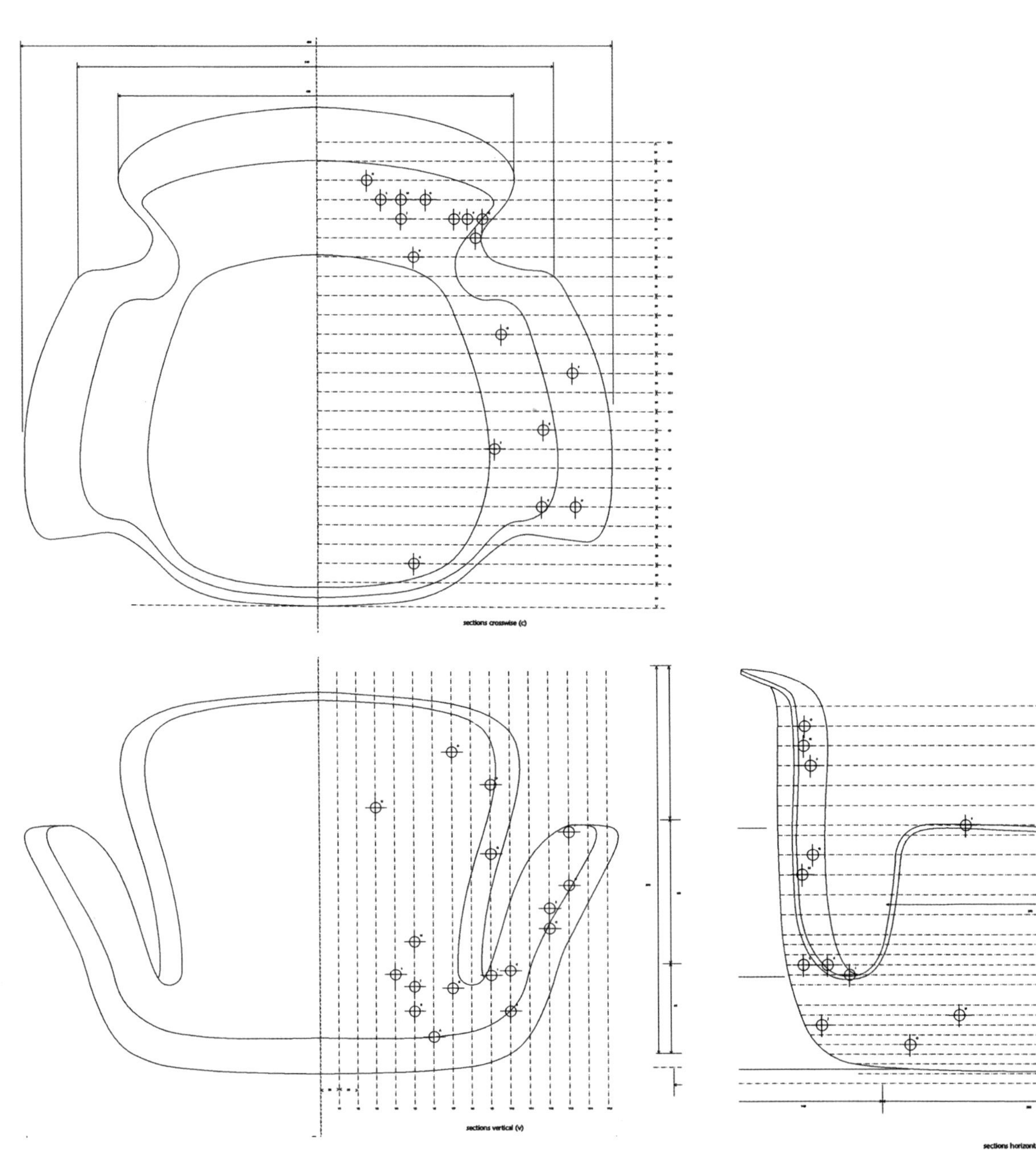

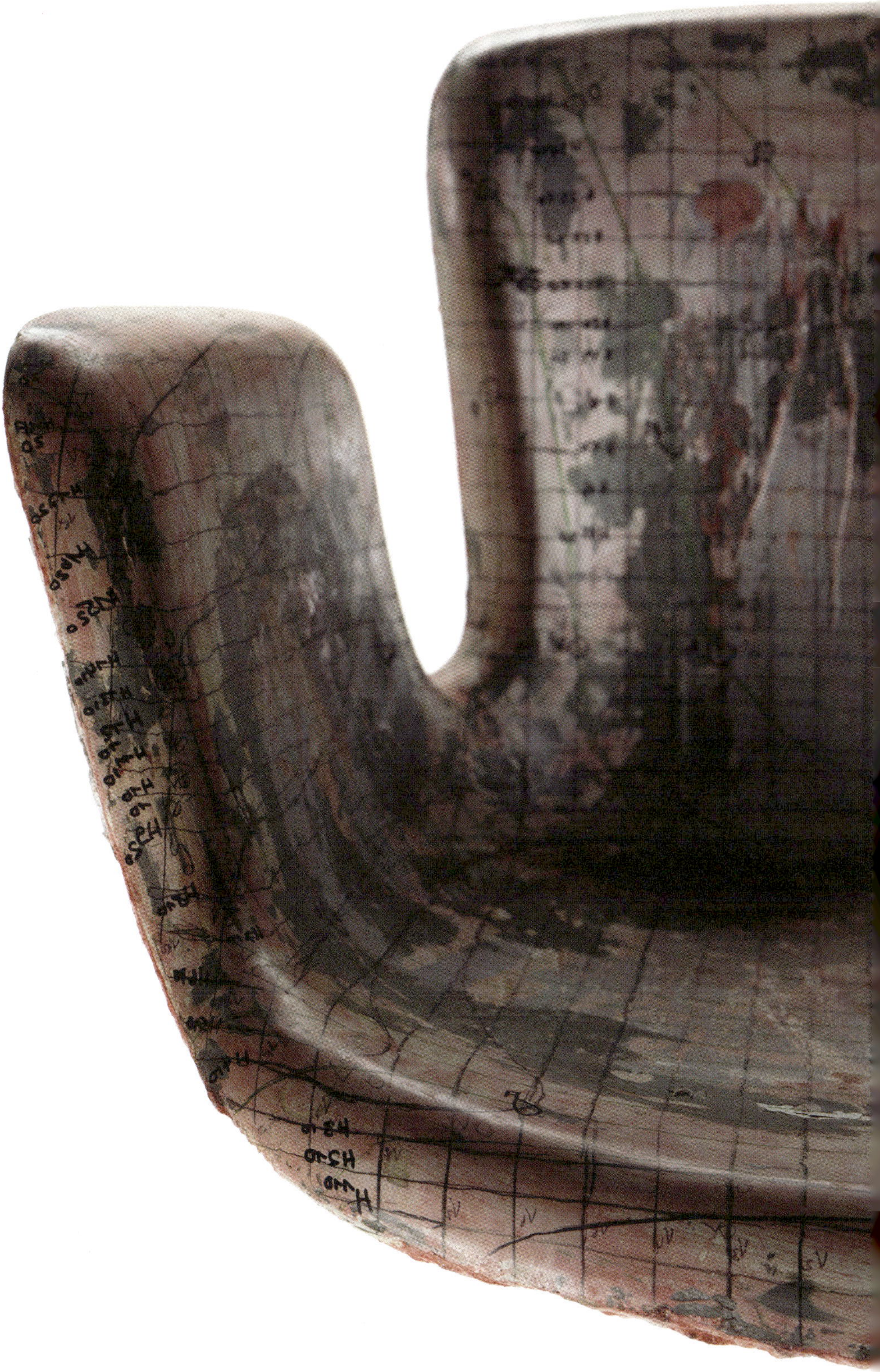

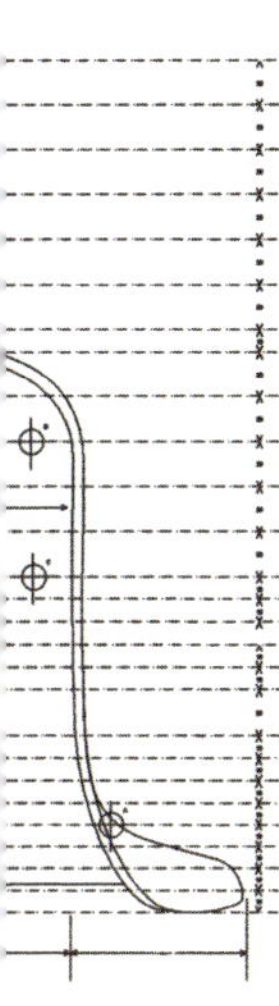

hand made juli chair mould for the first fibreglass handmoulded seatshells, Berlin 1995

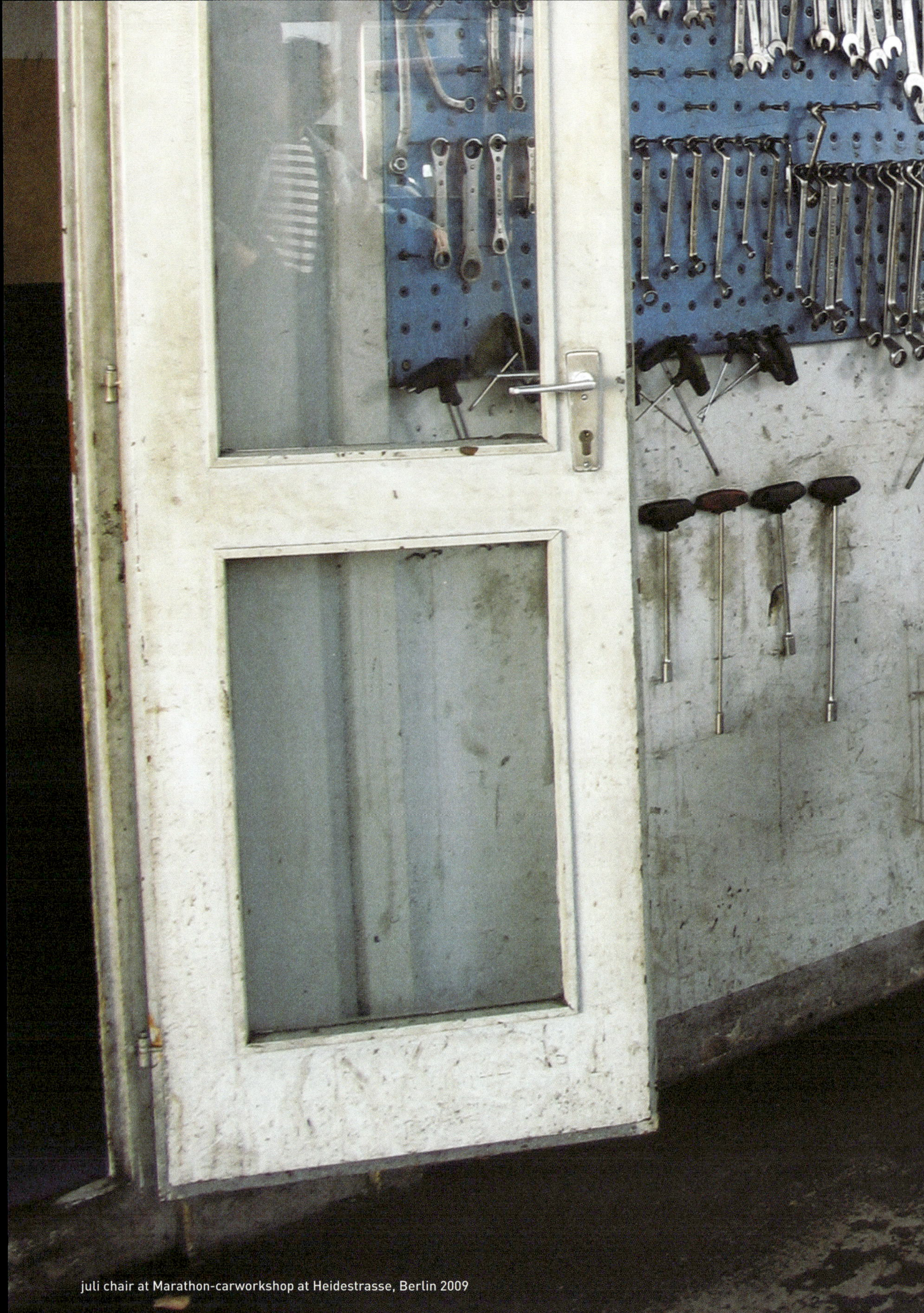

juli chair at Marathon-carworkshop at Heidestrasse, Berlin 2009

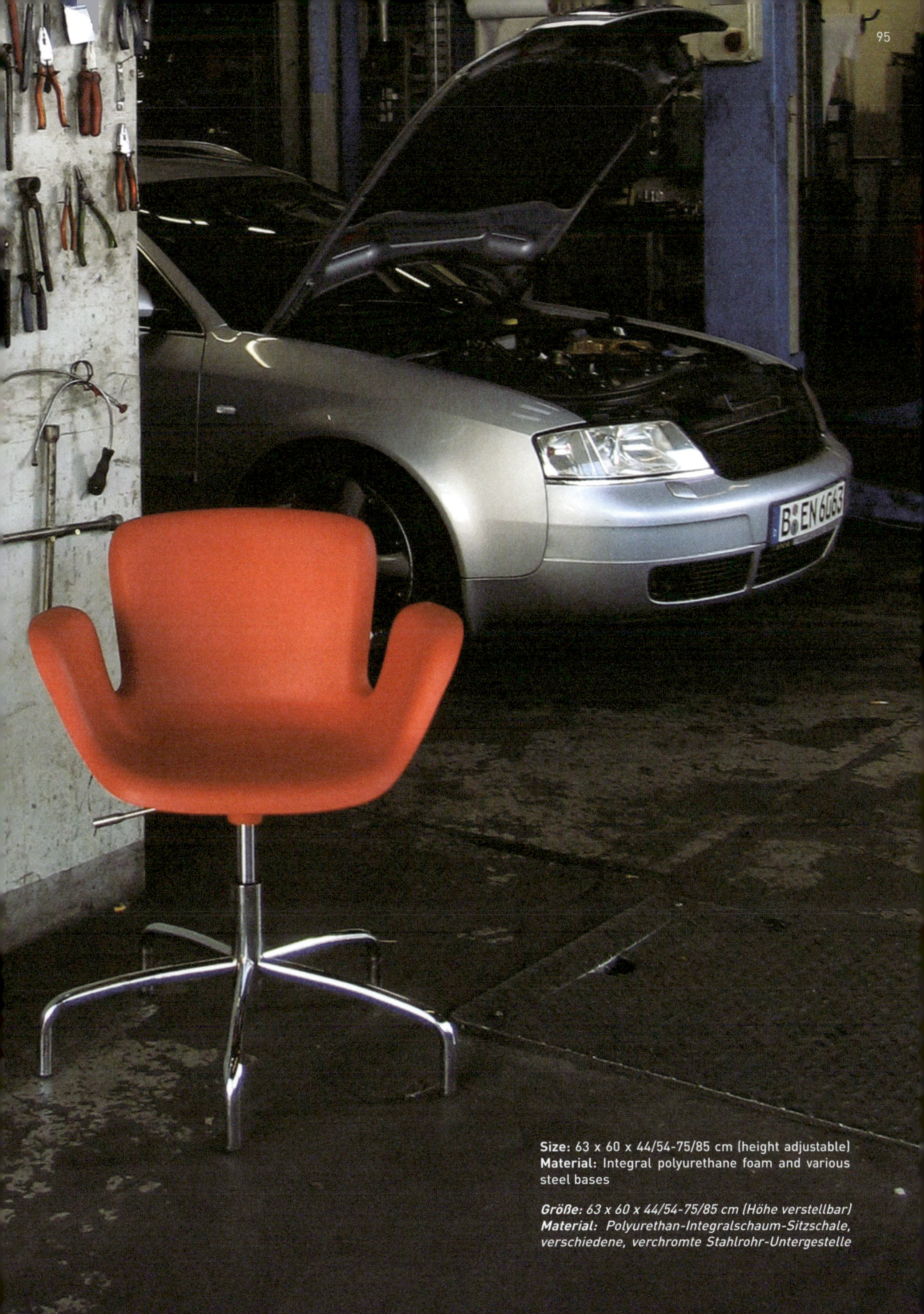

Size: 63 x 60 x 44/54-75/85 cm (height adjustable)
Material: Integral polyurethane foam and various steel bases

Größe: *63 x 60 x 44/54-75/85 cm (Höhe verstellbar)*
Material: *Polyurethan-Integralschaum-Sitzschale, verschiedene, verchromte Stahlrohr-Untergestelle*

soft cell

edition 1999

The soft cell collection is a limited edition of seating furniture which was ground-breaking because it was the first ever use of polyurethane gel in the furniture world. Aisslinger discovered the material in an exhibition in the MoMA curated by Paola Antonelli with the title "Mutant Materials" in the nineties: a soft translucent blue bicycle gel saddle. After some research, he approached Royal Medica close to Padua in Italy who used gel for operation desk mattresses and other medical applications. Together they developed the pads for a seating family which was presented in 1999 in a group show during the salone di mobile in Milan. Chemically, gel is a fluid molecular structure with a new upholstery dimension: 1 cm of gel provides the same degree of comfort as 5 cm of traditional foam.

Die Soft Cell Kollektion ist eine limitierte Edition von Sitzmöbeln, die aufgrund ihrer erstmaligen Verwendung von Polyurethan-Gel in der Welt der Möbel bahnbrechend war. Werner Aisslinger stieß in einer von Paola Antonelli kuratierten Ausstellung im MoMA, die „Mutant Materials" hieß und Ende der 1990er-Jahre dort zu sehen war, auf das Material: Ausgestellt war ein weicher transluzenter Fahrradsattel aus Gel. Nach einiger Recherche wandte er sich an die in der Nähe von Padua gelegene Firma Royal Medica, die Gel für Operationstisch-Auflagen und andere medizinische Anwendungsfelder einsetzte. Gemeinsam entwickelten sie die Gel-Pads für eine Sitzmöbelserie, die auf dem Salone del Mobile 1999 in einer Gruppenausstellung präsentiert wurde. Chemisch betrachtet hat Gel eine flüssige, molekulare Struktur mit einem speziellen fließenden Polsterverhalten: 1 cm Gel bietet den gleichen Komfort wie eine 5 cm dicke Schicht klassischen Schaums.

soft cell on rooftop at Heidestrasse, Berlin 2009

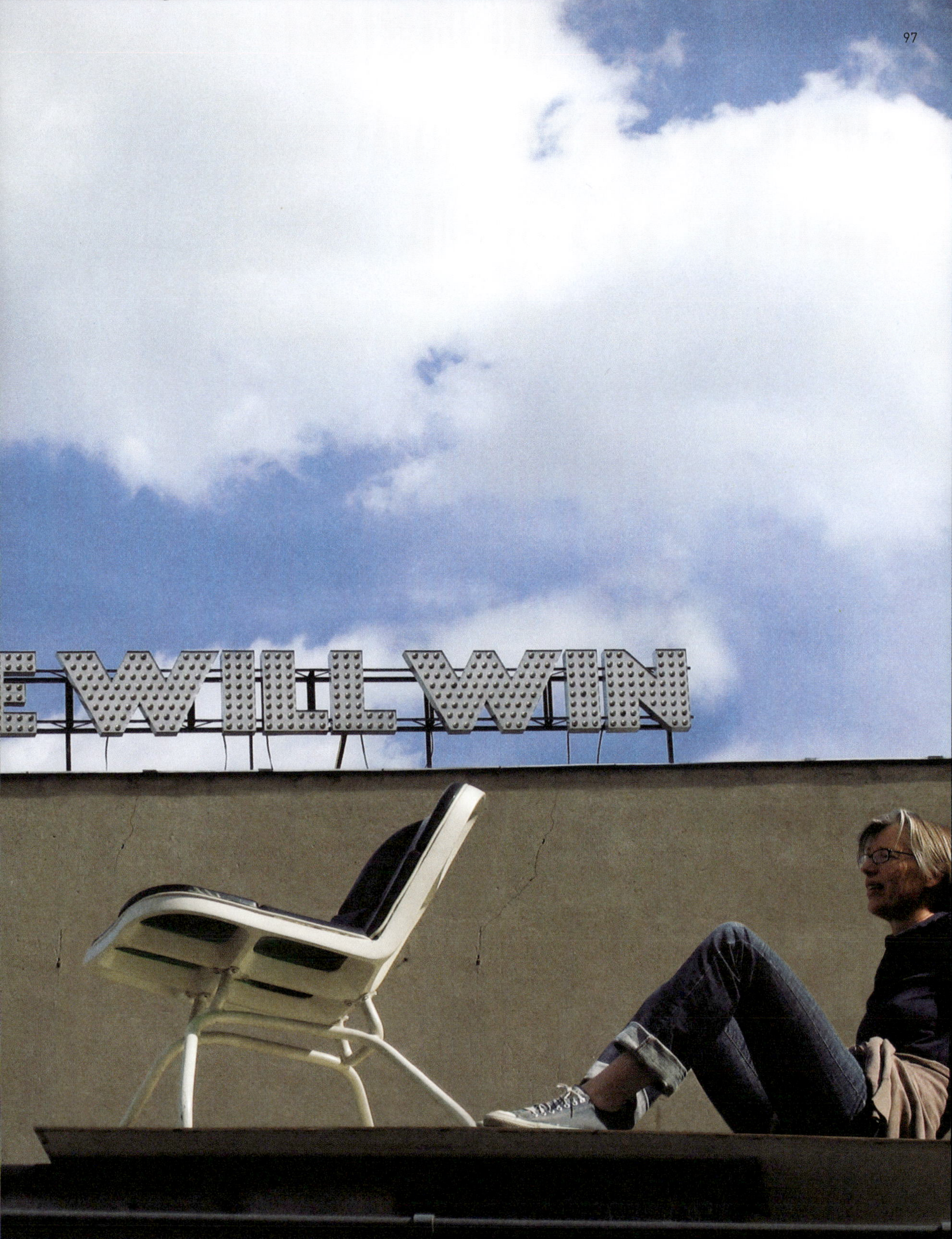
WILL WIN

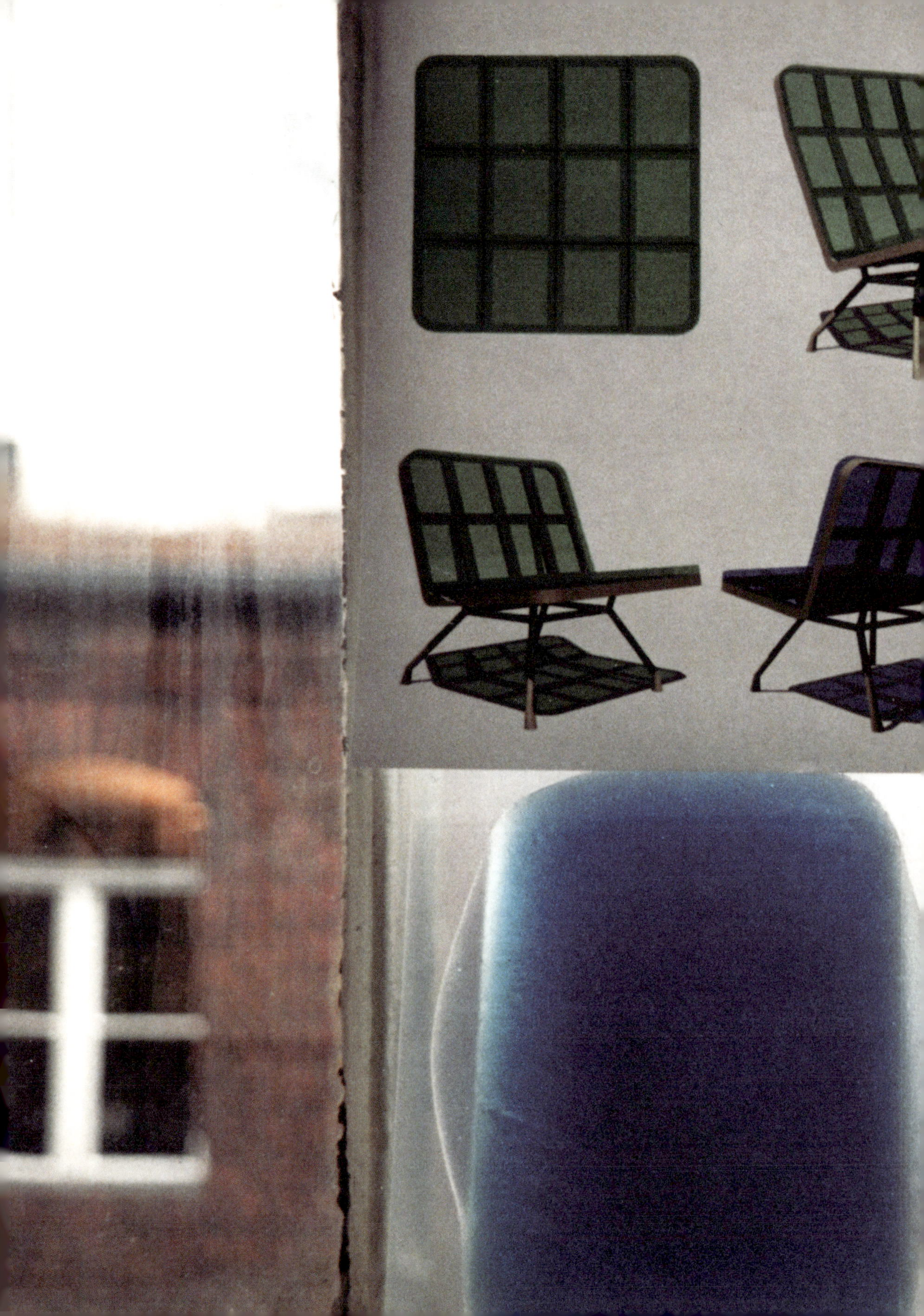

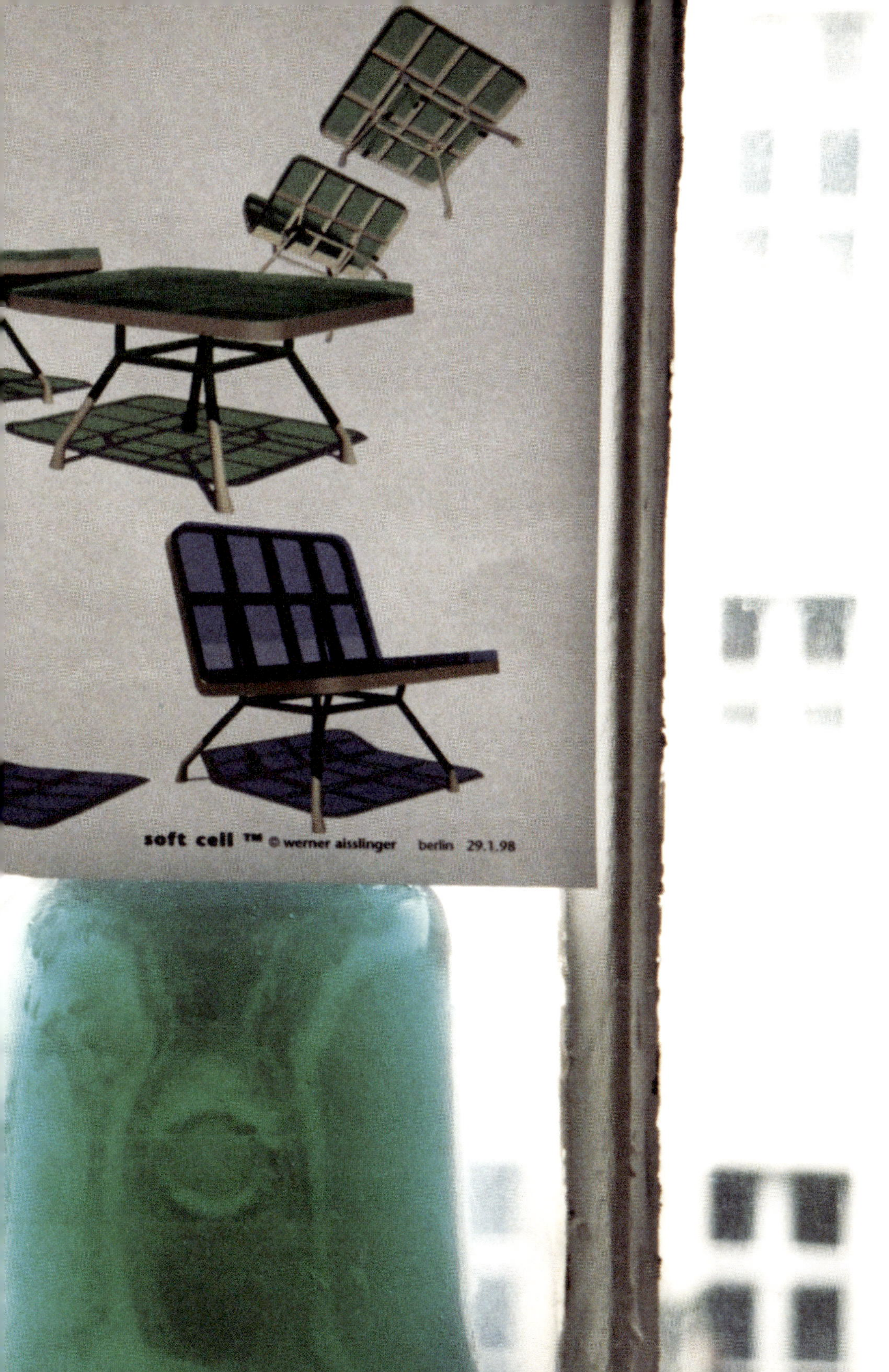

first renderings and material samples for soft cell prototypes at studio Leibnizstrasse, Berlin 1998

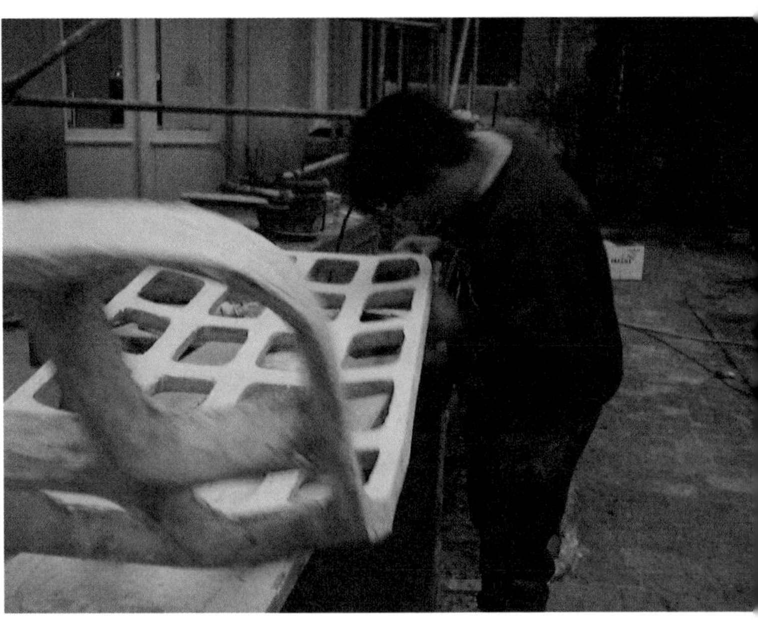

The aim of the formal concept was to create a project that displayed the same self-evidence as high-tech sneakers and combine it with the notion of using medical gel in the furniture world. The combination of the specially developed gel pads produced with a transparent spherical base-plate makes the furniture of soft cell totally transparent. The supporting moulded fibreglass honeycomb frame structures were made by the studio aisslinger team itself.

Formales Ziel war es, eine Ästhetik zu schaffen, die so selbstverständlich wirkt wie Hightech-Sneakers und die Gel aus dem Bereich der medizinischen Anwendung in die Welt der Möbel überträgt. Die Anordnung der speziell entwickelten Gelpolster auf einer sphärisch geformten transluzenten Trägerplatte verleiht den Soft Cell Möbeln ein durchweg transparentes Erscheinungsbild. Die wabenförmig aufgebauten Rahmenstrukturen aus Fiberglas wurden vom studio aisslinger team selbst hergestellt.

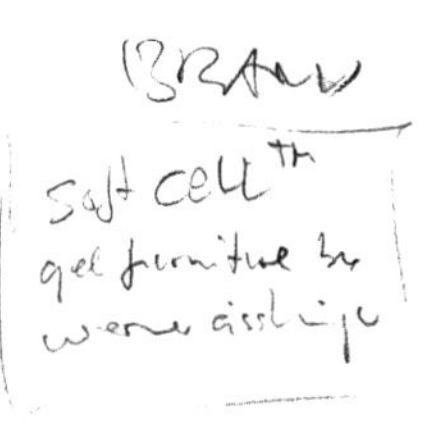

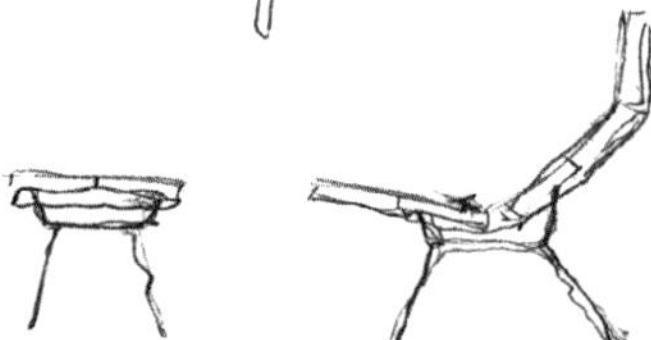

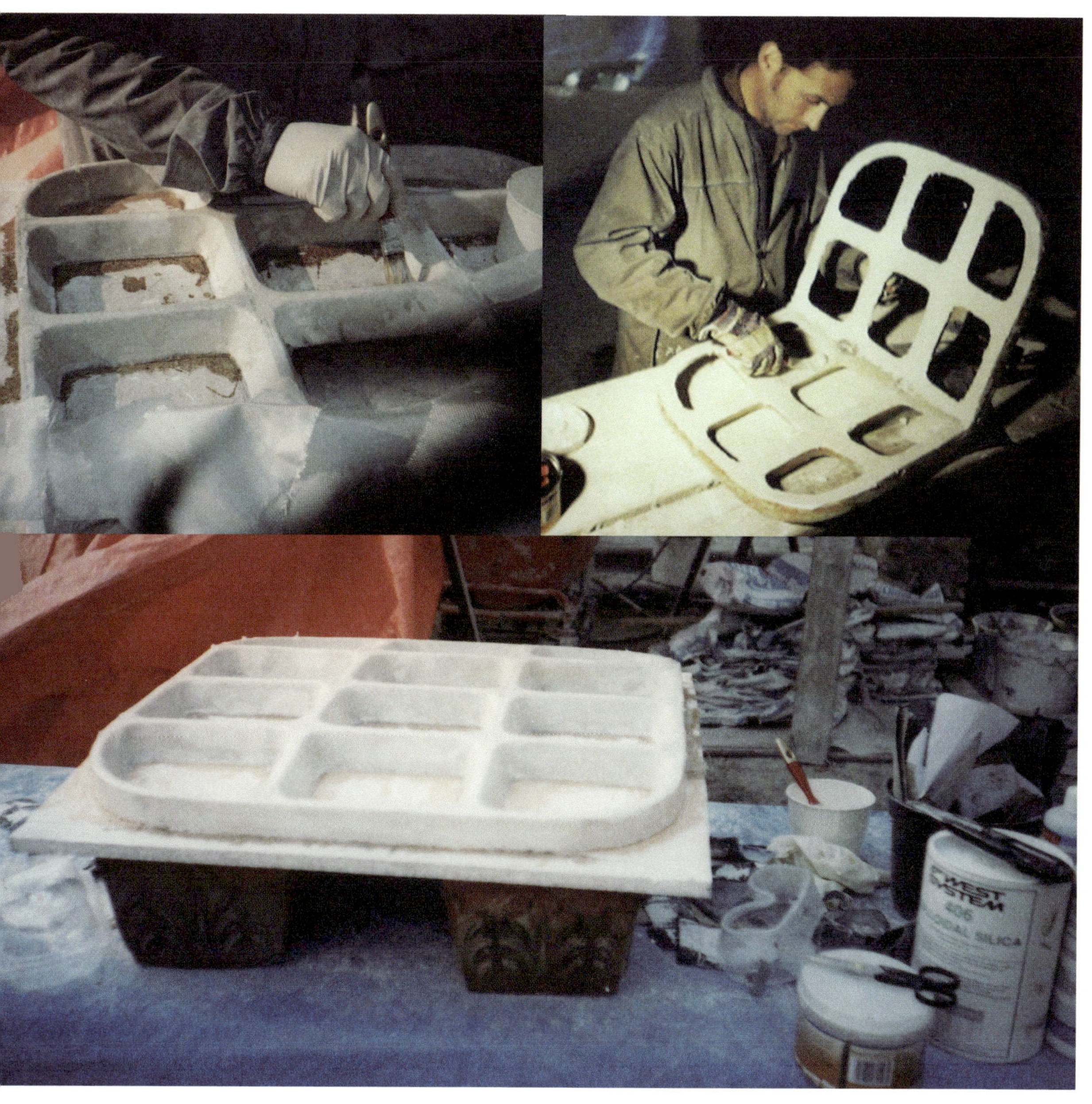

outdoor prototyping with Steve Morgan at Lückhoffstrasse , Berlin 1999

final moulded fibreglass frame structures, outdoor prototyping with Stefan Legner at Lückhoffstrasse, Berlin 1999

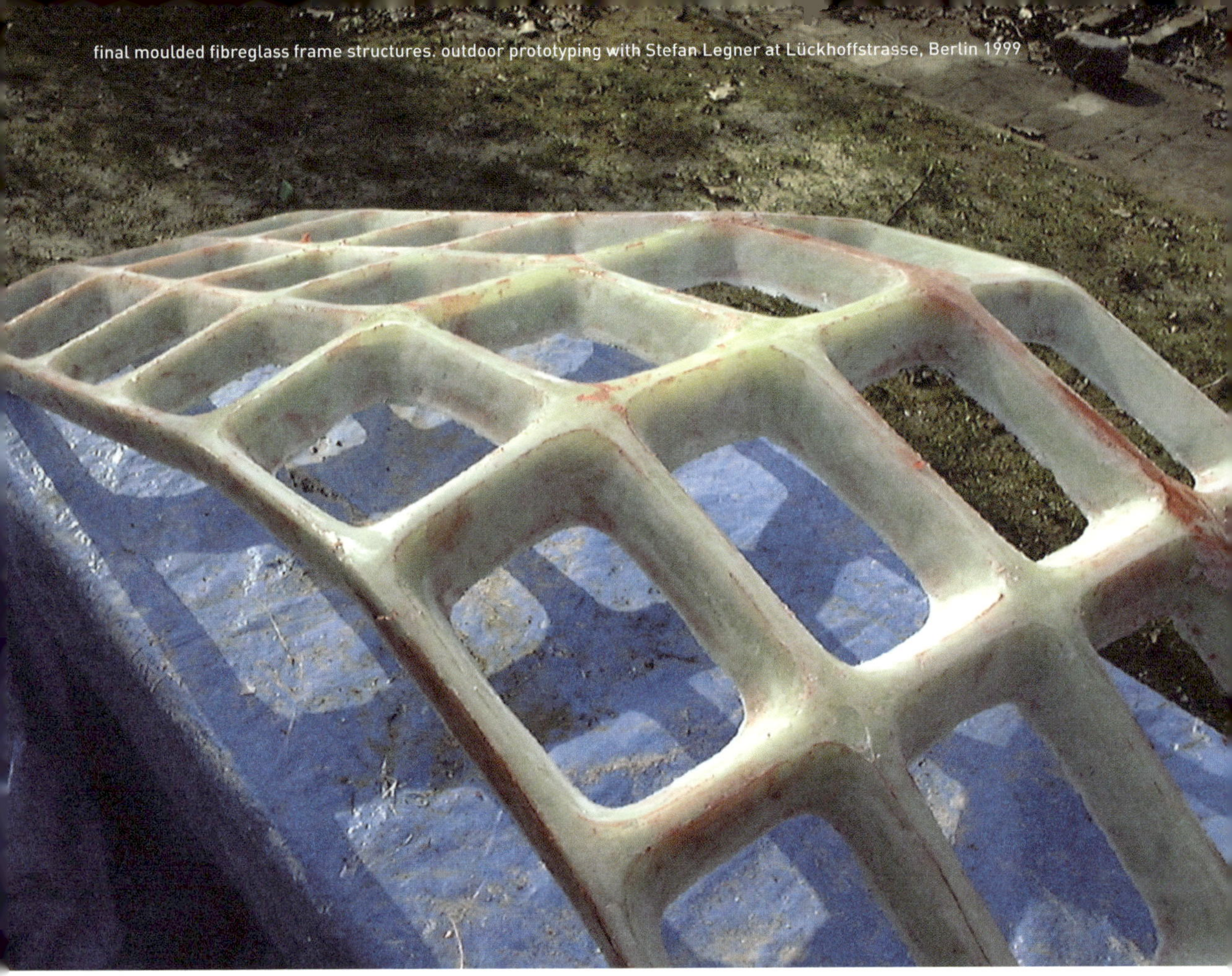

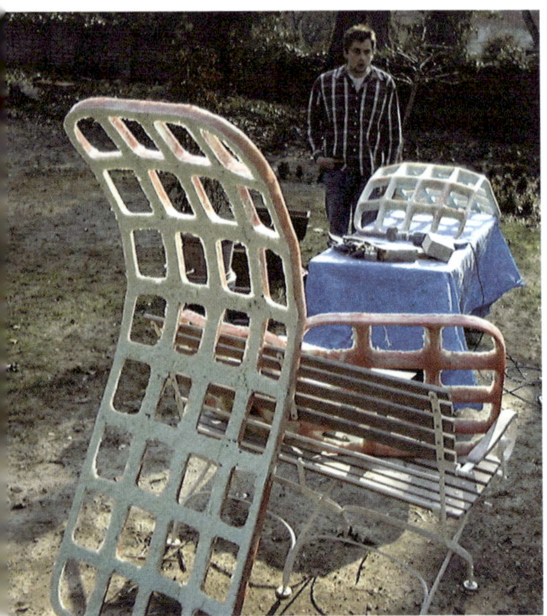

Size: 60 x 70/180 x 75 cm
Material: Green, yellow or blue gel pads fixed to a fibreglass frame which rests on a white or black steel frame

Größe: *60 x 70/180 x 75 cm*
Material: *Grüne, blaue oder gelbe Gel-Pads, die auf einem Fiberglasmonorahmen liegen, Rahmenstruktur aus weiß oder schwarz lackiertem Stahlrohr*

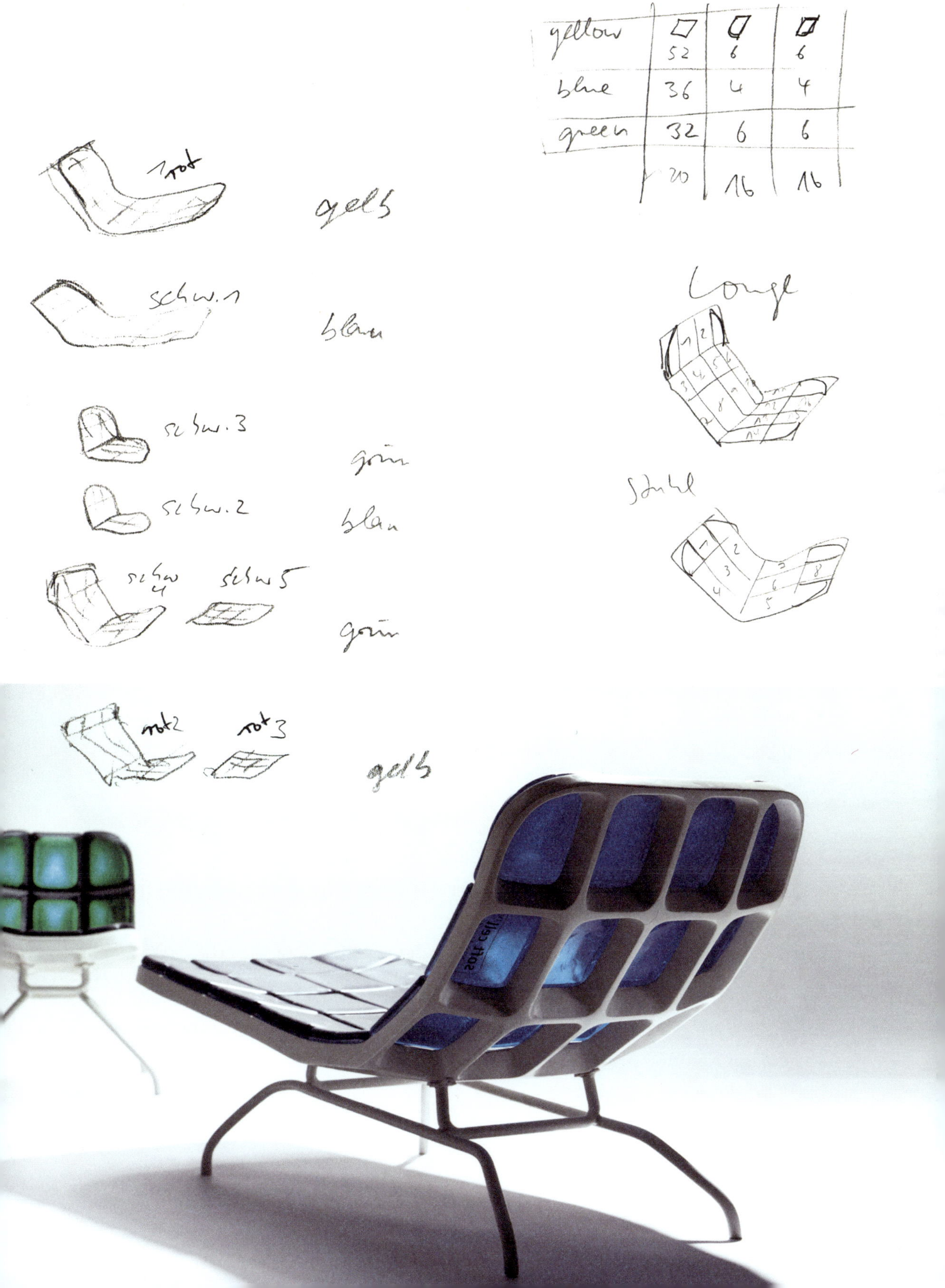

yellow	52	6	6
blue	36	4	4
green	32	6	6
	120	16	16

1 rot

gelb

schw. 1

blau

schw. 3

grün

schw. 2

blau

schw 4

schw 5

grün

rot 2

rot 3

gelb

Longe

Stuhl

soft chaise

Zanotta, Italy 2000

The soft chaise, presented at the Milan Furniture Fair in Milan 2000, was the first item of industrialised furniture that made use of gel. During the 1999 soft cell exhibition, Aisslinger talked to the Zanotta family about a more industrial and serial application of this new fascinating material. Together, they decided to design and develop a chaise which evolved into the 1999 soft-cell gel project. At the time, a new company called TechnoGel engineered a new production method with a matt self-coating film which is sprayed into the mould.

Der Soft Chaise war das erste industriell gefertigte Möbelstück aus Gel, das 2000 auf dem Salone del Mobile in Mailand vorgestellt wurde. Während der Soft Cell Ausstellung 1999 besuchte die Familie Zanotta Werner Aisslinger, um mit ihm über einen industrielleren und serienmäßigeren Einsatz dieses neuen, faszinierenden Materials zu sprechen. Sie beschlossen, gemeinsam eine Liege zu entwickeln, aufbauend auf dem Soft Cell Gel Projekt von 1999. Zu dieser Zeit arbeitete ein neues Unternehmen namens TechnoGel an einem optimierten Herstellungsverfahren, bei dem ein transluzenter Lack in die Werkzeugform gesprüht wird, der im self-coating Verfahren mit dem Gel eine resistente Haut bildet.

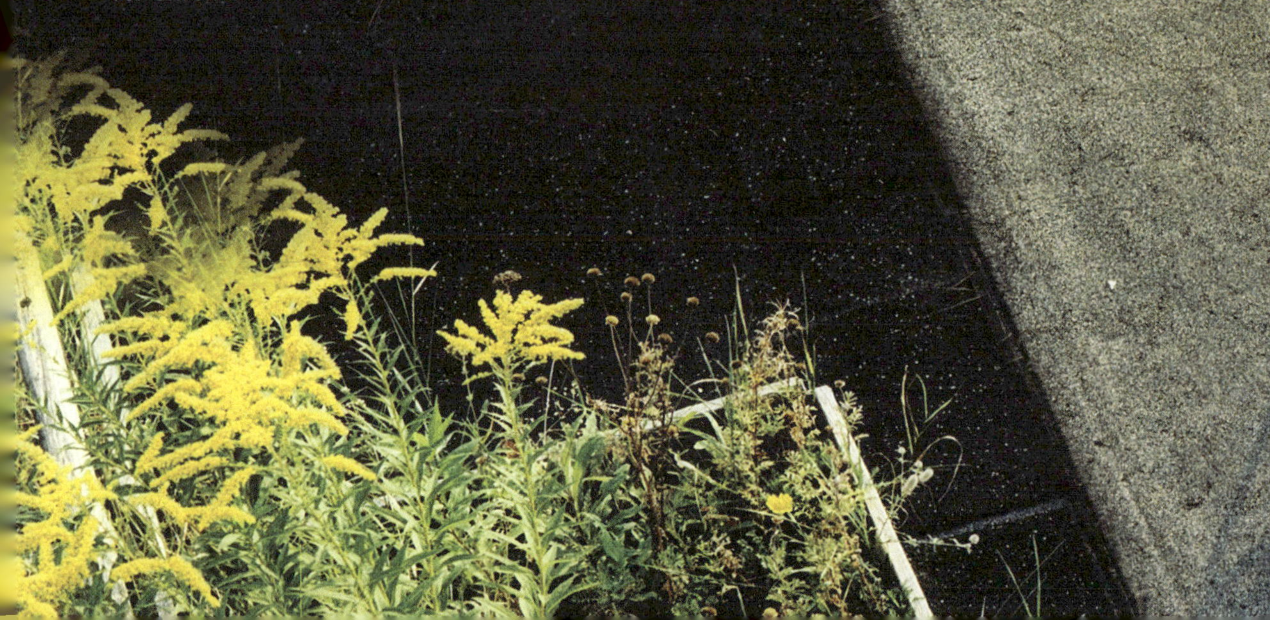

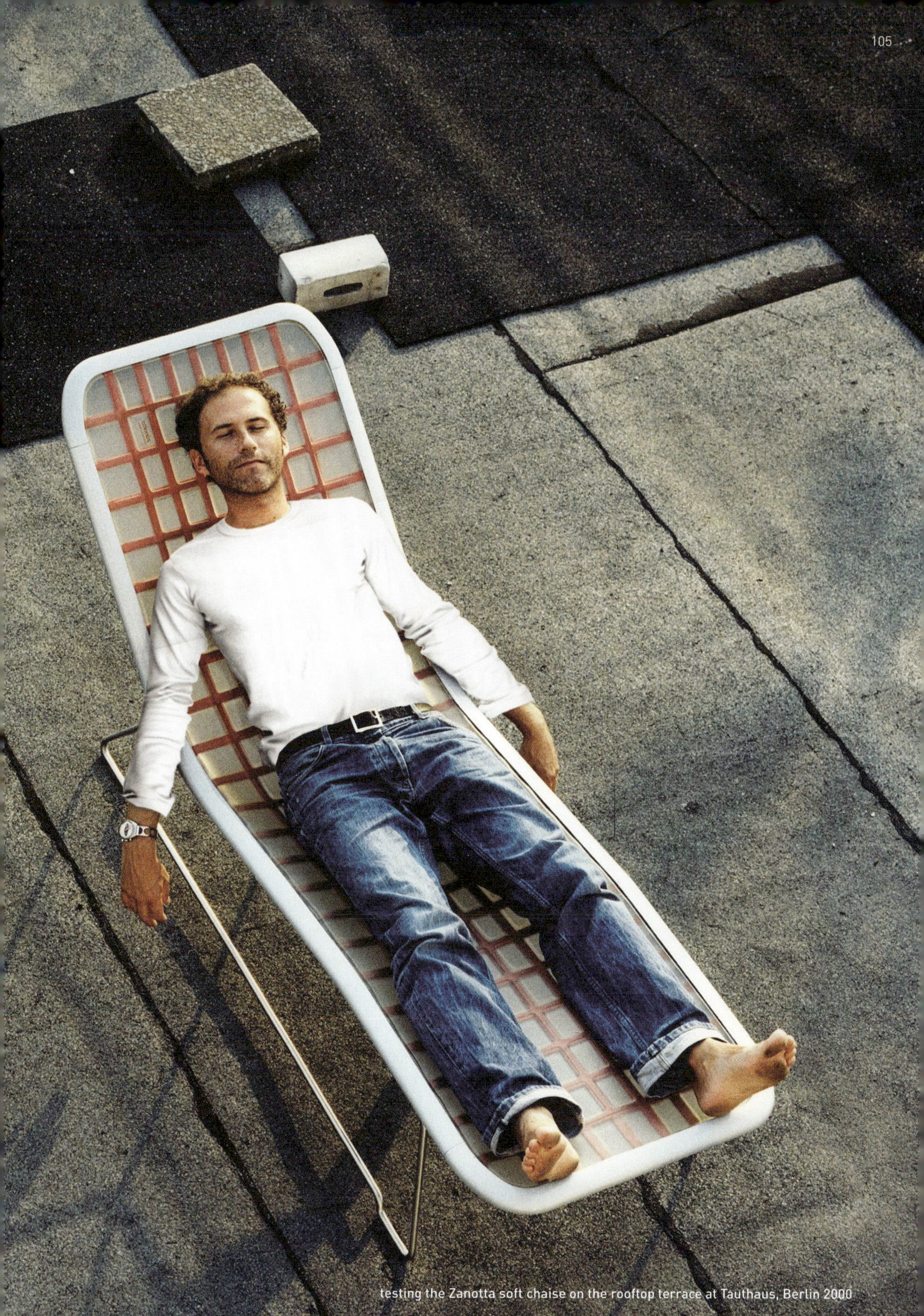

testing the Zanotta soft chaise on the rooftop terrace at Tauthaus, Berlin 2000

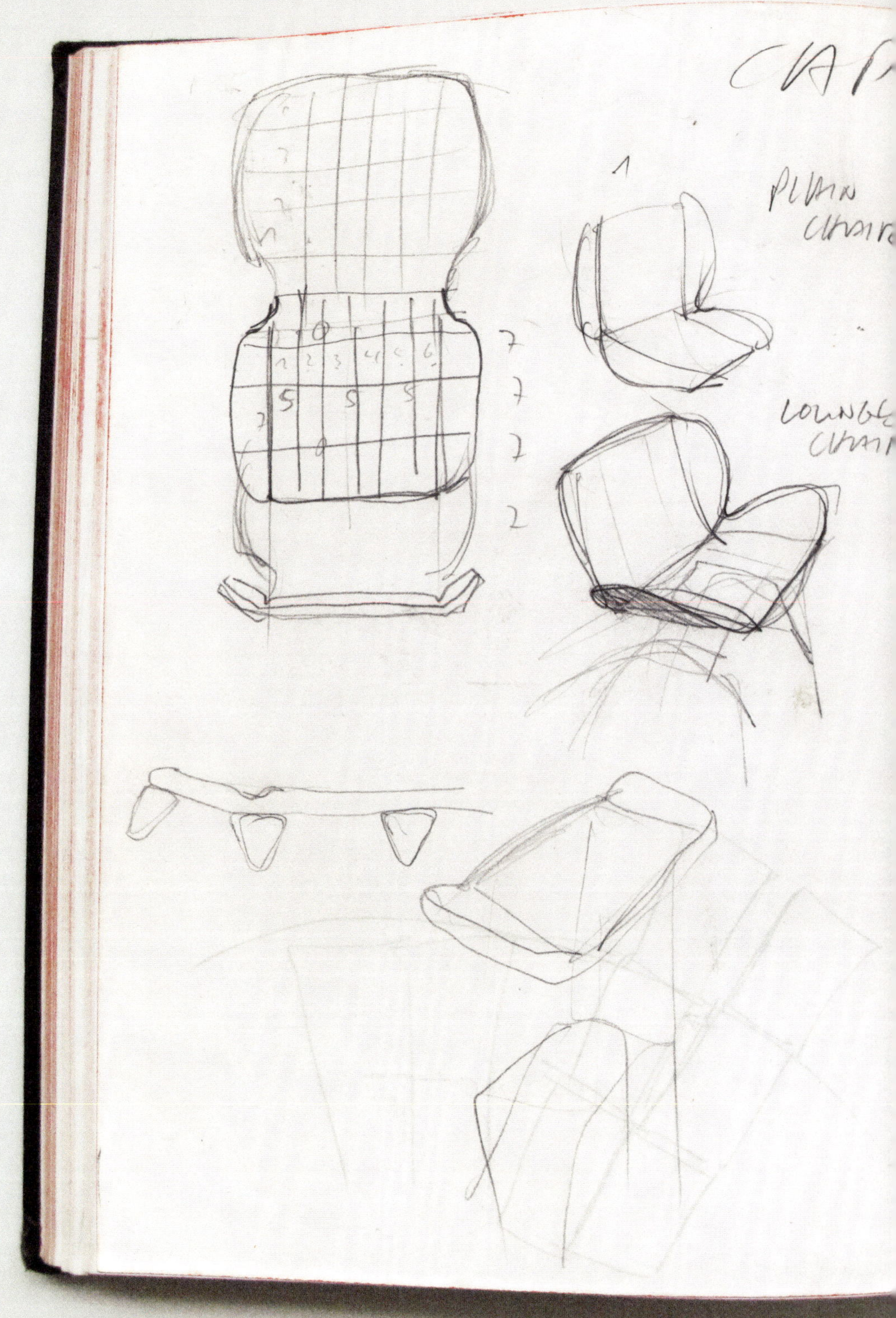

sketchbook pages for Zanotta soft chaise, Berlin 1999

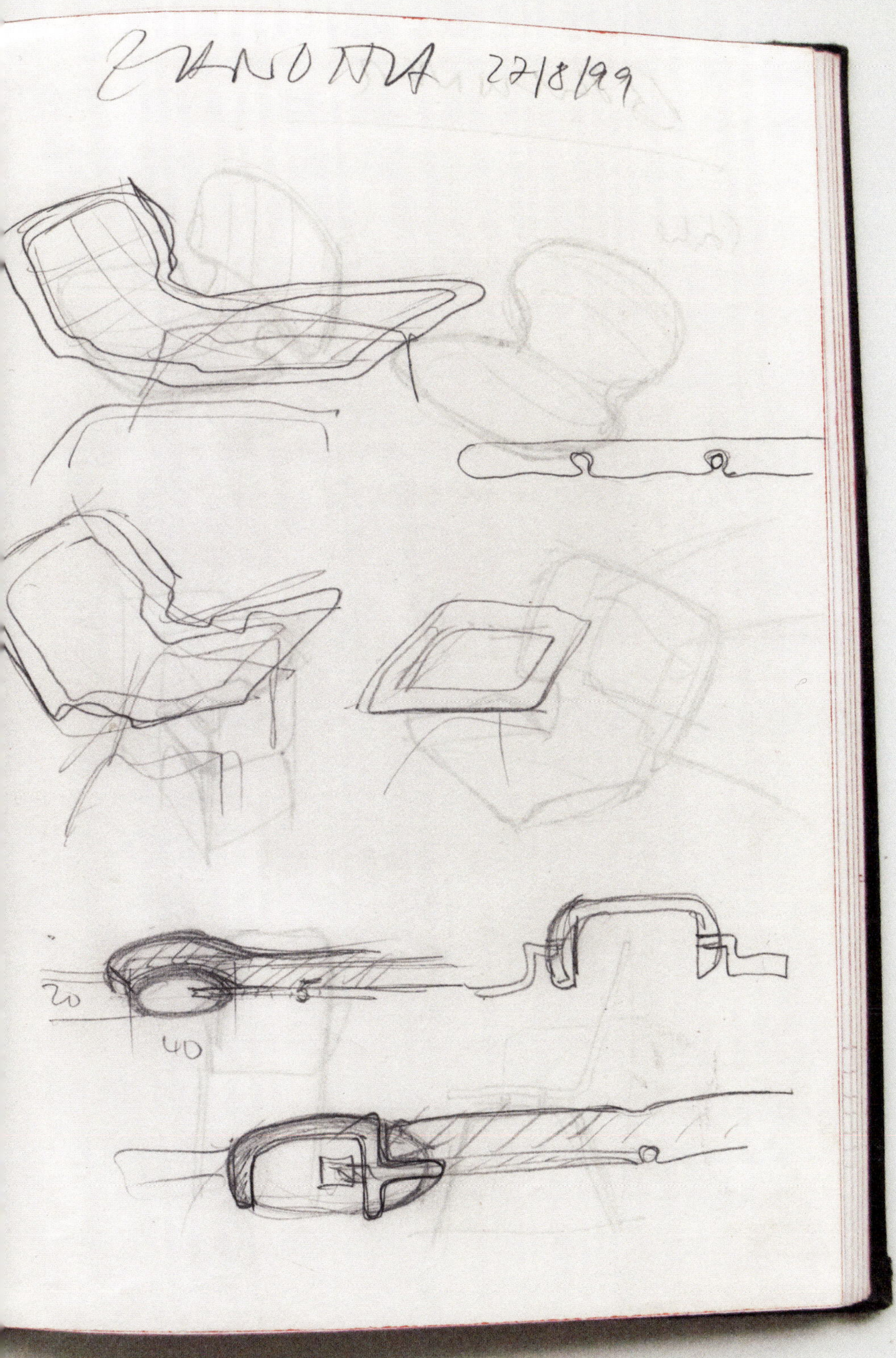

Werner Aisslinger designed a huge monopad surface which rests on top of a fabric grid framed by an aluminium alloy profile. The chaise soft became an iconic object and, in 2000, it was the second most published design-object worldwide. Zanotta stopped production four years later as the gel-colours turned out to be insufficiently UV-resistant when used outdoors.

Werner Aisslinger entwarf eine große Monopad-Gelmatte, die auf einem Gitter aus Textilbändern ruht, das wiederum in einem tragenden Rahmen aus Aluminiumprofilen gefasst ist. Die Soft Chaise wurde zu einer Designikone und war 2000 das am zweithäufigsten publizierte Designobjekt weltweit. Zanotta stellte die Produktion allerdings vier Jahre später ein, da sich herausstellte, dass die Gelmatten bei dauerndem Outdoor-Einsatz nicht ausreichend UV-resistent waren.

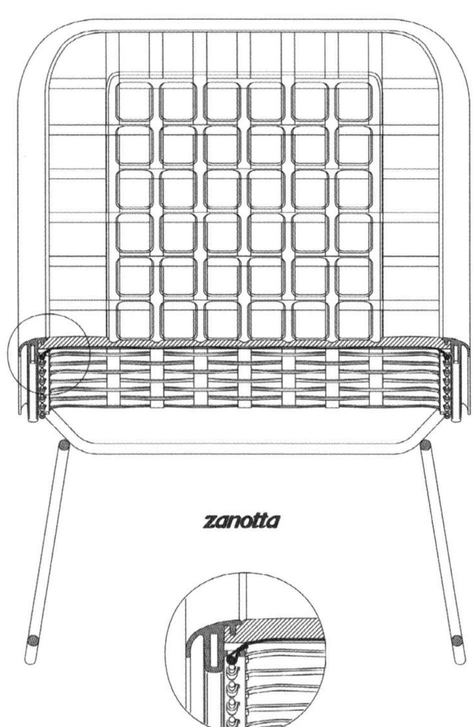

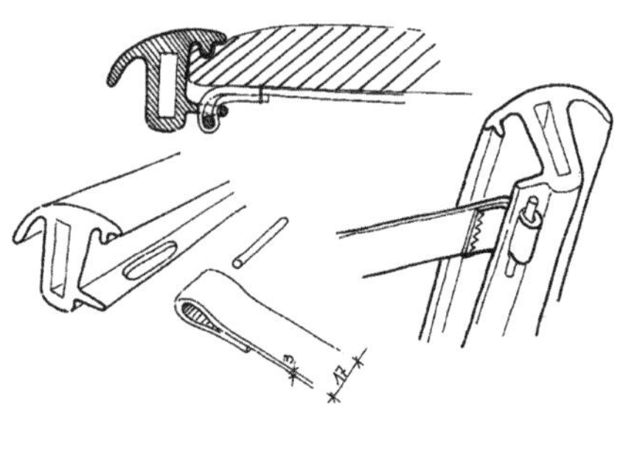

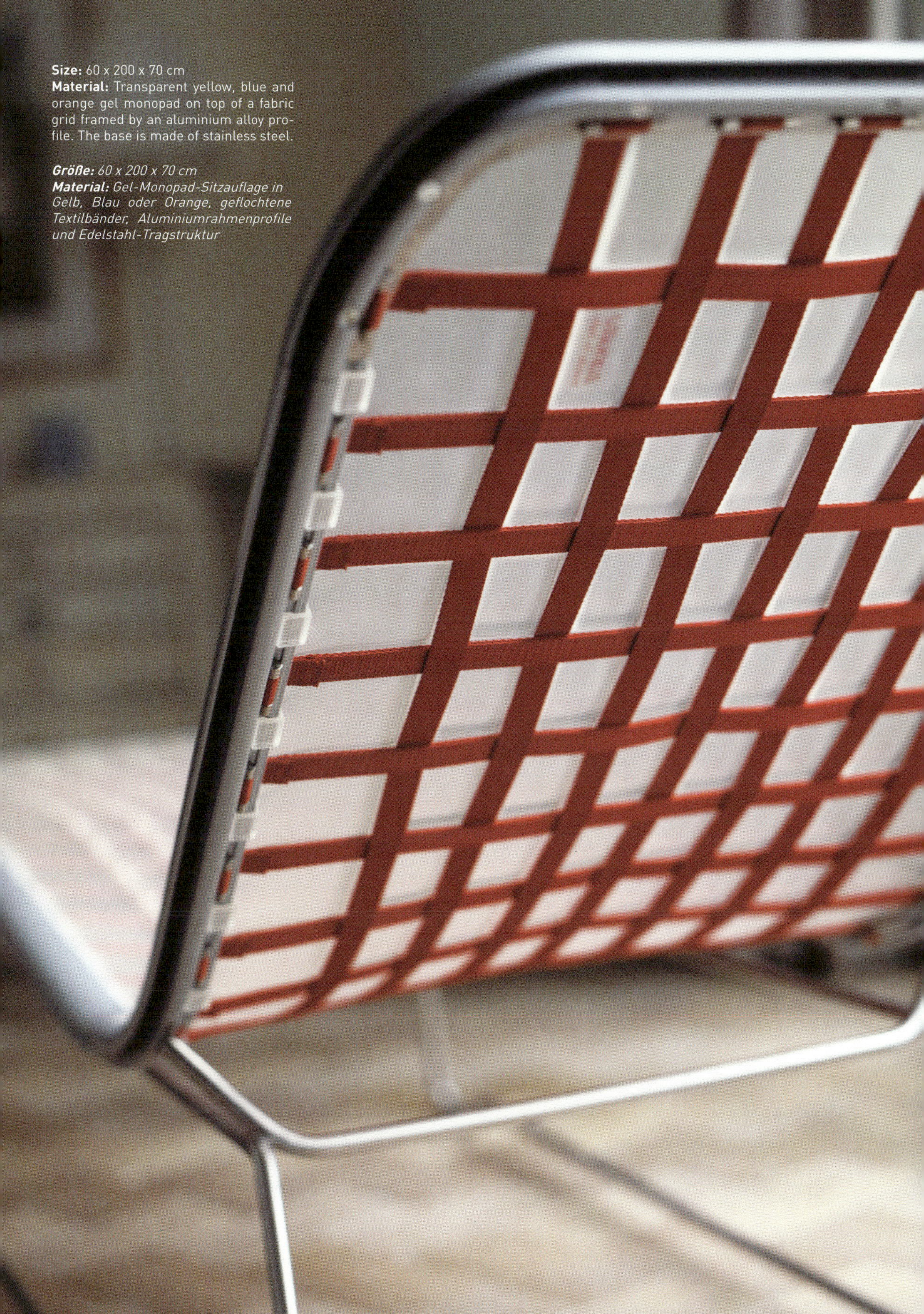

Size: 60 x 200 x 70 cm
Material: Transparent yellow, blue and orange gel monopad on top of a fabric grid framed by an aluminium alloy profile. The base is made of stainless steel.

Größe: *60 x 200 x 70 cm*
Material: *Gel-Monopad-Sitzauflage in Gelb, Blau oder Orange, geflochtene Textilbänder, Aluminiumrahmenprofile und Edelstahl-Tragstruktur*

gel chair

Cappellini, Italy 2001

The latest development with this fascinating material has been created with Cappellini and has evolved technologically. As with the leaves of a tree, the organic lattice structure shows through the translucent surface of the chairs, and depending on the light situation, their colour and appearance change. The gel-surface is matt and has a texture resembling human skin.

The Cappellini gel collection fascinated the design experts and is regarded as a quantum leap in material evolution in design – to quote Philippe Starck: "Here it became clear that there is no need for designing but simply for experimenting with a balanced minimum of no design which is only concerned with the material itself." Amongst the earliest design fans of the translucent high-tech chairs was Brad Pitt, who ordered thirty gel chairs from Cappellini in specially customized hues for his beach house in Santa Barbara.

Das technologisch komplexeste Designkonzept mit dem faszinierenden Werkstoff TechnoGel wurde mit Cappellini umgesetzt. Durch die transluzenten Flächen der Stühle scheint das organische tragende Gittermuster wie bei Blättern eines Baumes durch, je nach Lichteinfall ändern sich Farben und dadurch die Gesamterscheinung der Gel Chairs. Die Gel-Oberfläche ist matt und mit einer Textur beschichtet, die der menschlichen Haut nachempfunden ist.

Die Cappellini-Gel Kollektion, von der Philippe Starck sagt, „dass hier verstanden wurde, mit einem Minimum zu experimentieren und sich ganz aufs Material zu konzentrieren" faszinierte die Designexperten und wird als Quantensprung in der Materialevolution im Design gesehen. Unter den ersten Designfans der transluzenten High-Tech-Stühle war Brad Pitt, der sich gleich 30 Gel Chairs in eigens für ihn produzierten Farbtönen für sein Strandhaus in Santa Barbara bei Cappellini bestellte.

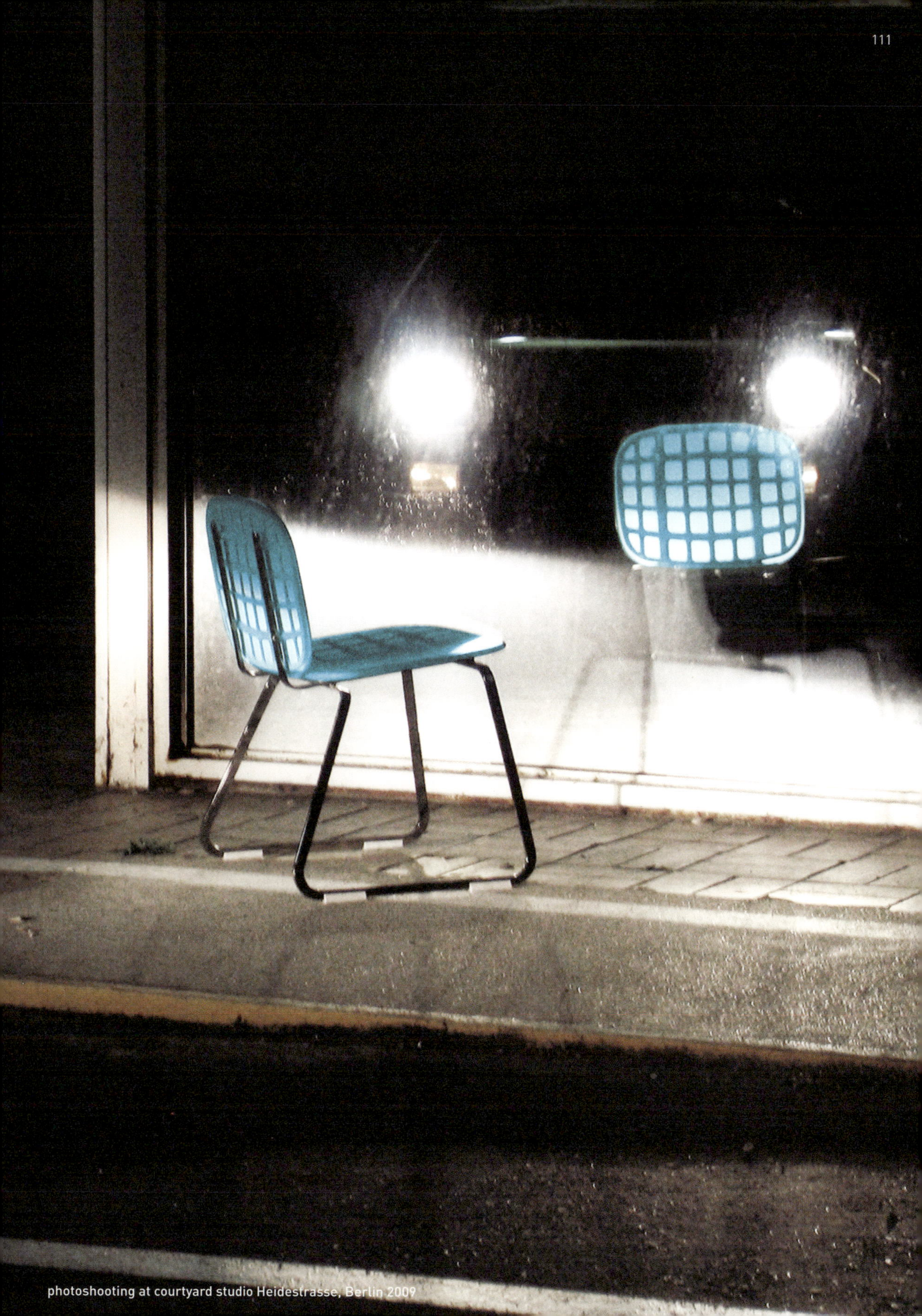

photoshooting at courtyard studio Heidestrasse, Berlin 2009

photos middle Giulio Castelli, founder of Kartell and Philippe Starck at the Cappellini exhibition in superstudio during the Milan Furniture Fair 2001

photo bottom gel chairs before shipping to Brad Pitt for his Santa Barbara house

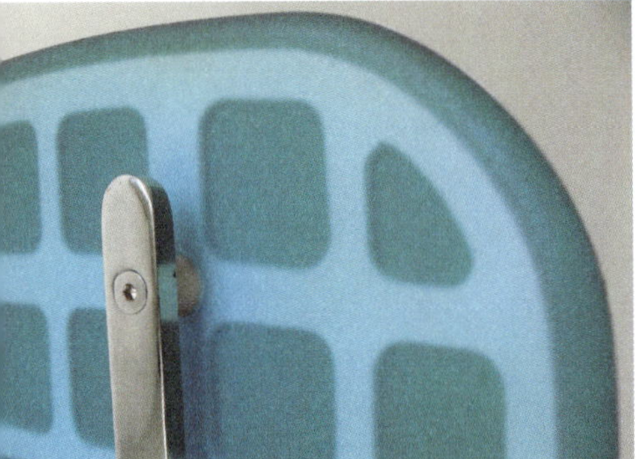

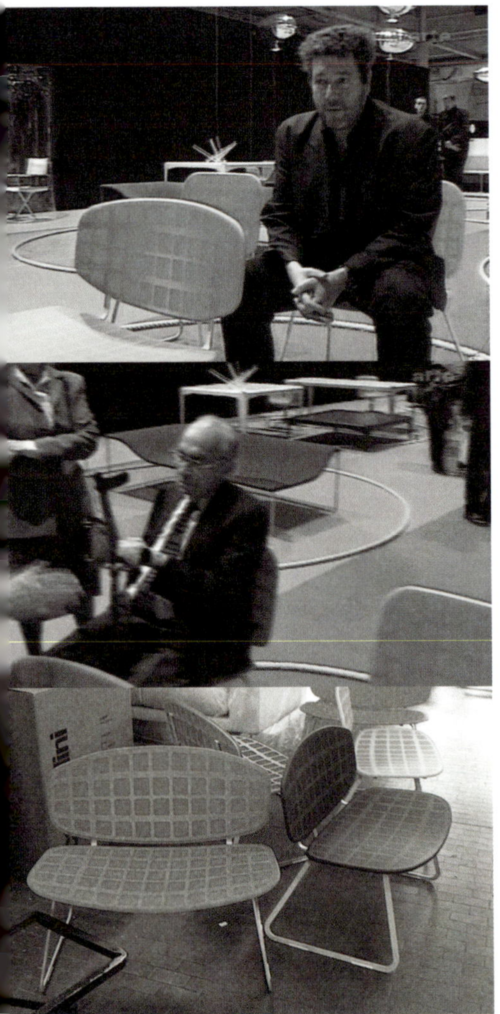

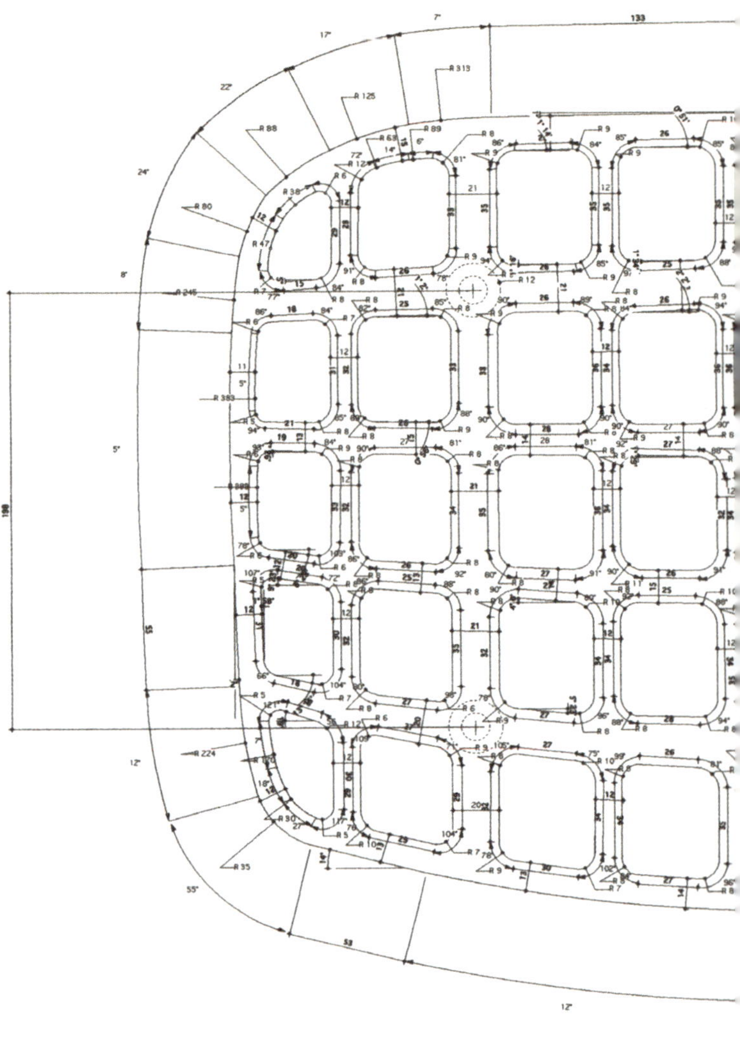

The seat and backrest of these chairs consist of a techno-gel sandwich made of a gel-coated weight-bearing nylon lattice (an elastic translucent minimal structure with surprising seating comfort) mounted on a chromium-plated metal subframe.

Die Stühle und Lounge-chairs der Gel Chair Kollektion von Cappellini bestehen aus einem verchromten linearen Metalluntergestell, auf das zwei flächige Module mit einem TechnoGel-Sandwich montiert werden. Dieses Sandwich besteht aus einem mit Gel ummantelten tragenden Nylongitter – eine elastische transluzente Minimalstruktur mit überraschendem Sitzkomfort.

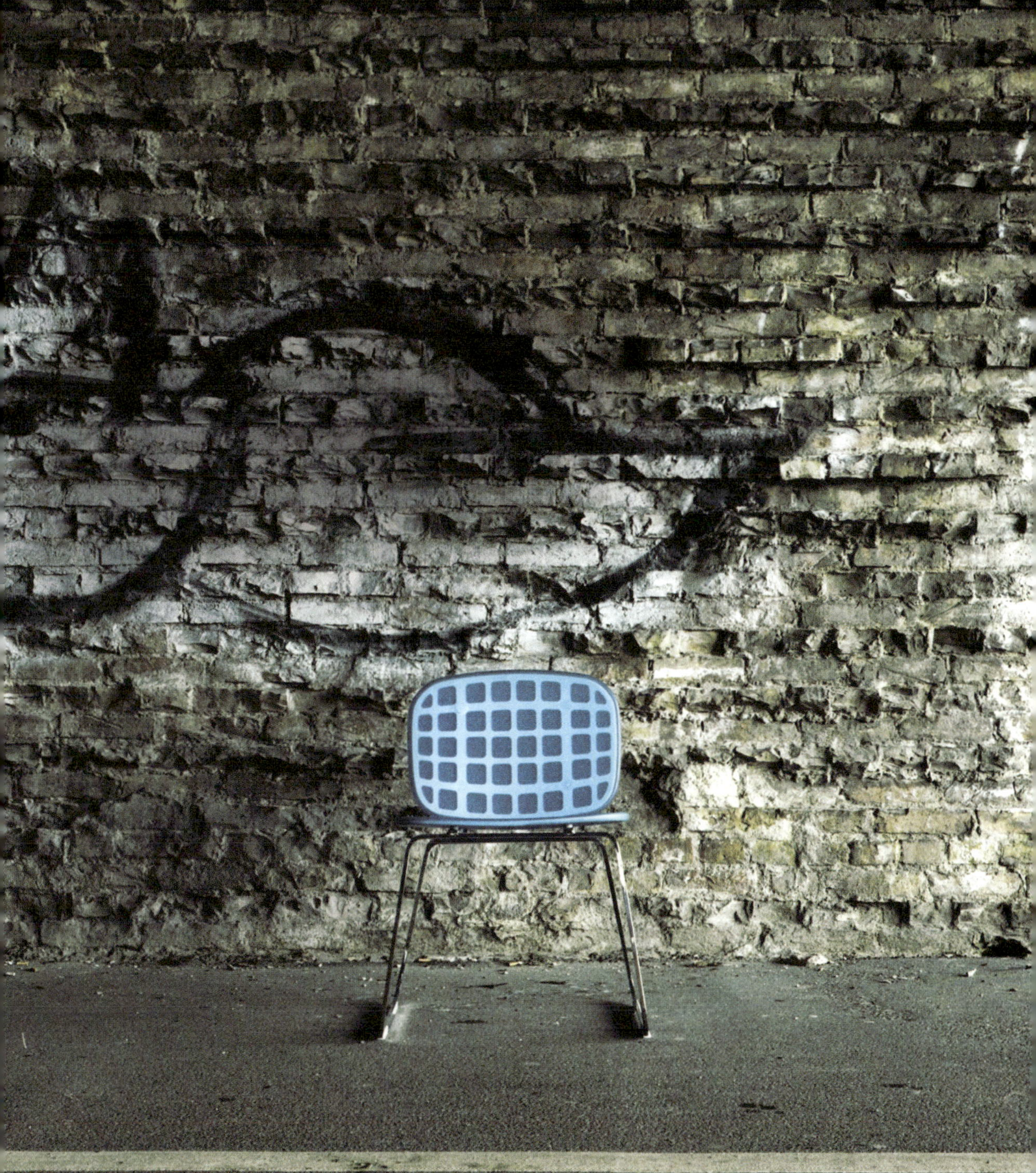

Size: 50/75 x 55 x 72 cm
Material: TechnoGel seats and backrests with nylon frame and chromed steel base
Ausführungen: Green, yellow, blue, red, grey and white Gel

Größe: *50/75 x 55 x 72 cm*
Material: *Sitz und Rückenpolster aus TechnoGel-Nylon Sandwich, Basis aus verchromtem Stahl*
Ausführungen: *Grüne, gelbe, blaue, rote, graue und weiße Gelflächenmodule*

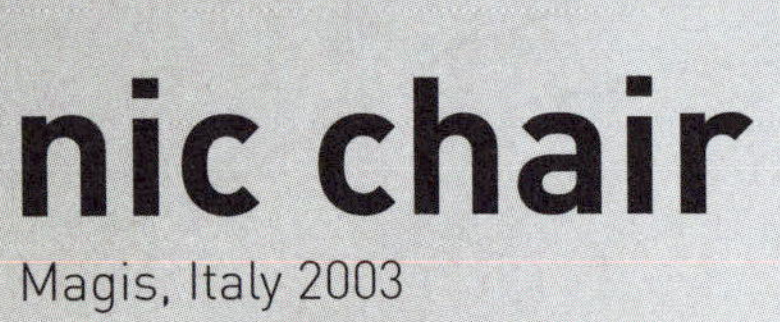

nic chair

Magis, Italy 2003

After four years of development, production of the nic chair finally started in 2004. Its complicated gas-injection/air-moulding production process, which has only been successfully implemented for the market by two companies worldwide (one of them being Magis), is a revolution in the world of plastic production.

Nach einer Entwicklungszeit von vier Jahren ging der Nic Chair 2004 in Produktion. Sein kompliziertes Spritzguss-Herstellungsverfahren im Gasinnendruckverfahren/Air-Moulding, das weltweit von nur zwei Firmen (eine davon ist Magis) auf dem Markt erfolgreich eingeführt wurde, stellt eine Revolution in der Welt der Kunststoffherstellung dar.

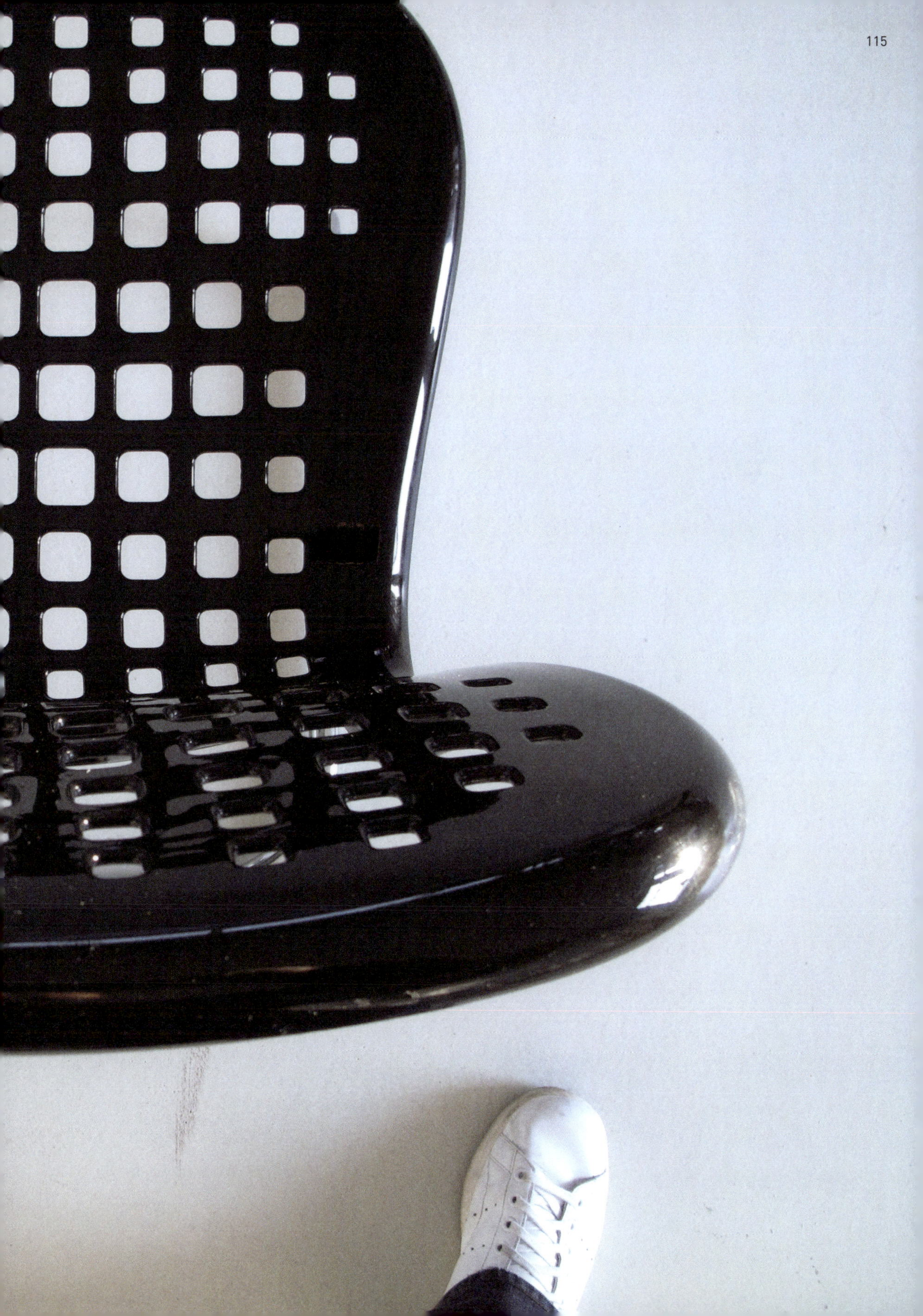

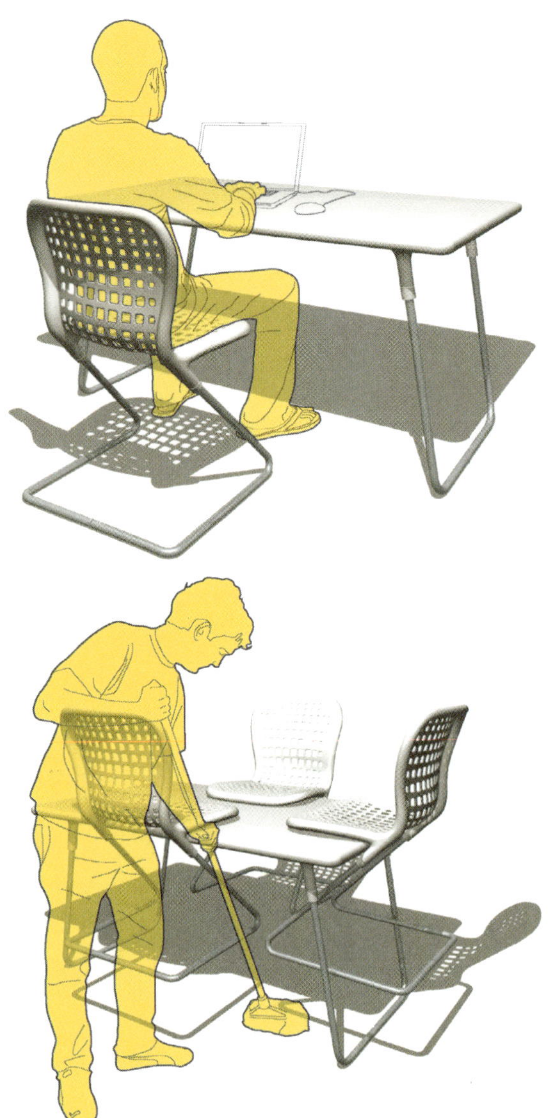

"...Werner Aisslinger believes that new innovative design is driven by technology, which is an attitude in tune with the philosophy of Magis. His new chair, Nic, pushes the potential of technology to make a designer's vision reality. Chairs don't need to look like this and, at least theoretically, it is entirely wrong to cantilever a seat in this way so as to maximise the stress on the connection between seat and frame. But it is an elegant solution to chair design, and, since the 1930s, designers have wanted chairs where the seat seems to be suspended freely in space on two legs. Moreover, Aisslinger wanted to explore the springiness of a chair, this being the result of this type of structure. Magis has been at the forefront of plastic-moulding technology: air-moulding technology, minutely plotted by computer, introduces pockets of air within the plastic to form tubes and chambers that add strength and reduce the weight of the chair. In addition, less material is required to make the chair. In order to strengthen the structural joints at the rear of the seat, nylon sheaths are inserted into the plastic frame."

Eugenio Perazza, the founder of Magis

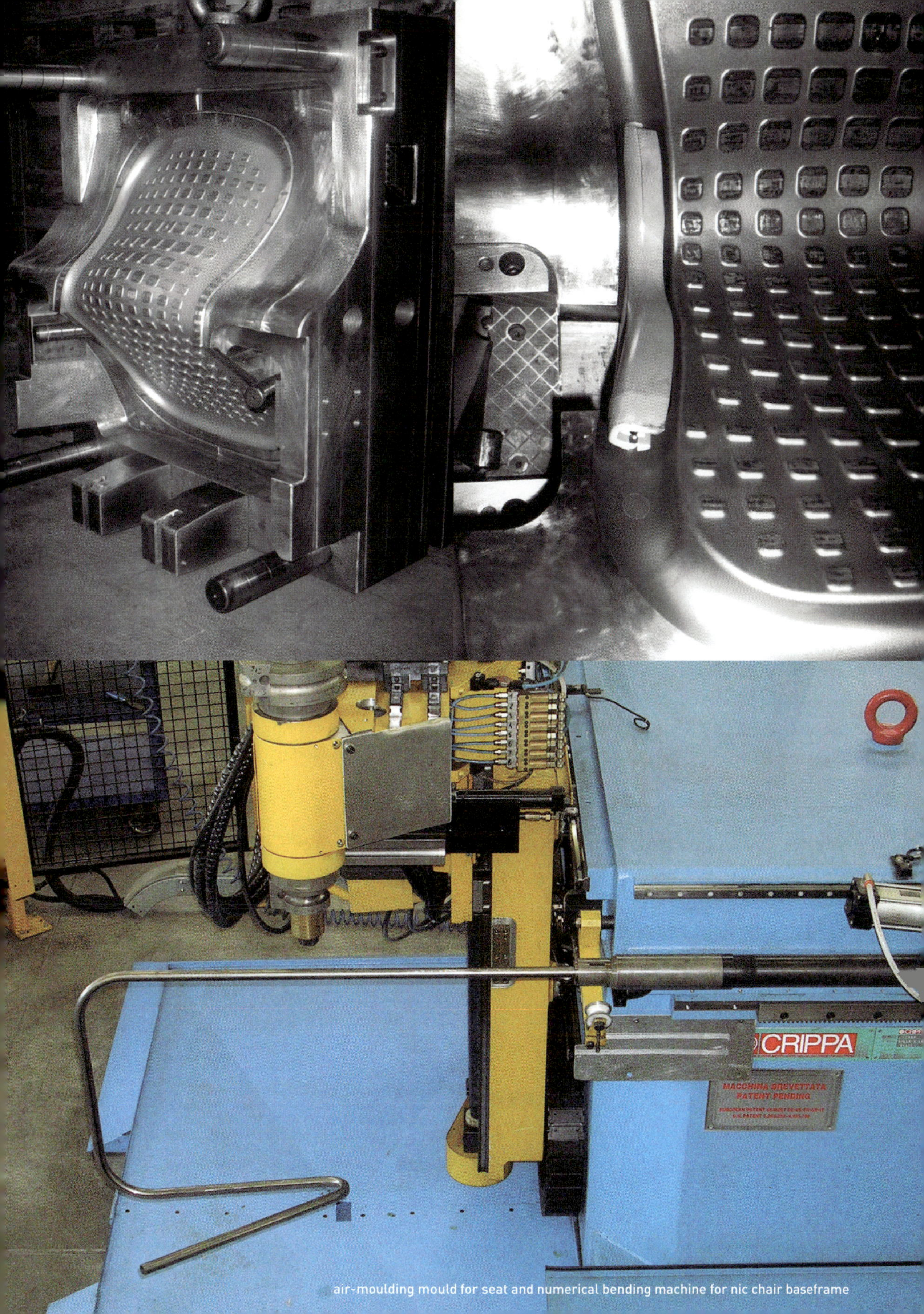

air-moulding mould for seat and numerical bending machine for nic chair baseframe

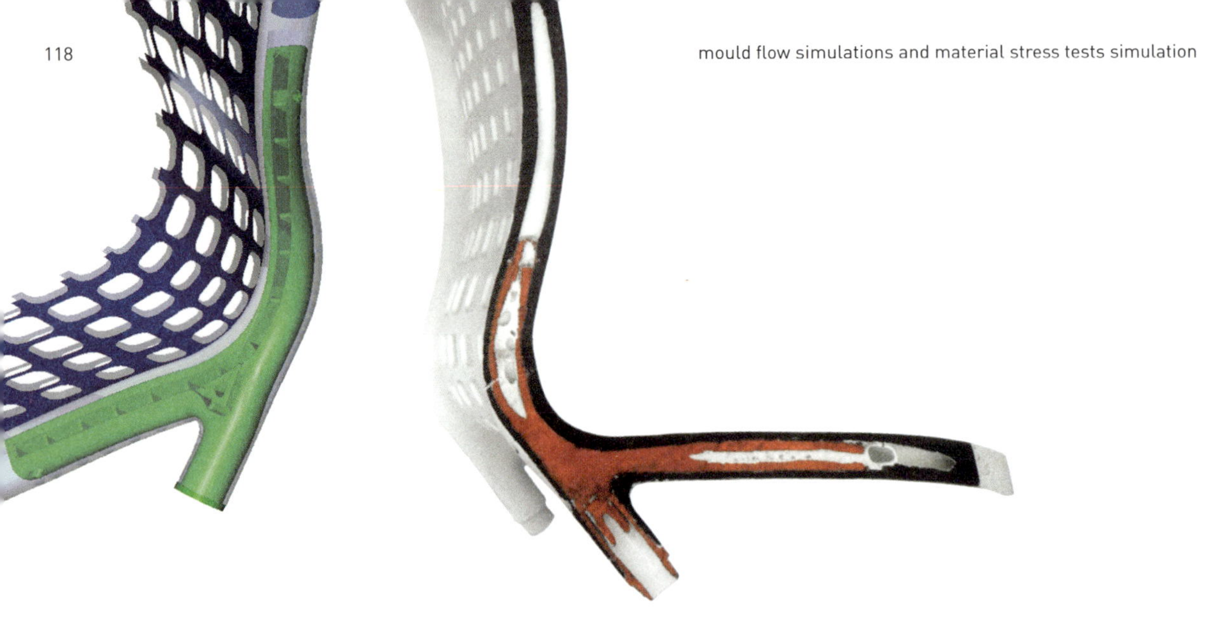

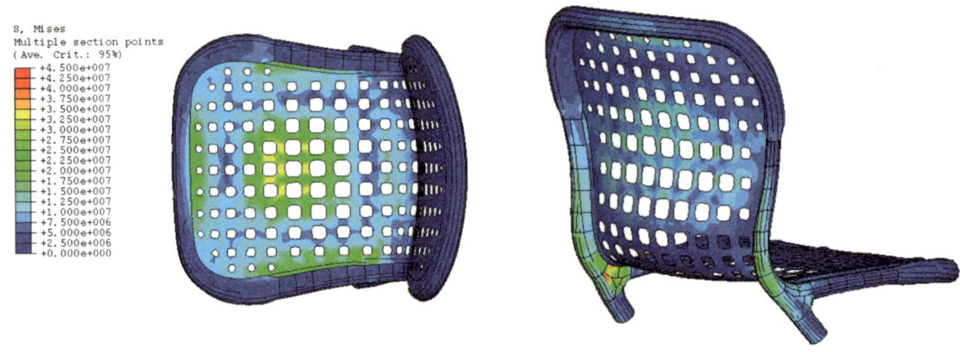

Hollow like bamboo, the plastic seat is highly stable, light and elastic and requires a minimum of material input. To reduce the transport size, the nic chair's steel base can be detached and packaged with the seat into a 40 cm³ cube.

Die Sitzschale ist innen hohl wie Bambus, äußerst stabil, leicht und elastisch und wird mit einem geringen Materialaufwand hergestellt. Der Stahlrohrrahmen kann demontiert werden, so dass sich seine Größe reduziert und er zusammen mit dem Sitz in eine 40 cm³ große Kiste hineinpasst und kompakt transportiert werden kann.

Size: 47 x 51 x 81 cm
Material: Frame in chromed steel tube, seat in polypropylene with glass fibre added
Versions: Various colours (orange, green, grey, white)

Größe: *47 x 51 x 81 cm*
Material: *Untergestell in Stahlrohr, Sitz aus glasfaserverstärktem Polypropylen*
Ausführungen: *Verschiedene Farben (orange, grün, grau, weiß)*

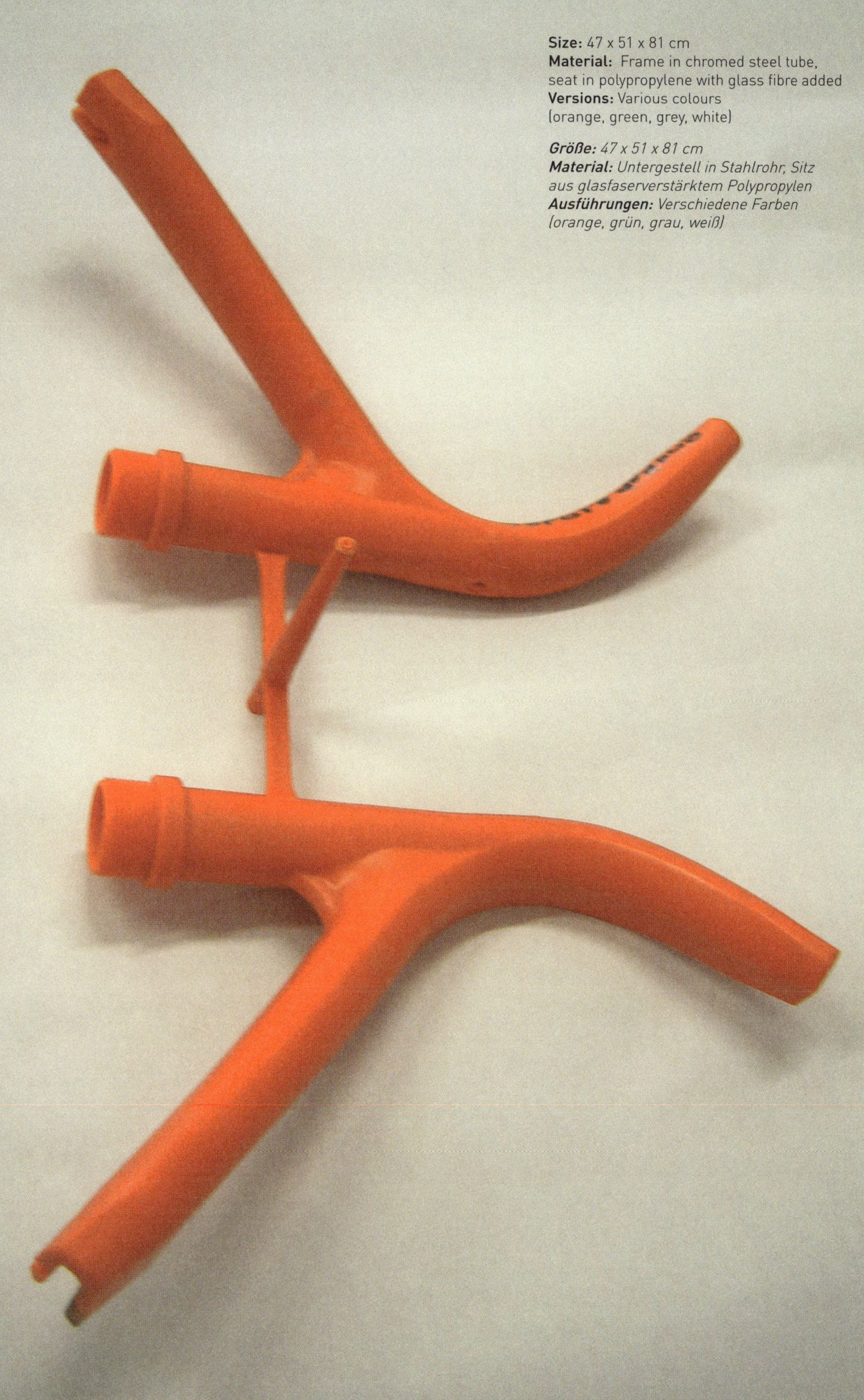

strengthening glass fibre reinforced insert for connecting point of tubeframe with seat

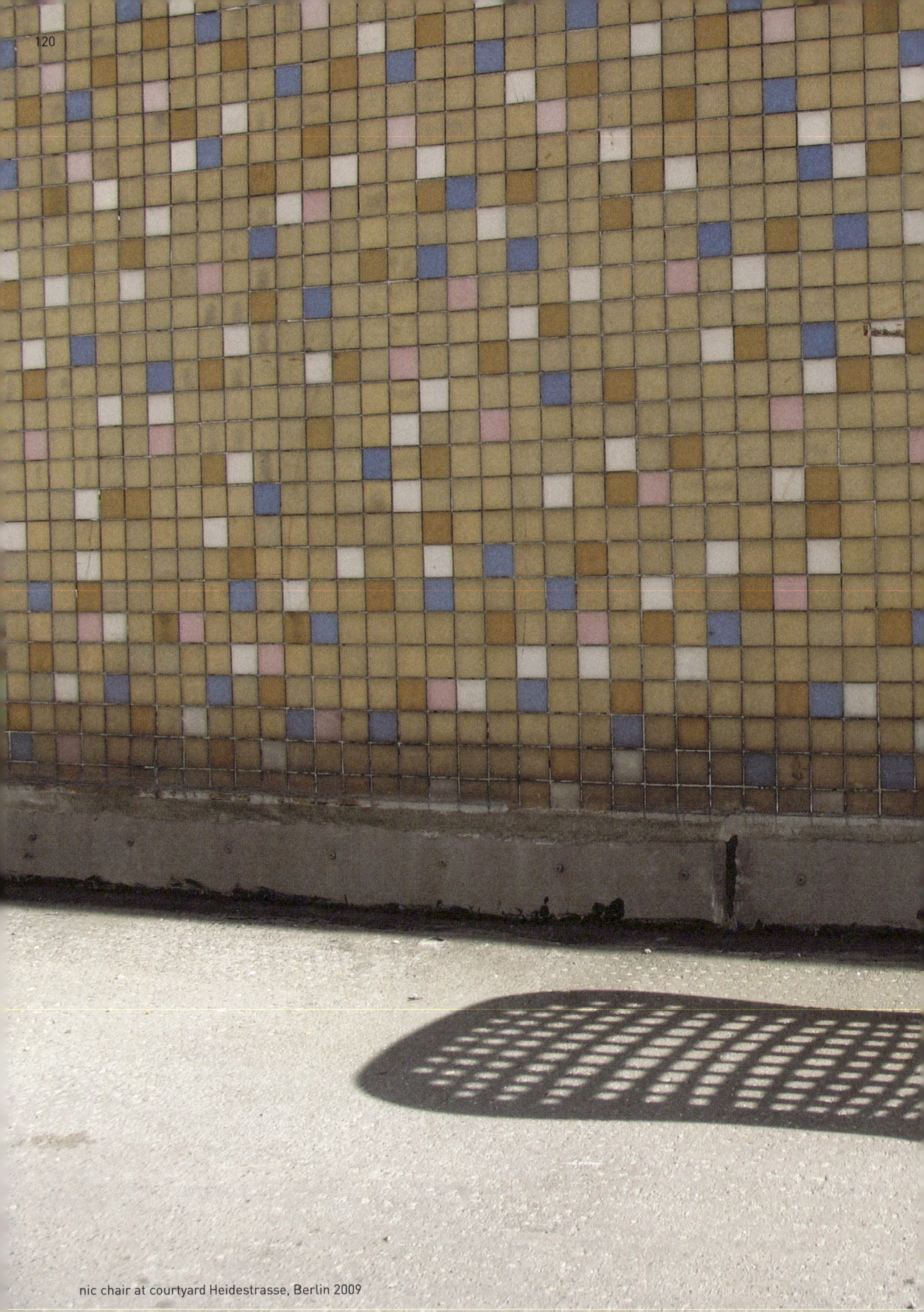

nic chair at courtyard Heidestrasse, Berlin 2009

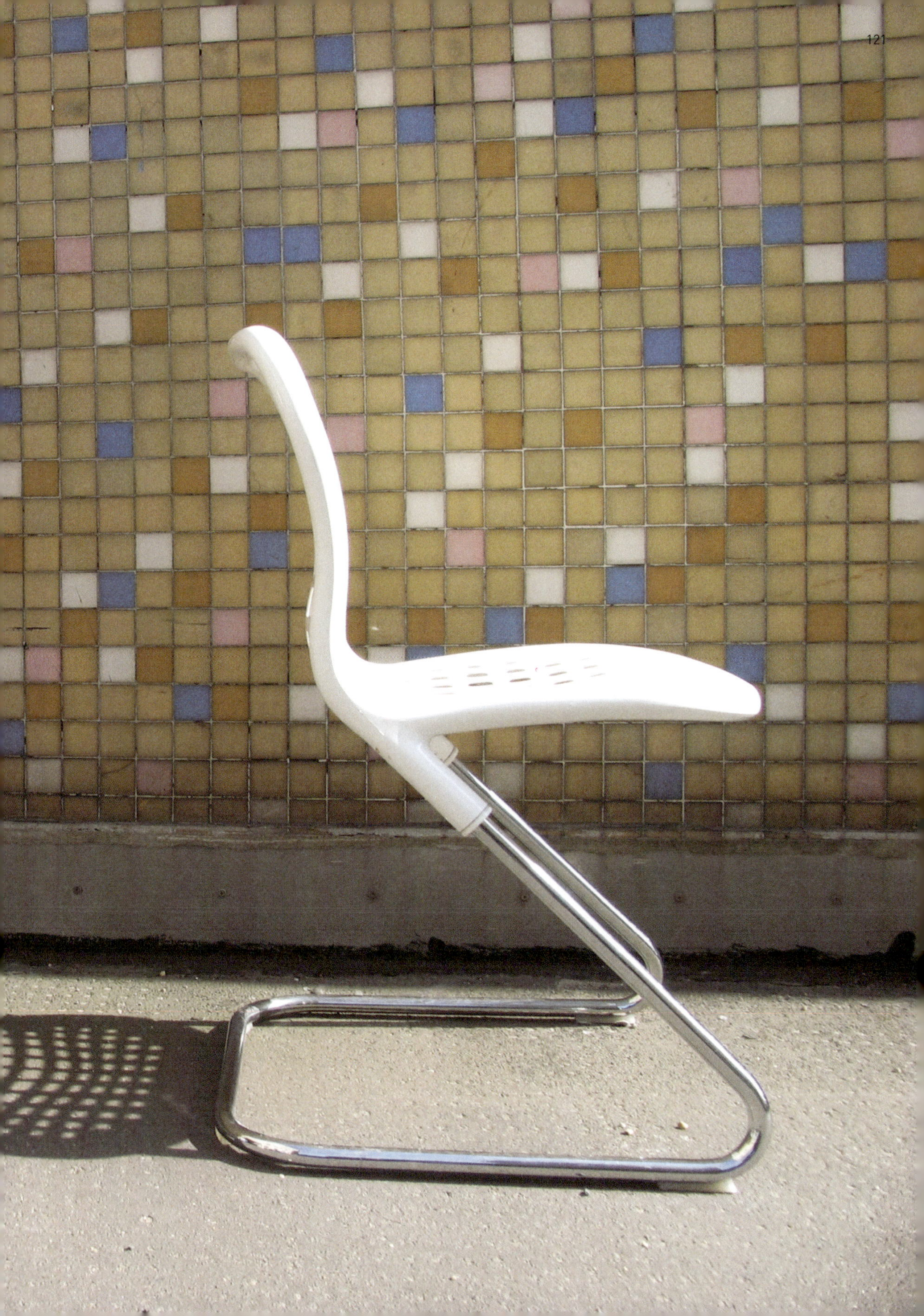

mesh

edition/installation for the "nature design" exhibition Museum für Gestaltung Zürich 2007

The architectural concept of mesh is based on organic spaces which are interwoven in a light and minimalistic way to form perspectives, densifications and overlays. Added to one another, the translucent and osmotic modular structure divides open architectural spaces or creates subspaces without a complete opaque separation.

Organische Räume, die nicht aus festen soliden Strukturen bestehen, sondern wie ein Blätterdach leicht und minimalistisch verwoben sind, mit Durchblicken, Verdichtungen und Überlagerungen bilden das Grundkonzept des Mesh Wabenprojektes. Mesh liegt die räumliche Vision zugrunde, transluzente und osmotische Textilmodul-Strukturen frei zu addieren, dadurch offene Architekturen zu unterteilen oder Subräume erzeugen zu können, ohne diese blickdicht abschirmen zu müssen.

mesh prototype installation at studio Heidestrasse, Berlin 2009

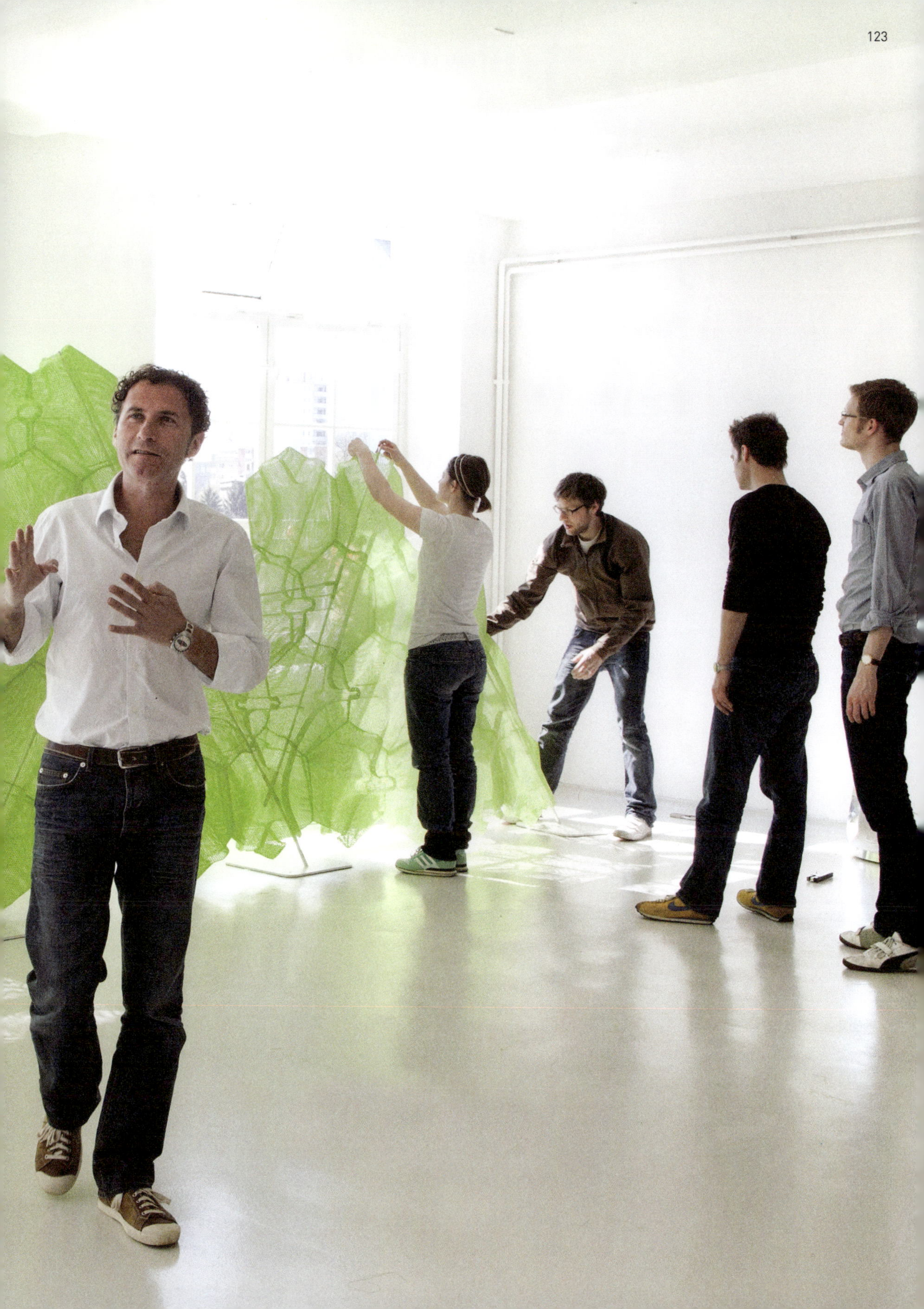

The textiles are knitted and three-dimensionally shaped in a high-tech procedure to form lightweight, buttressed combs that can be added endlessly to form walls, space shells, screens or tunnels.

The three different types of relief structures on the combs make it possible to generate organic tree-like structures inspired by a macro-zoom picture of a vegetal leaf. The variations in colour of the fibre and changing of the weave direction create perforated and condensed surface textures. Material-wise, the mesh-knitting structure is a technological evolution: The fibres of the mesh are partly made from adhesive fibres which under heat blend into a stiff textile microstructure.

Die in einem Hightech-Verfahren strickgewebten und durch Erhitzen dreidimensional verformten textilen, extrem leichten Wabenmodule werden durch Verketten zu Wänden, Raumschalen, Paravents oder Tunnelgebilden verbunden und können nach dem Endlosprinzip erweitert werden.

Die drei Wabenmodultypen sind mit einer Reliefstruktur dreidimensional verformt und somit ausgesteift. Bei der Addition generieren sie organische, baumähnliche Strukturen, dem Macro-Zoom eines pflanzlichen Blattes ähnlich. Unterschiedliche Farben der verwebten Fasern und wechselnde Webrichtungen erzeugen perforierte und verdichtete Oberflächentexturen.

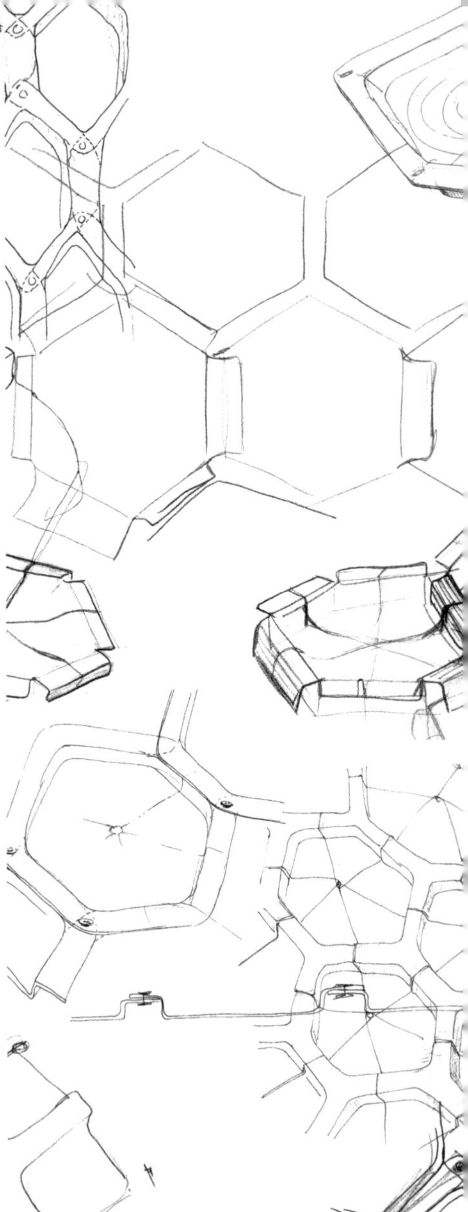

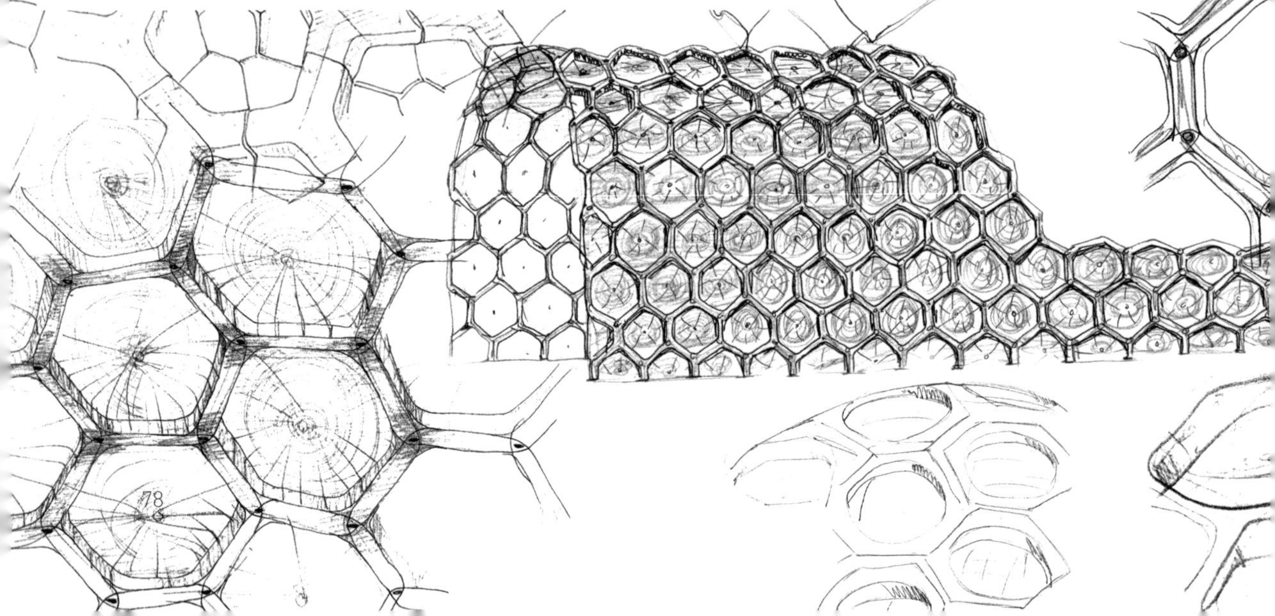

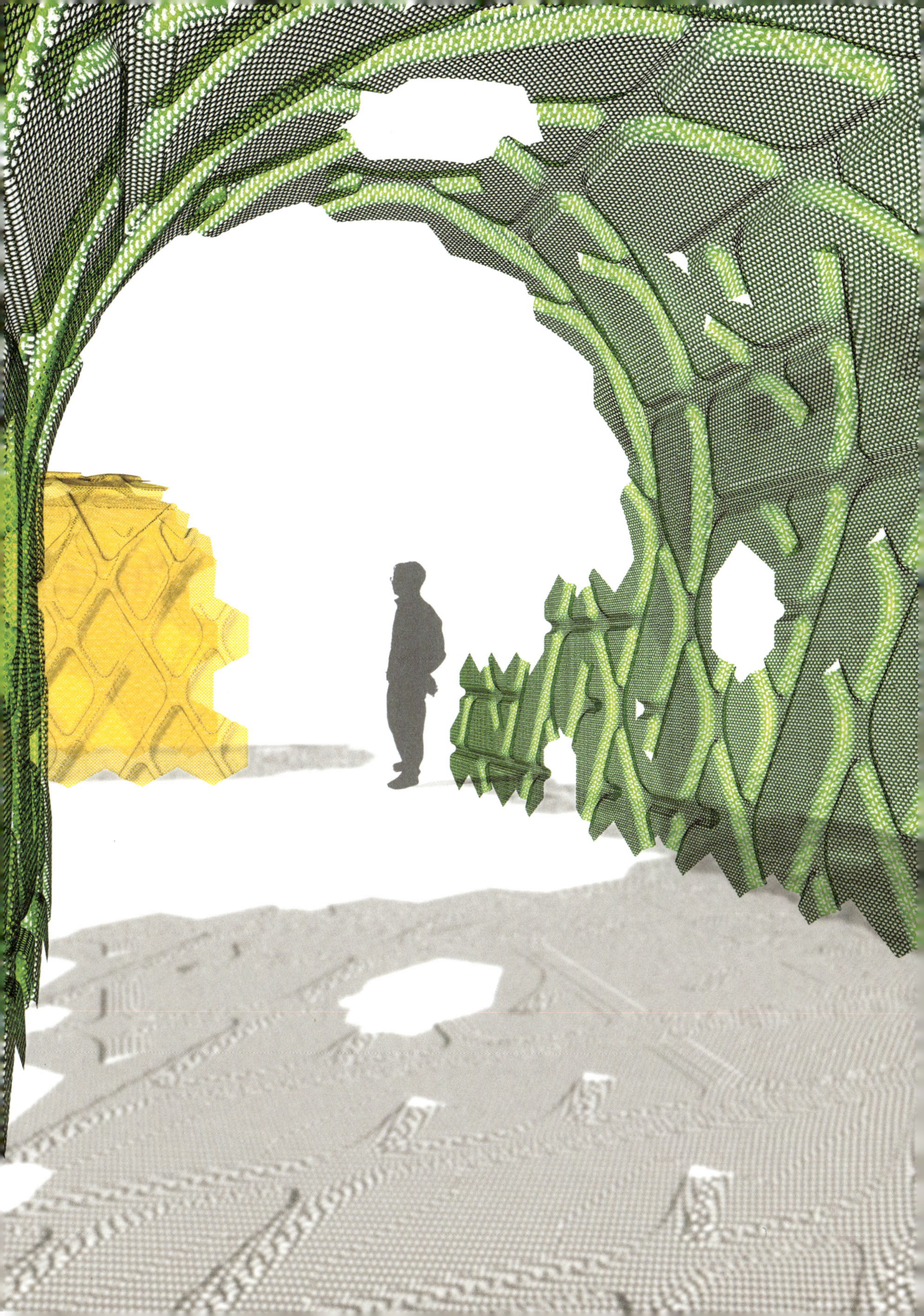

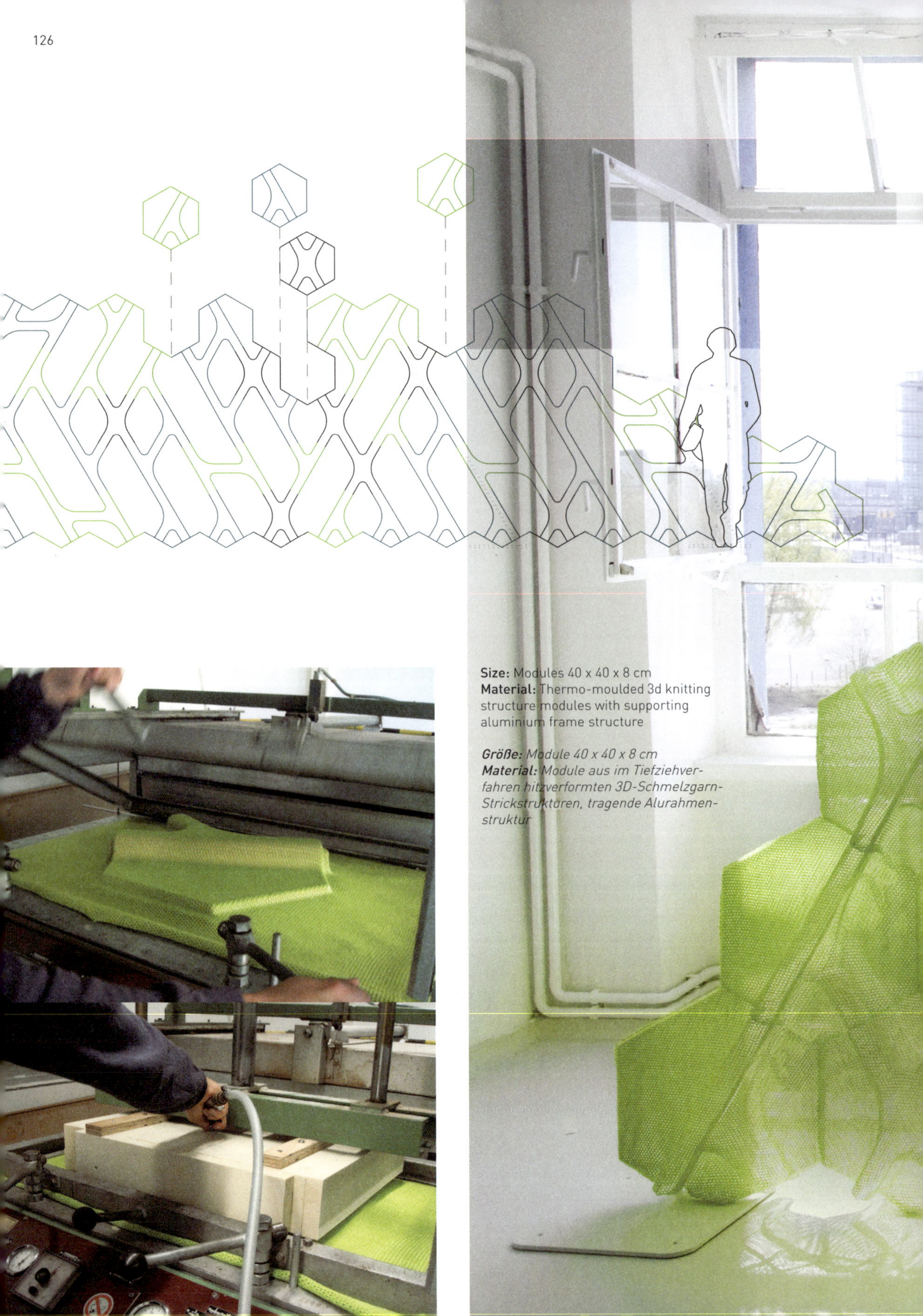

Size: Modules 40 x 40 x 8 cm
Material: Thermo-moulded 3d knitting structure modules with supporting aluminium frame structure

Größe: *Module 40 x 40 x 8 cm*
Material: *Module aus im Tiefziehverfahren hitzverformten 3D-Schmelzgarn-Strickstrukturen, tragende Alurahmenstruktur*

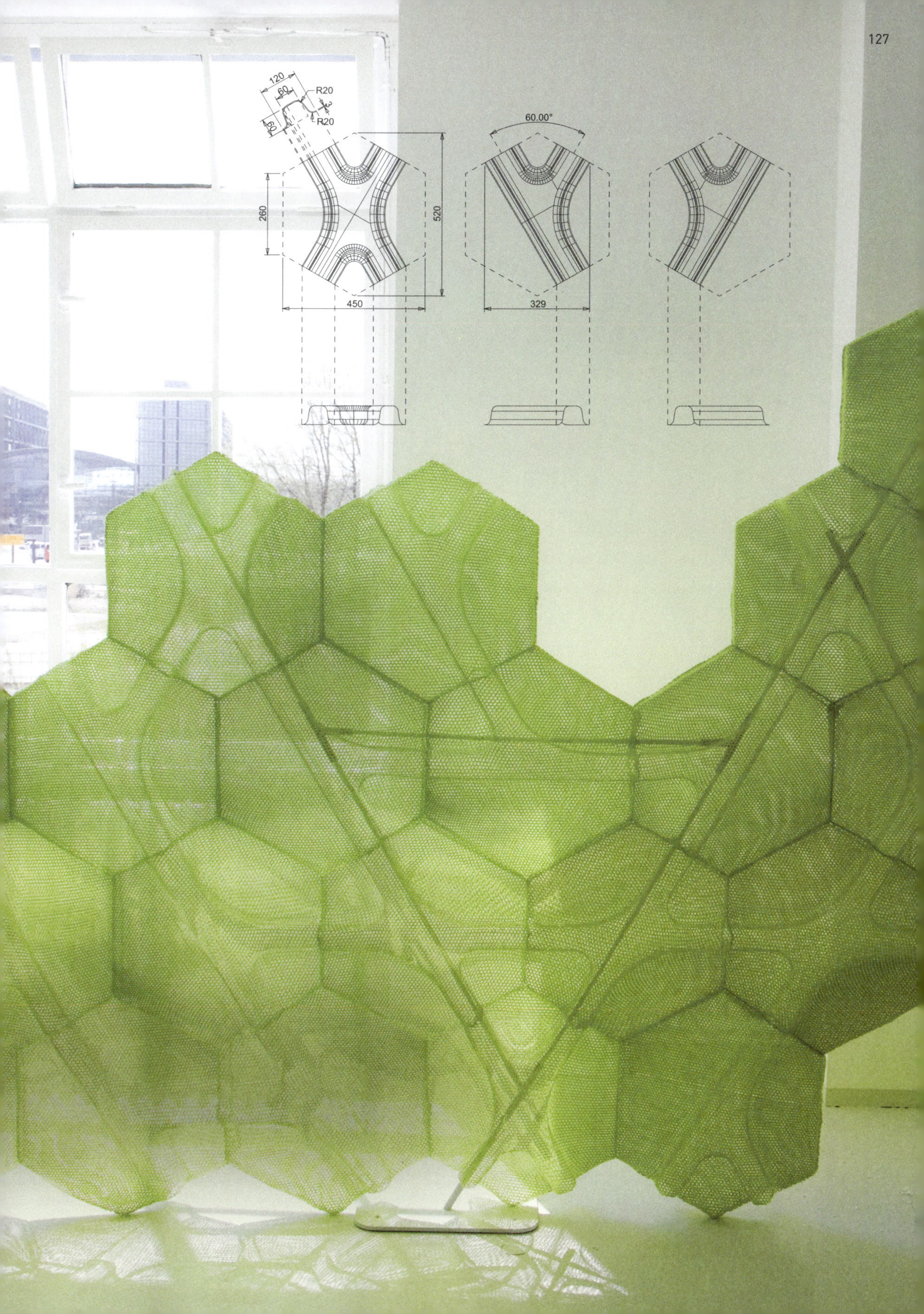
120
60
R20
3
R20
60
60.00°
260
520
450
329

NETwork

3D stitching furniture edition 2010

The NETwork 3D stitching furniture project combines new technologies with traditional stitching techniques to create a collection of textile objects. It transforms 2-dimensional embroidery into a furniture object.

Since Gaetano Pesce's UP-collection from 1969, the switch of dimensions has been a challenge for designers and design concepts. The pieces of the NETwork stitching furniture edition–armchairs, stools and lamps – are volumes carefully designed for later flattening with software support. The objects created are extremely light and transparent and they seem to flow in space as 3D textile meta-networks.

Das NETwork Projekt – eine Edition textiler Objekte – vereint modernste Technologien mit traditionellen Sticktechniken. Aus zweidimensionalen Stickereien werden dreidimensionale Sitzobjekte generiert.

Seit Gaetano Pesce 1969 seine UP-Kollektion vorstellte, ist der Dimensionswechsel von 2D zu 3D eine Herausforderung für Designer und Designkonzepte. Die Objekte der NETwork 3D Stitching Furniture Edition – Sessel, Hocker und Leuchten – sind sorgfältig berechnete Volumina, die später mit Hilfe einer Software zu flächigen, maschinell stickbaren Mustern umgerechnet werden. Die resultierenden abgeformten 3D-Objekte sind extrem leicht und transparent und scheinen als textile 3D-Meta-Netze im Raum zu schweben.

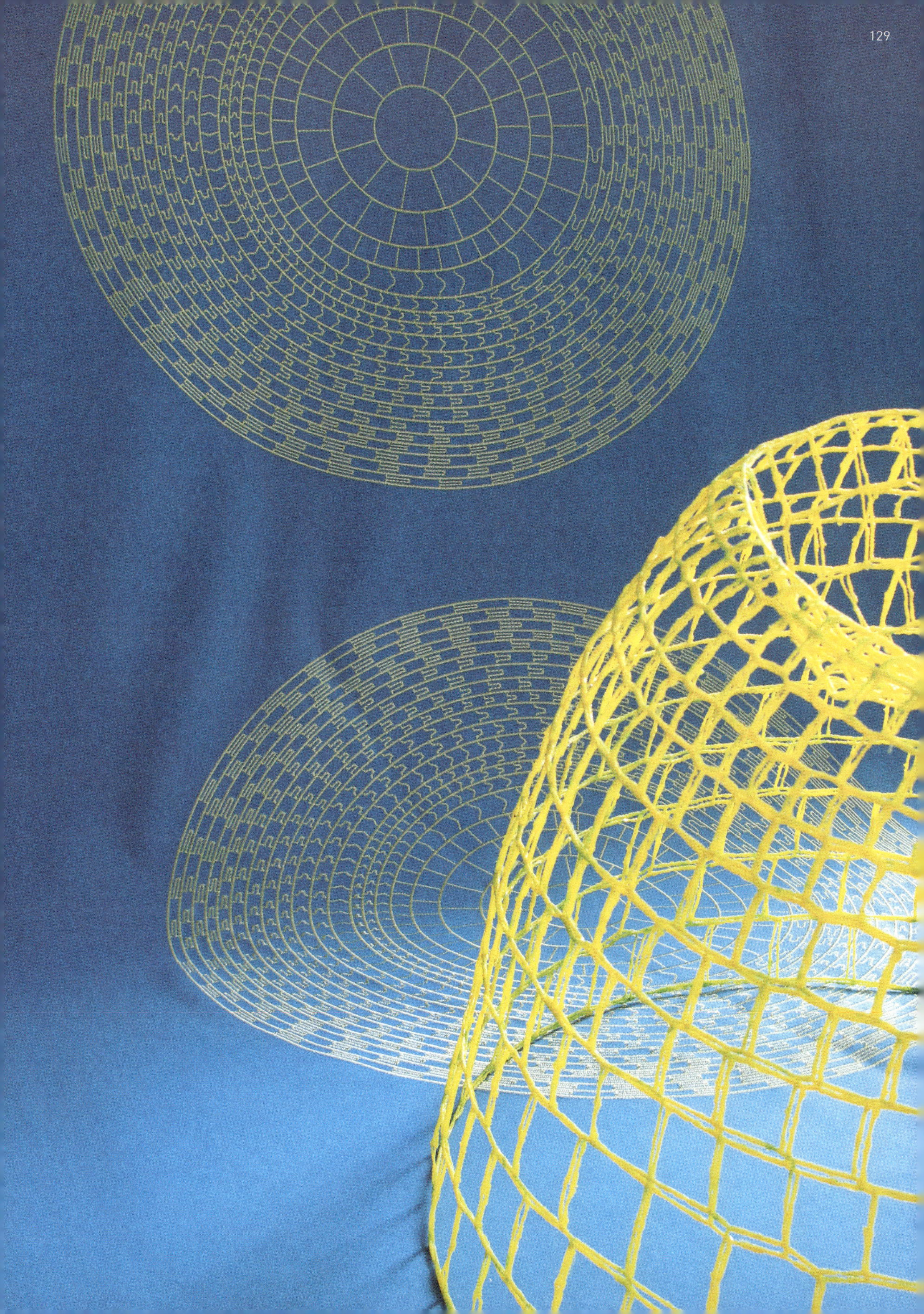

This new 3D textile pop-up technology is the result of research conducted with a traditional German manufacturer in Plauen, a region with a long tradition in stitching and embroidery. The combination of experimental design with a hidden traditional production is always an exciting field for new concepts. Nowadays, the know-how of specialized technologies is more often found in the supplying industries than in the design brands themselves.

Diese neue textile 3D-Pop-up-Technologie ist das Ergebnis einer Forschungsarbeit, die gemeinsam mit einem traditionellen Stickereihersteller aus Plauen entwickelt wurde, einer Region, die über eine lange Tradition im technischen Sticken verfügt. Die Symbiose aus experimentellem Design mit traditionellen Herstellungsmethoden ist generell ein aufregendes Gebiet für neue Designkonzepte. Heutzutage ist das Know-how spezialisierter Technologien häufiger in der Zulieferindustrie zu finden als bei den Designmarken selbst.

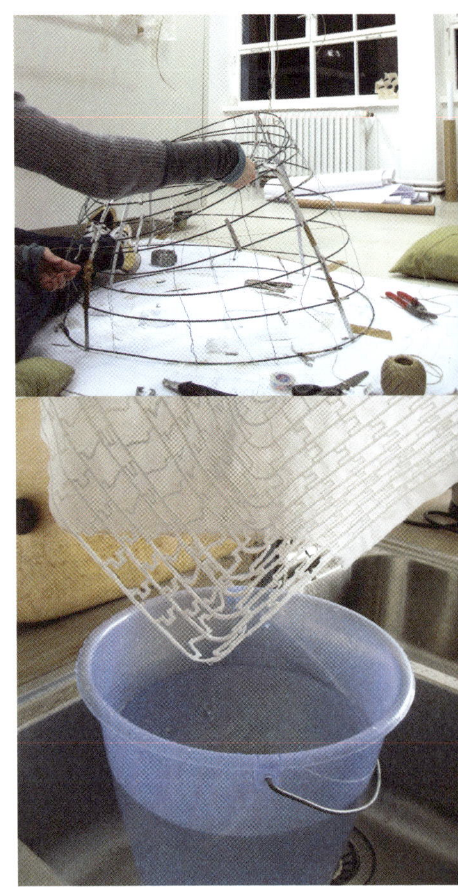

dissolving of stitched grid from carrying cellulose

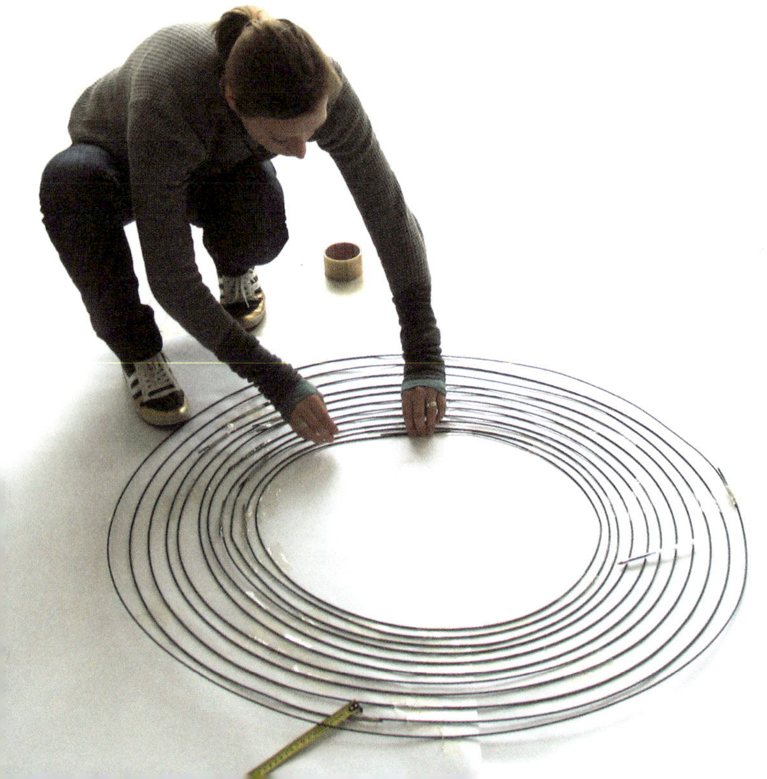

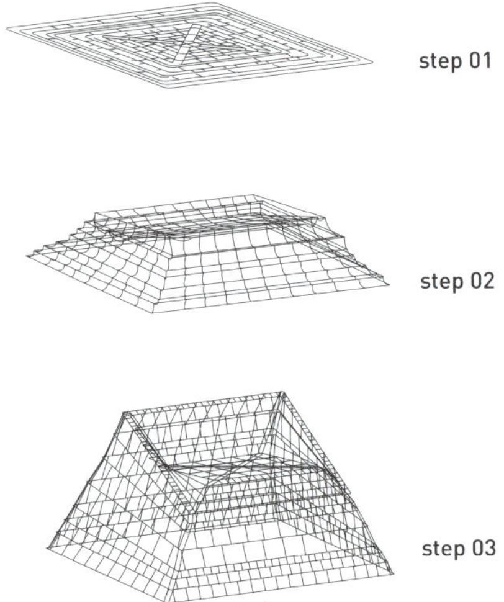

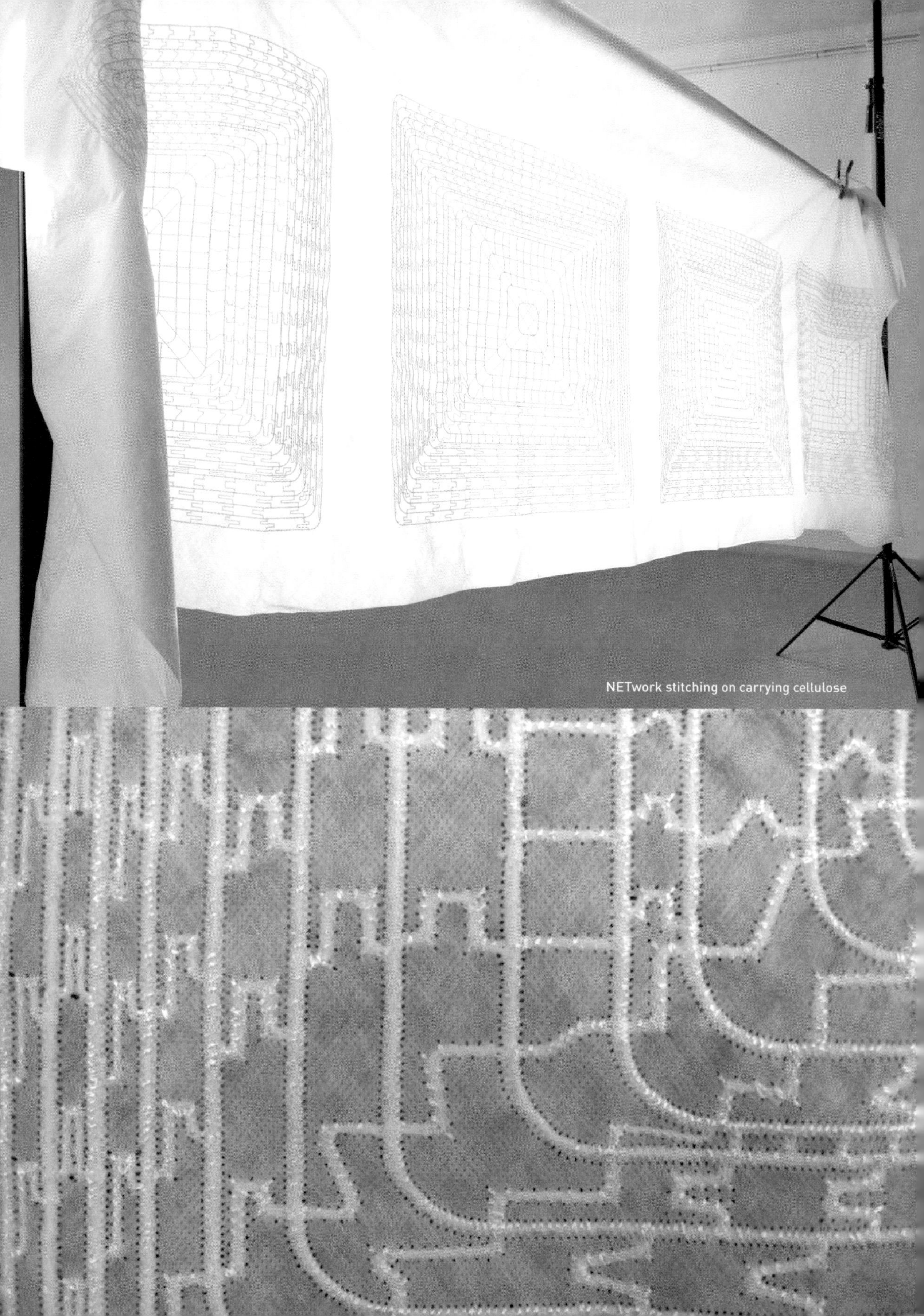

NETwork stitching on carrying cellulose

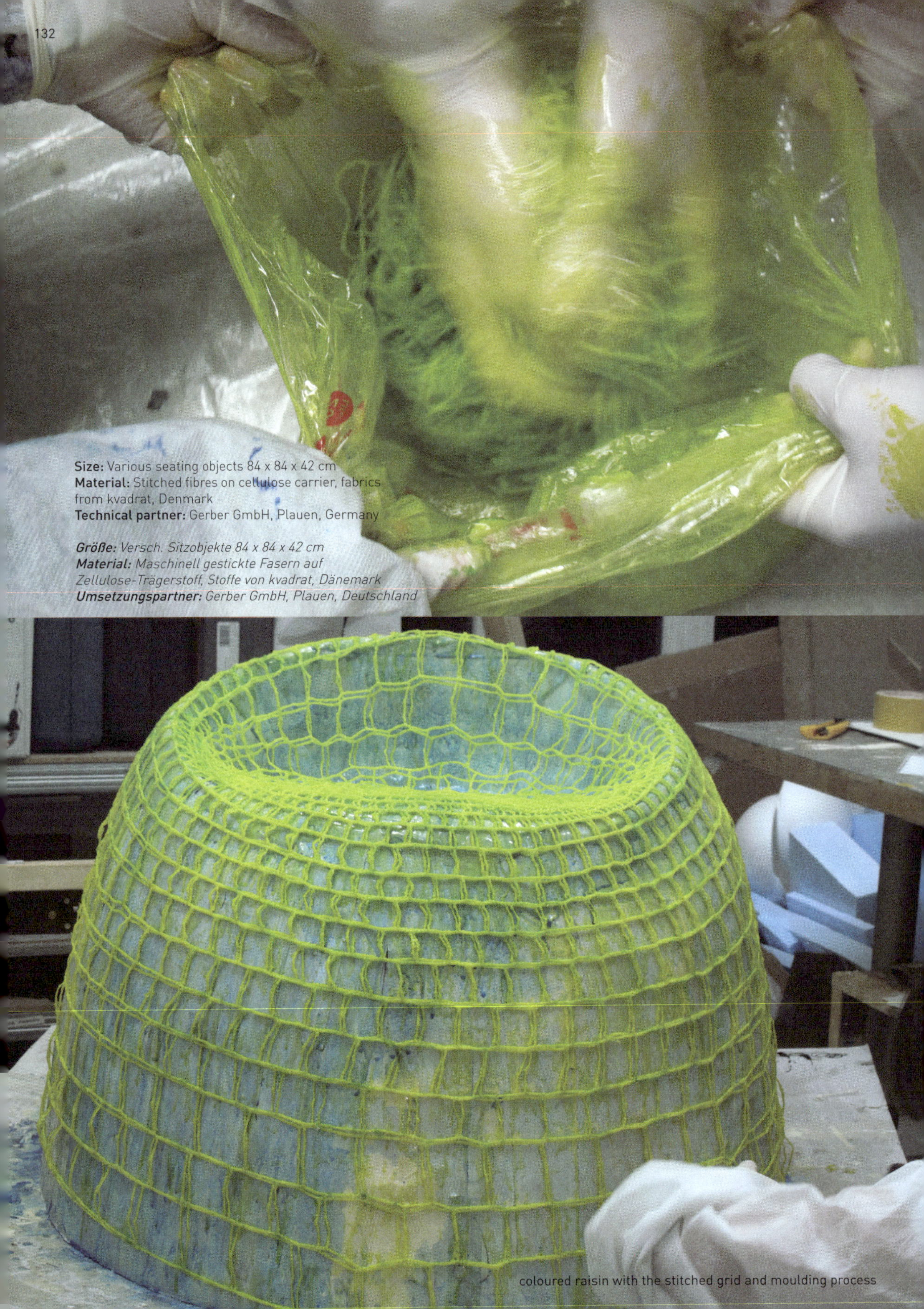

Size: Various seating objects 84 x 84 x 42 cm
Material: Stitched fibres on cellulose carrier, fabrics from kvadrat, Denmark
Technical partner: Gerber GmbH, Plauen, Germany

Größe: *Versch. Sitzobjekte 84 x 84 x 42 cm*
Material: *Maschinell gestickte Fasern auf Zellulose-Trägerstoff, Stoffe von kvadrat, Dänemark*
Umsetzungspartner: *Gerber GmbH, Plauen, Deutschland*

coloured raisin with the stitched grid and moulding process

The volumes are first translated with software into 2D projections of themselves which can be directly programmed into the machines that stitch the pattern into a carrying surface. The carrying surface is then dissolved and the embroidered 2D pattern becomes free to form a 3D object. Finally, the objects formed by the stitched honeycomb structures are fixed over a fibreglass mould and impregnated with resin in order to make them rigid and suitable for construction.

Die Volumina werden zunächst mit Hilfe einer Software in 2D-Projektionen verwandelt, die direkt in die Stickmaschinen einprogrammiert werden. Diese sticken das Muster auf die textile Trägerfläche, die dann durch Wasserzusetzen abgelöst wird. Das gestickte 2D-Muster wird freigelegt und formt sich dadurch zu einem 3D-Objekt. Die gestickten Gitterwabenstrukturen werden über eine Form aus Fiberglas gezogen und der Abguss mit Harz imprägniert und gehärtet, um die nötige konstruktive Festigkeit zu erlangen.

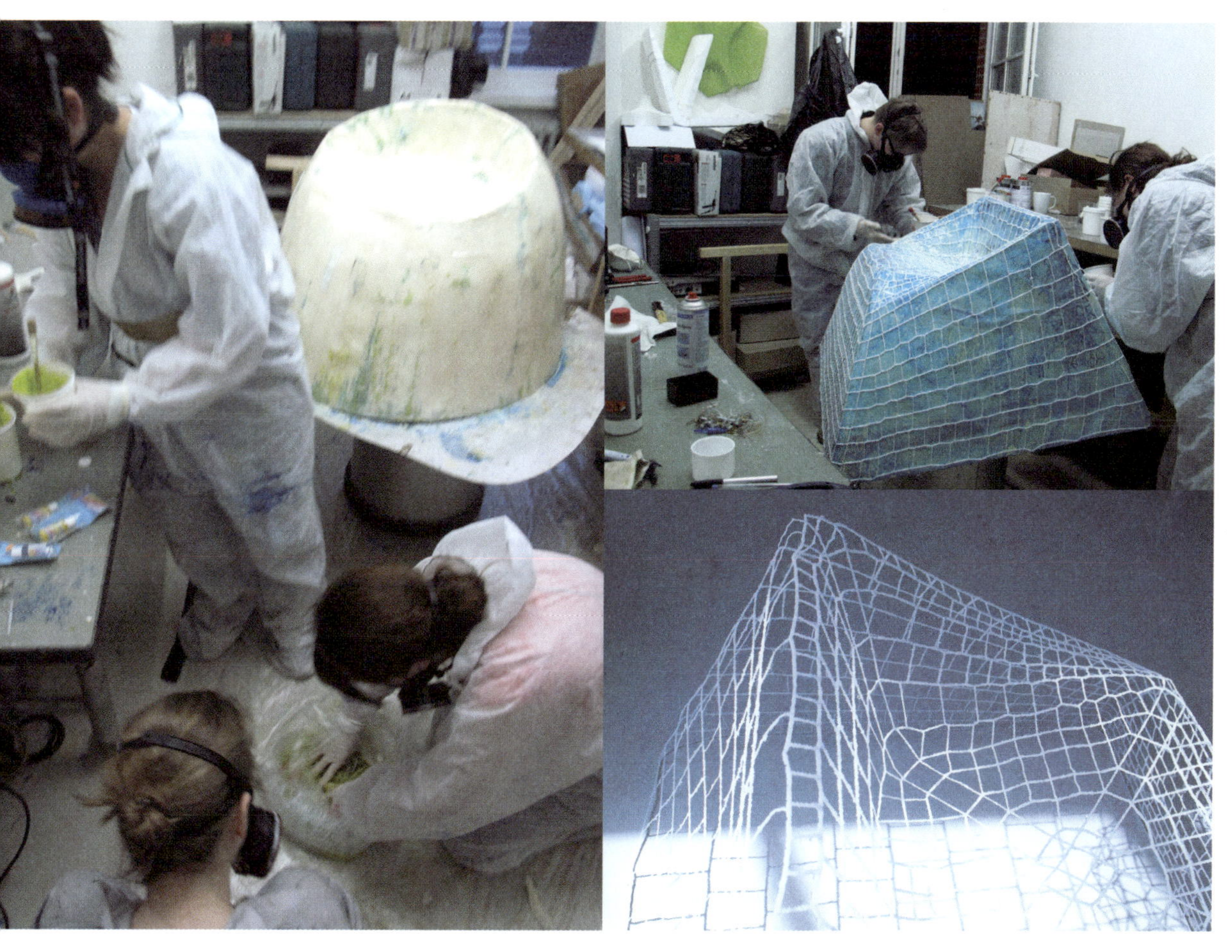

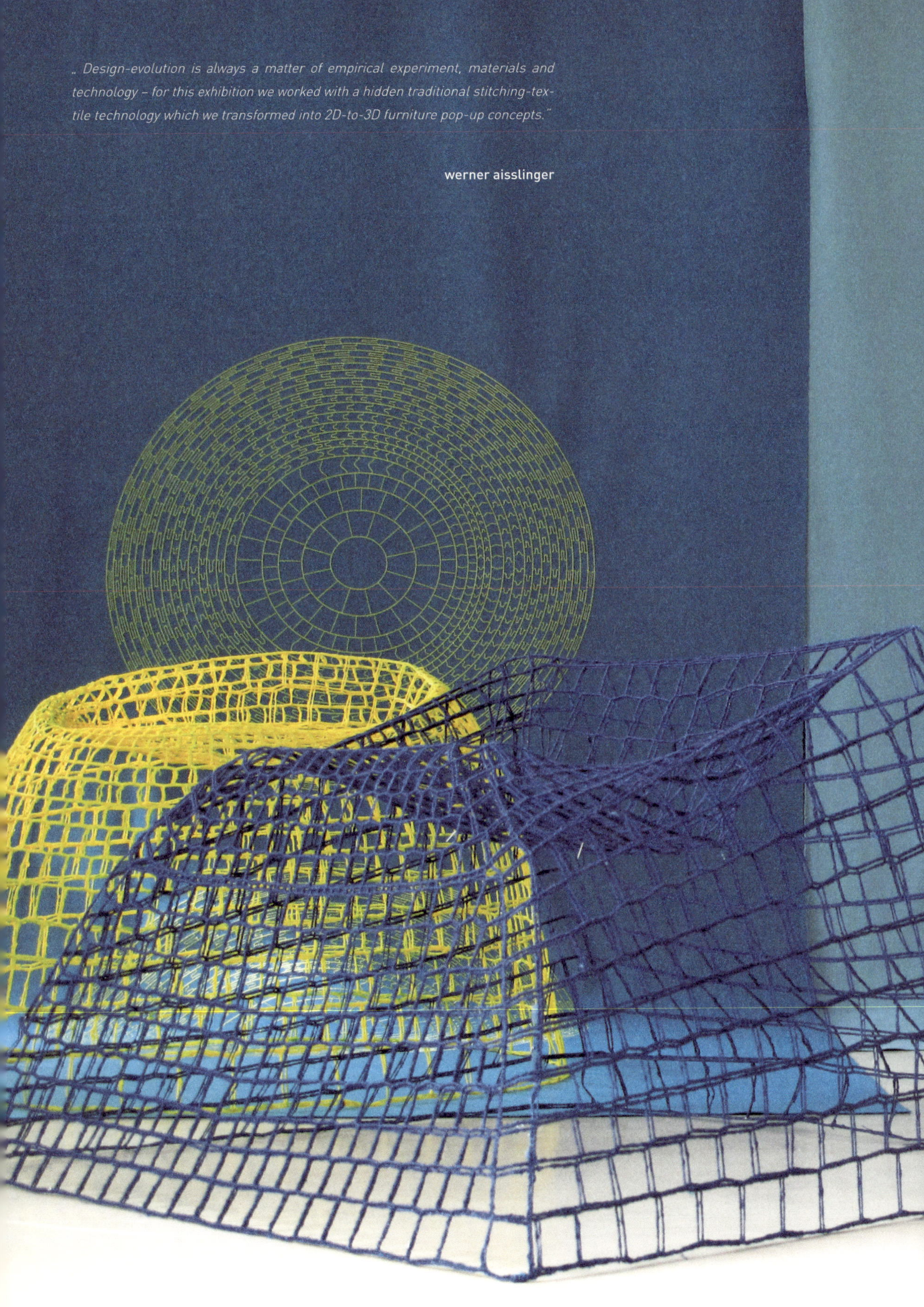

„ Design-evolution is always a matter of empirical experiment, materials and technology – for this exhibition we worked with a hidden traditional stitching-textile technology which we transformed into 2D-to-3D furniture pop-up concepts."

werner aisslinger

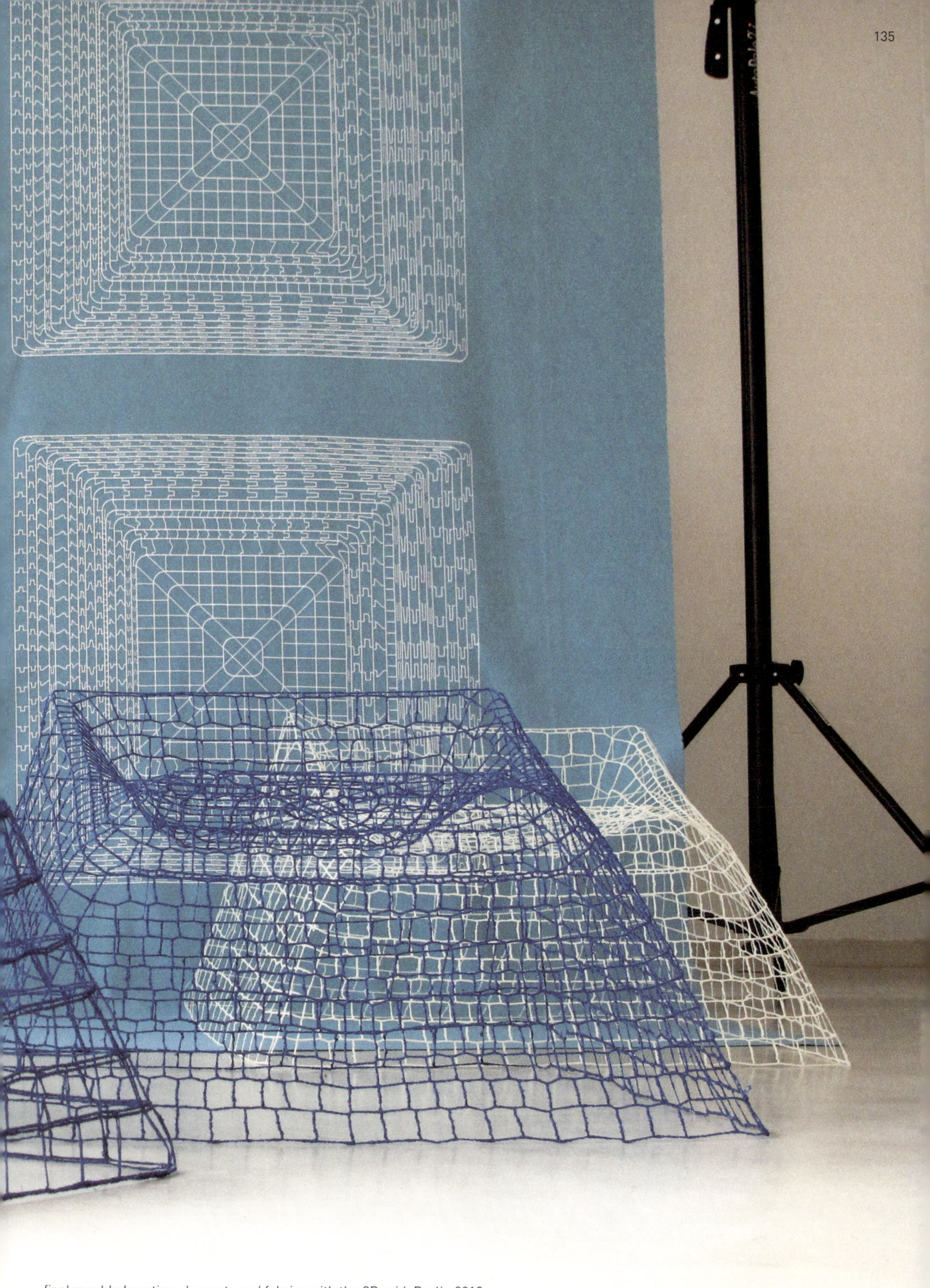

final moulded seating elements and fabrics with the 2D grid, Berlin 2010

MAKING

experimental design approach through the making of editions

"Designing by making" is a growing tendency in the design scene as a response to a debate that sees the increasing development of technology orientated high-end product design leading to a worldwide levelling. As such, the boring standardisation and globalisation of industrial products makes not only designers but also consumers miss the touch and feel of the creator, maker or craftsperson that has been involved in the process of making things.

Real-time experienced empirical processes, experiments with materials and technologies or traditional crafts often are the source of new ideas. Doing things in the workshops and factories and combining the outcomes with the experience of sophisticated manufacturers is inspiring, energising and positively unpredictable.

„Designing by making" ist eine wachsende Tendenz in der Designszene – als Reaktion auf eine zunehmend perfekter organisierte High-End-Produktentwicklung, die zu einem Global Style führt und eine weltweite Nivellierung des Designs mit sich bringt. Langweilige Standardisierung und Globalisierung industrieller Produkte hinterlassen nicht nur bei den Designern, sondern auch bei den Konsumenten das Gefühl, keine Einflüsse und Spuren der Kreativen, Erfinder, Verarbeiter oder Handwerker mehr vorzufinden, die an dem Entstehungsprozess beteiligt sind.

In Echtzeit erprobte empirische Herstellungsverfahren, Experimente mit Materialien und Technologien oder die Auseinandersetzung mit traditionellem Handwerk stellen eine Quelle neuer Ideen für Designer dar. Prozesse in Werkstätten und Fabriken auszuprobieren und die Resultate mit der Erfahrung hoch entwickelter Verarbeiter zu verbinden, ist eine inspirierende, unkalkulierbare Herangehensweise, die viele Energien freisetzt.

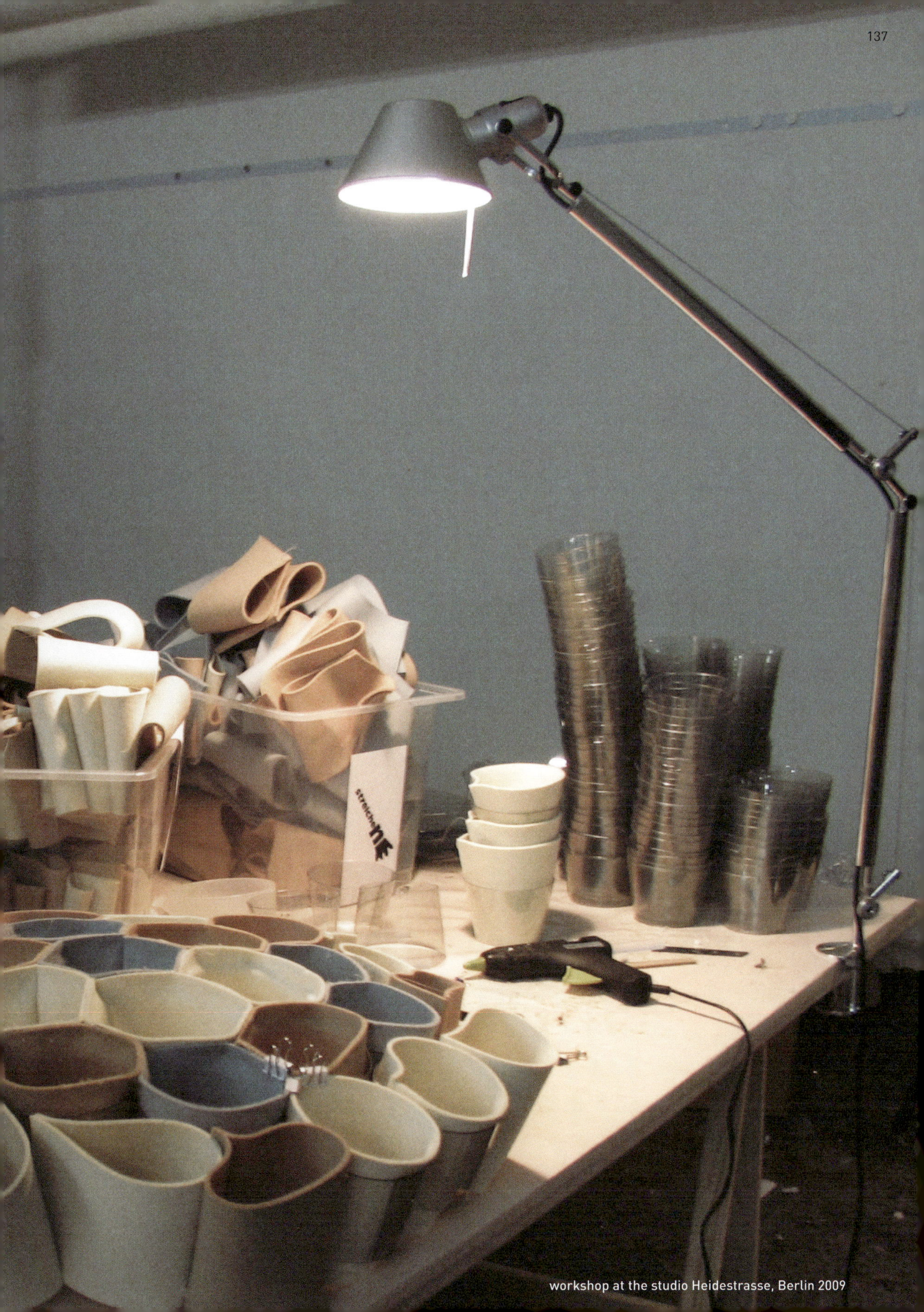

workshop at the studio Heidestrasse, Berlin 2009

coral modules

studio edition 2009

In the age of the collage-living scenario, the coral modules are a transparent and open kind of geodetic structure with a strong sculptural appearance. Influenced by the shapes of micro-organisms of marine life such phytoplankton, coral cell-structures and honeycombs, the overall shape is a multiple duplication of sub-modules which create the "coral" shape.

Im Zeitalter Collage-artiger Innenarchitekturen sind die Coral Seating Module eine transparente und offene geodätische Struktur mit einem intensiven skulpturalen Erscheinungsbild. Beeinflusst von den Formen der Mikroorganismen aus dem Meer wie Phytoplankton, korallenförmigen Zellstrukturen und Wabenmustern, beruht die insgesamt „korallenförmige" Ästhetik auf der multiplen Addition von Einzelmodulen.

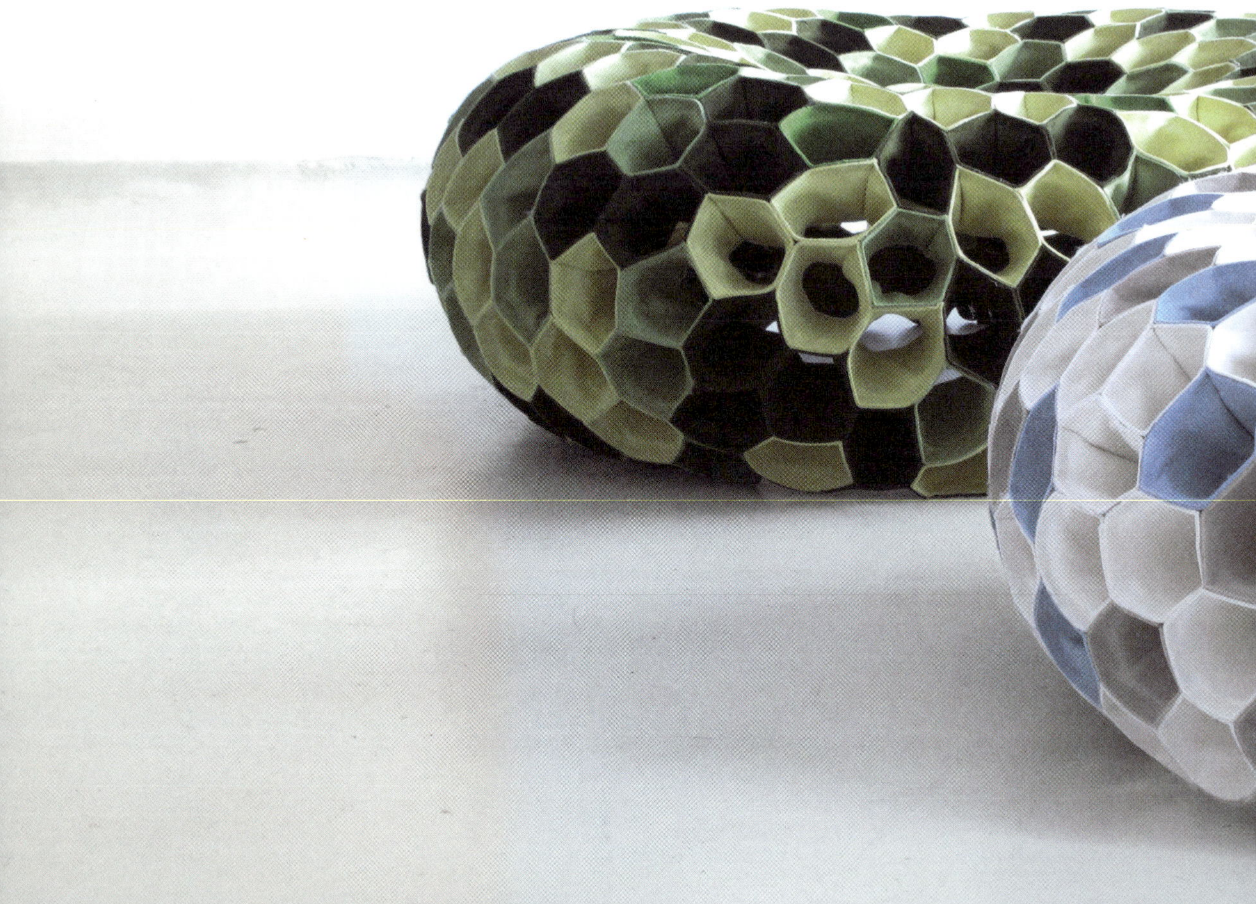

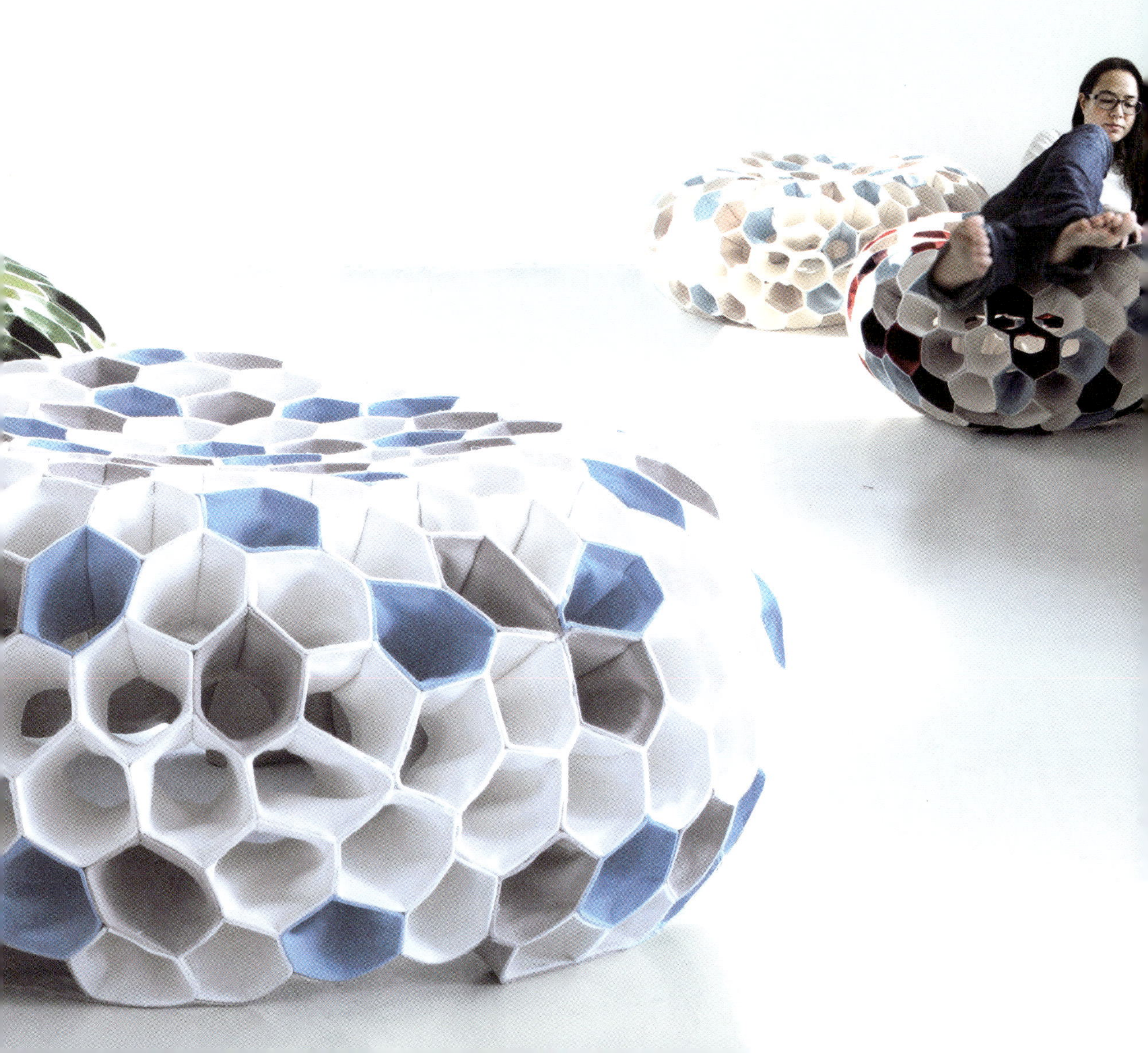

Made from a combination of hexagon funnels which are a hybrid of felt and polycarbon hexagons, comfortable and elastic seating modules in various shapes are created. For the "making", the studio team set up a workshop zone within the office with several workstations for the production process of the edition.

Die Kombination sechseckiger, aus Filz und Polycarbonat bestehender Trichtermodule bildet unterschiedlich geformte, komfortable und elastische Sitzmodule. Zur manufakturellen Herstellung wurden im Studio Workshop-Bereiche für den Produktionsprozess der Edition geschaffen.

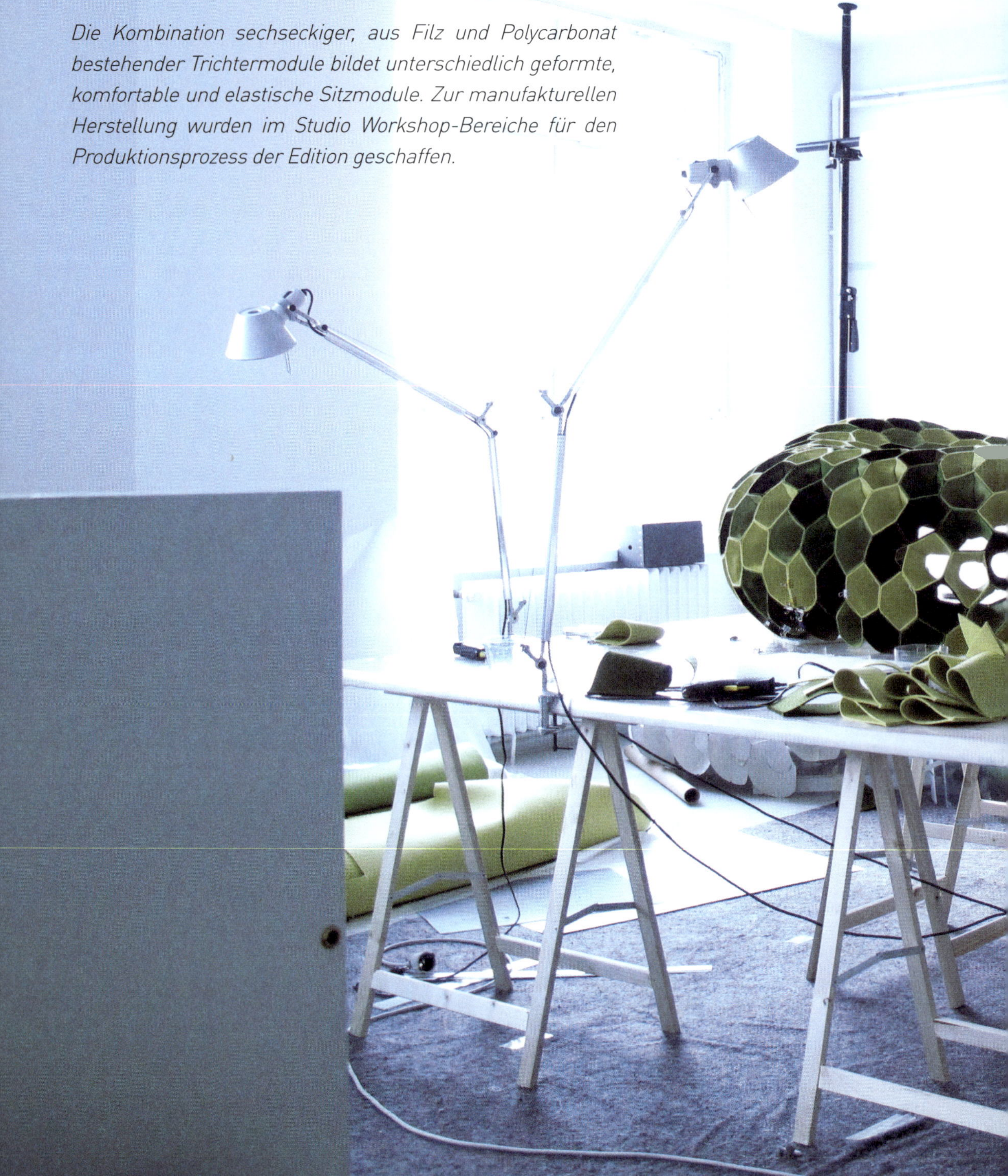

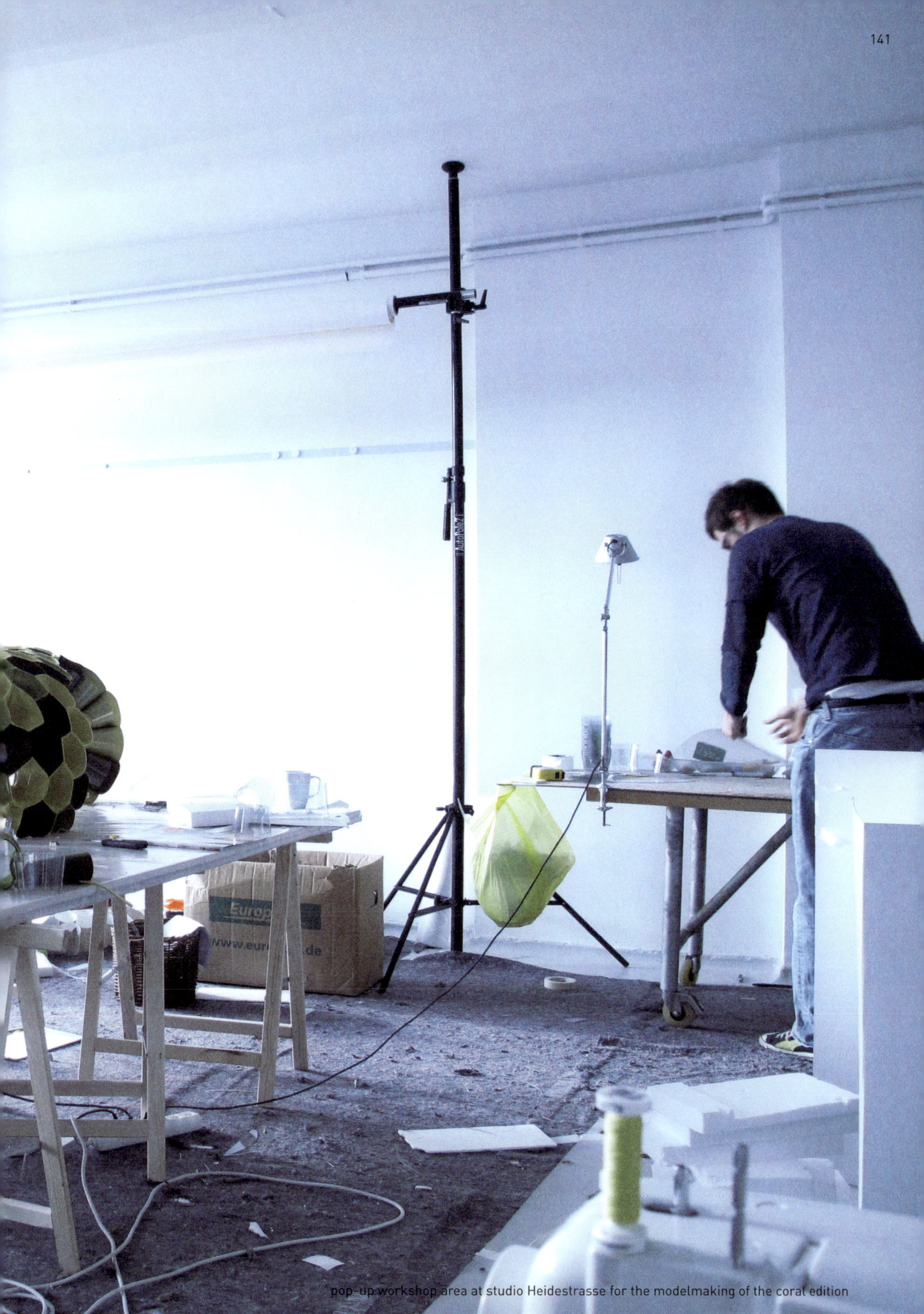

pop-up workshop area at studio Heidestrasse for the modelmaking of the coral edition

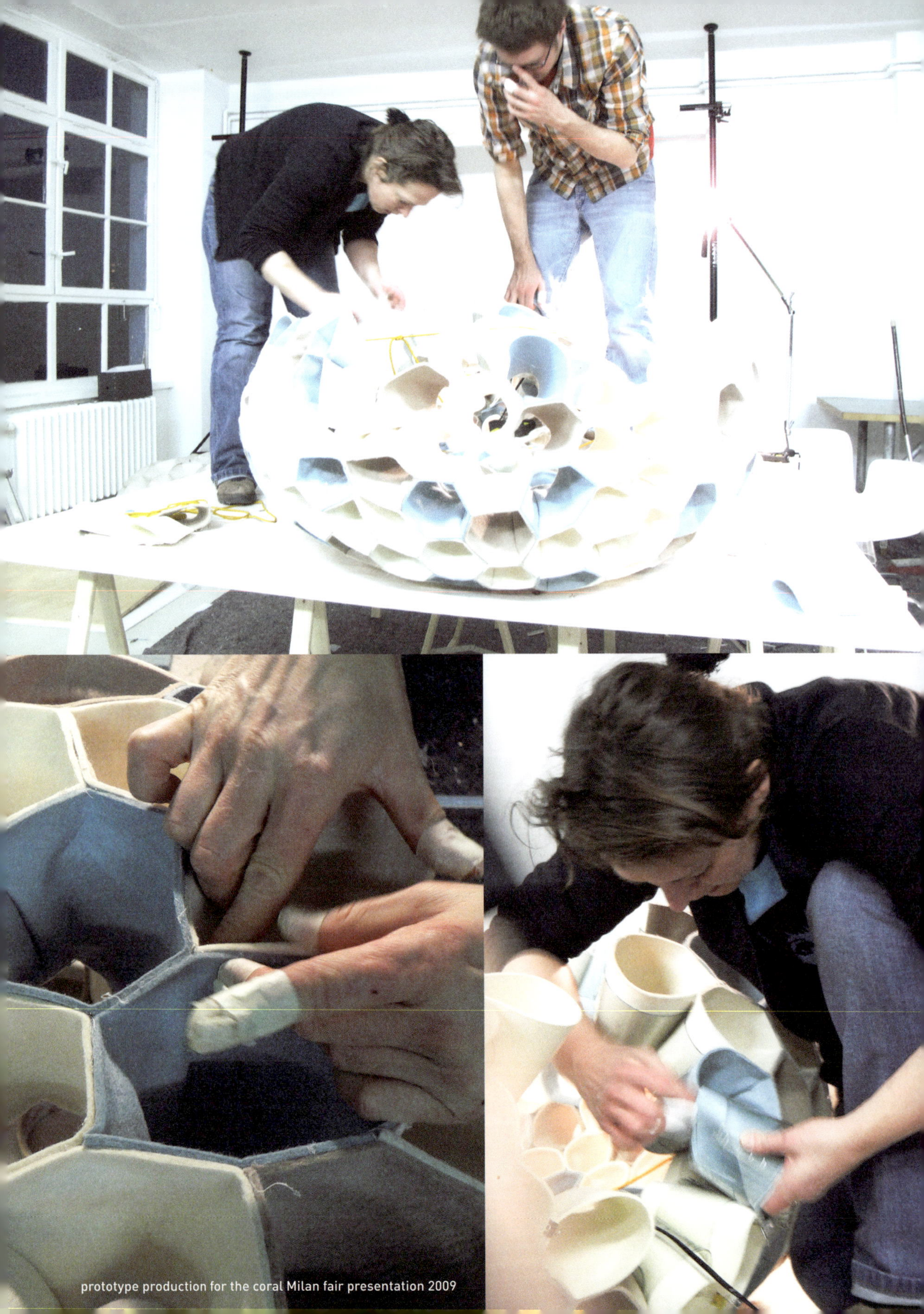

prototype production for the coral Milan fair presentation 2009

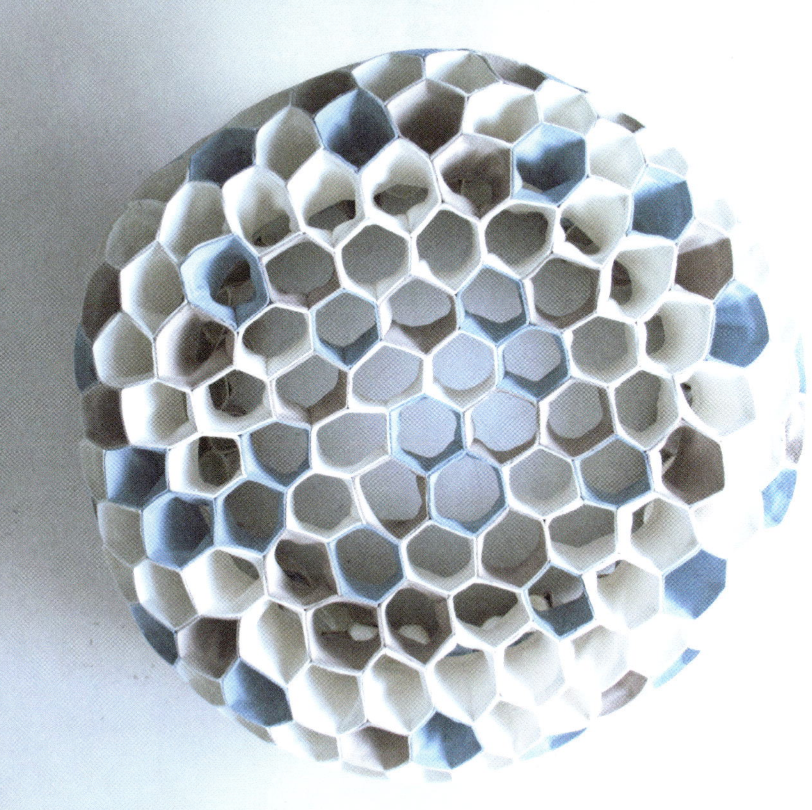

Sizes: Diameter 75-130 cm, height 38-46 cm
Material: Felt & polycarbon sandwich modules in various colour combinations

Größen: *Durchmesser 75-130 cm, Höhe 38-46 cm*
Material: *Filz & Polycarbonat-Sandwich-Module in verschiedenen Farbkombinationen*

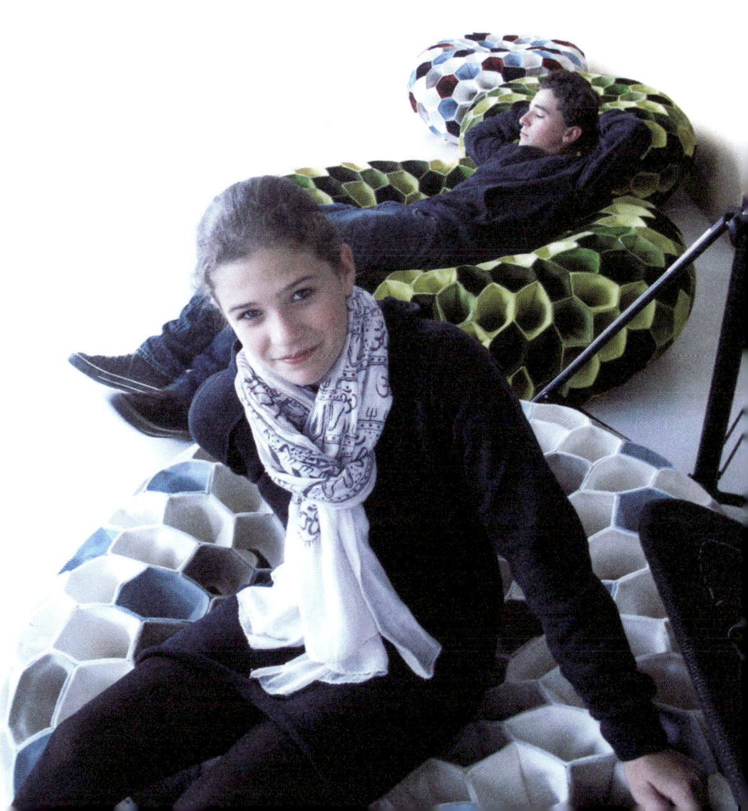

coral light

edition 2009

The coral suspension lamp is a large lighting sculpture made of a methodical repetition of hexagonal units created with a fine layer of reinforced felt. The amorphous form of the geodetic ball shape is reminiscent of the coral seating modules of sea-life coral structures. The light source is as if it were invisibly hidden within the geometric construction and produces an indirect lightshade as well.

Die korallenförmige Hängeleuchte ist eine große Leuchtskulptur, hergestellt durch die methodische Wiederholung sechseckiger Submodule aus einer dünnen Schicht harzverstärkten Filzes. Die amorphe, geodätische Kugelform erinnert genauso wie die Coral Seating Sitzmodule an Korallenstrukturen aus dem Meer. Die Lichtquelle liegt verborgen innerhalb der geometrischen Konstruktion und generiert in der Wabenschale eine indirekte Lichtwirkung.

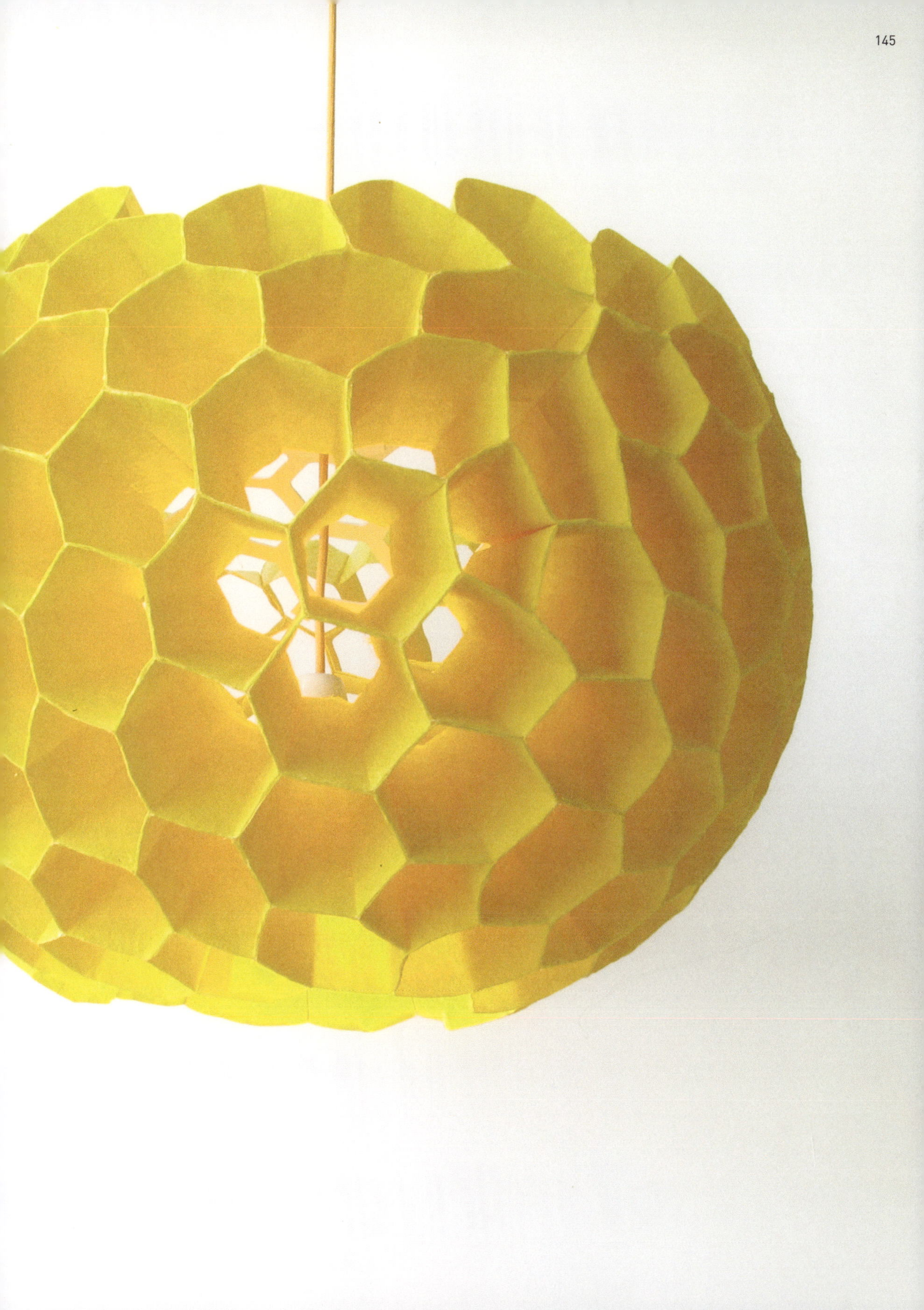

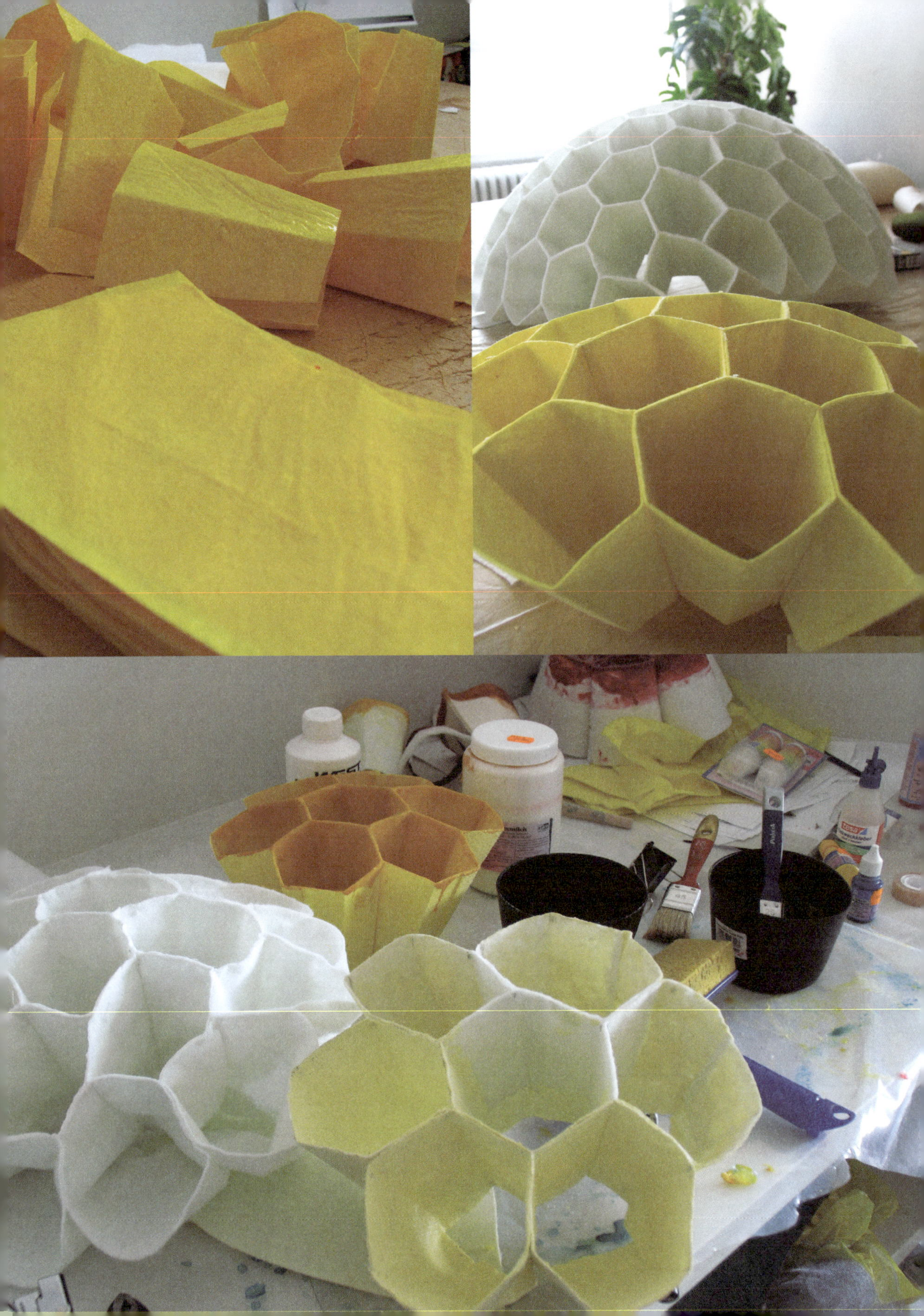

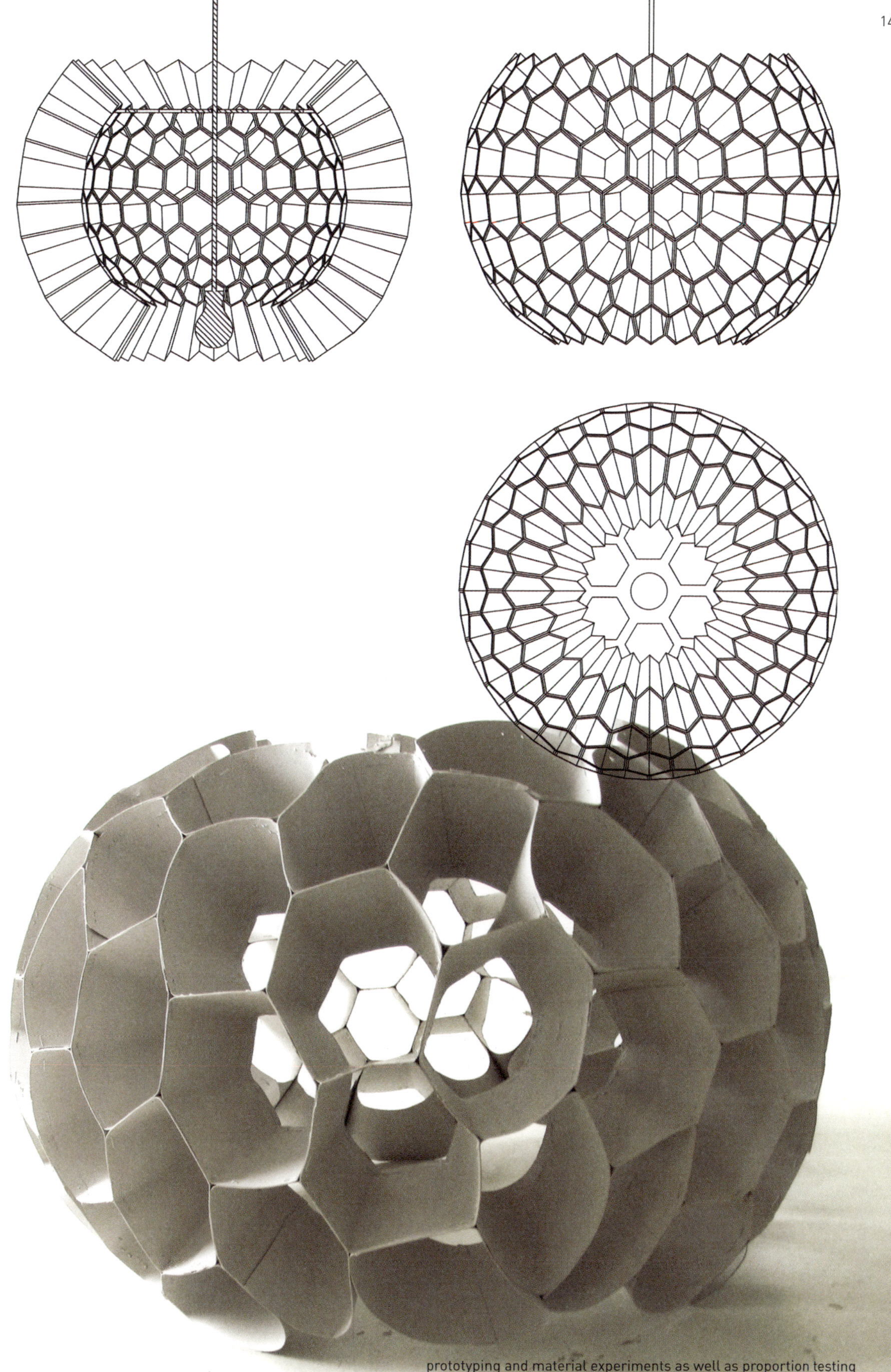

prototyping and material experiments as well as proportion testing

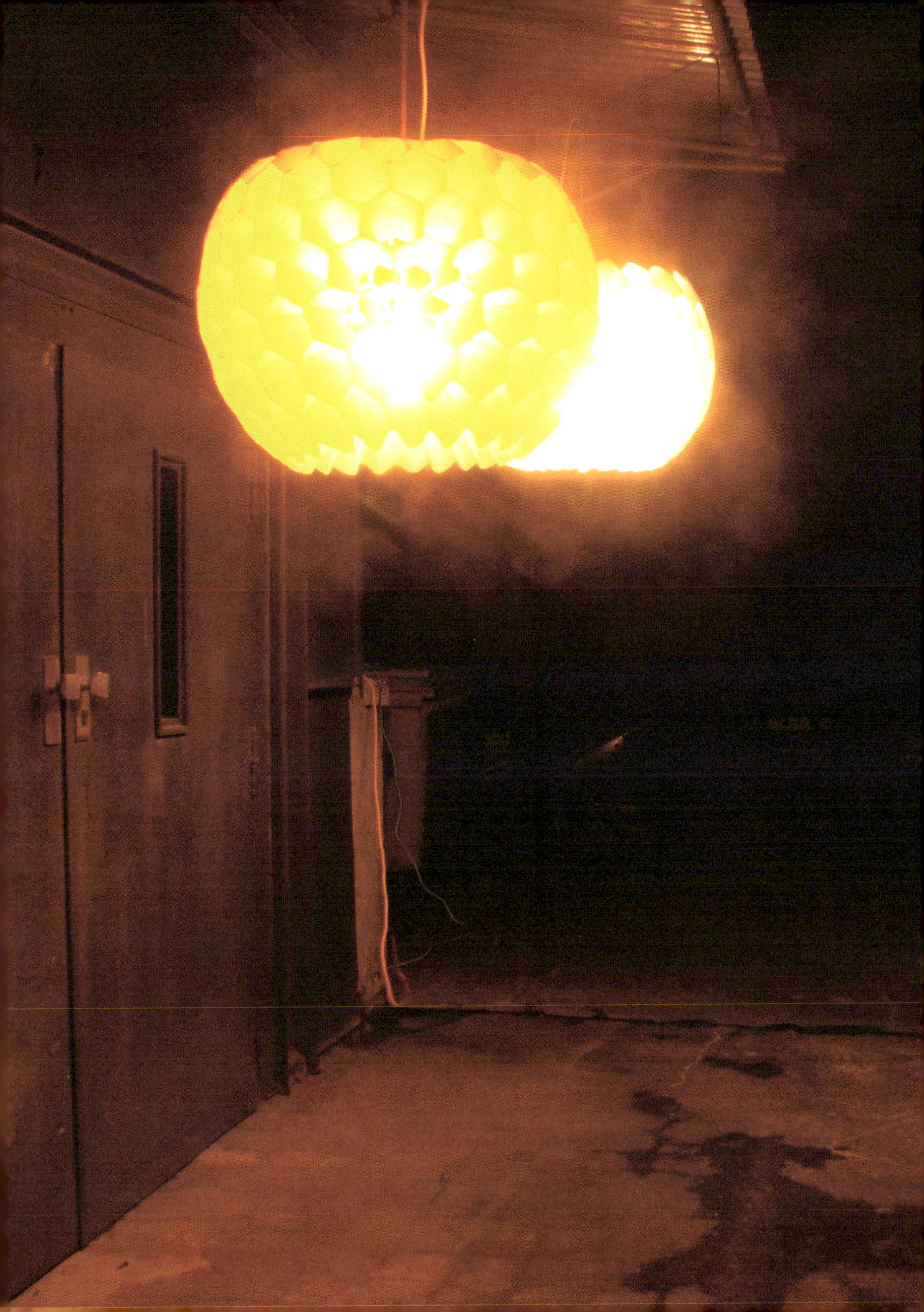

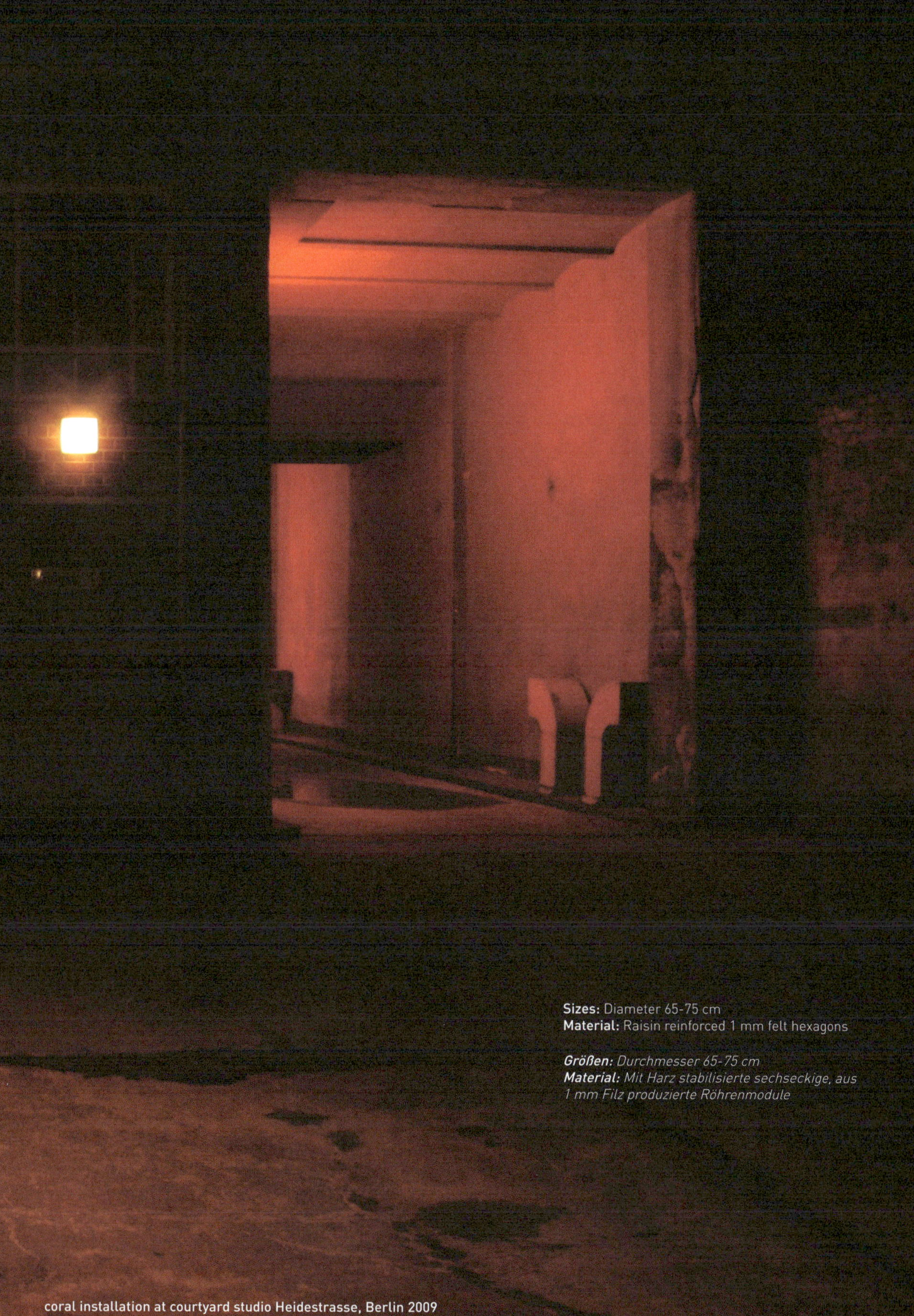

Sizes: Diameter 65-75 cm
Material: Raisin reinforced 1 mm felt hexagons

Größen: *Durchmesser 65-75 cm*
Material: *Mit Harz stabilisierte sechseckige, aus 1 mm Filz produzierte Röhrenmodule*

coral installation at courtyard studio Heidestrasse, Berlin 2009

basket

concept study for Vitra 2008

In conjunction with Vitra, basket was developed as a pilot project for an "office reset concept". The starting point comprised three versions that had been created as 1:1 models in studio aisslinger. Basket makes intentional use of the analogy with a Hollywood swing. After all, what kind of seating furniture is the epitome of laid-back, recuperative, unforced relaxation if not the Hollywood swing?

In the office, gently swinging back and forth is a way of escaping from stressful tasks for a while in order to absorb new ideas and fresh viewpoints and allow them to take effect. These quiet phases of concentration are not only a brief timeout but, above all, a change of context that enhances the ability to focus on subsequent work activities. Ideally, they are a "reset" of the spirit.

Zusammen mit Vitra wurde Basket als Pilotprojekt für ein „Office-Reset-Konzept" entwickelt. Ausgangspunkt waren drei Versionen, die als 1:1 Modelle im studio aisslinger entwickelt wurden. Basket bedient sich bewusst der Analogie einer Hollywoodschaukel, denn: Welches Sitzmöbel ist der Inbegriff vom lässigen, erholsamen und ungezwungenen Verweilen, wenn nicht die Hollywoodschaukel?

Im Bürobetrieb kann man sich durch das sanfte Hin- und Herschaukeln eine Weile von seinen Aufgaben loslösen, um neue Ideen und frische Impulse aufzunehmen und wirken zu lassen. Diese stillen Konzentrationsphasen sind nicht nur eine kleine Auszeit, sondern vor allem ein Kontextwechsel, der die Fokussierung auf die nachfolgenden Arbeitsaktivitäten erhöht. Im Idealfall eben ein „Reset" des Geistes.

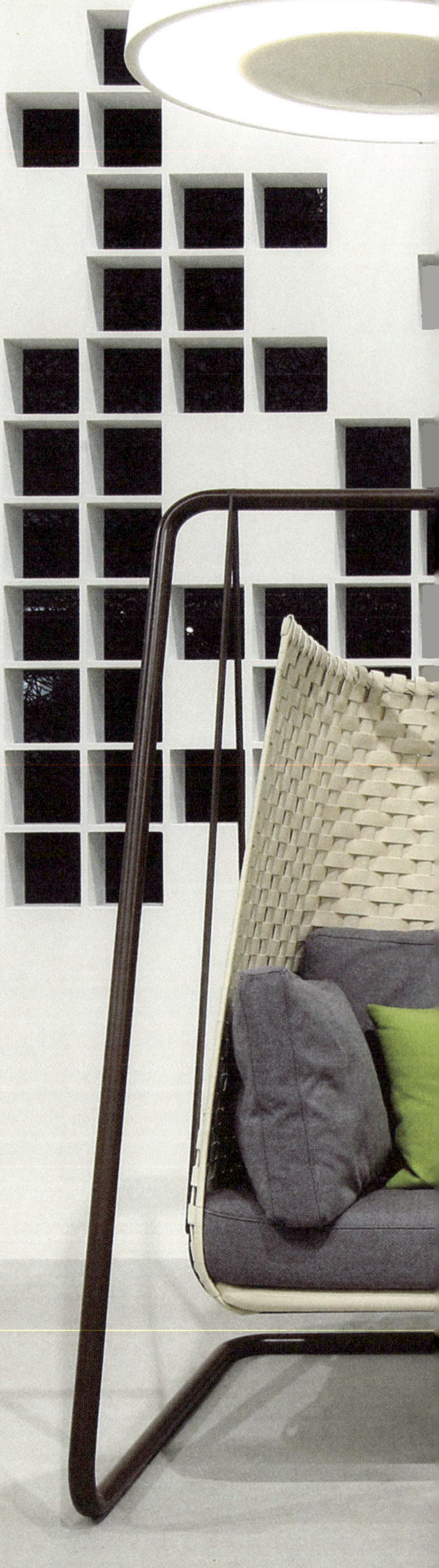

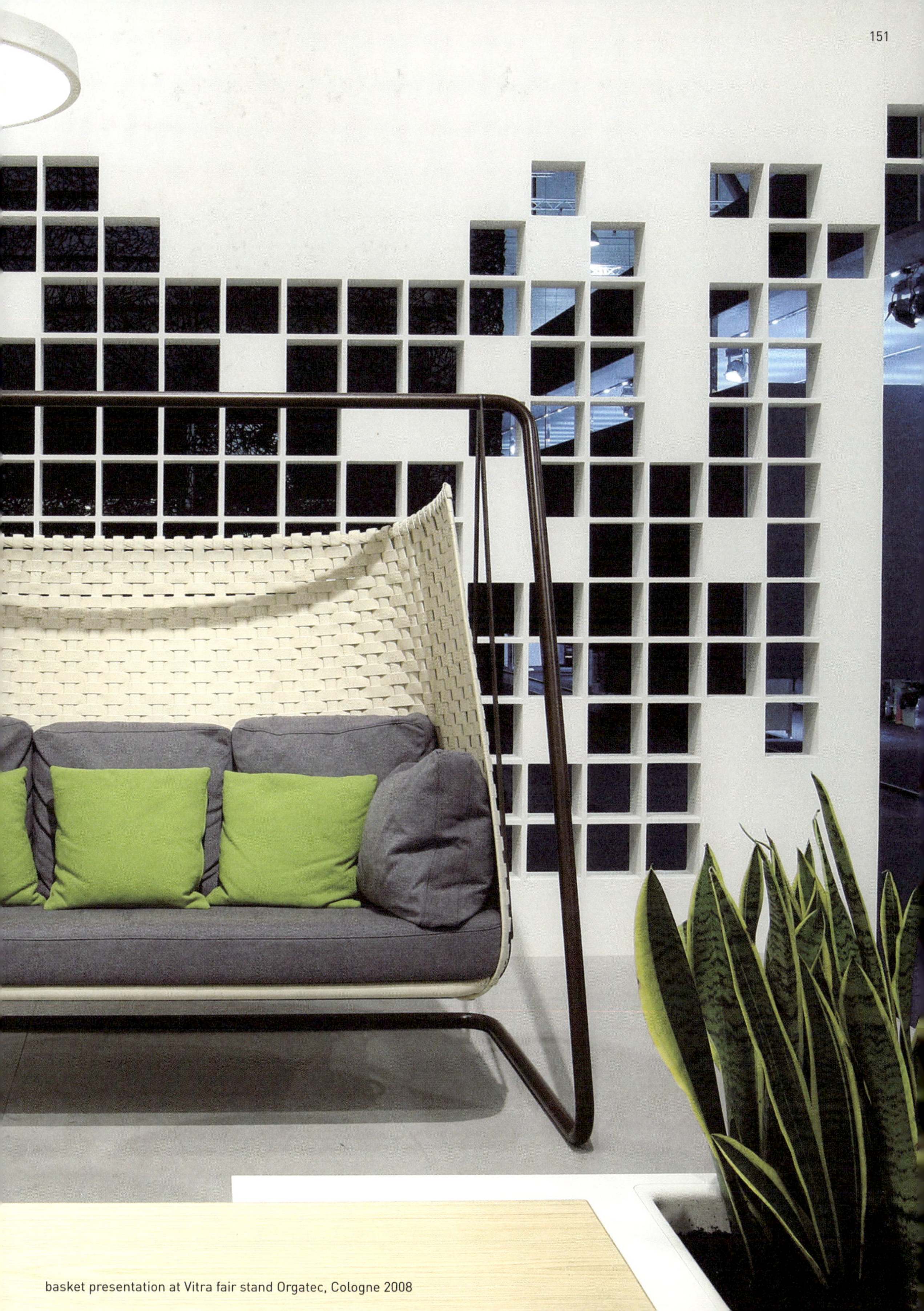

basket presentation at Vitra fair stand Orgatec, Cologne 2008

prototyping of one of the 3 concepts for the basket project

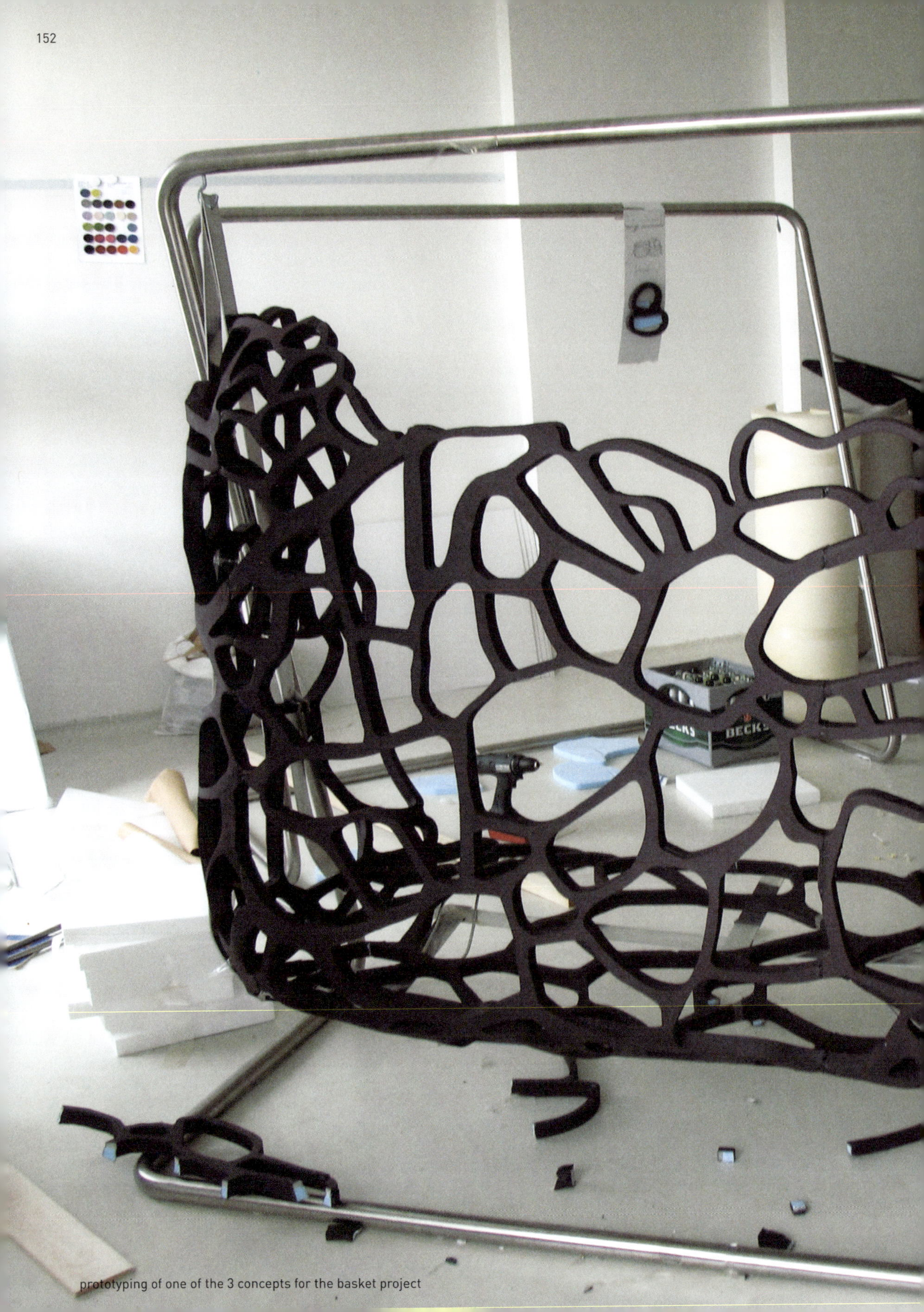

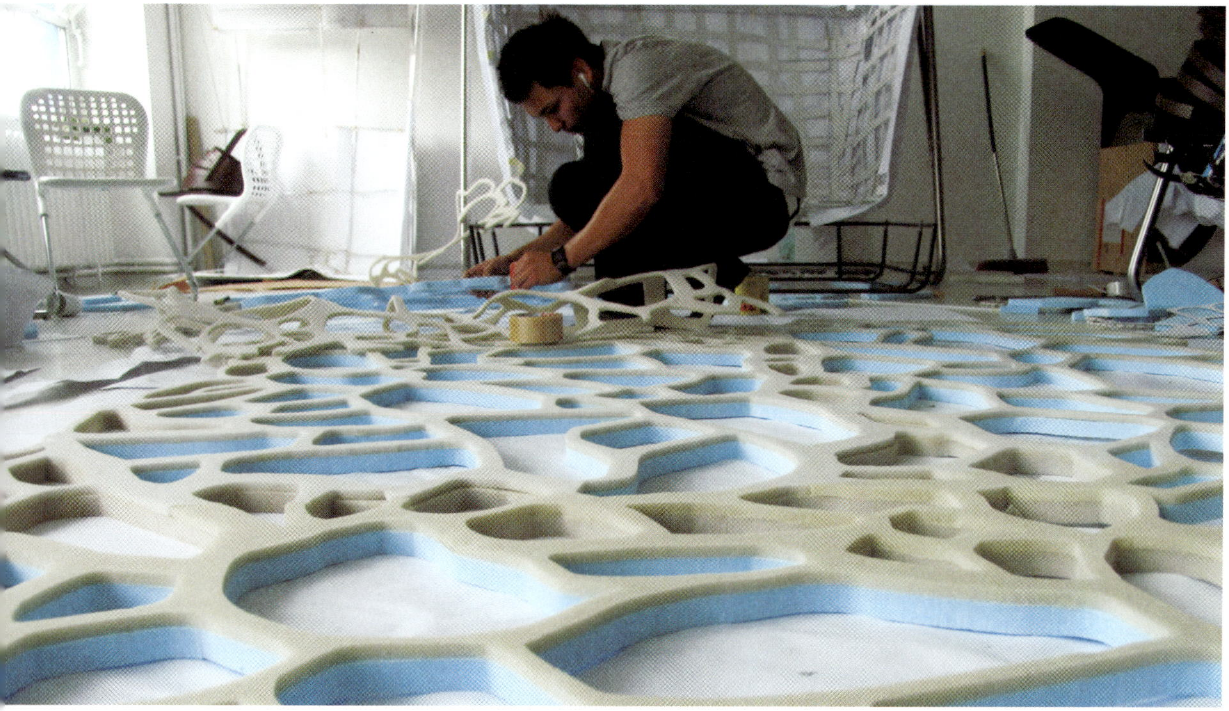

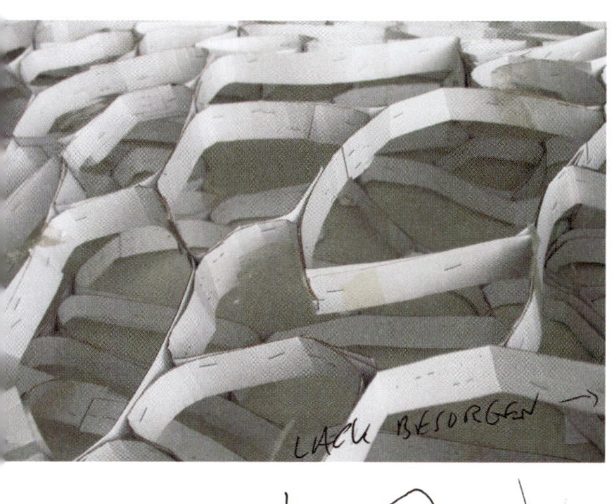
LACK BESORGEN

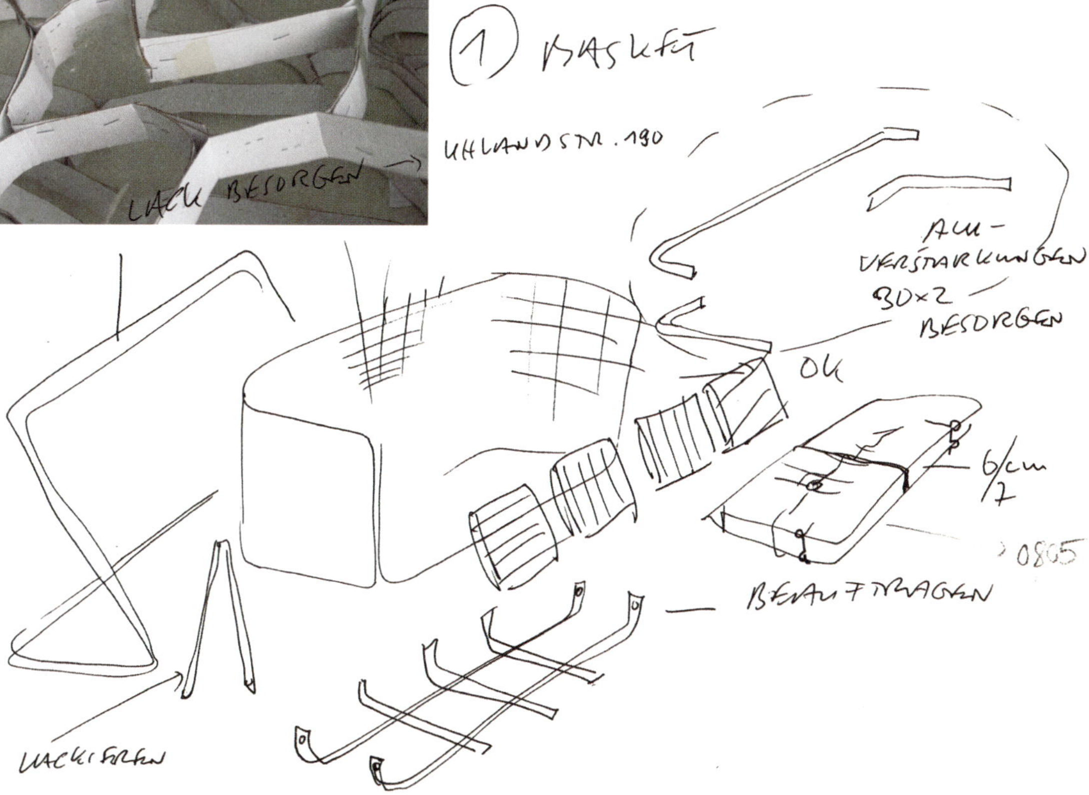

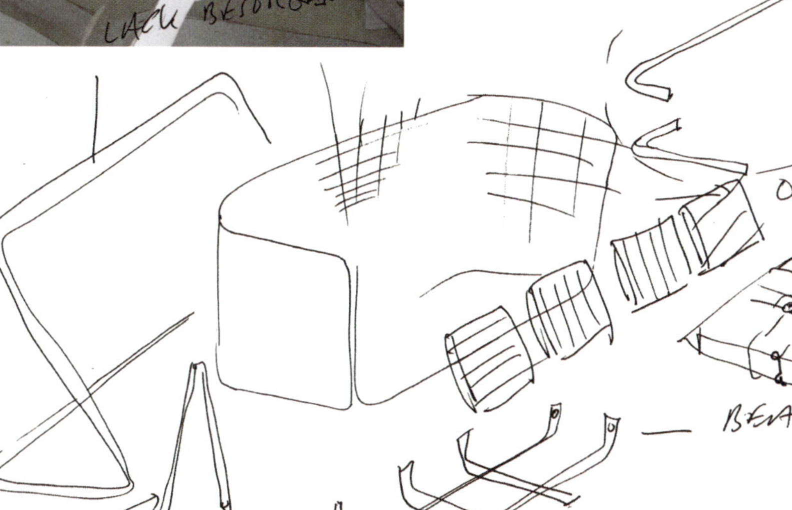
1 BASKET
UHLANDSTR. 190
ALU-
VERSTÄRKUNGEN
30x2
BESORGEN
OK
6/cm
7
0805
BEAUFTRAGEN
LACKIEREN

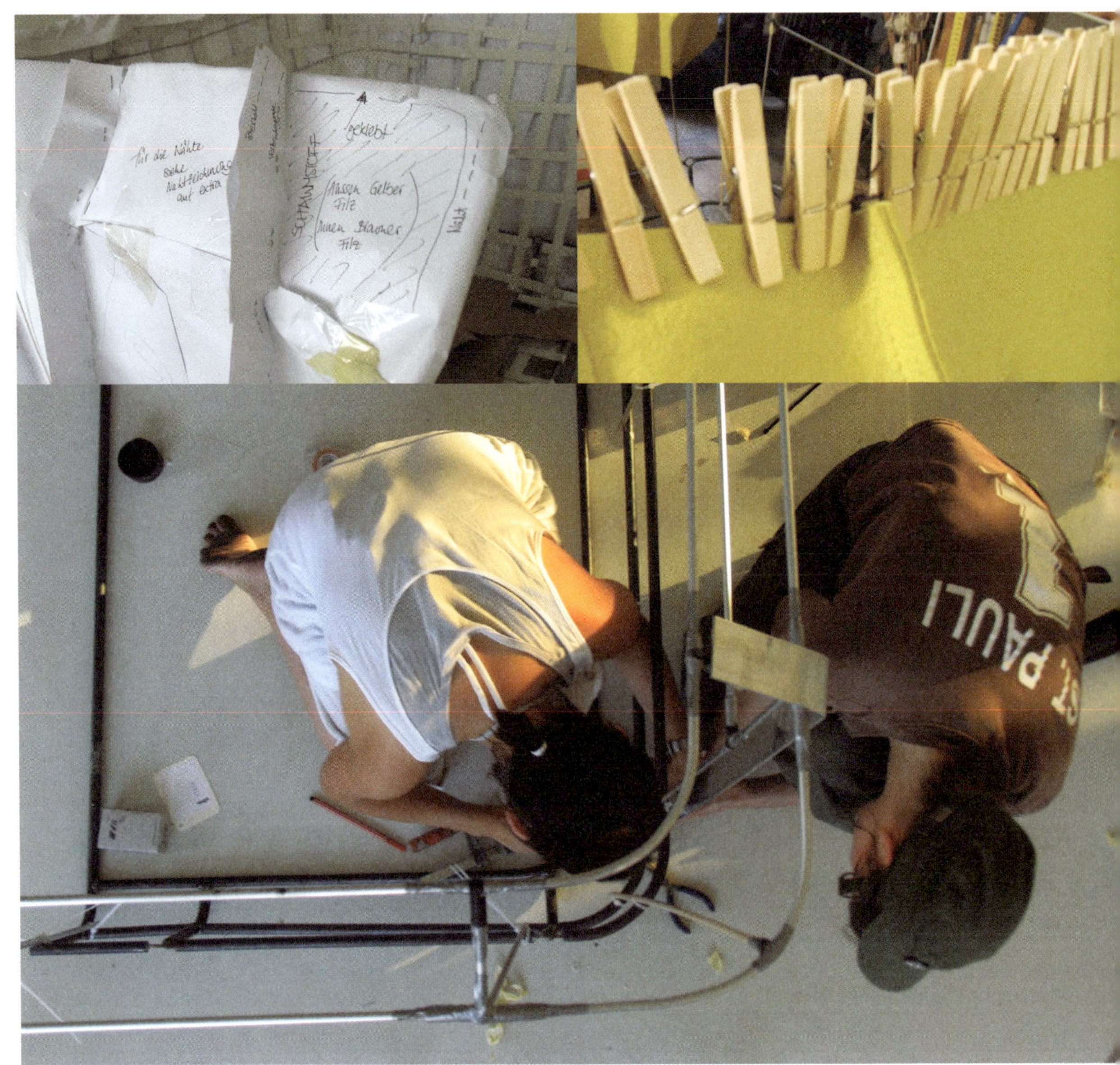

prototyping of a felt version for the basket project at studio Heidestrasse, Berlin 2008

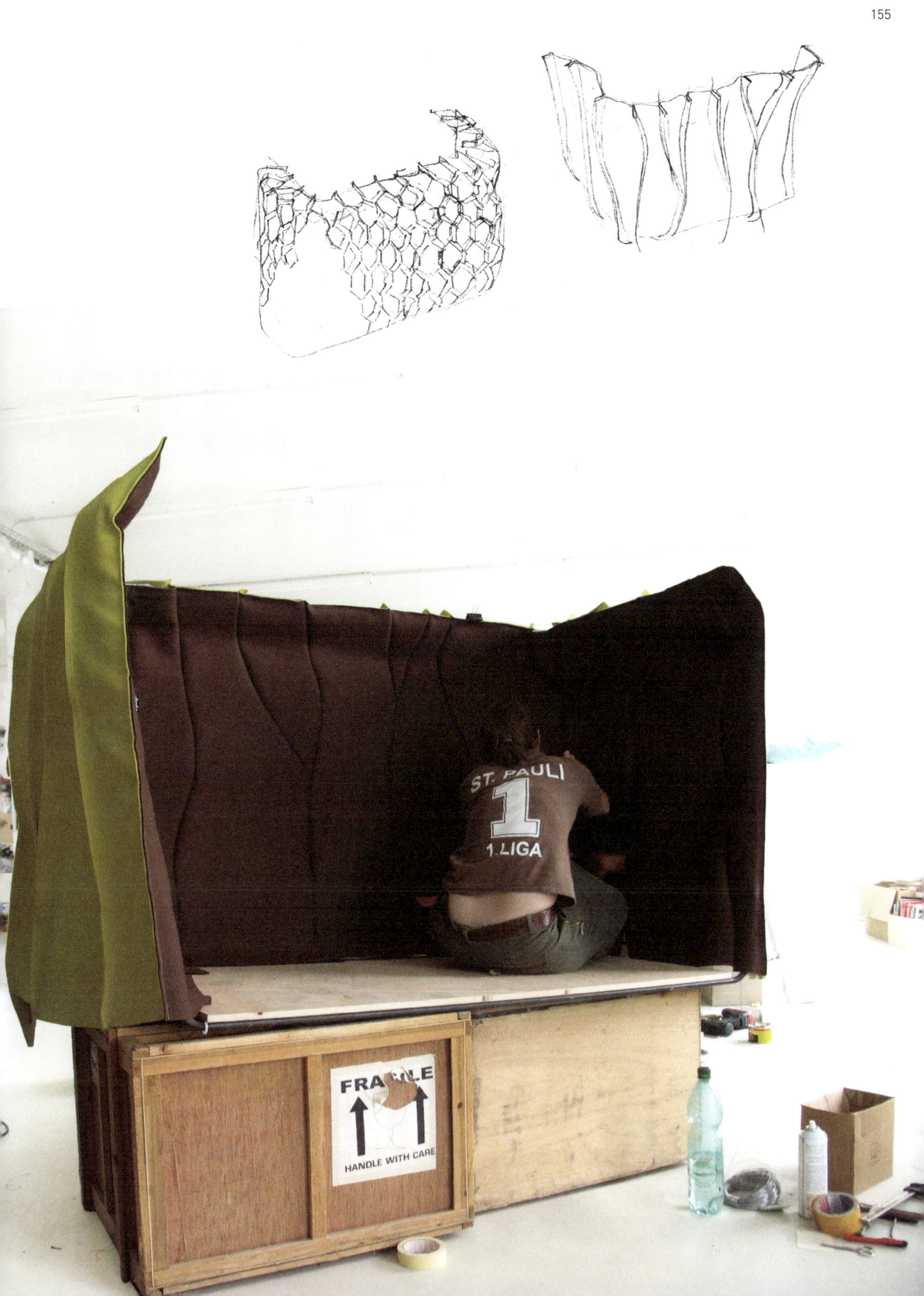
ST. PAULI
1
1.LIGA
HANDLE WITH CARE

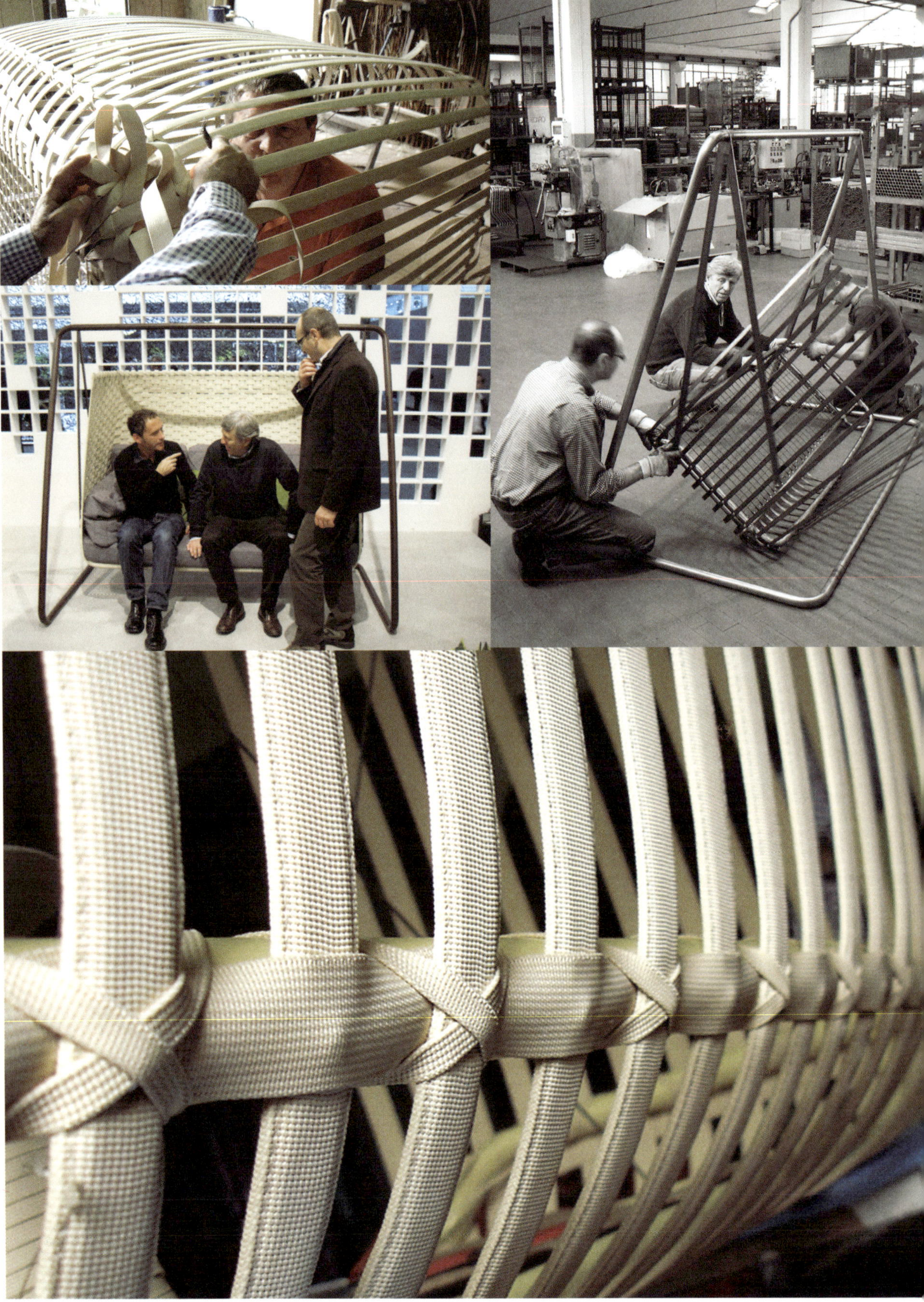

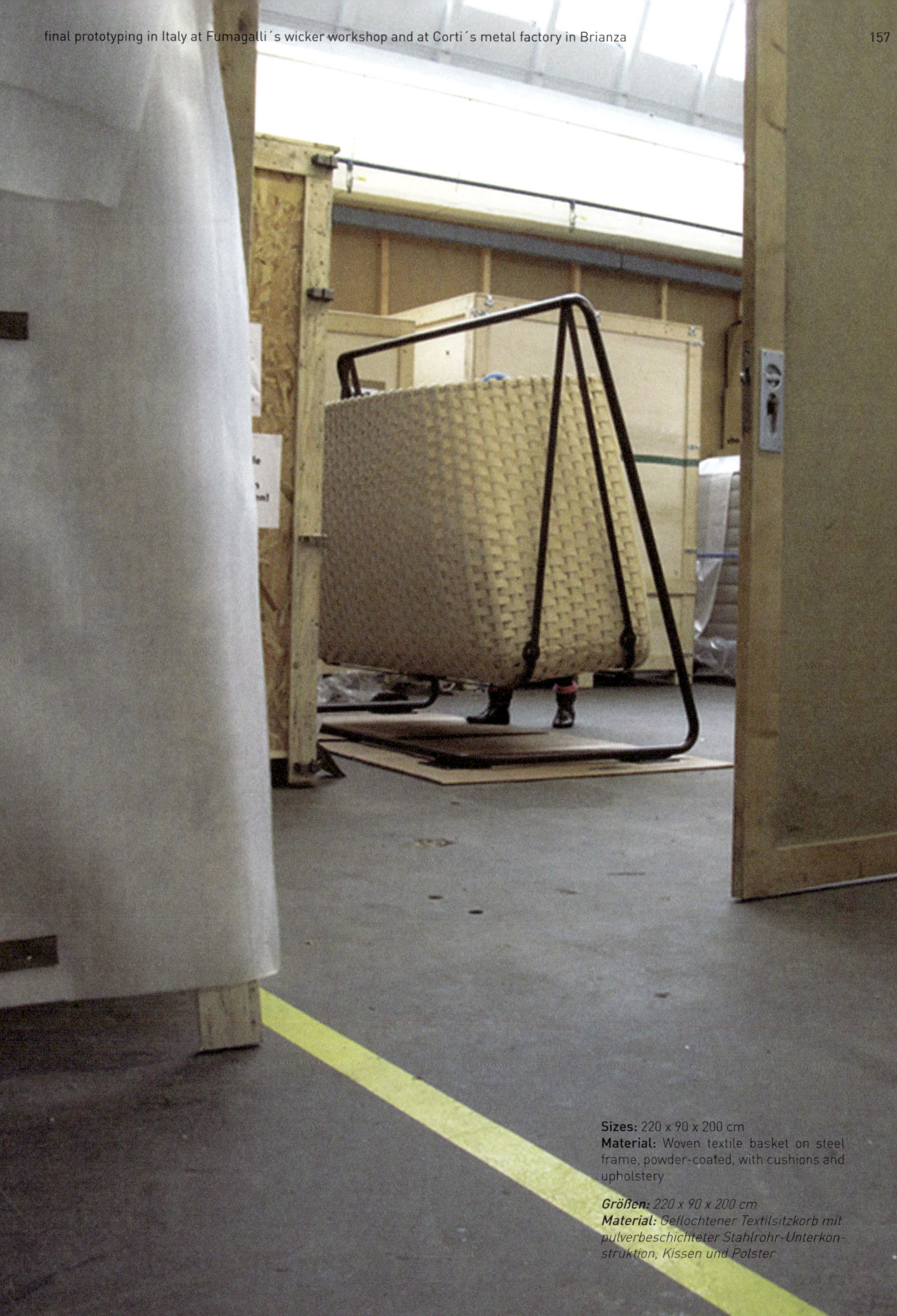

Sizes: 220 x 90 x 200 cm
Material: Woven textile basket on steel frame, powder-coated, with cushions and upholstery

Größen: *220 x 90 x 200 cm*
Material: *Geflochtener Textilsitzkorb mit pulverbeschichteter Stahlrohr-Unterkonstruktion, Kissen und Polster*

tree light

dab, Spain 2008

The tree light family is designed as a linear, sculptural, standing and suspension lighting concept with its aesthetical origin in the abstraction of shapes in nature. The underlying concept of this series of lights is a stem that forks out into roots and various branches to form the foot and the shade fixtures respectively.

The lamp shade can be seen as an abstraction of a treetop similar to architectural tree scale models. The overall form of the treetop is a sphere, which has been distorted in various planes. Five laser-cut sheet metal strips create the lamp shade. Each individual strip extends into the third dimension simply by being bent.

Das Design der Tree Light Familie basiert auf einem linearen, skulpturalen Konzept von Steh- und Hängeleuchten, deren formaler Ursprung in der Abstraktion von Formen aus der Natur liegt. Ästhetisch basiert das Design auf der Natur-Analogie eines Stammes, der in Wurzeln und Ästen verläuft, die den Lampenfuß beziehungsweise die Halterung für den Lampenschirm bilden.

Der Lampenschirm kann als Abstraktion einer Baumkrone gesehen werden, ähnlich wie in Architektur-Maßstabsmodellen. Die Baumkrone ist in horizontale Bänder, die unregelmässige Wellenlinien beschreiben, unterteilt. Technisch baut sich der Lampenschirm aus fünf mit einem Laser ausgeschnittenen streifenförmigen Metallblechen auf. Jeder Streifen wird gewalzt und gebogen und nimmt dadurch eine dreidimensionale Form an.

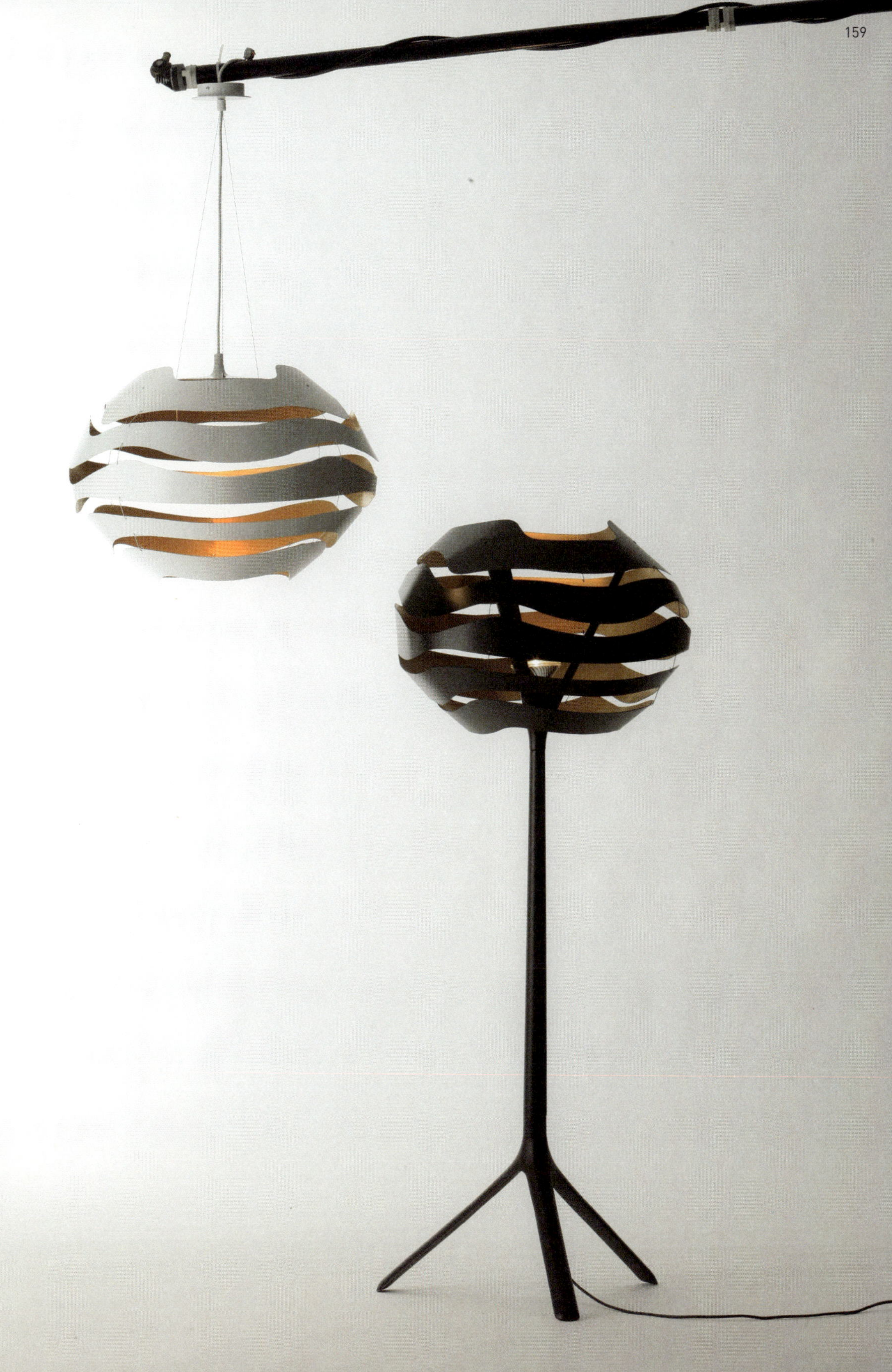

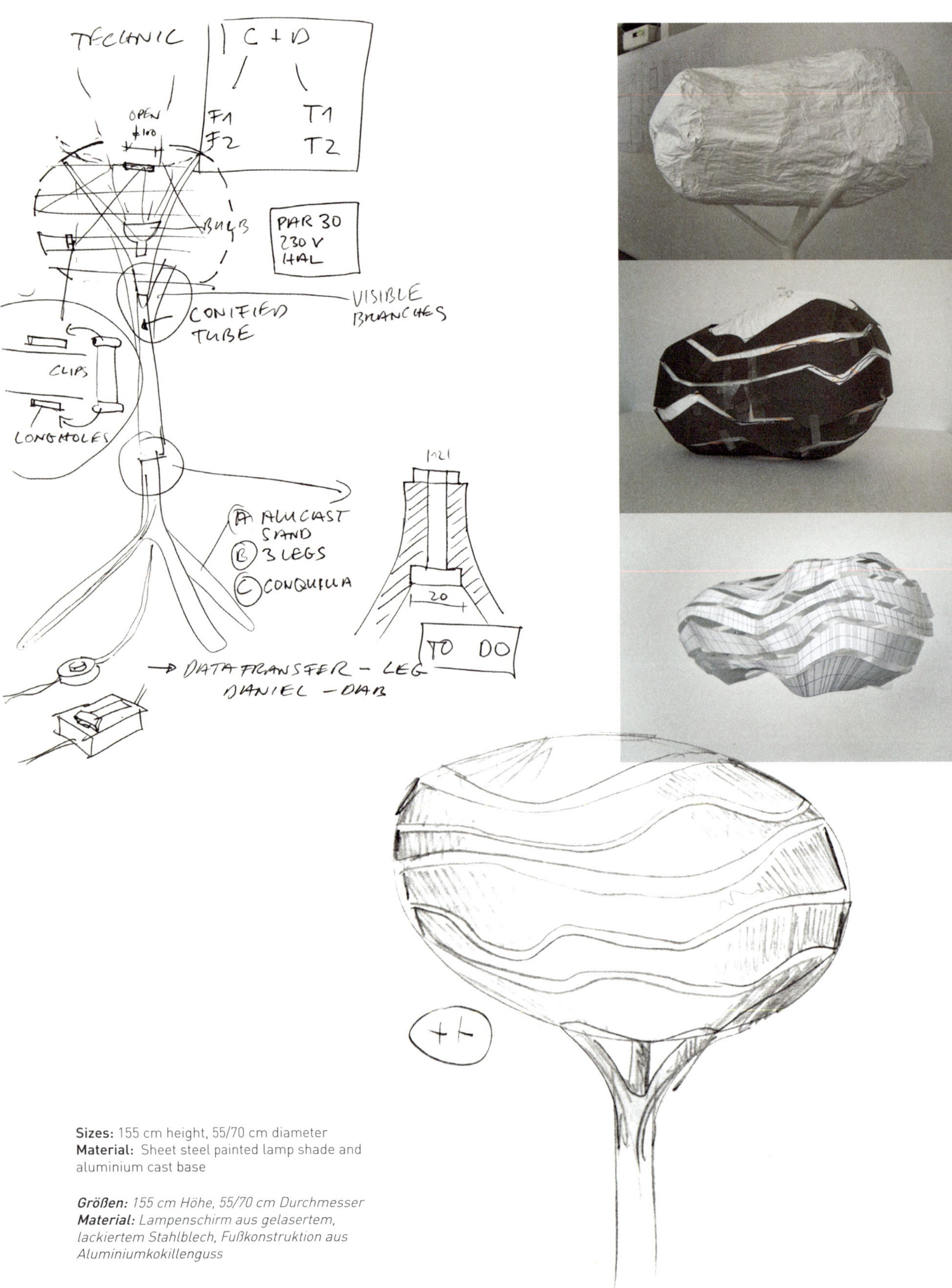

Sizes: 155 cm height, 55/70 cm diameter
Material: Sheet steel painted lamp shade and aluminium cast base

Größen: *155 cm Höhe, 55/70 cm Durchmesser*
Material: *Lampenschirm aus gelasertem, lackiertem Stahlblech, Fußkonstruktion aus Aluminiumkokillenguss*

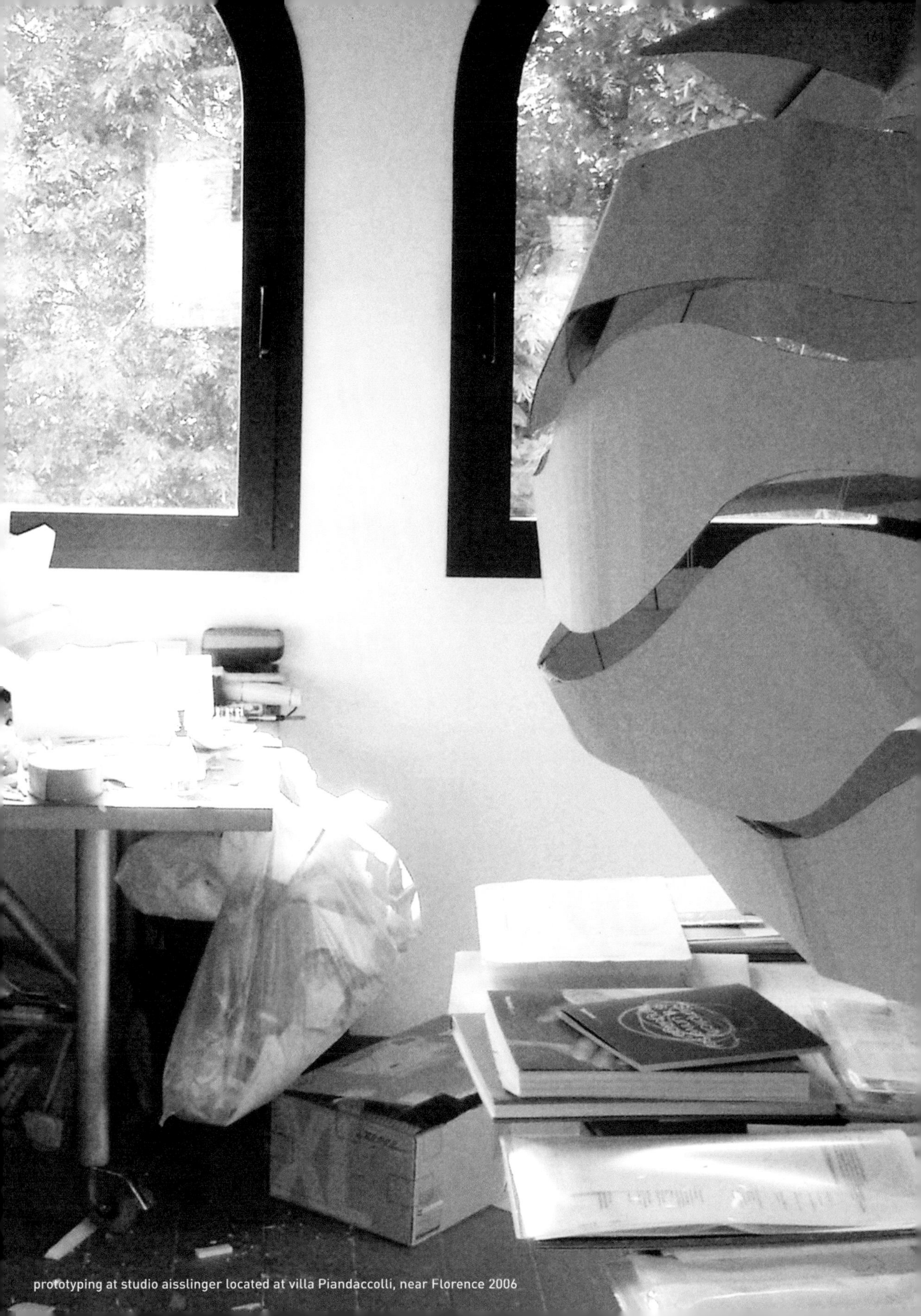

prototyping at studio aisslinger located at villa Piandaccolli, near Florence 2006

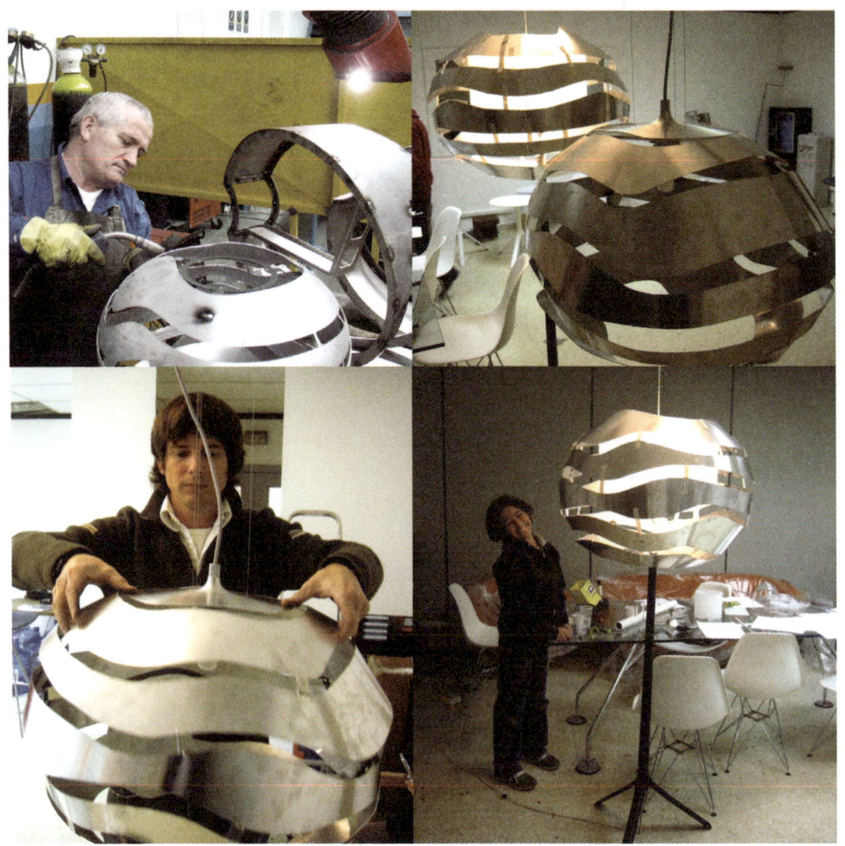

The intriguing detail of the tree lamp is its unusual source of light, hidden in the top part of the light stem. The light was thought of as an indirect source which would be reflected around inside the lamp shade before it leaves its origin. All the onlooker will see when the lamp is turned off is an empty space, while, when it is switched on, an abundant play of reflections ricochets inside the lamp shade and exits it at various, random angles. The clue is the reflective surface finish inside the lamp shade. A mirror-like golden surface is lit and reflects the light due to its irregular shape at various angles.

Das Faszinierende an der Tree Light ist ihre ungewöhnliche Lichtreflexion. Das Licht ist als indirekte Quelle konzipiert, die innen im Lampenschirm Reflexionen erzeugt, bevor die Strahlen den ursprünglichen Lichtraum verlassen. Ist die Lampe ausgeschaltet, sieht der Betrachter nur ein leeres Kugelvolumen, ist sie jedoch eingeschaltet, reflektiert das Licht innen auf den golden lackierten Bändern des Lampenschirms und tritt in unterschiedlichen Winkeln aus.

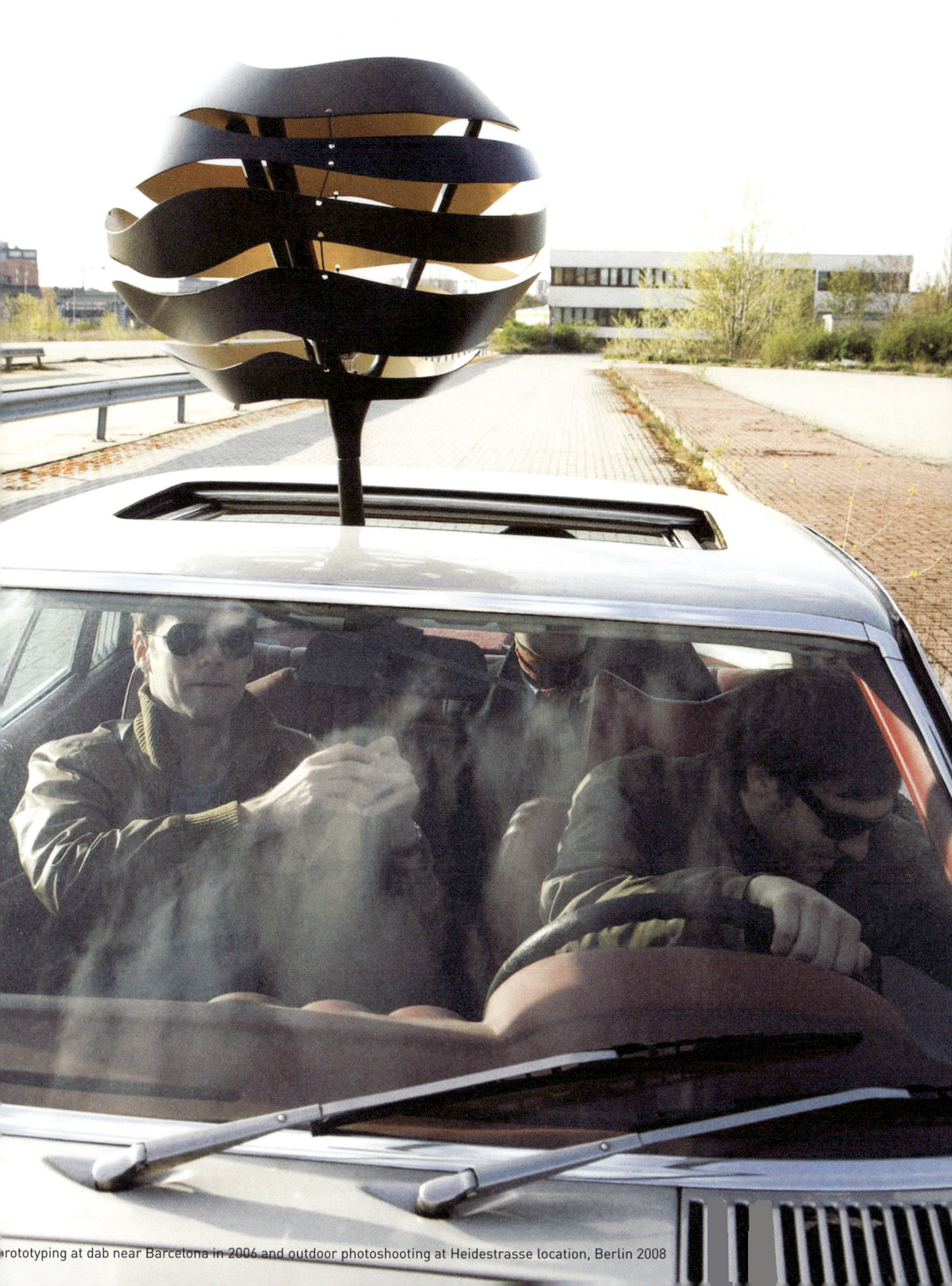

rototyping at dab near Barcelona in 2006 and outdoor photoshooting at Heidestrasse location, Berlin 2008

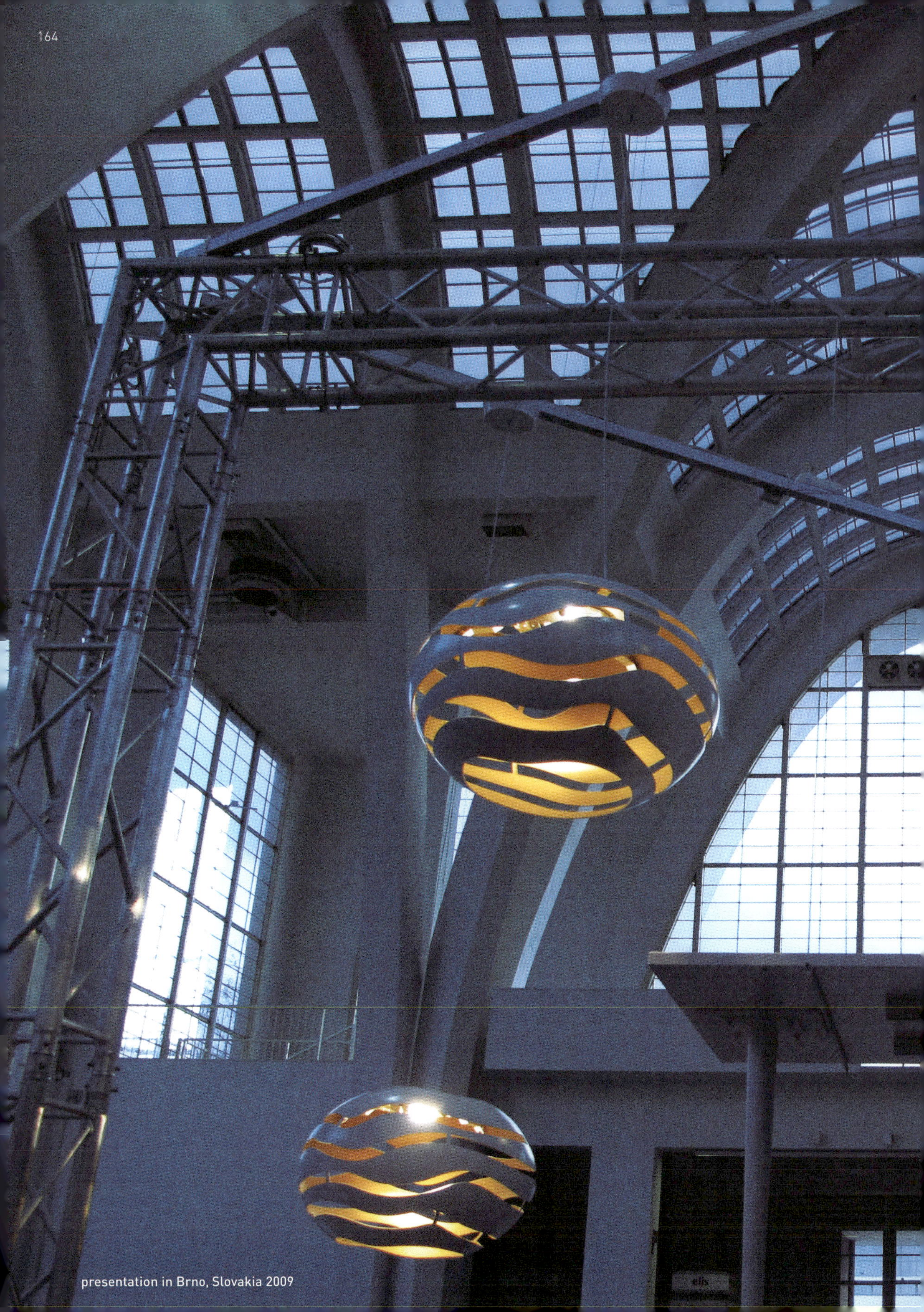

presentation in Brno, Slovakia 2009

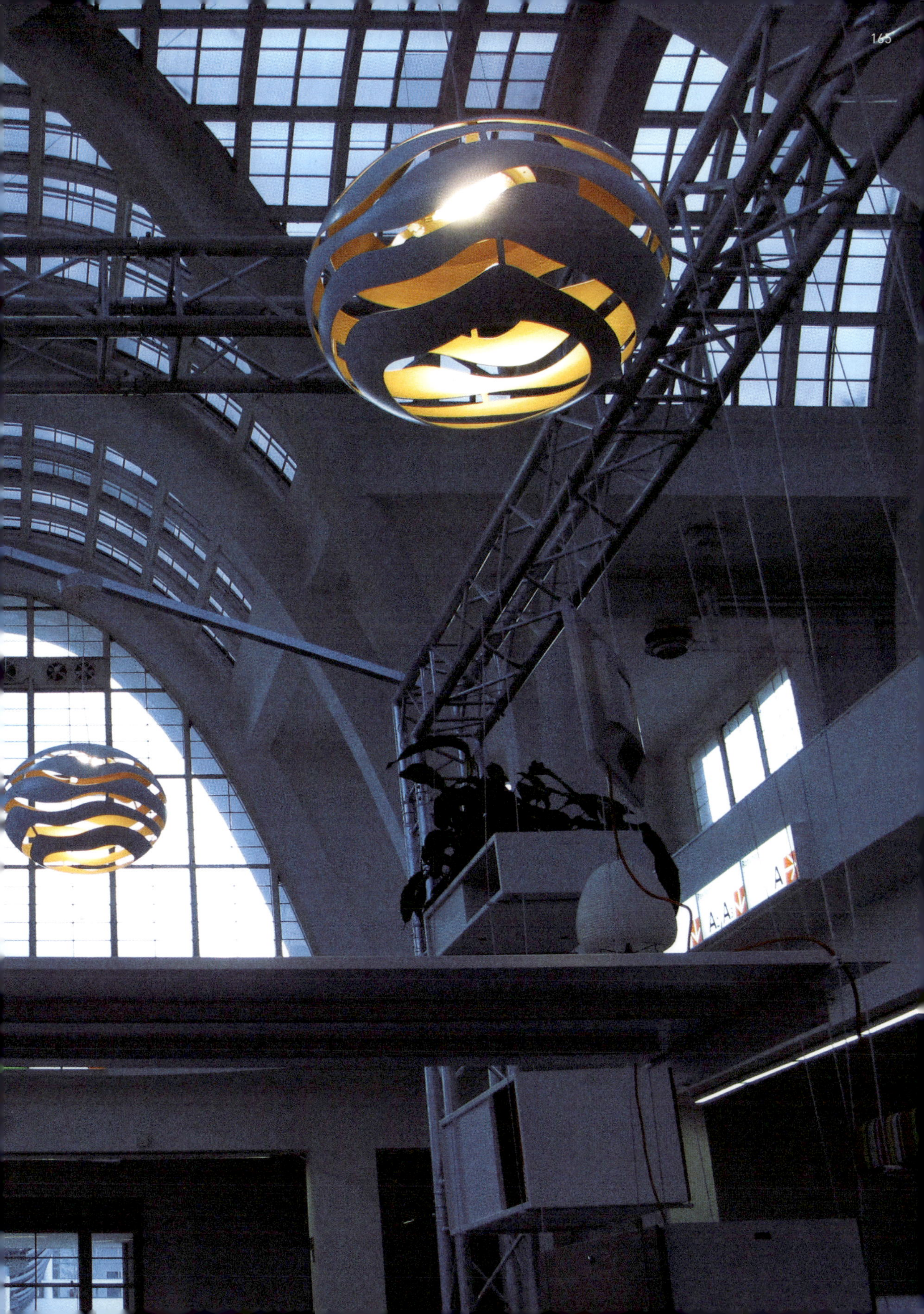

mesh vases

edition with CIAV, Meisenthal 2008

The mesh vases were developed together with CIAV Meisenthal, an experimental laboratory for hand-blown glass in France. With CIAV, a new fabrication concept was developed by blowing the glass into a bag of glass-fibre textile which is fixed in a iron rack. The grid of the glass-fibre textile, which is removed after the glass is blown, gives the vase its unknown texture grid.

Die Mesh Vasen wurden zusammen mit CIAV Meisenthal entwickelt, einem experimentellen Labor für mundgeblasenes Glas in Frankreich. Das CIAV und Werner Aisslinger entwickelten gemeinsam ein neues Herstellungskonzept, bei dem Glas in eine aus Glasfasertextilien hergestellte netzartige Tütenform geblasen wird, die in einem Gestell aus Eisen verankert ist. Nach dem Glasblasen wird die Glasfasertüte entfernt, die als Abdruck der Vase ihre spezielle Textur verleiht.

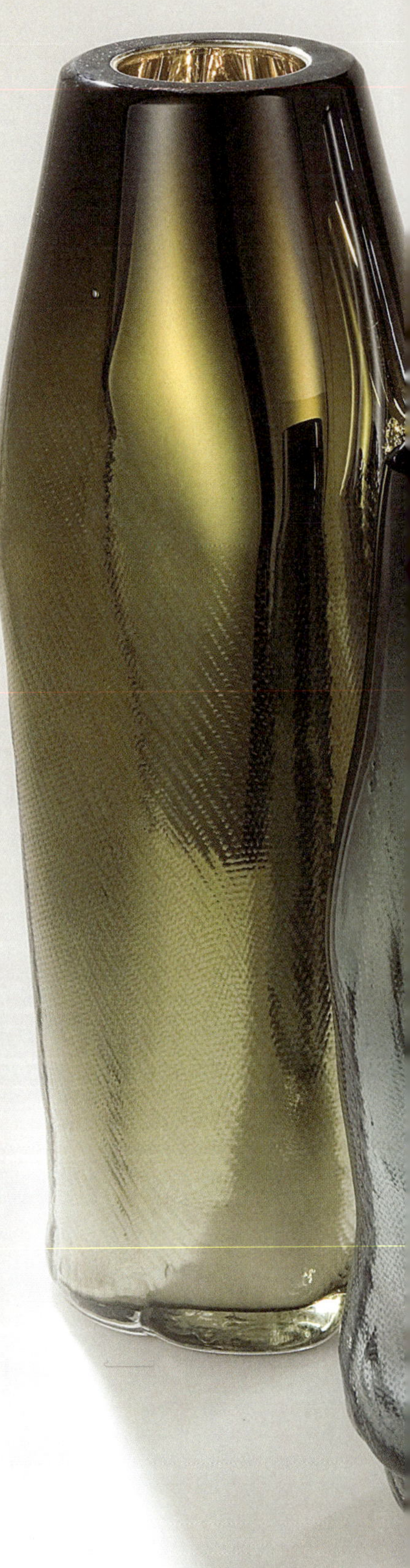

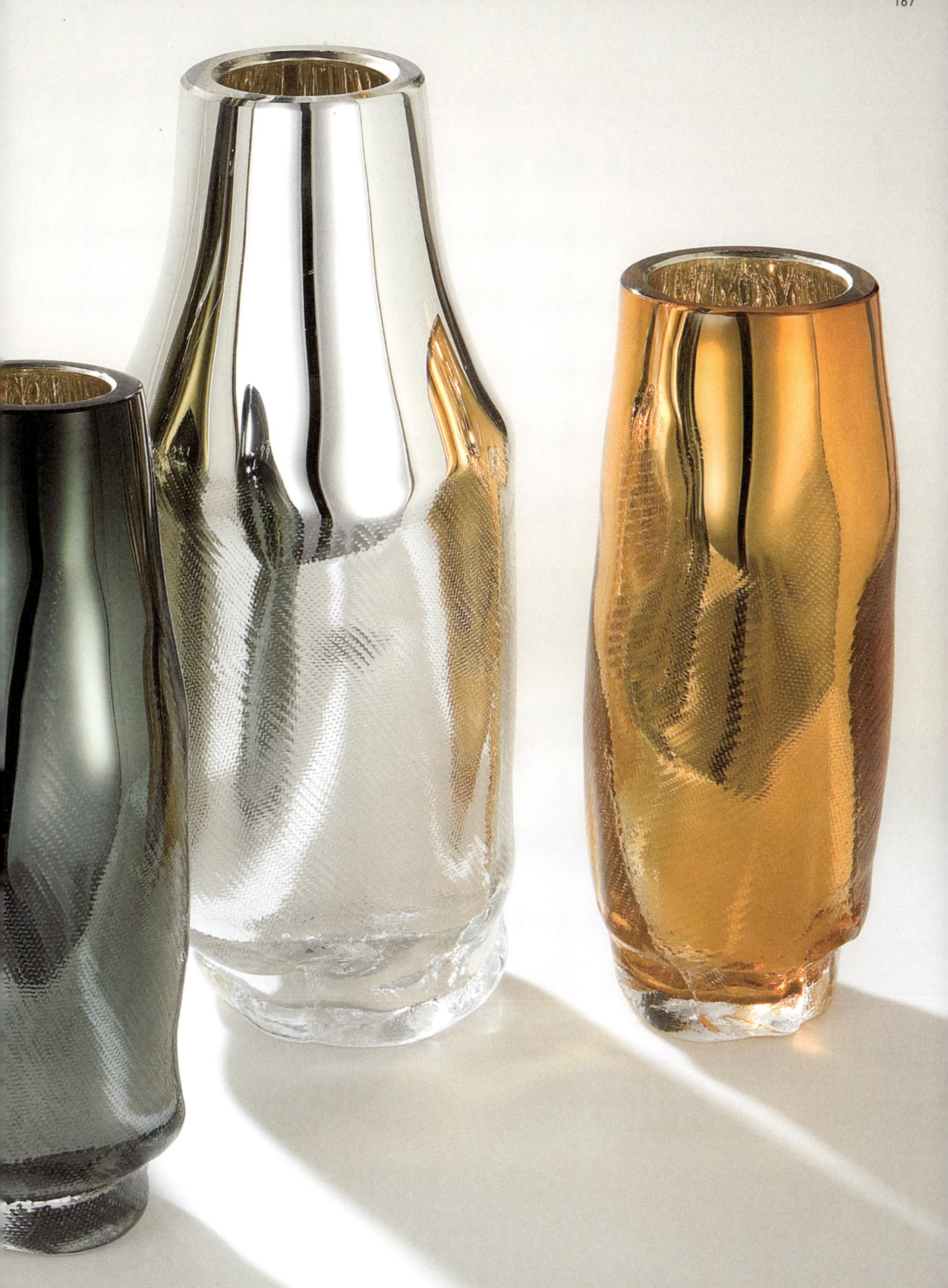

With the process, every vase becomes a different sculpture so that the project is finally a balancing act between a serial method and an unpredictable creative process that leads formally to one-offs in terms of shape and proportions.

Jede Vase erhält durch den Verarbeitungsprozess ihre individuelle skulpturale Form. Das Projekt ist letztendlich ein Balanceakt zwischen Serienanfertigung und einem unberechenbaren kreativen Prozess, der in Bezug auf Form und Proportion zu Unikat-Produkten führt.

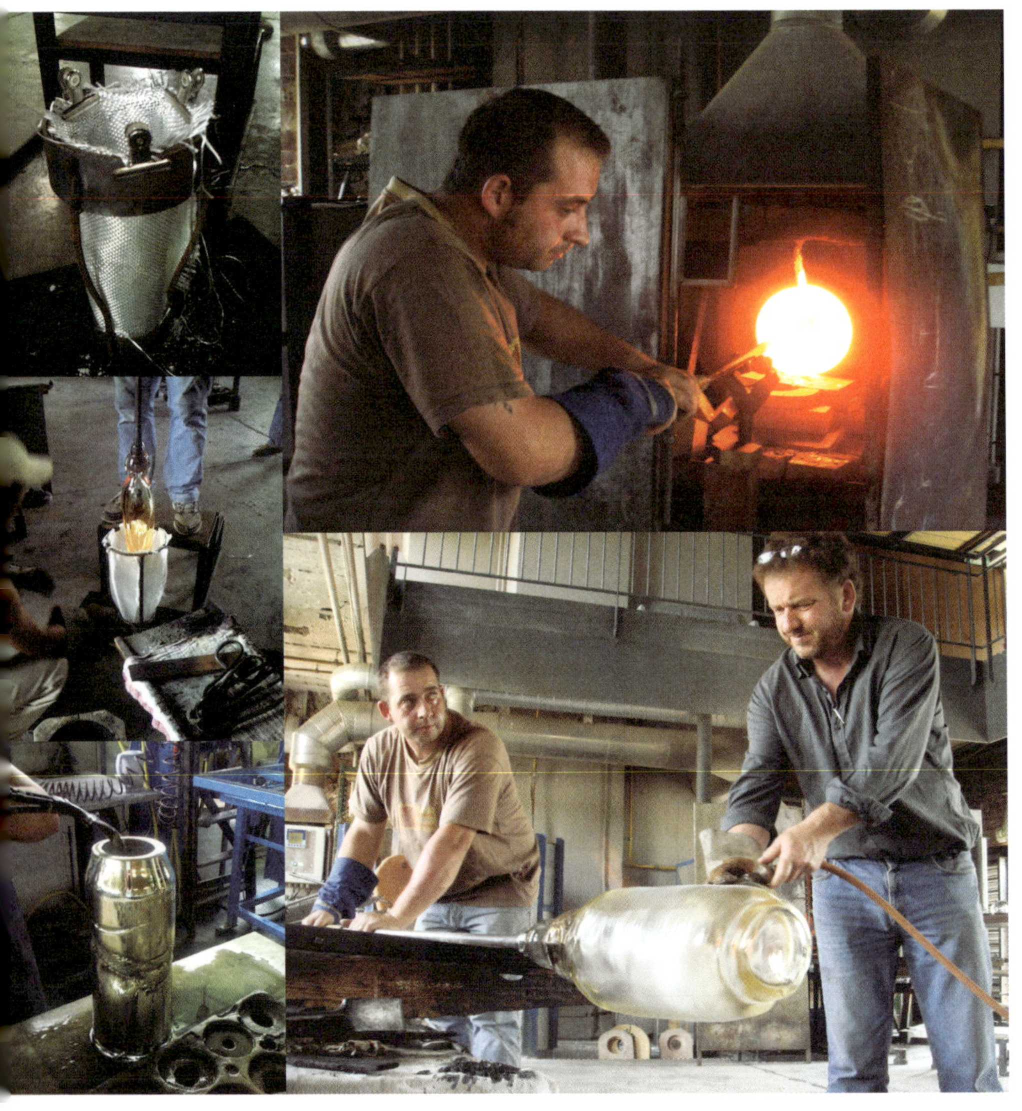

Jean Marc and Bernard of CIAV Meisenthal during the first prototyping

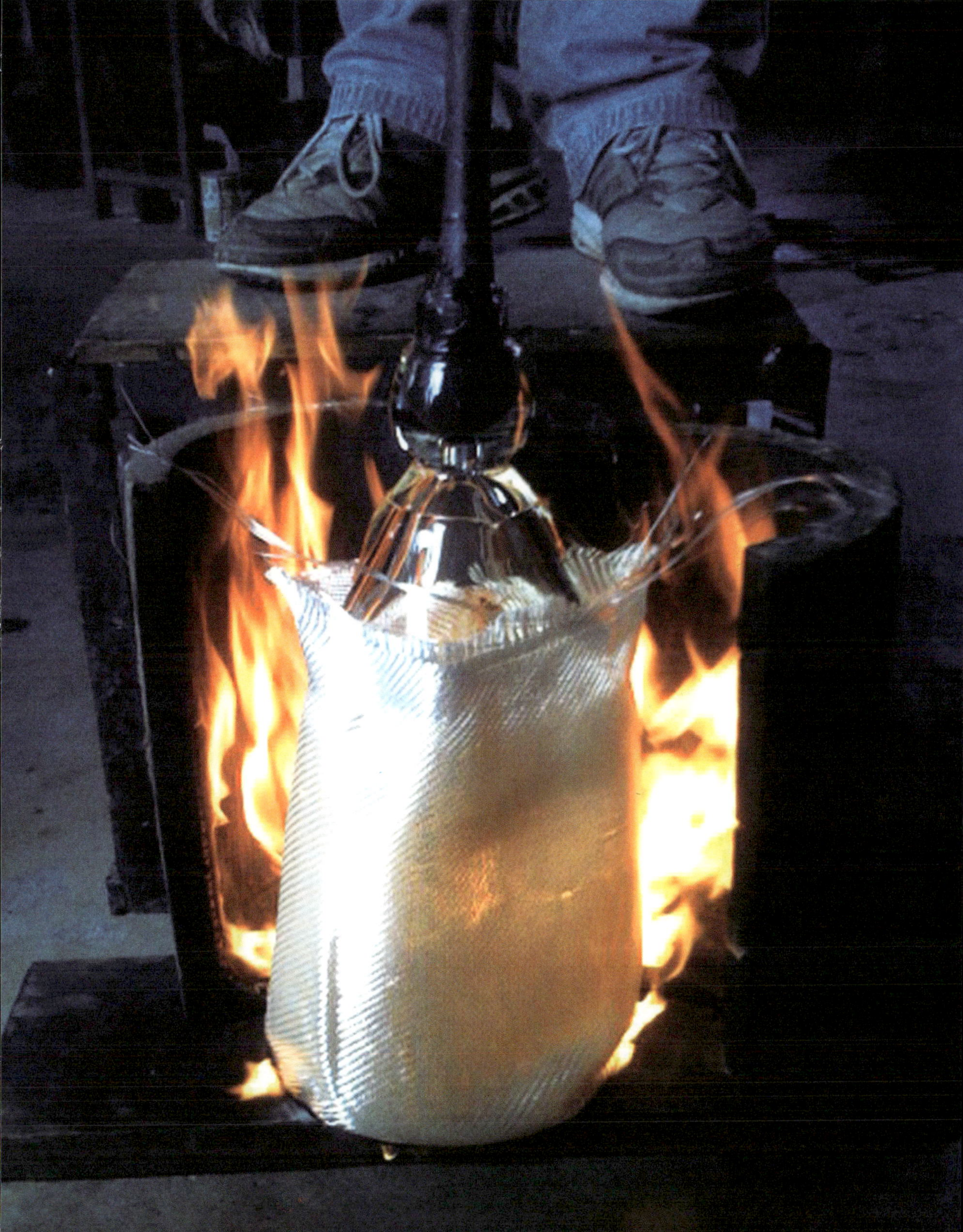

Sizes: 36 and 44 cm height
Material: Hand-blown coloured glass with glass-fibretextil mesh print, inside silver-coated
Colours: Orange, dark green, grey, red

Größen: *36 und 44 cm Höhe*
Material: *Mundgeblasenes farbiges Glas mit Glasfasertextilabdruck, innen versilbert*
Farben: *Orange, dunkelgrün, grau, rot*

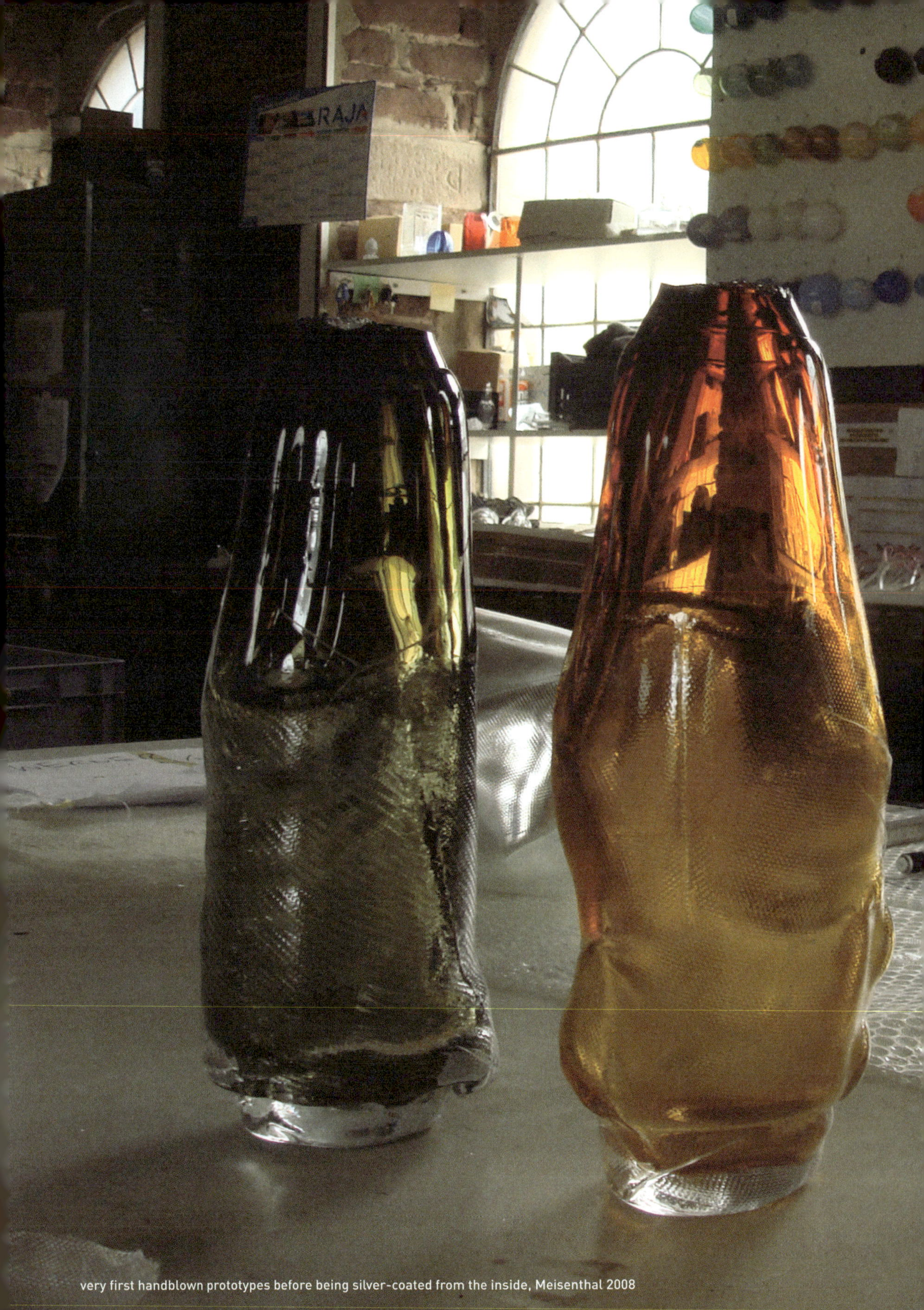

very first handblown prototypes before being silver-coated from the inside, Meisenthal 2008

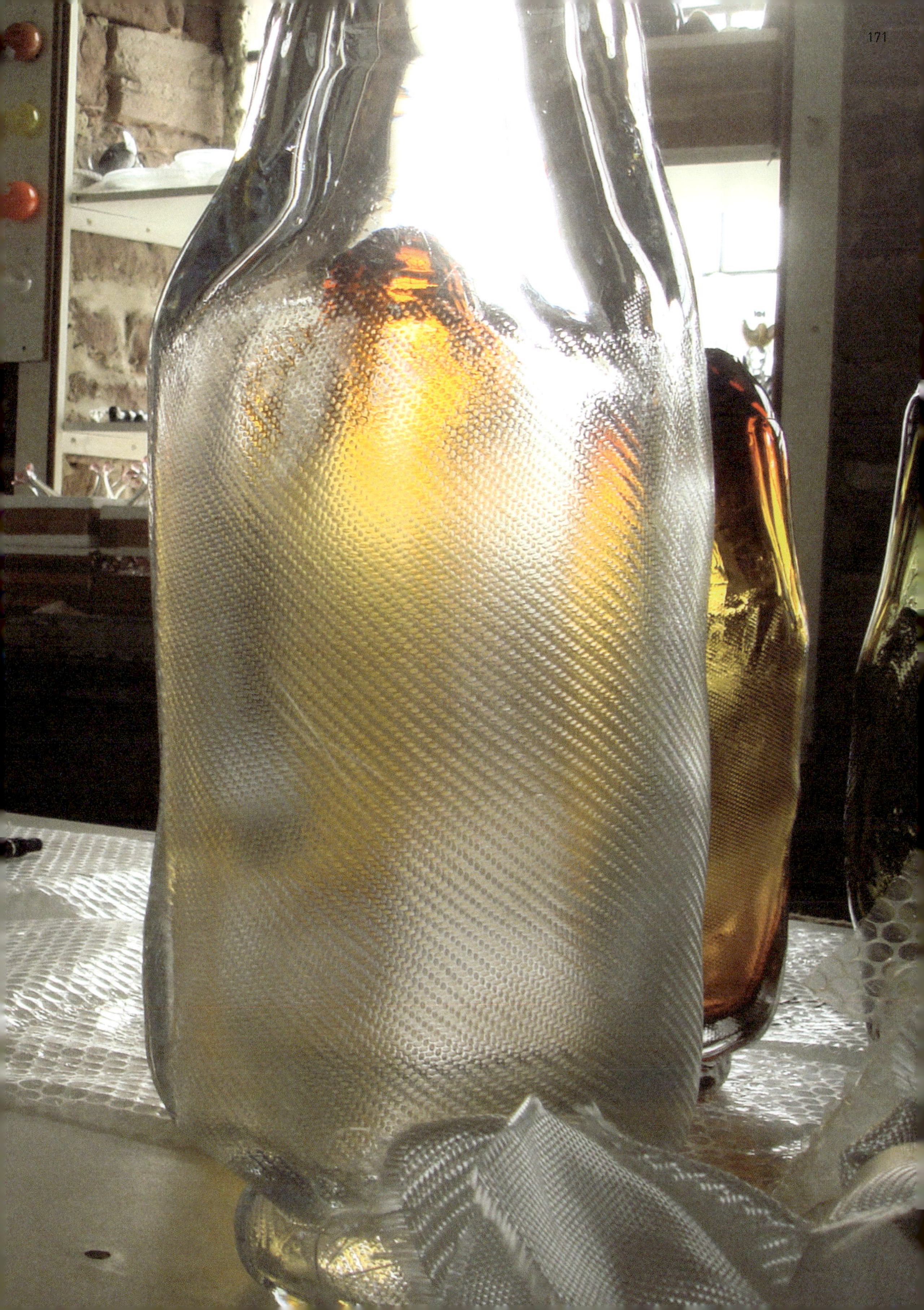

HOSPITALITY DESIGN

holistic design projects

Hospitality design, retail design and brand architecture projects are always challenging for designers. These projects provide an opportunity to incorporate product designs in a larger-scale environment and to design a holistic ambience. The designer is then less involved in mechanical engineering as in actual product design processes but more in the synchronisation of colours, materials, the mix of vintage and actual design and general architectural circumstances. In contrast to product designs, interior projects are rapid processes and are much more dependent on communication and interaction with architects, building engineers, construction managers, craftsmen and technical crews.

Projekte in den Bereichen Hospitality Design, Retail Design und Markenarchitektur stellen für Designer immer Herausforderungen dar. Sie bieten ihnen die Möglichkeit, Produktentwürfe in ein größeres Environment einzubinden und eine holistischere räumliche Umgebung zu gestalten. Der Designer beschäftigt sich dann zwar weniger mit Engineering oder Produktionsverfahren wie bei eigentlichen Produktdesignprojekten, dafür mehr mit der Synchronisierung der Farben und Materialien, der Symbiose von Vintage und aktuellem Design sowie mit architektonischen und baukonstruktiven Fragestellungen. Innenarchitekturprojekte sind im Gegensatz zum Produktdesign extrem schnelle und komplexe Prozesse, bei denen die Kommunikation und Interaktion mit Architekten, Bauingenieuren, Bauleitern, Handwerkern und Technikern im Vordergrund stehen.

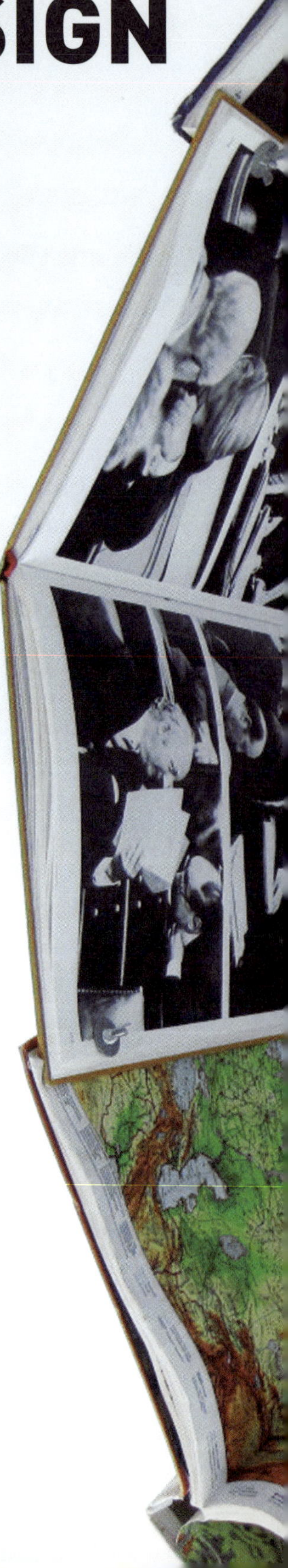

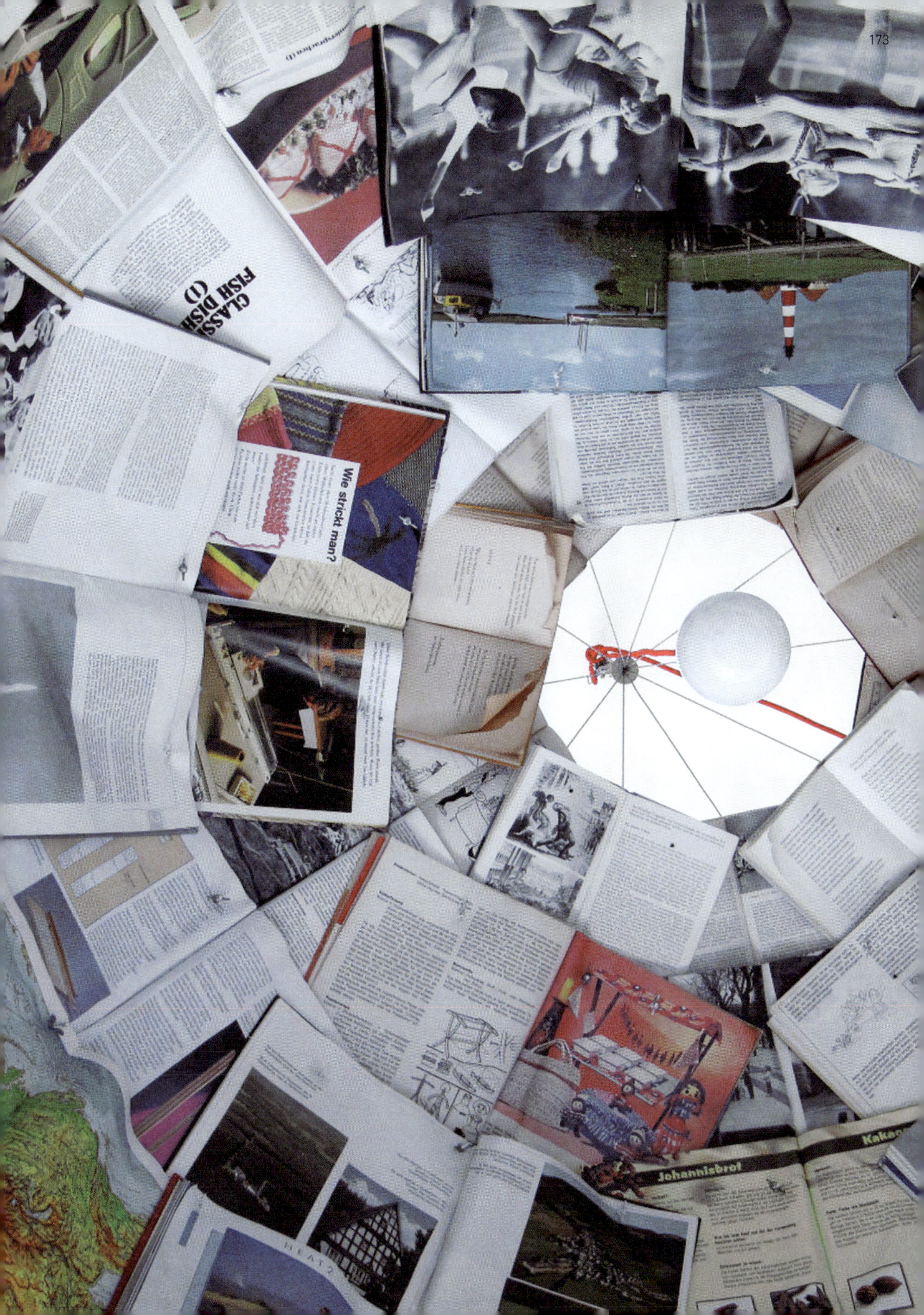
CLASSIC FISH DISH (1)
Wie strickt man?
Johannisbrot
Kakao

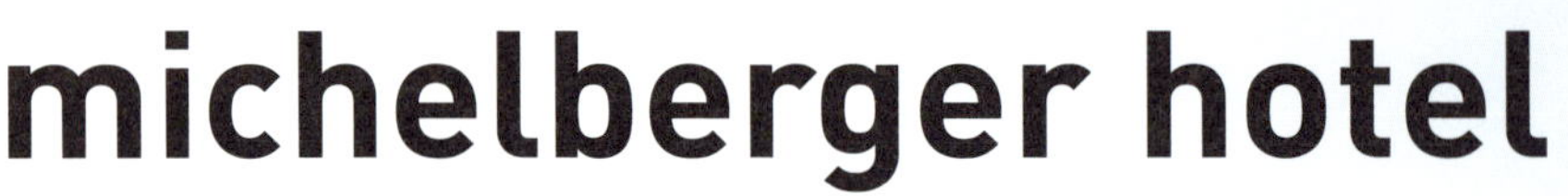

michelberger hotel

concept of a new hotel typology, berlin 2009

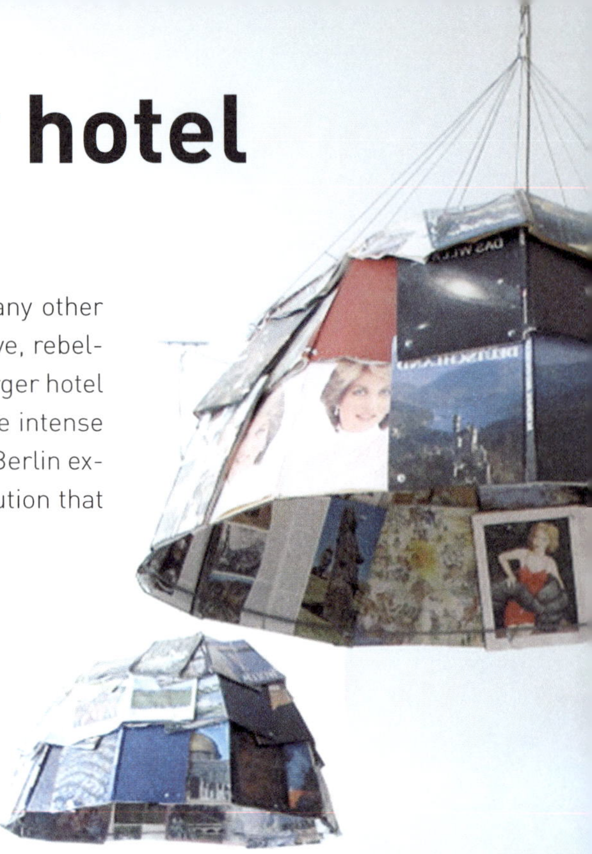

The former east part of Berlin is still different to any other tourist destination in Europe: it is unrefined, creative, rebellious and constantly recreating itself. The michelberger hotel was designed to revel in Berlin's roughness and the intense creative flow. The michelberger tries to extend the Berlin experience within the hotel, in a casual, low-cost solution that features professional service and management.

Das frühere Ostberlin unterscheidet sich immer noch von anderen bekannten touristischen Destinationen Europas. Es ist rau, kreativ, rebellisch und erfindet sich immer wieder neu. Das Michelberger Hotel machte es sich zum Konzept, diese raue Atmosphäre und den kreativen Spirit Berlins zu betonen. Im Michelberger wird diese Stimmung als kompakter Mikrokosmos innerhalb eines Hotels verdichtet – auf lässige Art, als kostengünstige Lösung, die dennoch professionellen Service bietet.

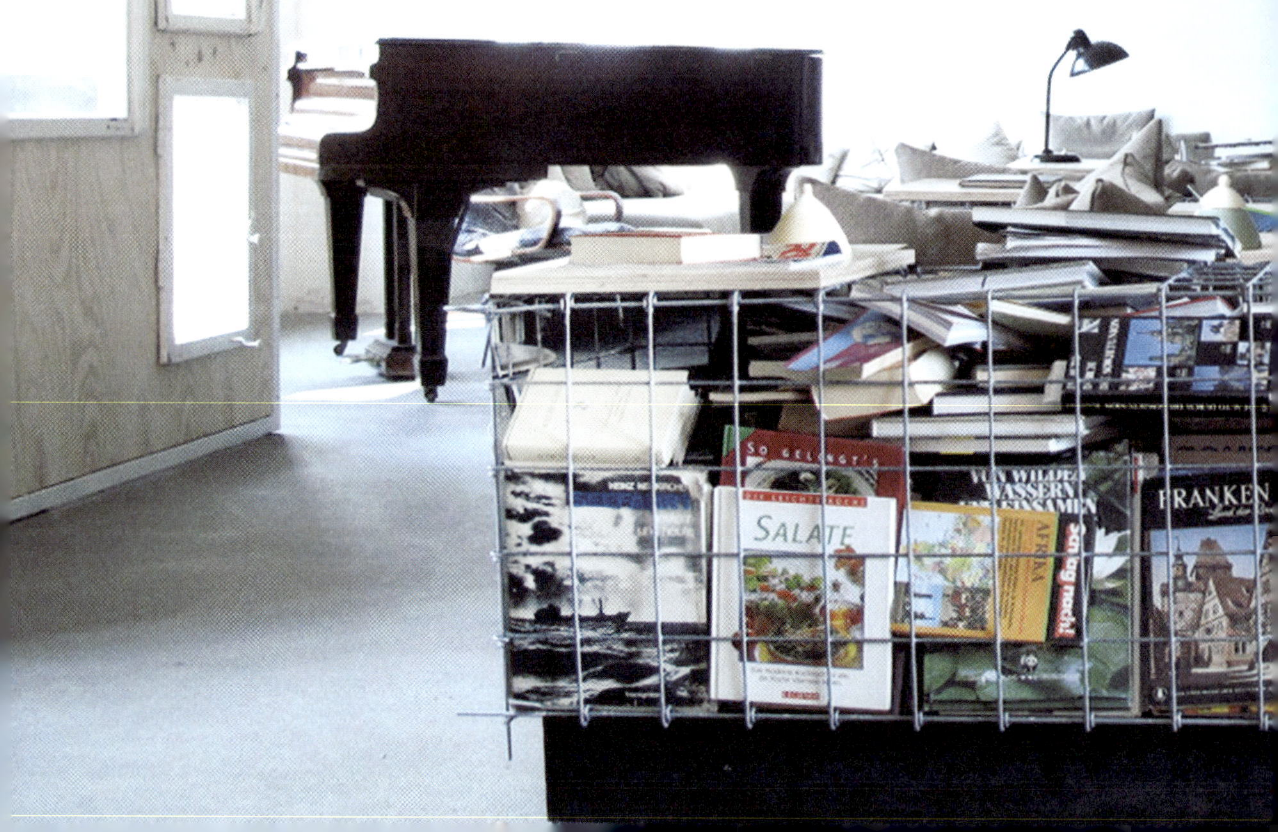

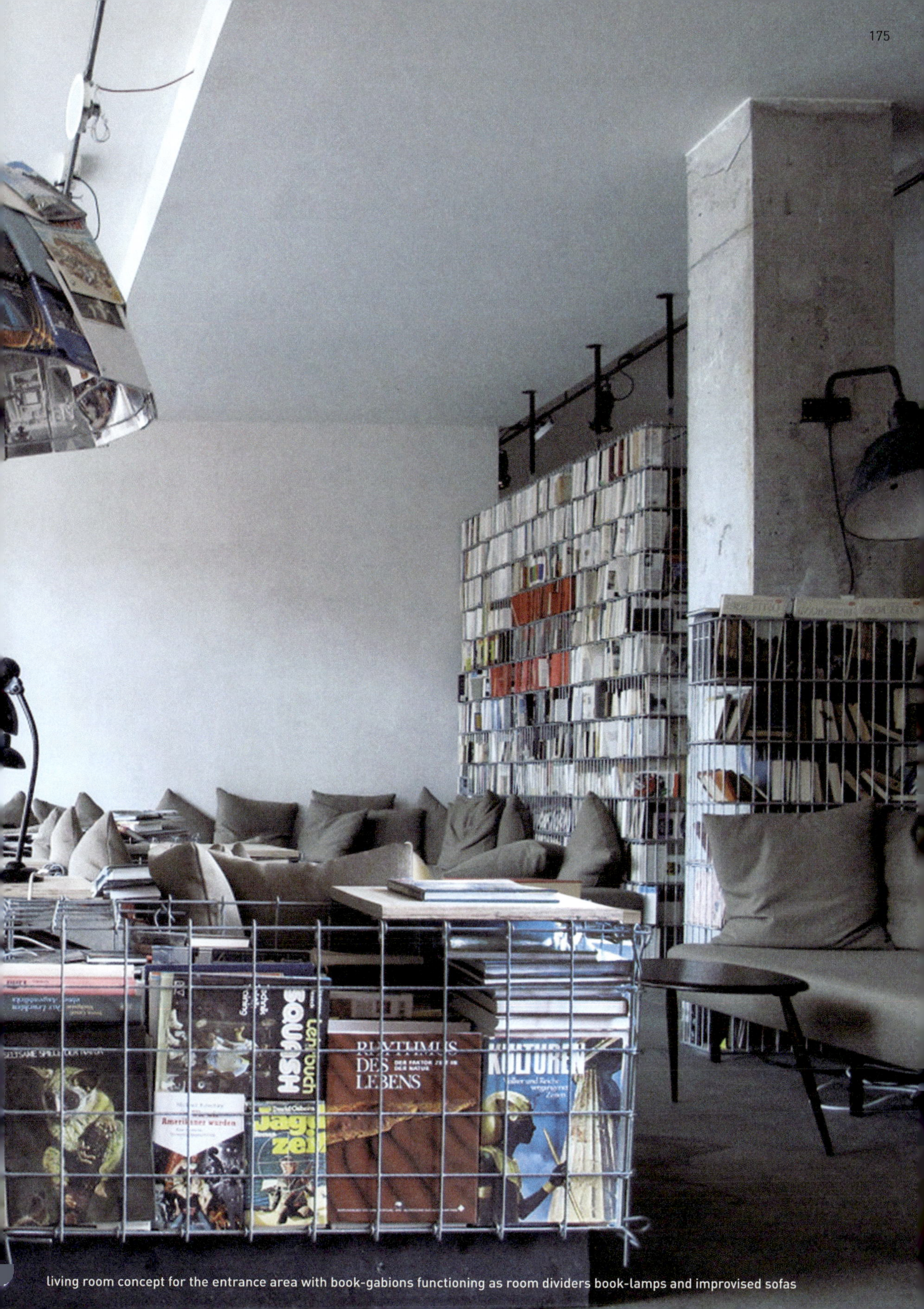

living room concept for the entrance area with book-gabions functioning as room dividers book-lamps and improvised sofas

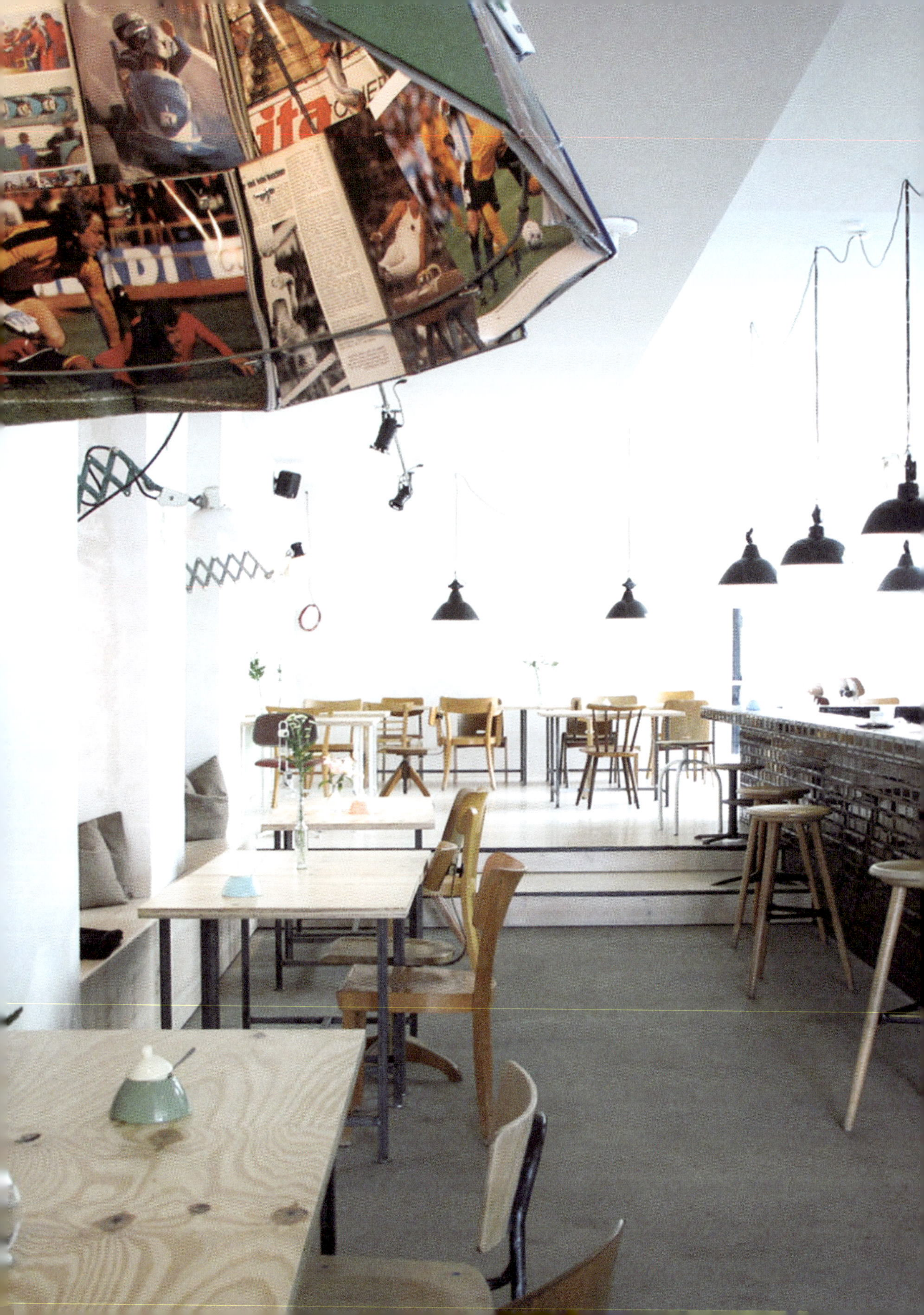

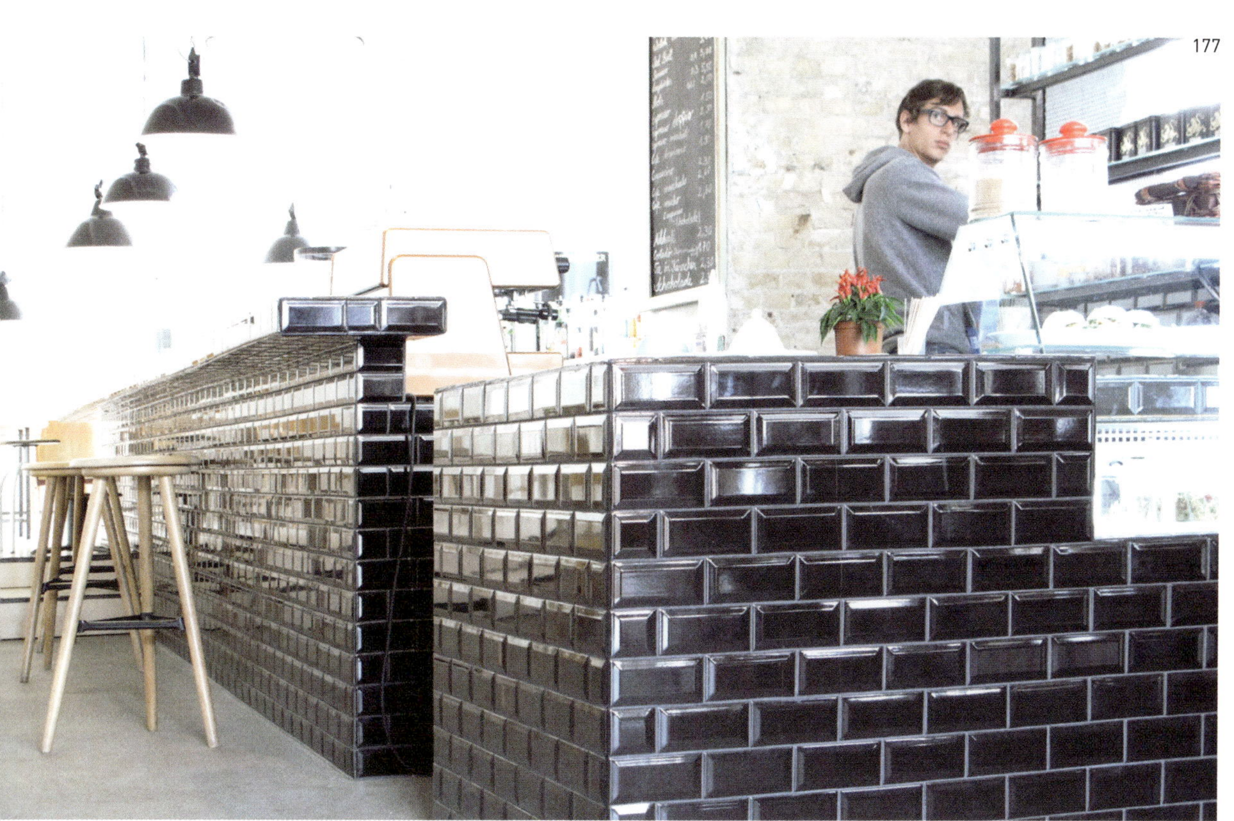

tiled bar with fleamarket chairs and vintage factory lamps

Werner Aisslinger's Berlin-based studio has designed this new hotel typology with a patchwork collage style. A place where one feels as if one is staying at a friend's house and that shows little interest in stereotypical ideas of hotel luxury. For Tom Michelberger, the 31-year-old organiser and owner, the aisslinger design team has created a cosmopolitan haunt, where they themselves would love to stay. The michelberger hotel is housed in a converted factory building displaying a brick facade, high ceilings, large windows and a courtyard that acts as the social hub of the hotel.

Werner Aisslingers Berliner Designstudio hat diesen neuen Hoteltypus in einem Patchwork-Collage-Stil entworfen. Entstanden ist ein Ort, der dem Gast das Gefühl gibt, im Haus von Freunden zu sein, und der kein großes Interesse an klischeehaften Ideen von Luxus zeigt. Das Aisslinger Designteam entwickelte für Tom Michelberger, den 31-jährigen Organisator und Eigentümer, einen weltoffenen, aber dennoch bodenständigen Ort, an dem sich nicht nur Gäste, sondern auch die Macher selbst gerne aufhalten würden. Architektonisch befindet sich das Michelberger in einem umgebauten Fabrikgebäude mit Ziegelsteinfassade, hohen Decken, großen Fenstern und einem Innenhof, der als sozialer Dreh- und Angelpunkt des Hotels dient.

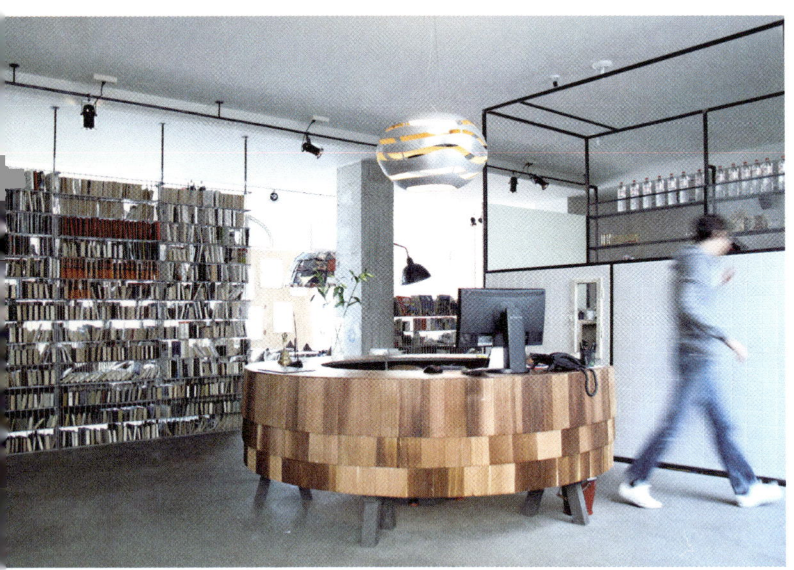

The hotel's public rooms heighten the person-to-person experience. From the façade with a Hollywood-style marquee sign, guests enter a short corridor filled with oversized light bulbs, letting them know they're entering a special place. The courtyard, bar and restaurant areas flow into one another. Instead of building an imposing reception desk, studio aisslinger team created an inviting circular welcome island, placed in the centre of the bar and mingle zone. A relaxed and laid-back refuge from the bustling city during the day evolves into a lively night bar, featuring a stage for musical or other performances – a setting that will attract local scene-makers and tourists alike.

Die Public Areas des Hotels verstärken das direkte, persönliche Hotelerlebnis. Vom Eingang mit dem Vordach im Stil à la Hollywood gelangt der Gast in einen kurzen Gang, der mit überdimensional großen Glühbirnen versehen ist, den Weg zum Hof beschreibt und gleichzeitig lichtdramaturgisch zum Hoteleingang leitet. Der Innenhof, die Bar und das Restaurant gehen ineinander über. Anstatt einer imposanten Hotelrezeption entwarf das studio aisslinger eine einladende, runde Willkommensinsel, in der Mitte der Bar positioniert. Während das Hotel tagsüber ein entspannter und lockerer Rückzugsort von der geschäftigen urbanen Umgebung ist, verwandelt es sich abends in eine lebendige Bar mit einer Bühne für Konzerte oder andere Veranstaltungen – ein Rahmen, der sowohl heimische Szenemacher als auch Touristen anlockt.

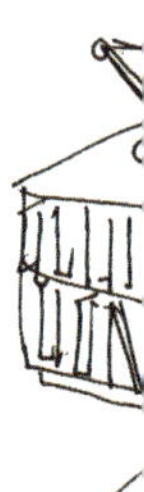

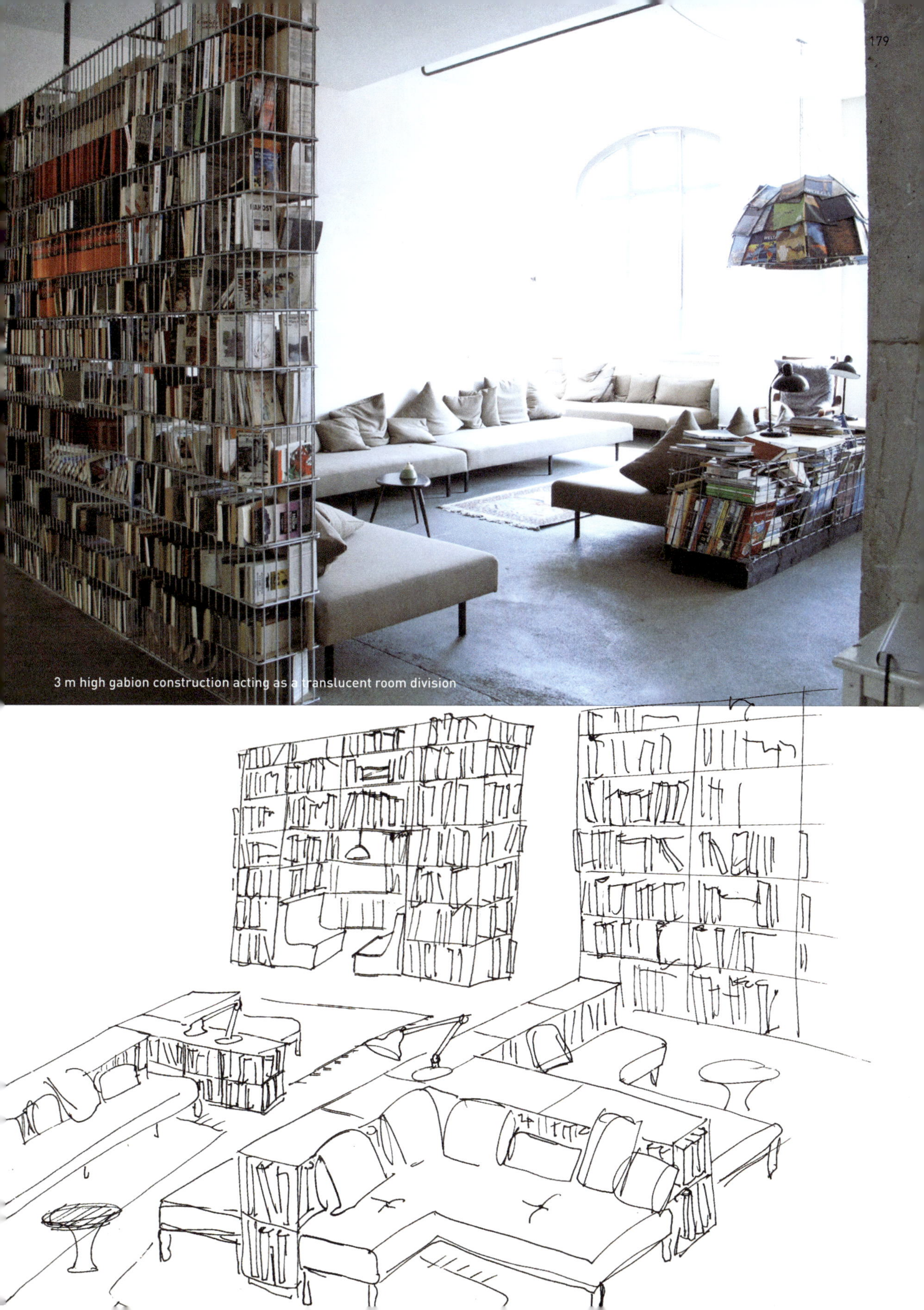

3 m high gabion construction acting as a translucent room division

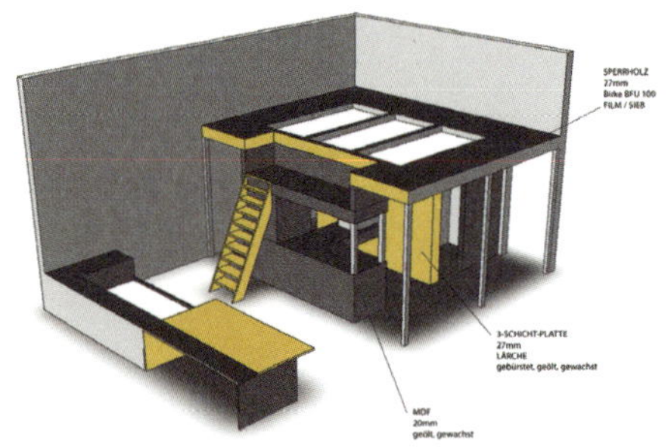

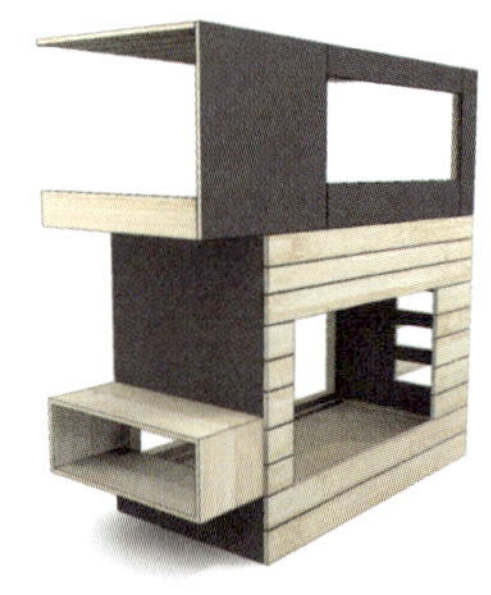

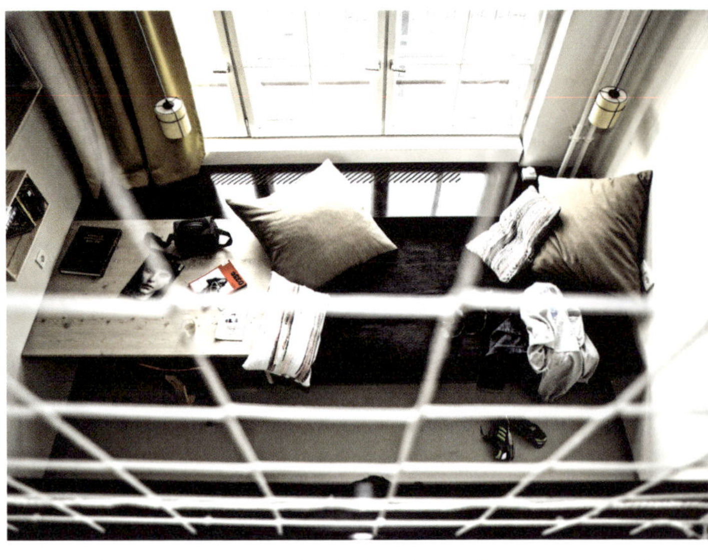

computer simulations of the upper bed levels and group-"band"rooms with 9 beds

The rooms are based on a totally new approach to hotel rooms: the astonishing two level room concept offers a living-area basement and a second level bedroom-platform. The result of this design-concept is a funky, communally organized social space that blends the best elements of hostel and hotel. Five different room categories offer a range of different layouts. The rooms display a high level of space efficiency and lots of vertical drama and airiness – a feat allowed by the placing of loft bed areas above the bathrooms. Most rooms fall into the category of "33m³" and "55m³" rooms for singles, couples and threesomes but other options including "The Big One" allow groups of four or even more to room together. The core rooms feature king-sized beds on brushed larch-wood platforms, glass-walled bathrooms, free WIFI access, and flat-screen. All rooms sport soothing grey tones and sunflower-yellow curtains, as well as custom-made wallpaper.

Der Ansatz bei den Hotelzimmern ist grundlegend neu: Das Raumkonzept der mit zwei Ebenen ausgestatteten Zimmer bietet auf der unteren Ebene einen unkonventionellen Wohnbereich und auf der zweiten Ebene ein Podest mit Schlafbereich. Zusammen ergibt das eine lässige Atmosphäre, die die besten Elemente eines Hostels und Hotels miteinander verbindet. Fünf unterschiedliche Zimmerkategorien bieten eine Reihe von erstaunlichen Grundrissen. Alle zeichnen sich durch ein hohes Maß an effizienter Raumausnutzung, vertikale 2-Ebenennutzung und große Luftigkeit aus – ein Kunststück, das durch die Positionierung der Schlafbereiche über den Badzellen gelungen ist. Die meisten Zimmer fallen unter die Kategorie „33m³"und „55m³" Zimmer für ein, zwei oder drei Personen. Außerdem gibt es „The Big One", in dem Gruppen von vier und mehr Personen untergebracht werden können. Die Hauptzimmer verfügen über King-Size-Betten auf Podesten aus gebürstetem Lärchenholz, gläserne Badezimmer, freien WIFI-Zugang und einen Flachbildschirm. Alle Zimmer sind in beruhigenden Grautönen gehalten, haben sonnenblumengelbe Vorhänge und individuell gefertigte Tapeten.

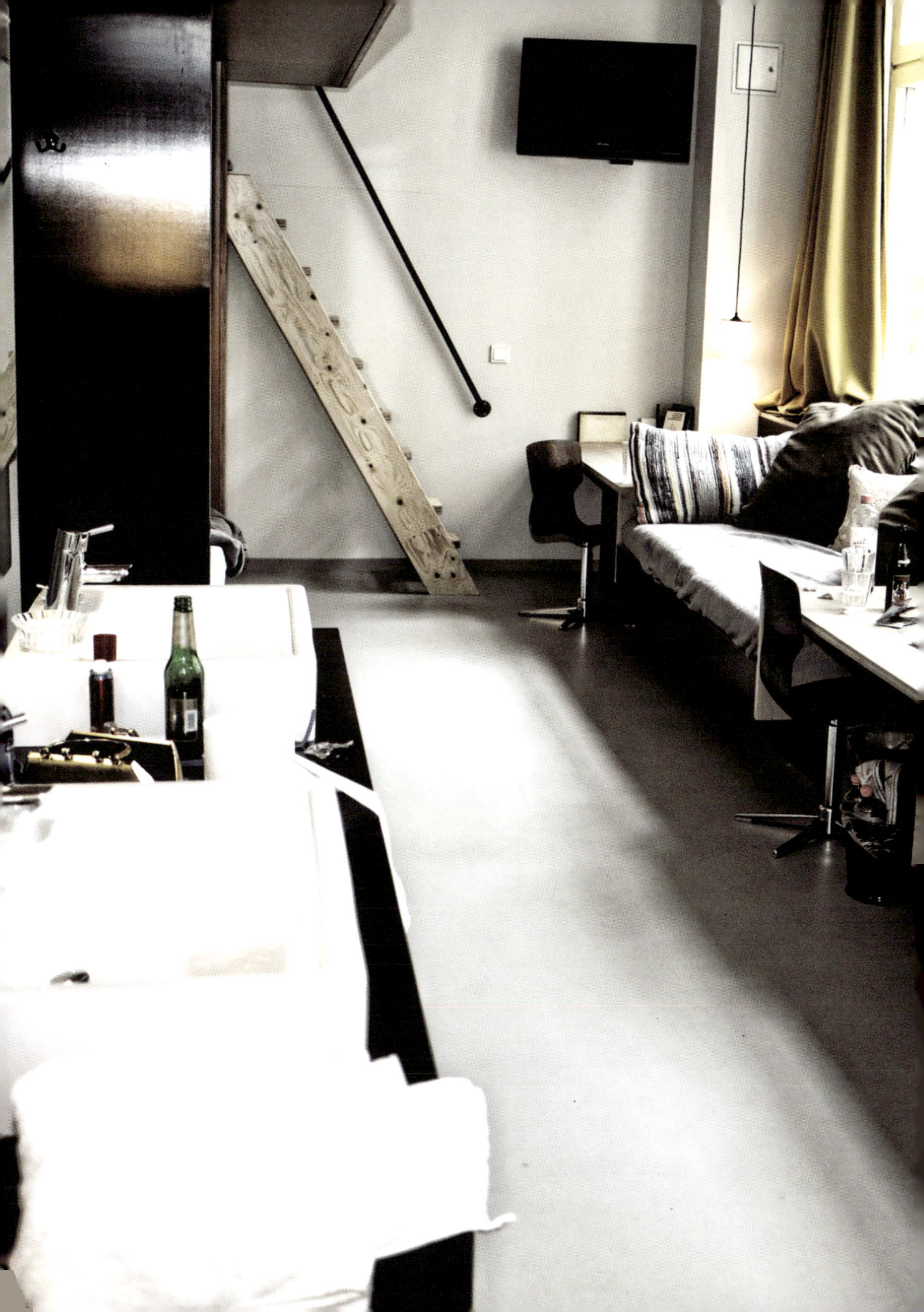

SHOWCASES

1990 - 2010

1990

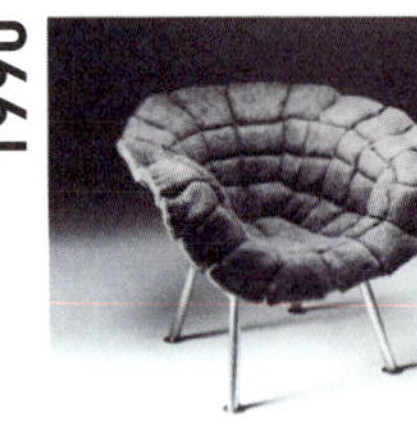

Felt Lounge Chair
edition

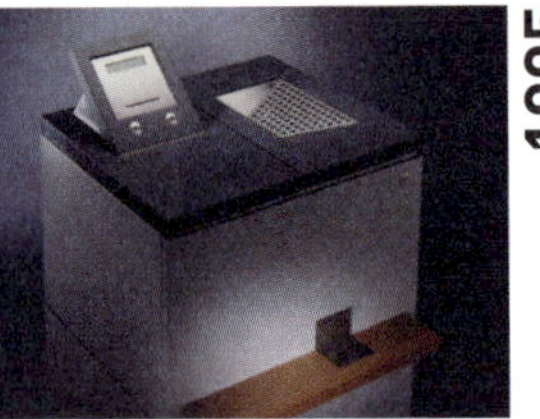

NGZ Cash Automation
Terminal

1995

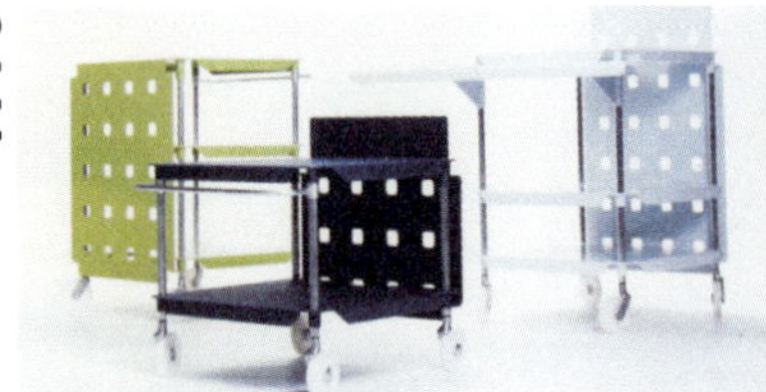

Trolley System
edition

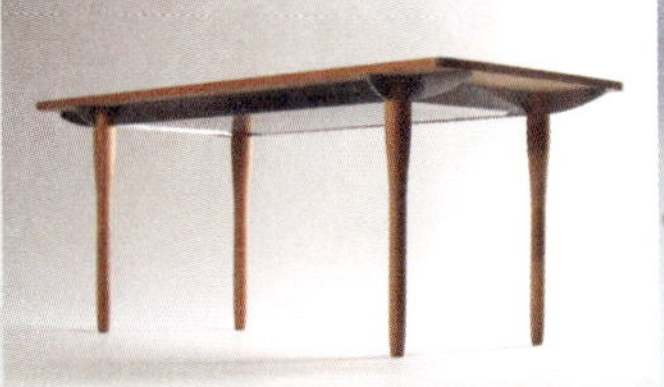

Extension Table
prototype, Porro

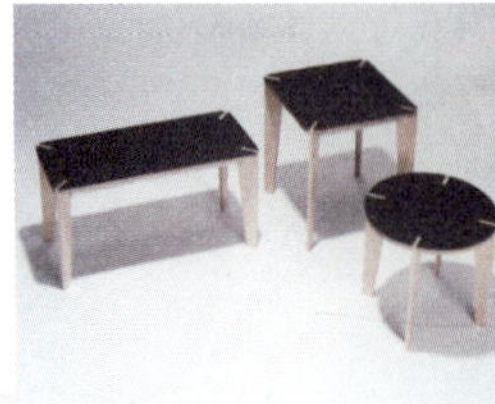

Low Table
edition

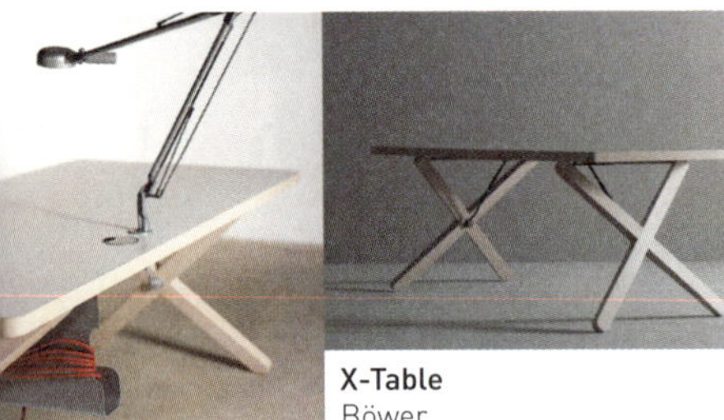

X-Table
Böwer

1999

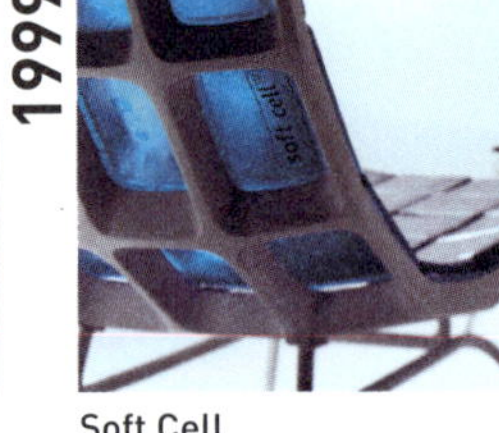

Soft Cell
gel furniture edition

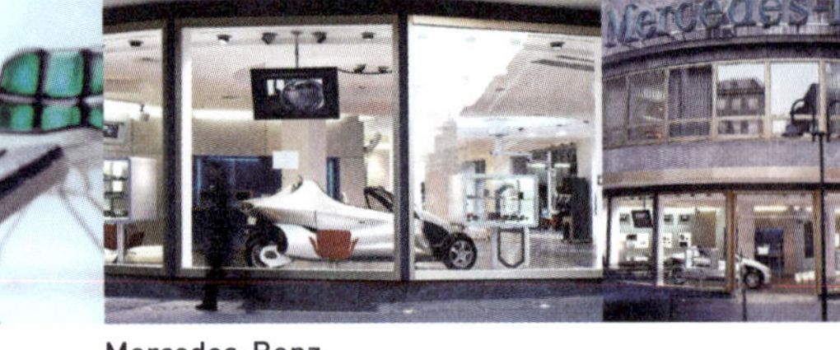

Mercedes-Benz
concept store, Frankfurt

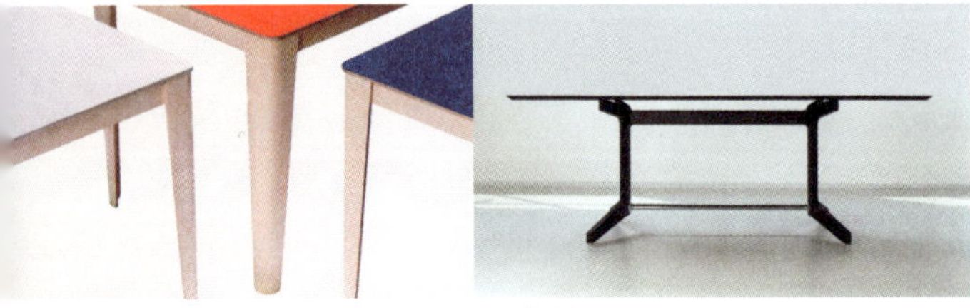

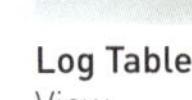

Linn Table
Jonas & Jonas

Log Table
View

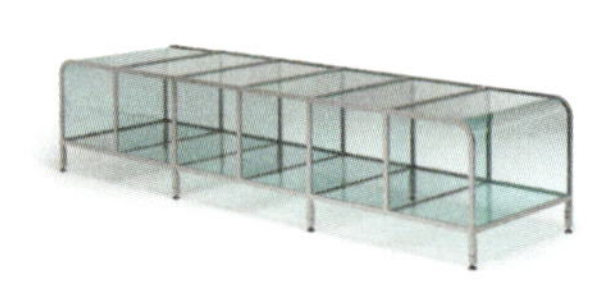

Cell System
Zeritalia

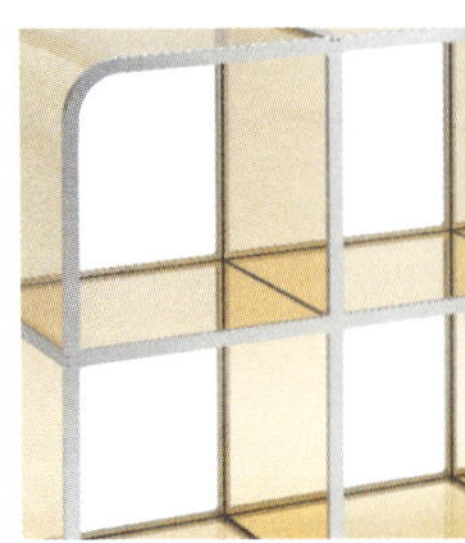

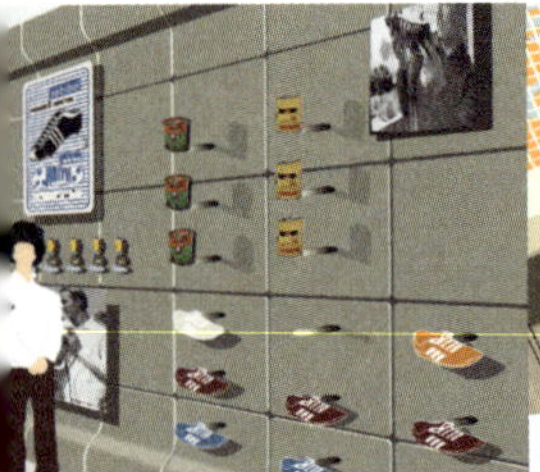

Adidas Originals Store
concept, Adidas

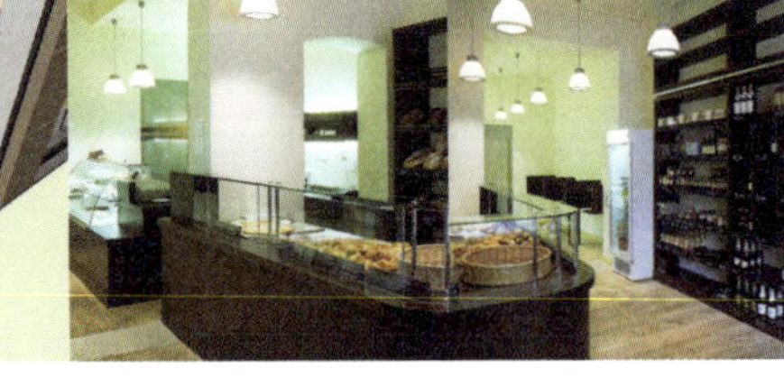

Coffeeshop
Delices Normand, Berlin

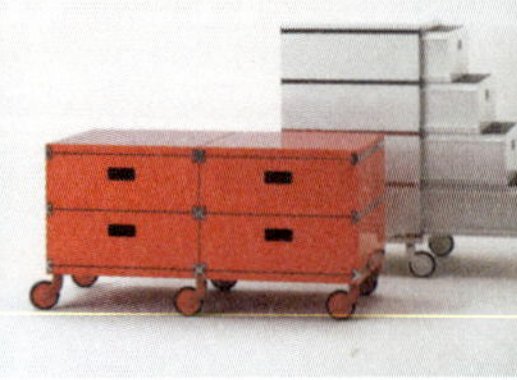

Plus Unit
Magis

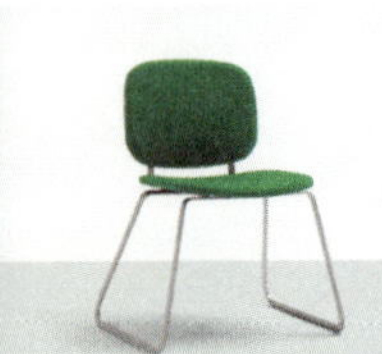

Map Chair
Cappellini

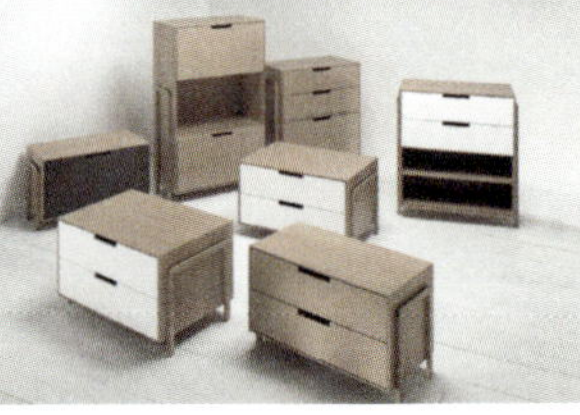

Box Unit
Ideal Form Team

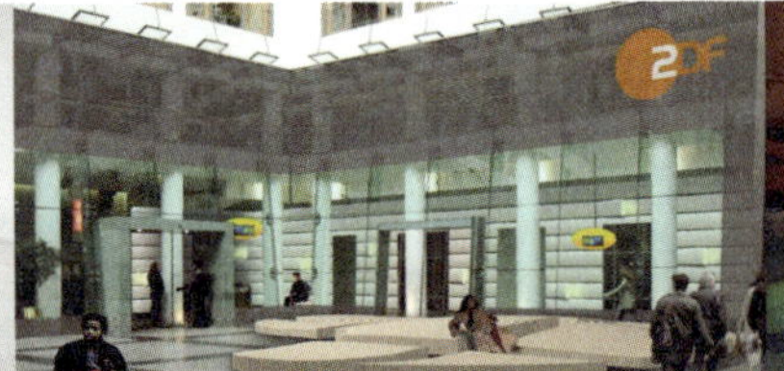

ZDF Hauptstadtstudio Berlin
Redesign winner competition

X-type Lounge
Jaguar

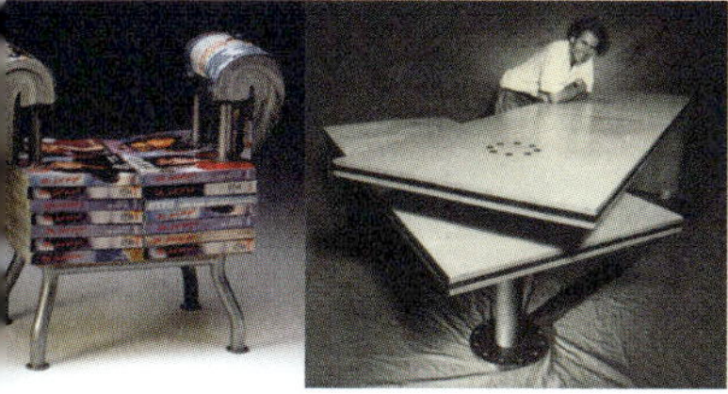

Otto Chair
edition

Bramigk Design Store
radial counter

1991

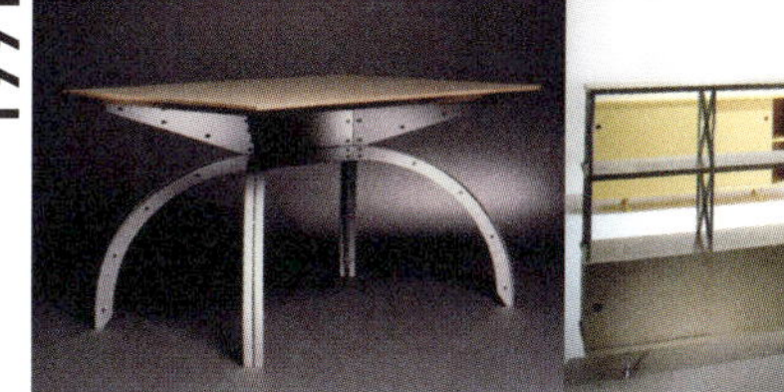

Steel Table
prototype

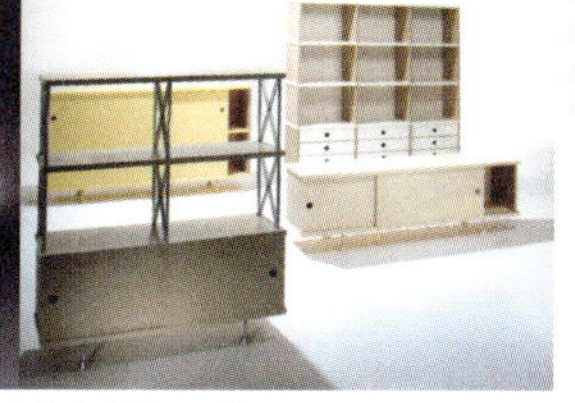

Global Board System
edition

1994

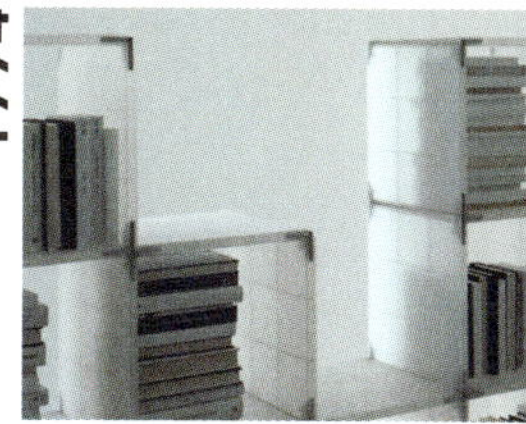

Endless Shelf
Porro

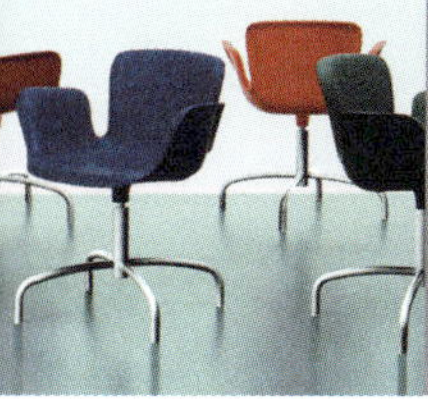

Juli Chair
Cappellini

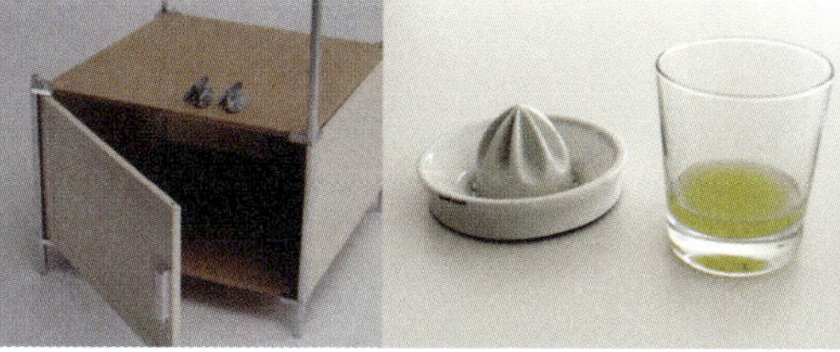

Modular Wardrobe System
edition

Lemon Squeezer
Smart China edition

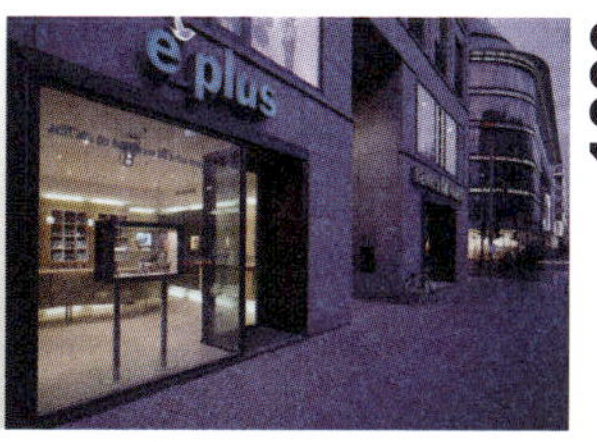

E-Plus Shopconcept
E-plus

1998

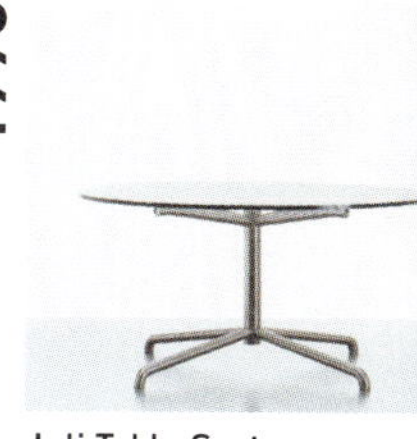

Juli Table System
Cappellini

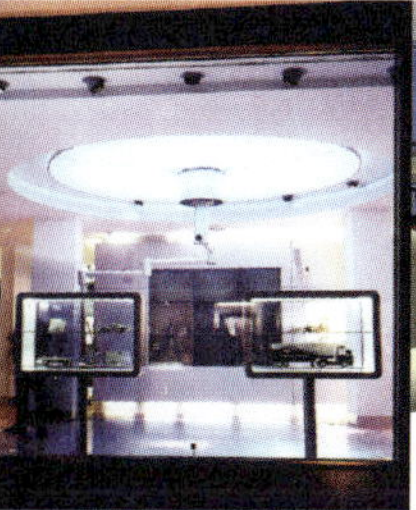

Expo 2000 Exhibition
concept, Bertelsmann

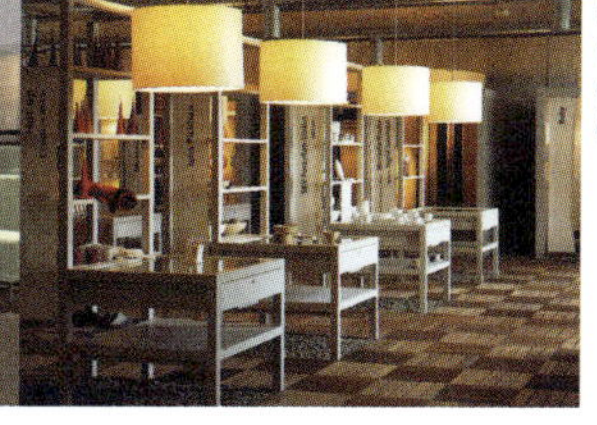

Stilwerk Designplatform
Stilwerk Berlin

2000

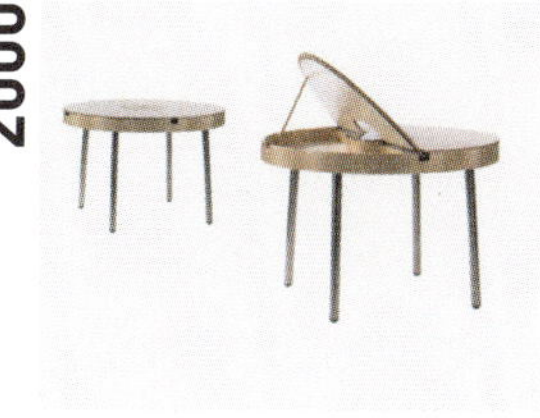

Lid Table
Jonas & Jonas

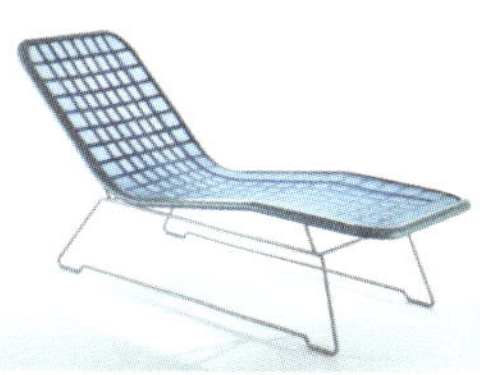

Soft Chaise
Zanotta

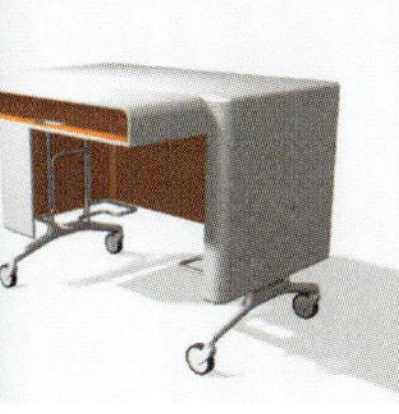

Trolley
concept, Zanotta

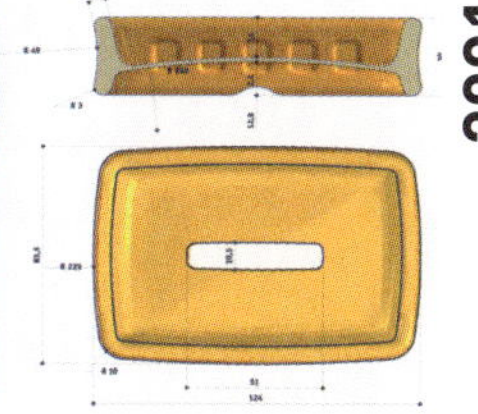

Safety Glasses
Global Vision / Uvex

Gel Objects
concept, Authentics

2001

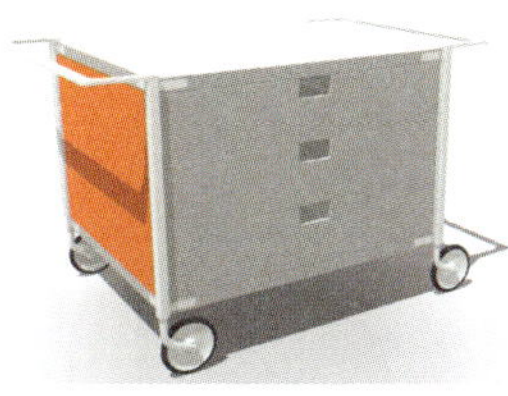

Flo System
Cappellini

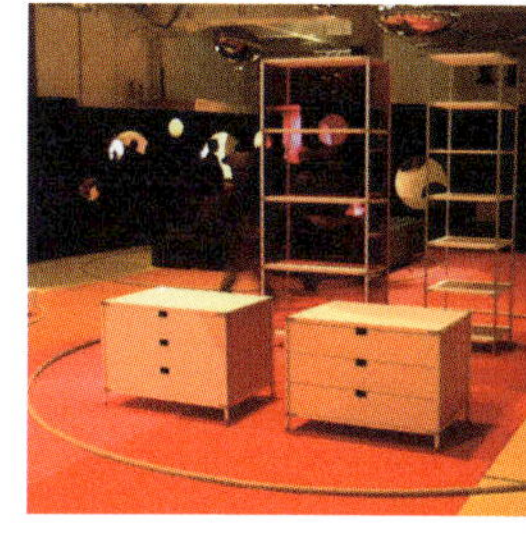

Gel Chair
Cappellini

2002

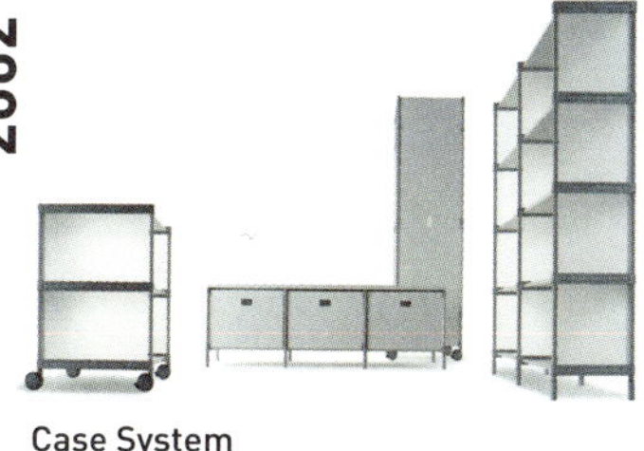

Case System
Interlübke

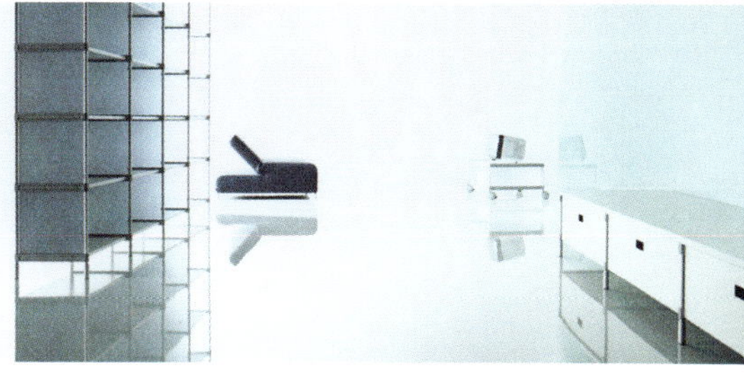

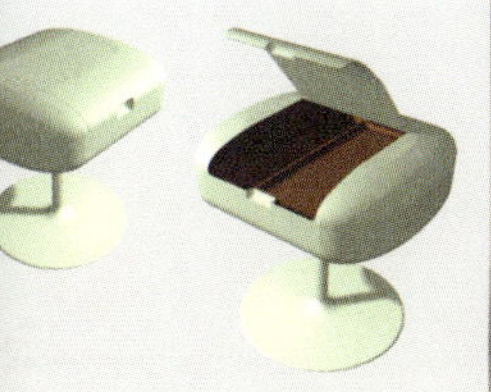

Humidor
concept, Cappellini

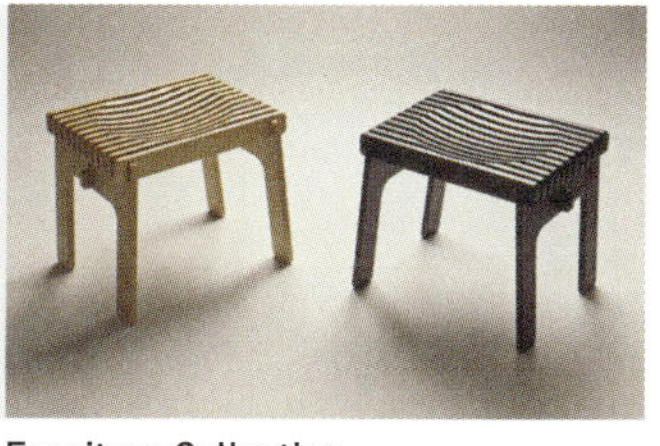

Furniture Collection
Purple South, New Zealand

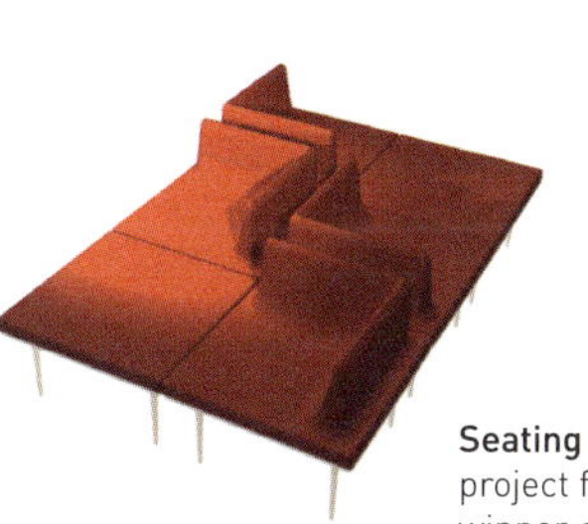

Seating Landscape
project for Wallraf-Richartz-Museum, Cologne
winner competition

2003

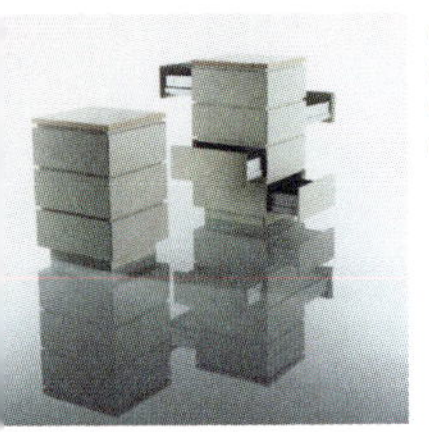

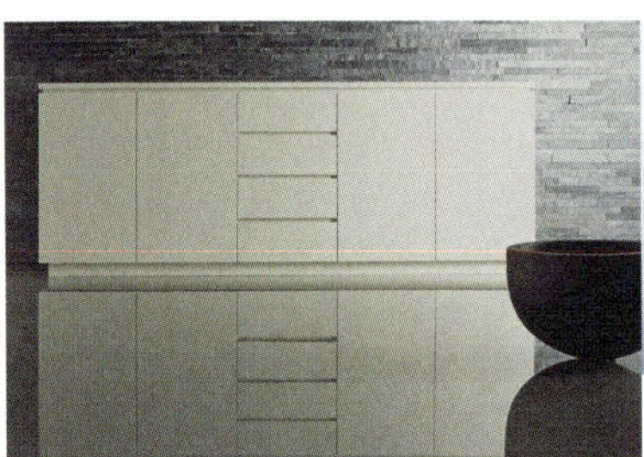

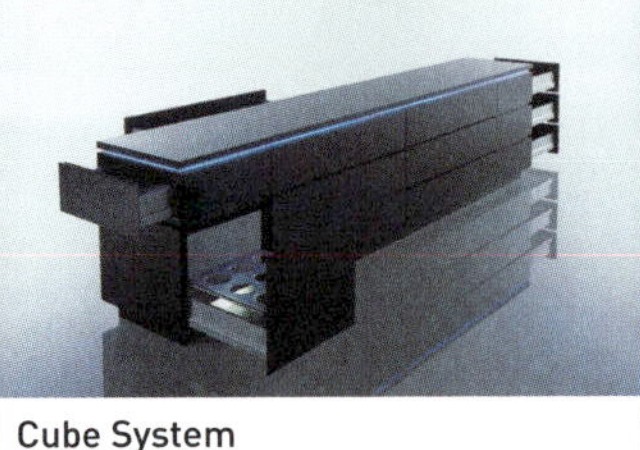

Cube System
Interlübke

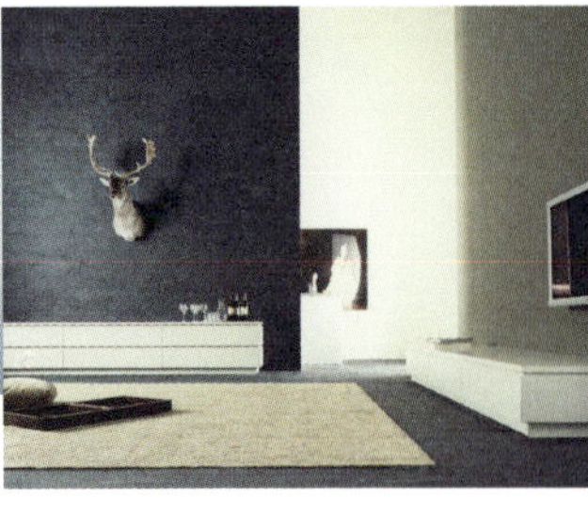

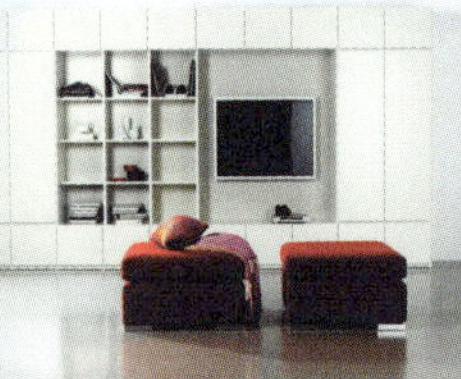

Frame System
Interlübke

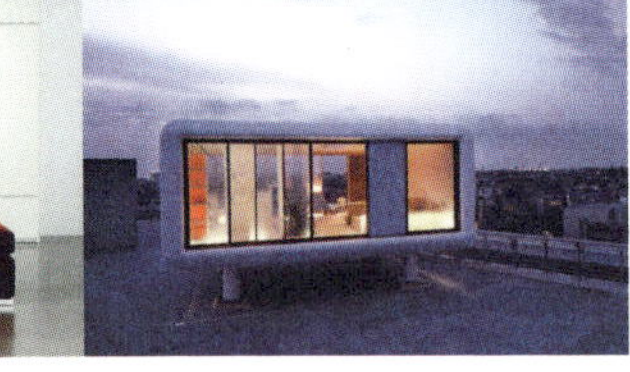

Loftcube

2004

EU+ Exhibition
Designmai, Berlin

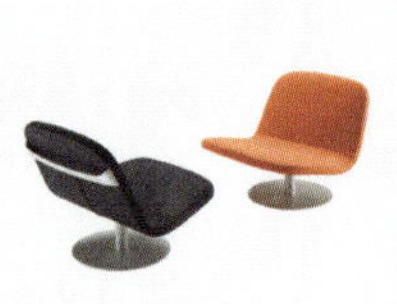

Flori Lounge Chair
Zanotta

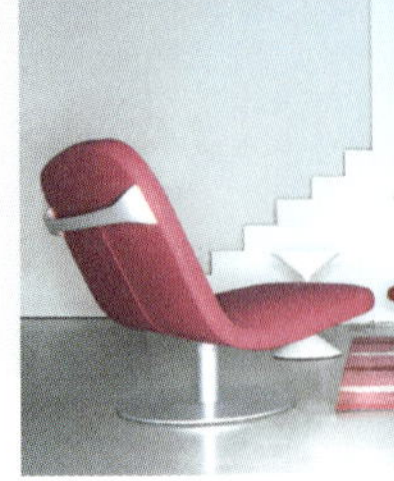

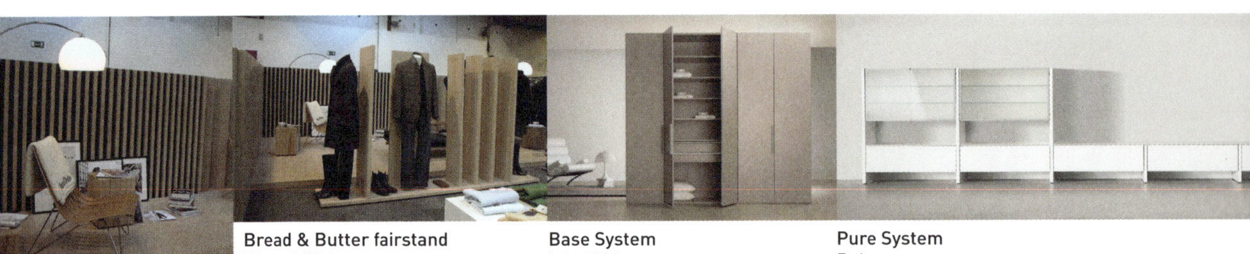

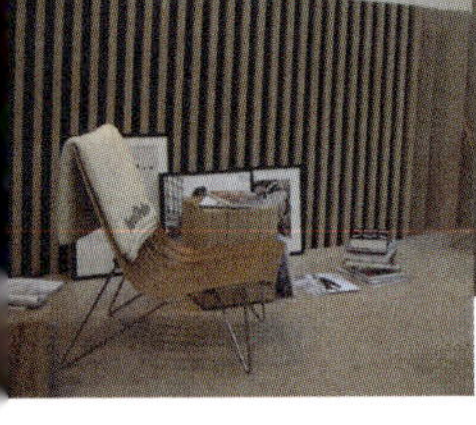

Bread & Butter fairstand
Marc O´Polo

Base System
Interlübke

Pure System
Behr

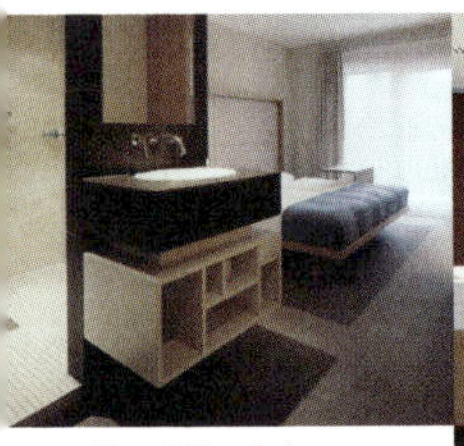

Hotel Daniel
Weitzer Group, Graz

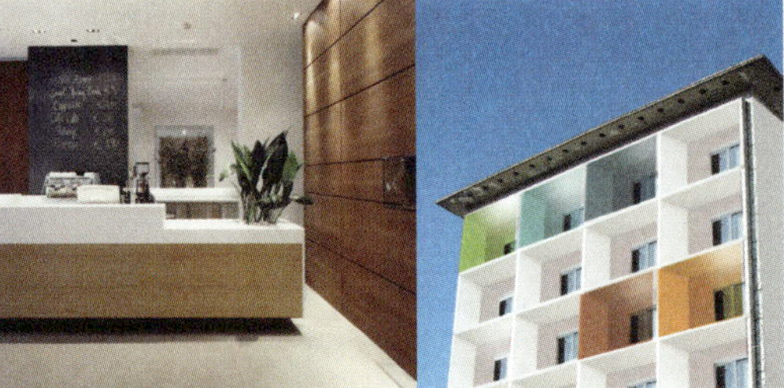

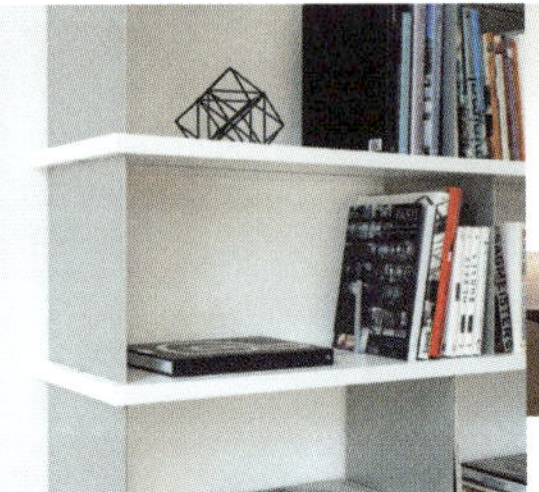

Gliss
Piure

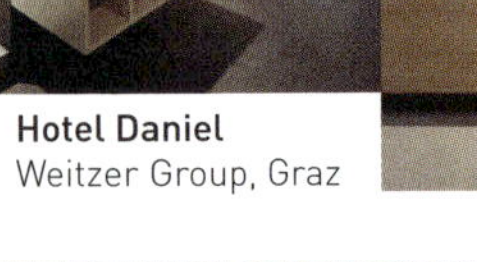

Alape Brand Island
Alape

Knit Chair
edition

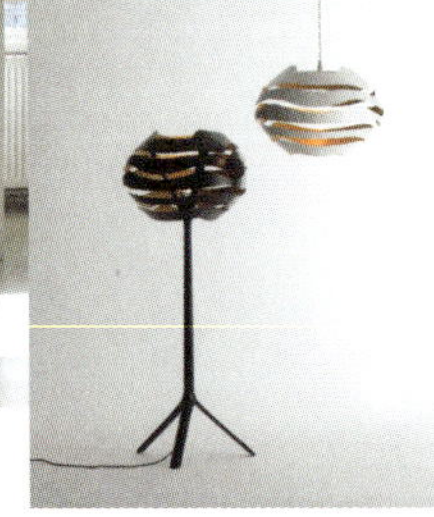

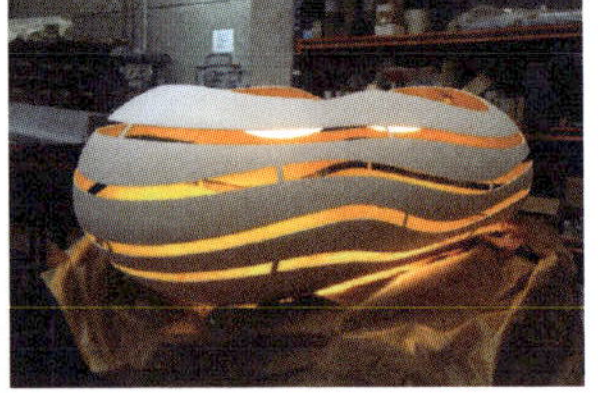

Tree Light and Tree Potato
dab

2006

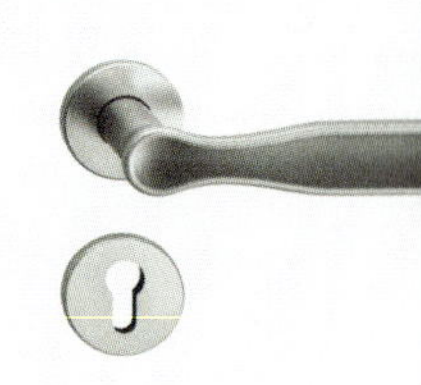

Concave-Convex Handle
FSB

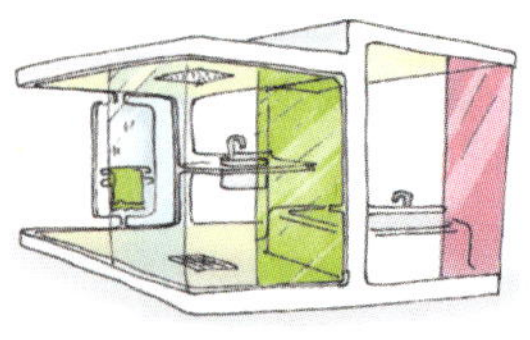

Alape
Bathroom concepts

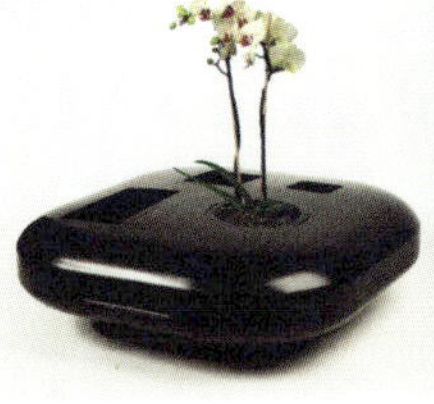

Tablehub
DuPont Corian

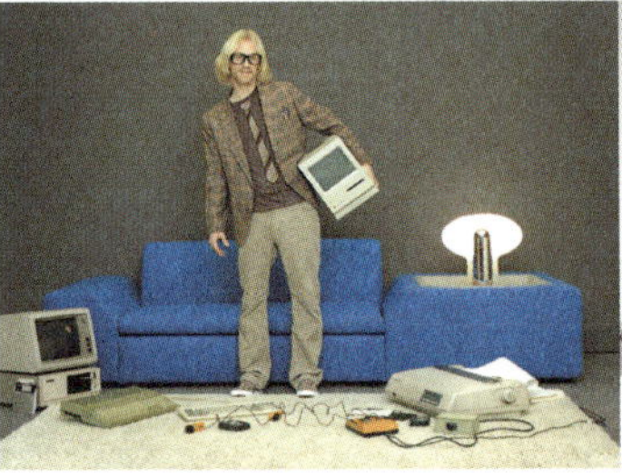

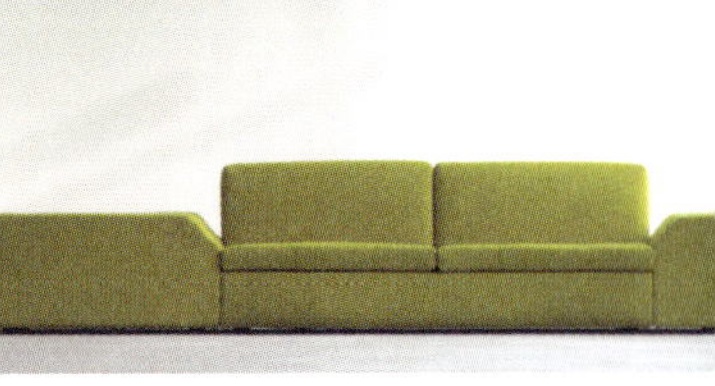

Low Sofa
Joquer

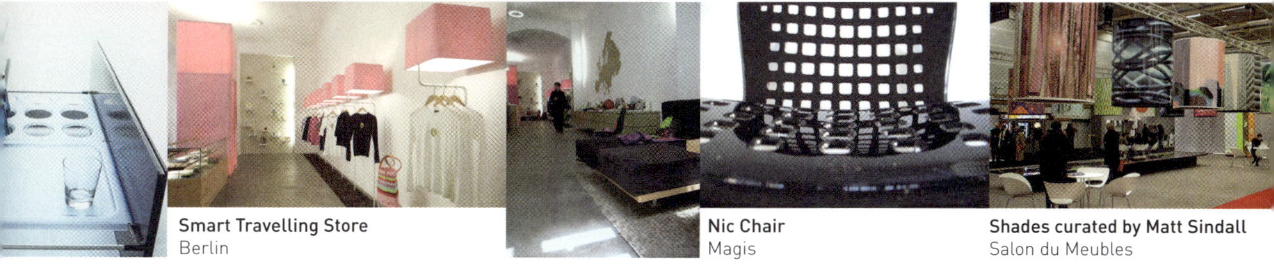

Smart Travelling Store
Berlin

Nic Chair
Magis

Shades curated by Matt Sindall
Salon du Meubles

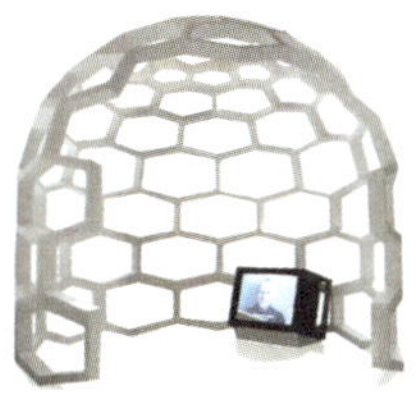

Microdome
edition

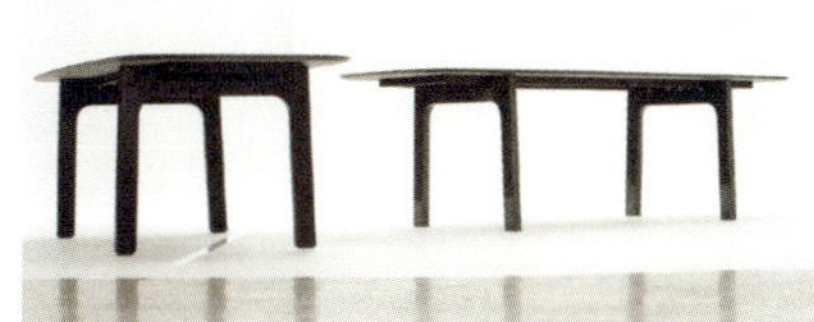

Loop, Stone Table
Draenert

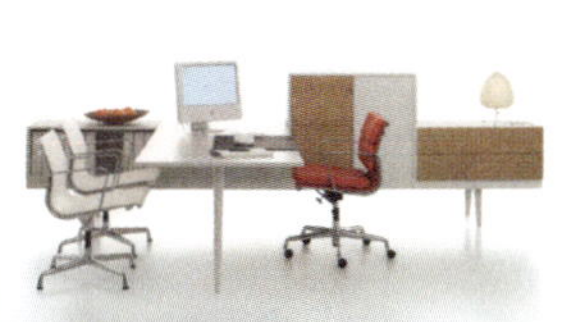

Level 34
Vitra

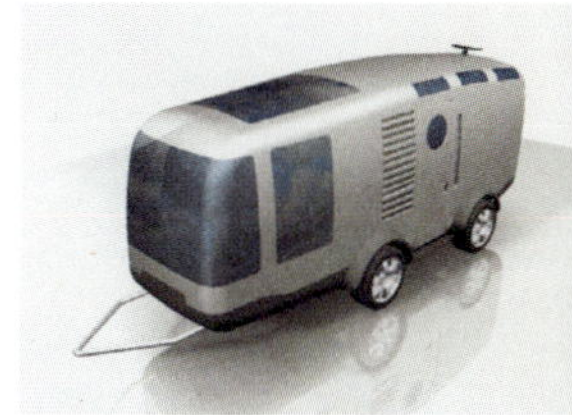

SUT-Trailer
concept, Crossmobil

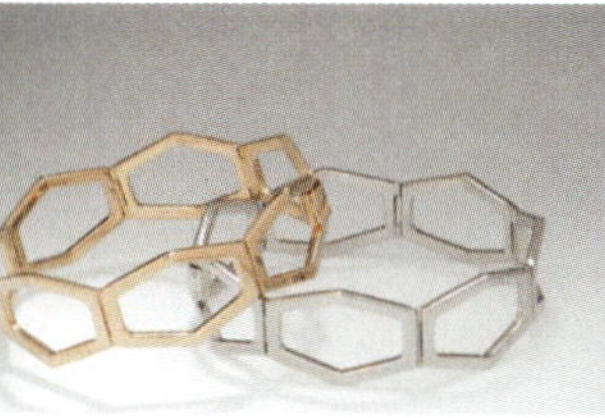

Dome Collection
Biegel Jewellery

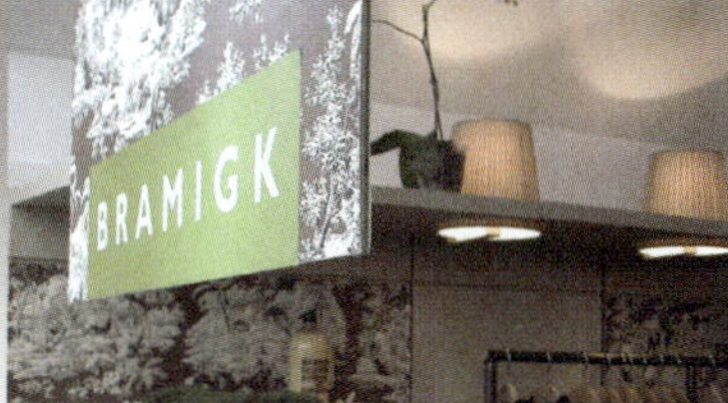

Bramigk Design Store
Berlin

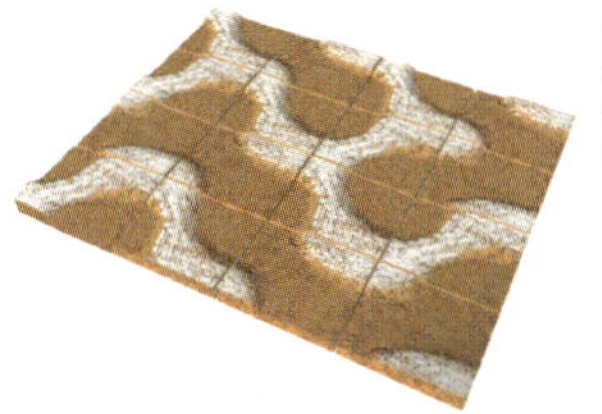

Modular Cookie Landscape
Pappilan, Bolzano

2005

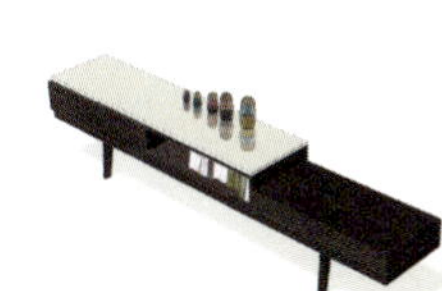

Home Bench
Vitra

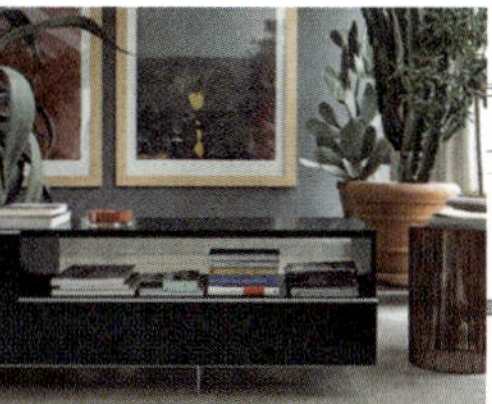

Horizon
Piure

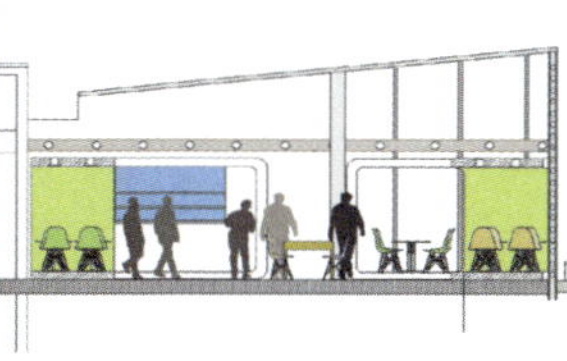

Wolfsburg Wallino
Museum coffee shop concept

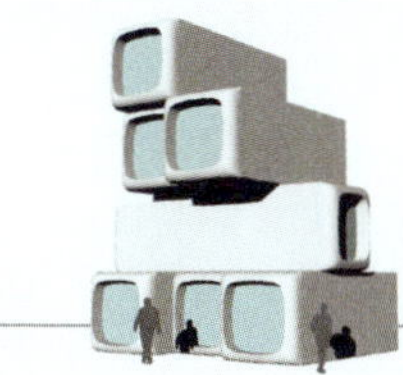

Container Houses
concept, GE

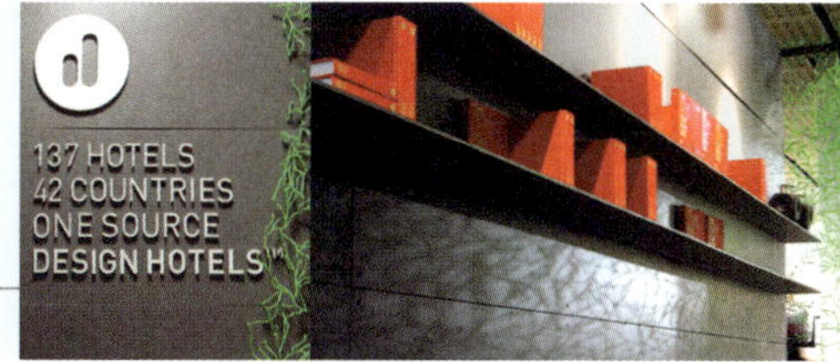

Designhotels Fair Stand ITB Berlin
Designhotels

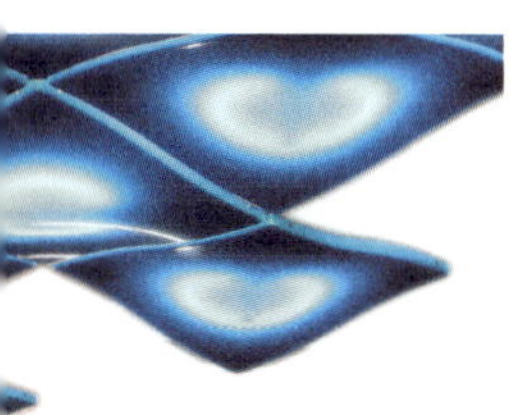

Light Wave Installation
Bombay Sapphire

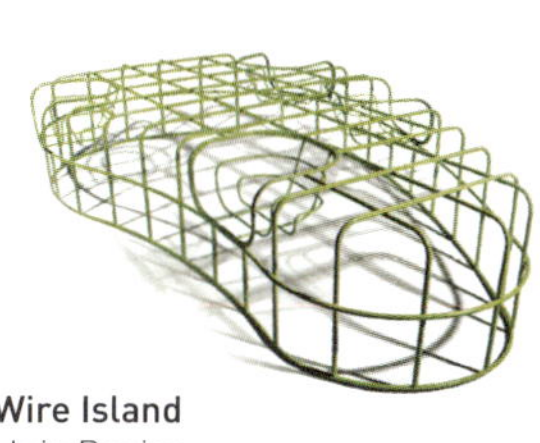

Wire Island
Unic Design

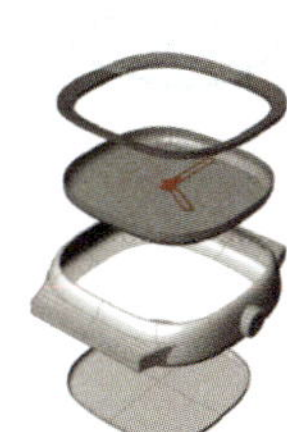

Softsquare
concept, Lorenz

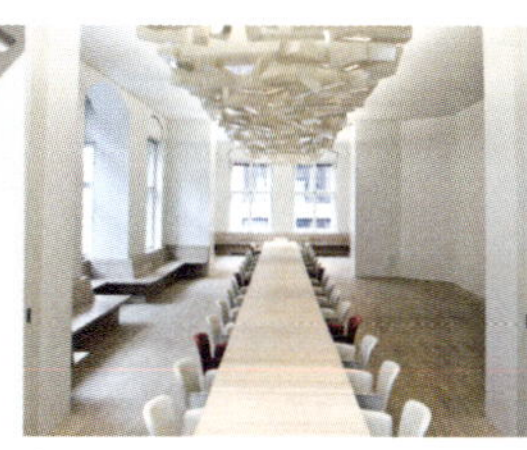

School of Governance Berlin
Interior design

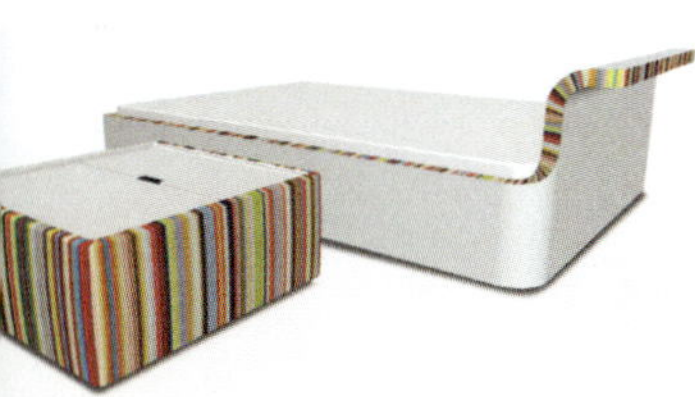

Low Bed and Pouff
Joquer

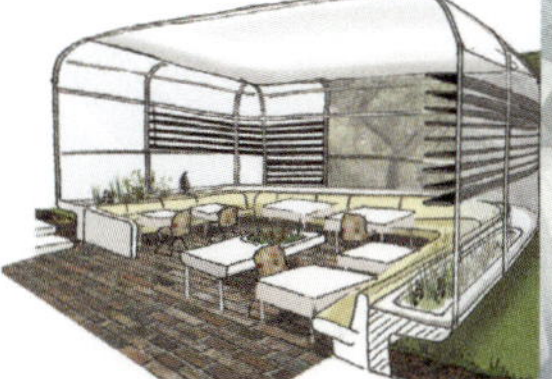

Hotel St. George HH
concept for Gastwerk GmbH

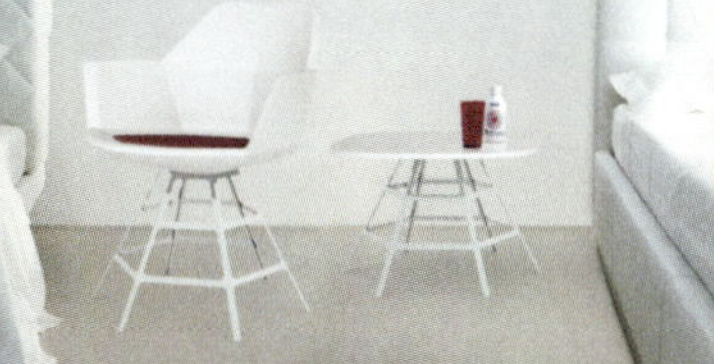

ROL Armchair
Viccarbè

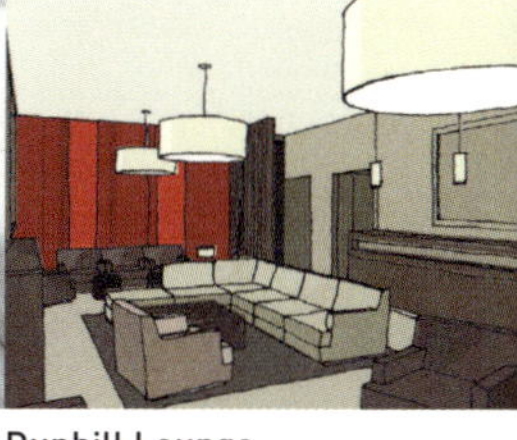

Dunhill Lounge
concept, Berlin

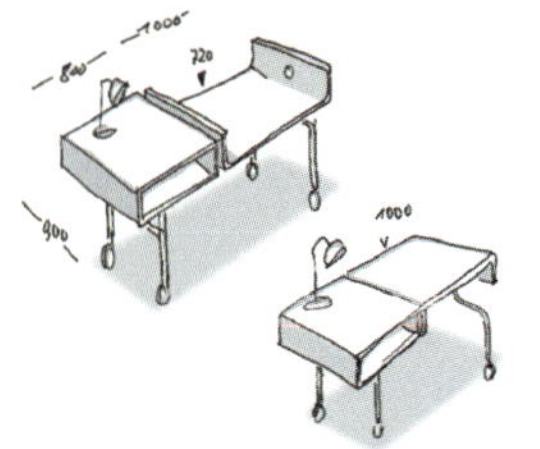

student furniture concept, Kortrijk
Hogeschool West-Vlaanderen

2007

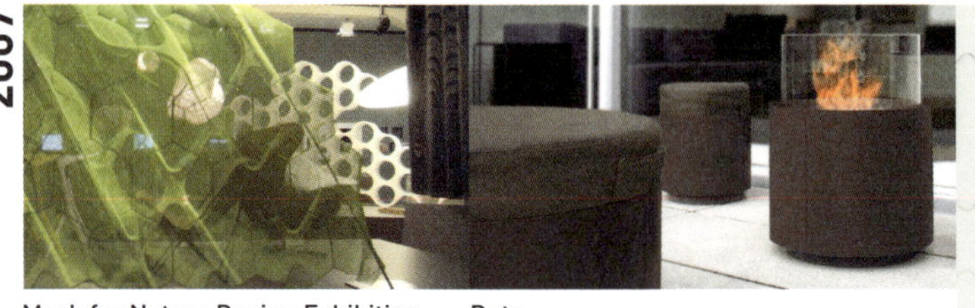

Mesh for Nature Design Exhibition
Museum für Gestaltung Zürich

Dots
Conmoto

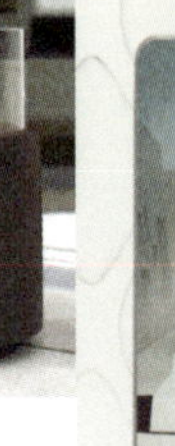

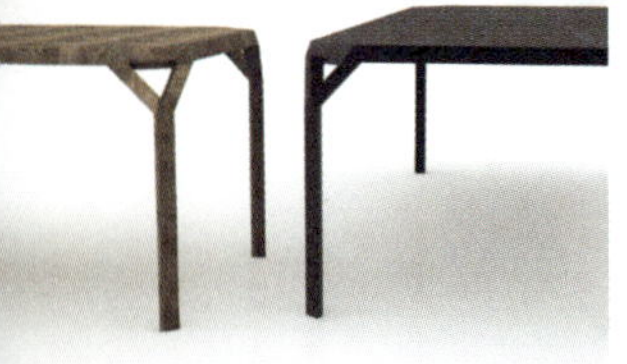

Porro Table
project, Porro

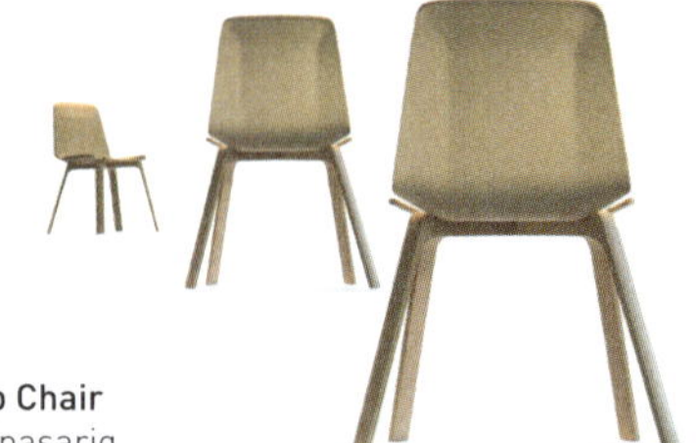

Gap Chair
Fornasarig

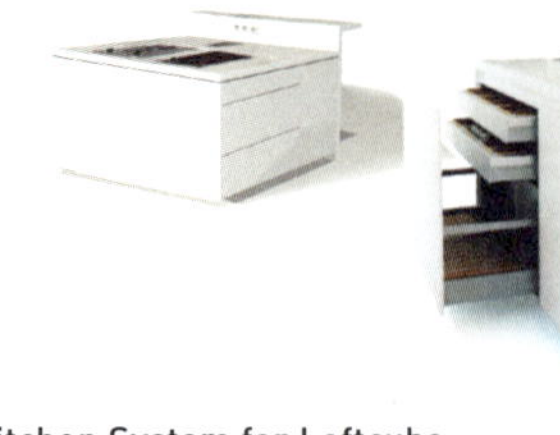

Bathroom System
DuPont - Loftcube

Kitchen System for Loftcube
Bulthaup

2008

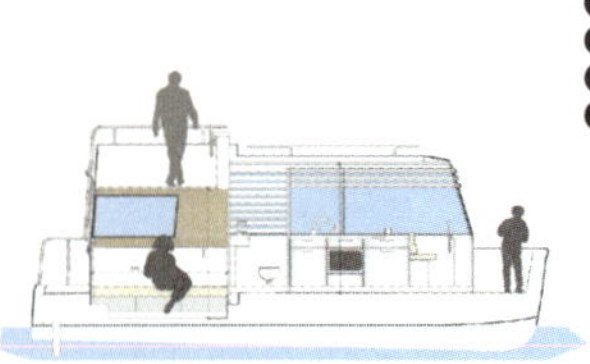

Houseboat
concept, Kuhnle Werft

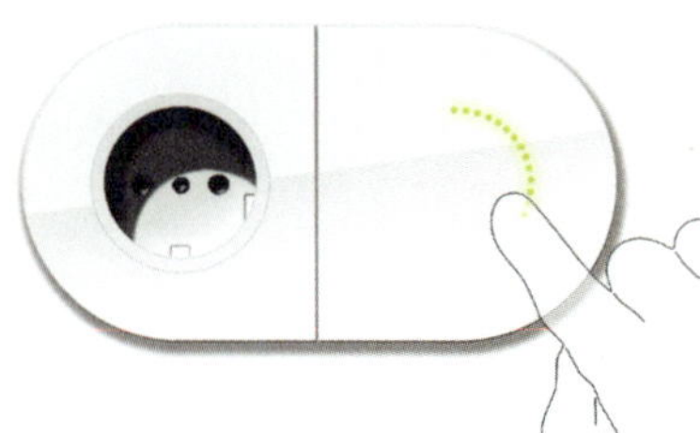

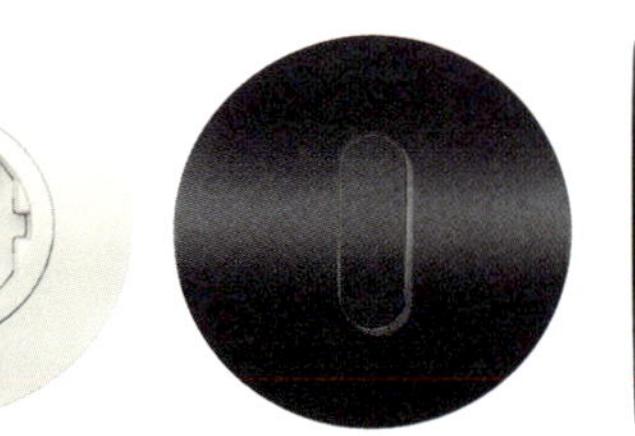

R1 - switch
concept, Berker

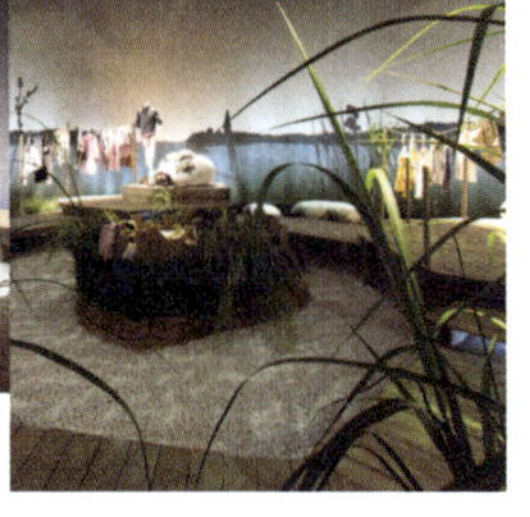

Marco Polo - Fair Presentations
Firenze (autumn/spring)

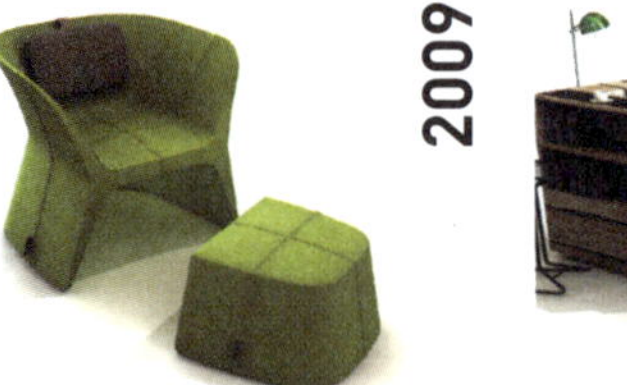

Coalesse Seating
project

2009

Boss Orange Shop
concept, Hugo Boss

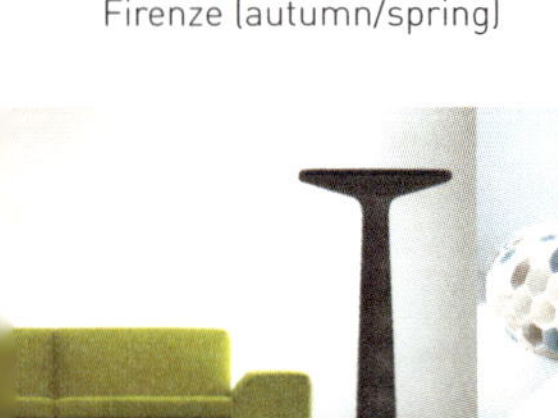

Meshlight
edition

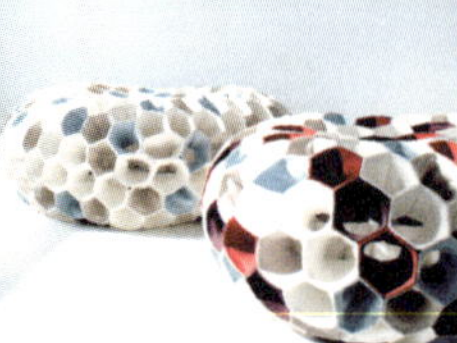

Coral Seating Modules
edition

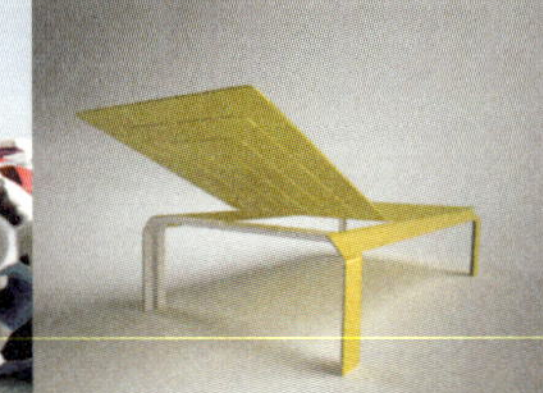

Samoa Chaise outdoor
Samoa

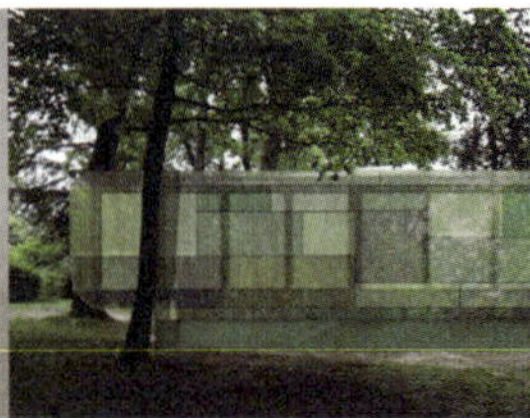

Pavilion Museum
concept Haus am Waldsee

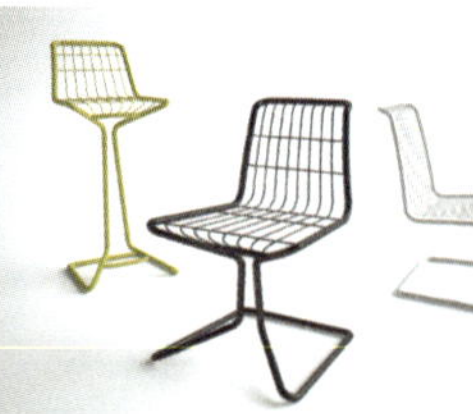

A-Chair with Tina Bunyaprasit
L´abbate

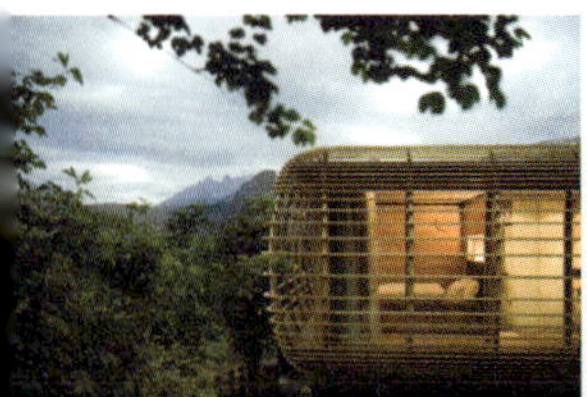

Fincube
nomadic house, South Tyrol

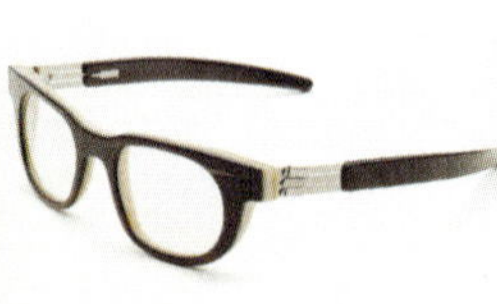

Onono Collection
ic-berlin!

2010

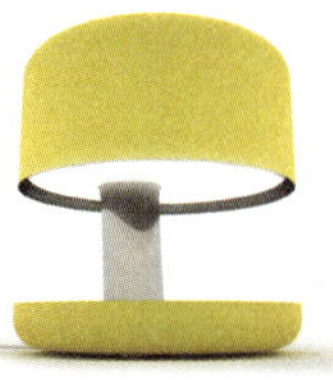

Glas Table Lamp
concept

A Chair Wood
L´abbate

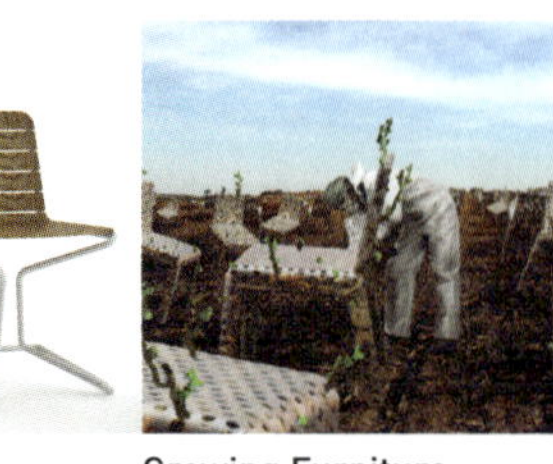

Growing Furniture
Plantation concept

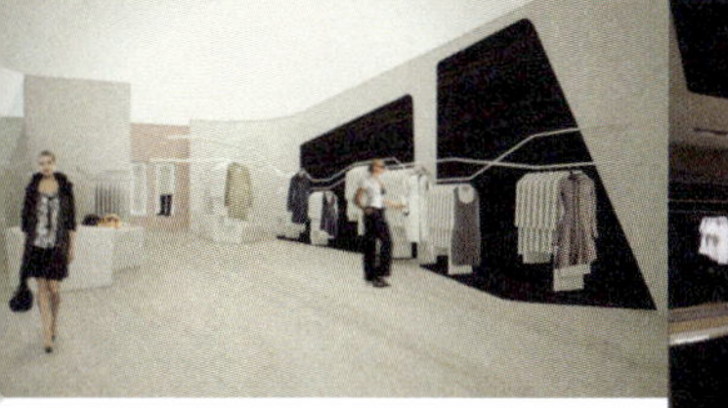

Laurel Shop
concept, Laurel

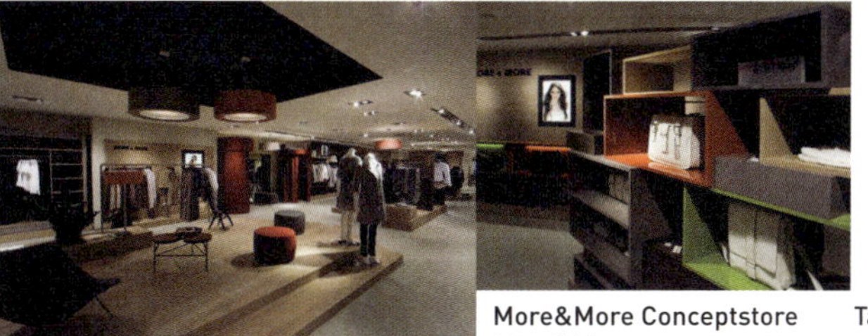

More&More Conceptstore
More&More

Table hub
concept, Alessi

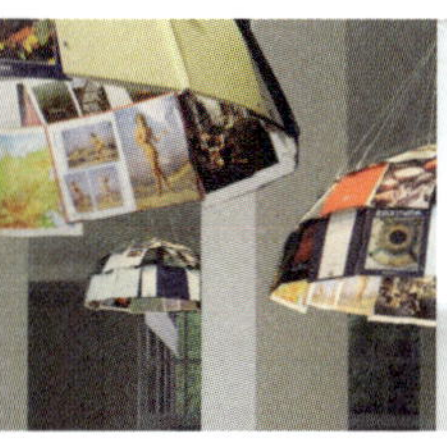

Books Lamp
edition

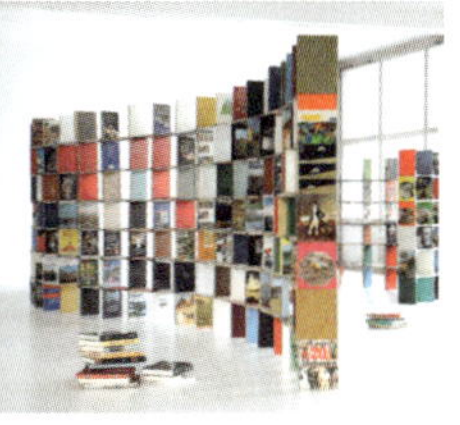

Books
edition

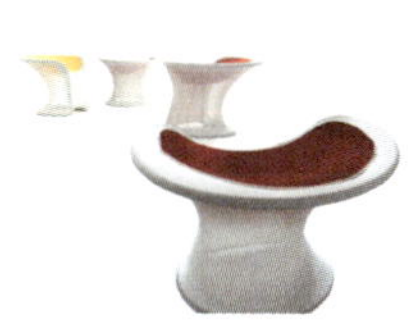

Knitted Chair
edition with Wörner GmbH

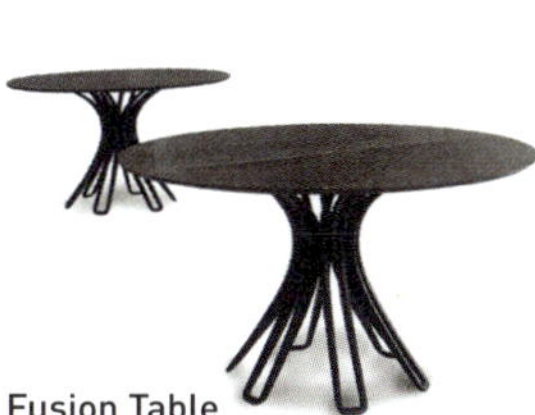

Fusion Table
Draenert

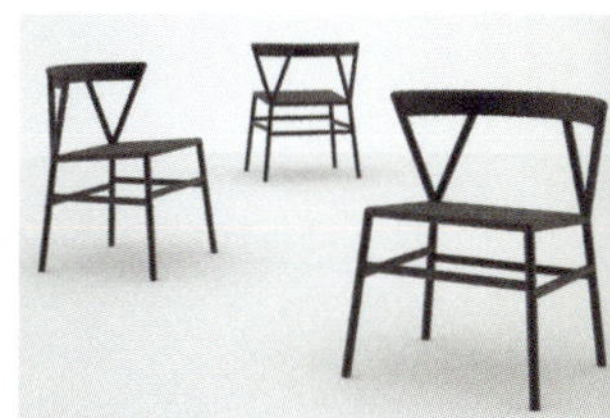

Wood Chair
concept, Porro

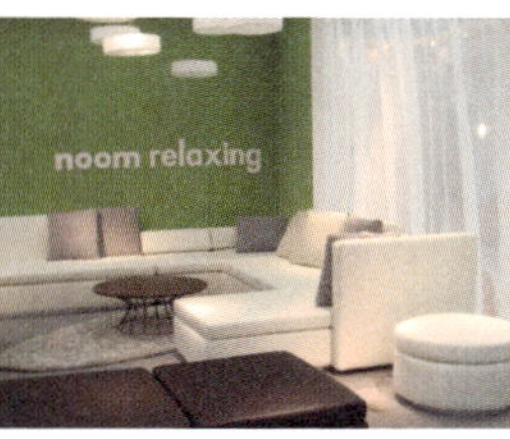

Noom Collection
Berdini Design

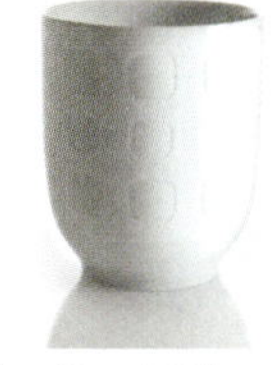

Berker Cup 2004
Berker

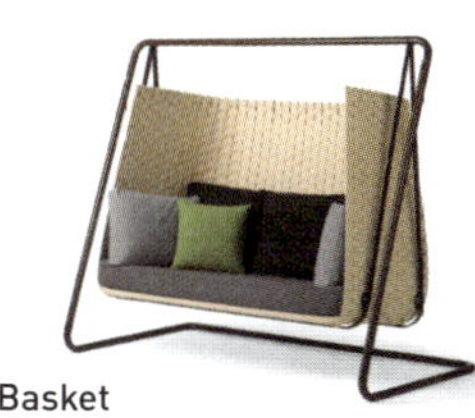

Basket
Vitra

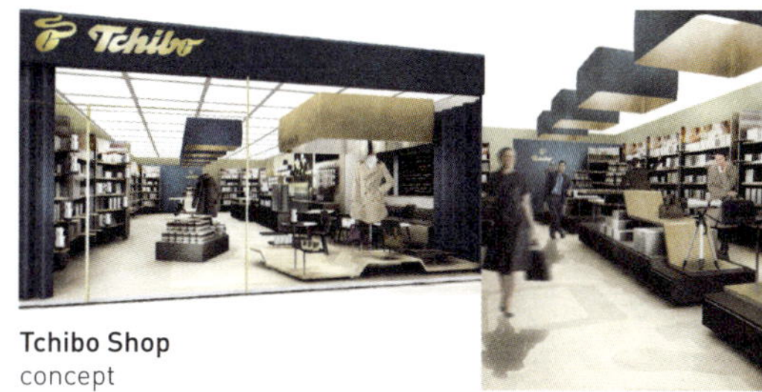

Tchibo Shop
concept

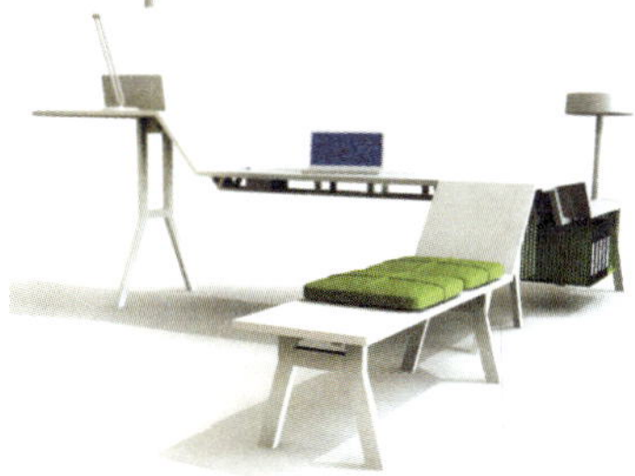

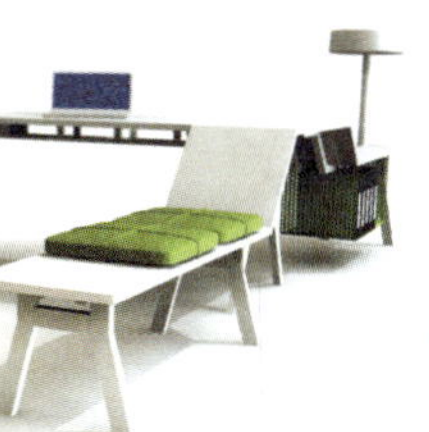

Flow - Office Landscape System
Office Planner, Singapore

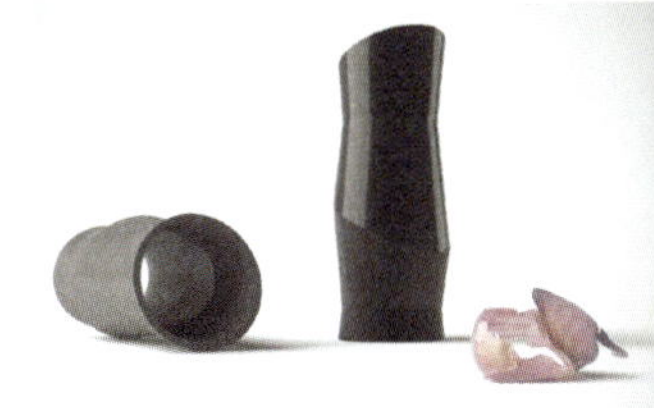

Garlic Peeler
project, Koziol

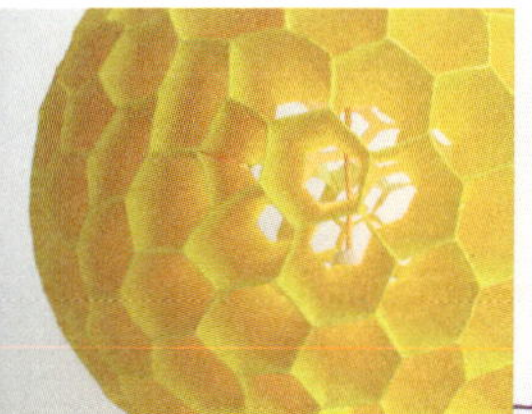

Coral Light
edition

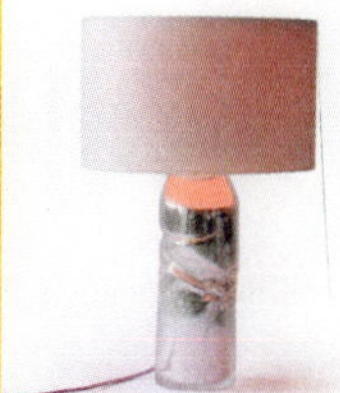

Mesh Vase Lamp
edition

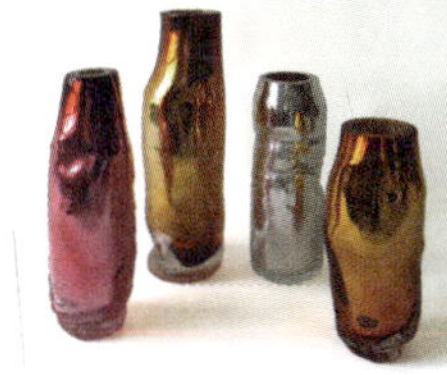

Mesh Vase
Lumas/CIAV Meisenthal

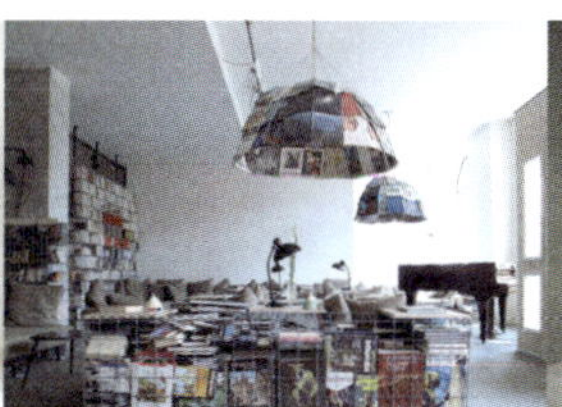

Michelberger Hotel, interior
Berlin

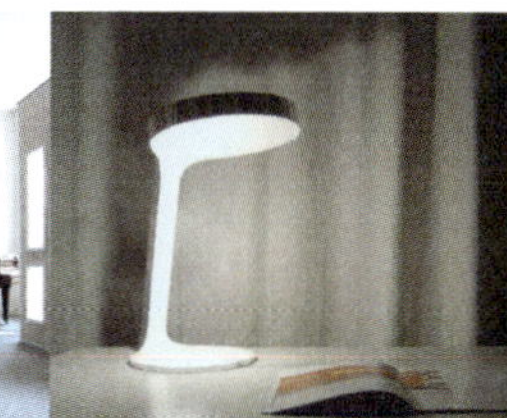

Screen Table Lamp
prototype

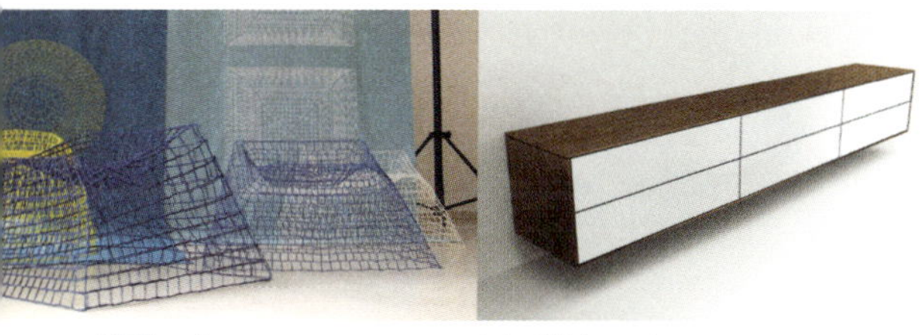

NETwork
edition with Gerber GmbH

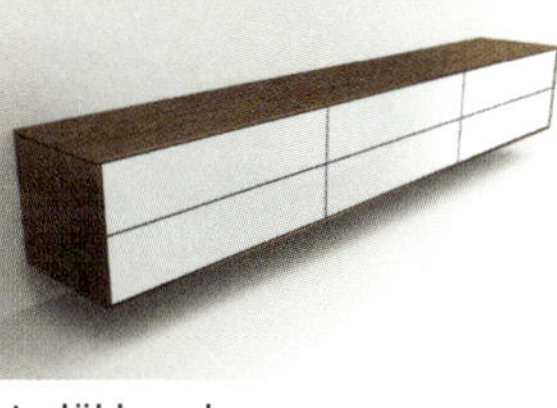

Interlübke cube x
2010

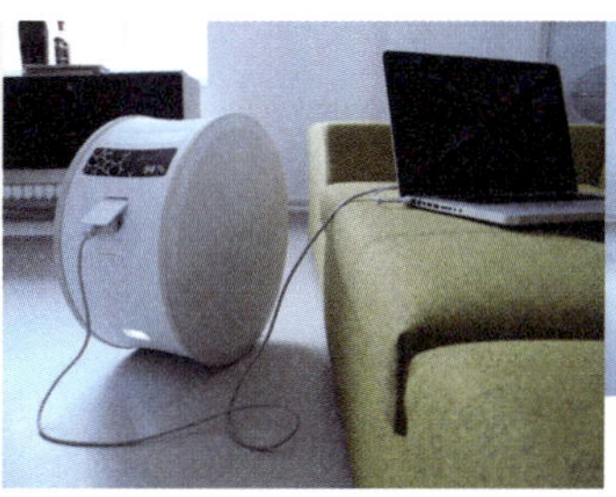

Yill office energy charger
Younicos AG

exhibitions 2010 »Schöner Sitzen. 50 Jahre Stuhldesign, Museum für Kunst und Gewerbe, Hamburg« »bewußt, einfach. Das Entstehen einer alternativen Produktkultur, Volker Albus and Institut für Auslandsbeziehungen e.V. (ifa), Mexiko City« »anders als immer. Zeitgenössisches Design und die Macht des Gewohnten, Volker Albus and Institut für Auslandsbeziehungen e.V. (ifa), Wellington - Auckland - Melbourne« »Design Deutschland 2010 - presented by German Design Council at the ICFF, International Contemporary Furniture Fair in New York and Milan« »DMY - Open Process, Made in Berlin 2010, Zona Tortona, Milan« »DMY - 2010, Berlin« »Vases vs. Vases, Helmrinderknecht contemporary design gallery, Berlin« **2009** »Solo exhibition "Designstory" at Mobitex, Brno, Slovakia« »New Olds, Institut für Auslandsbeziehungen e.V. (ifa), Stuttgart« »DMY - Made in Berlin 2009, Berlin« »Made in Berlin 2009, Create Berlin members in Milan, Italy« »Interieur/Exterieur – Wohnen in der Kunst – Kunstmuseum Wolfsburg, Germany« »Micro House, Bielefelder Kunstverein, Bielefeld, Germany« »Nullpunkt – Nieuwe German Gestaltung, MARTa Herford, Germany« »DMY Asia Exhibition Tour 2009, Taiwan, Tokyo, Seoul, Singapore« »40 Chairs - Invitational Exhibition of World renowned designers' works, CAFA Art Museum, Beijing« **2008** »ZKM Museum Karlsruhe, 2008, Vertrautes Terrain – Karlsruhe, Germany« »Spain Playtime – Fresh Air in Spanish Design, Zona Tortona, Milano« **2007** »Corian(R): 40 Years / 40 Designers, at Design Within Reach-Meatpacking/Chelsea Studio, New York City« »Suitcases from Berlin - Koffer aus Berlin, Ausstellung M Project Galery, New York« »Full house, Ausstellung im Haus am Waldsee, Designmai, Berlin« »loftcube, Ausstellung fuori salone, Exansaldo, Milan« »Corian(R): 40 Years /40 Designers, salone Milan« »design seating for design eating, fornasarig, Triennale, Milan« »books, Installation in der Christuskirche, Passagen Cologne« »Second Skin, Vitra Design Museum, Weil am Rhein, Germany« **2006** »Light Wave presentation, Blue Collection of Bombay Saphire, Lichtwerk Altona, Hamburg, Germany« »FSB, Paar Klinken, Exhibition Stilwerk, Berlin« »5x5 Project-Designers & Producers, Interieur, Designregio Kortrijk, Belgien« »Create Berlin "Best of Berlin", Ausstellung "Red Moscow", Moskau« »Sitzen ist Kunst, Kunstgewerbemuseum, Berlin« »Loftcube, ArchiSkulptur, Kunstmuseum, Wolfsburg« »Second Skin, Designausstellung Zeche Zollverein, Essen« »Loftcube, Eight Belgrade Triennal of World Architecture, Belgrad« **2005** »Loftcube, Woonmecca, Maastricht« »B to B Designausstellung, Brüssel« »Berlin Design / Designyoungsters, Seoul« »Jung + Deutsch, Hillside Terrace Gallery, Tokyo« »Vitra Level 34 presentation, Semperdepot, Wien« »Loftcube, Deutschlandschaft im Victoria & Albert Museum, London« »Vitra Level 34 show, Brüssel« »About Design Ausstellung auf der Tendence Fair, Frankfurt« »Vitra Level 34 showroom, London« »Anders als Immer, German design exhibition at Townhouse Gallery, Cairo« »Jung + Deutsch, design exhibition at edisonhöfe, designmai, Berlin« »Vitra Level 34 am Pfefferberg, designmai, Berlin« **2004** »Loftcube, Beitrag des deutschen Pavillons, 9. Architektur Biennale, Venedig« »Pappilan, Tendence Fair, Frankfurt« »Design Berlin!, Cube Gallery, Manchester« »Shades, Salon du Meuble de Paris« **2003** »Pappilan, Free University of Bozen-Bolzano« »Loftcube, t'Huis Front 2, Amsterdam« »Design Bloc, Prague« »Construire l'éphémère, EXPO.03, Neuchâtel« »Loftcube, Designmai, Berlin« »Design Berlin!, Vitra Design Museum, Berlin« »Habiter la lumière, French Cultural Center, Milan« »Take a Seat, Vitra Design Museum, Berlin« **2002** »Living in motion, Vitra Design Museum, Weil am Rhein« »milan in a van, Victoria & Albert Museum, London« **2001** »Exhibition Compasso D'Oro, Pallazzo Triennale, Milan« **2000** »Aperto Vetro 2000, Museo Correr, Venice« »soft cell-down light, Galerie Fiedler, Köln« **1999** »Identity crises, the 90's defined, Glasgow« »soft cellTM galleria la posteria, Mailand« **1998** »bewusst, einfach, Vitra Design Museum, Weil am Rhein« »bio 16 –industrial design biennale, Ljubjana« »Design-yearbook collection, Museum for Applied Arts, Cologne« **1997** »Design-time Bremen, Neues Museum, Weserburg« **1996** »Smart-China, 10 European Designer, Galerie Arosa 2000, Frankfurt« »Exhibition Bundespreis Produktdesign, Frankfurt« **1995** »Exhibition Compasso D'Oro, Pallazzo Reale, Milan« »Design-time Bremen, Neues Museum Weserburg« **1994** »Design Innovationen, Design Center, Essen« **1993** »Designer's Saturday, Düsseldorf«

awards 2008 »Mejor Diseño de Luminaria, Barcelona, for dab "tree series" Recognition from the Selci association, to the best product of lightning 2008 made in Spain« **2006** »Hotel of The Year, Expo Real, Munich, for "hotel daniel"« »Red Dot Award, Essen, for "loop"« **2005** »FX Award UK "Best System Furniture", London, for "level34", Vitra« **2004** »Premio Compasso D'Oro, Milan, for "plus unit"« »Red Dot Award, Essen, for "cube"« **2002** »Red Dot Award, Essen, for "plus unit"« **2001** »Compasso D'Oro-selection, Milano, for "soft chaise"« »Selection Centre Georges Pompidou "Carrefour de la création", Paris, for "soft chaise"« **2000** »ADI Design Index, Milan, for "soft chaise"« »Red Dot Award, Essen, for "x-table"« »Selection bio 17- design biennale, Ljubljana, with "soft cell"« »Blueprint 100 % Design Award, Lodon, for "soft chaise"« **1998** »Selection bio 16 - design biennale, Ljubljana, with "juli chair"« **1996** »Design Prize of the Federal Republic of Germany, German Design Council, Frankfurt, for "endless shelf"« **1995** »Compasso D'Oro selection, Milan, for "endless shelf"« **1994** »Design-selection Red Dot Award, Essen, for "endless shelf"« »Wogg Design Preis, Zürich for "x-system"« **1992** »Design Plus, Frankfurt, for "otto chair"«

museum collection 2010 Mesh Vases - Neue Sammlung, Pinakothek der Moderne, Munich, Germany **2008** Nic Chair, Magis - Permanent Collection MoMA, Museum of Modern Art, New York, USA **2008** Mesh Wall - Sammlung Museum für Gestaltung, Zürich, Switzerland **2006** Juli Chair, Cappellini - Neue Sammlung, Pinakothek der Moderne, Munich, Germany **2006** Nic Chair, Magis - Museum of Applied Arts, Kunstgewerbemuseum Berlin, Germany **2004** Plus Unit, Magis - Neue Sammlung, Pinakothek der Moderne, Munich, Germany **2003** Nic Chair, Magis - Fonds National d'Art Contemporain, Paris, France **2002** Soft Chaise, Zanotta - Fonds National d'Art Contemporain, Paris, France **2001** Soft Chaise, Zanotta - Permanent Collection Metropolitan Museum, New York, USA **2000** Soft Cell, Designcollection Vitra Design Museum, Weil am Rhein, Germany **1999** Juli Chair, Cappellini - Designcollection Vitra Design Museum, Weil am Rhein, Germany **1998** Juli Chair, Cappellini - Permanent Collection MoMA, Museum of Modern Art, New York, USA **1996** Endless Shelf, Porro - Neue Sammlung, Pinakothek der Moderne, Munich, Germany

Werner Aisslinger

Born in Nördlingen, Germany	**1964**
Grew up in Kempten/Allgäu in Bavaria	
Studied Design at University of Arts	**1987**
(Hochschule der Künste), Berlin	**1992**
Freelancer at Jasper Morrison and Ron Arad	**1989**
in London, and at Studio de Lucchi in Milan	**1992**
Founded "studio aisslinger" in Berlin,	**1993**
focusing on product design, design concepts	
and brand architecture	
Visiting teacher at the Berlin University	**1994**
of Arts and Lahti Design Institute, Finland	**1997**
Design Professor at Design College	**1998**
(Hochschule für Gestaltung), Karlsruhe	
(Department of Product Design) until 2004	
Cofounder of DESIGNMAI - designfestival Berlin	**2003**
Project supervisor at Designlabor Bremerhaven	**2005**
Permanent Jury Member and Curator	**2006**
of the Raymond Loewy Foundation and	since
Jury of the Lucky Strike Design Award	**2006**
Guest Professorship at Design College	
(Hochschule für Gestaltung), Karlsruhe	**2008**
Creative Curator of DMY Festival	**2010**

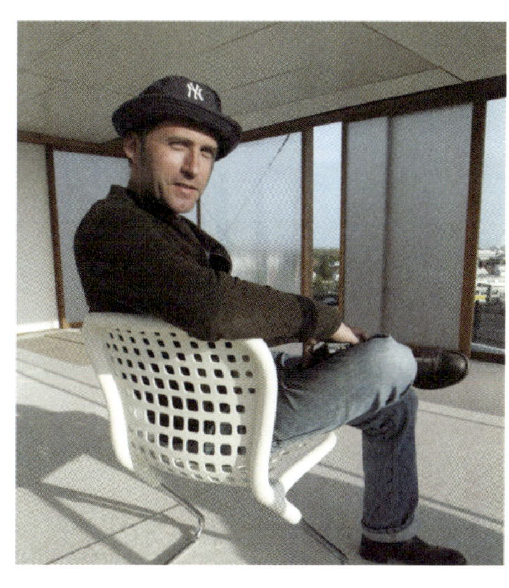

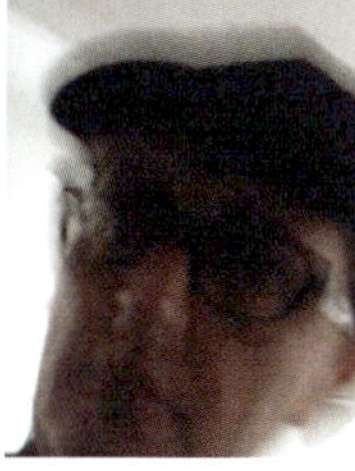

Volker Albus studied architecture. Since 1982 he has been working as a freelance architect and designer and since 1994 teaching as professor for product design at the Karlsruhe University of arts and design. He is an internationally renowned design journalist, co-editor of various design books and contributes to numerous magazines of architecture and design.

Volker Albus *studierte Architektur, ist seit 1984 freiberuflich als Architekt und Designer tätig und lehrt seit 1994 als Professor für Produktdesign an der Hochschule für Gestaltung in Karlsruhe. Als international bekannter Designpublizist ist er Mitherausgeber verschiedener Designbücher und für zahlreiche Architektur- und Designzeitschriften tätig.*

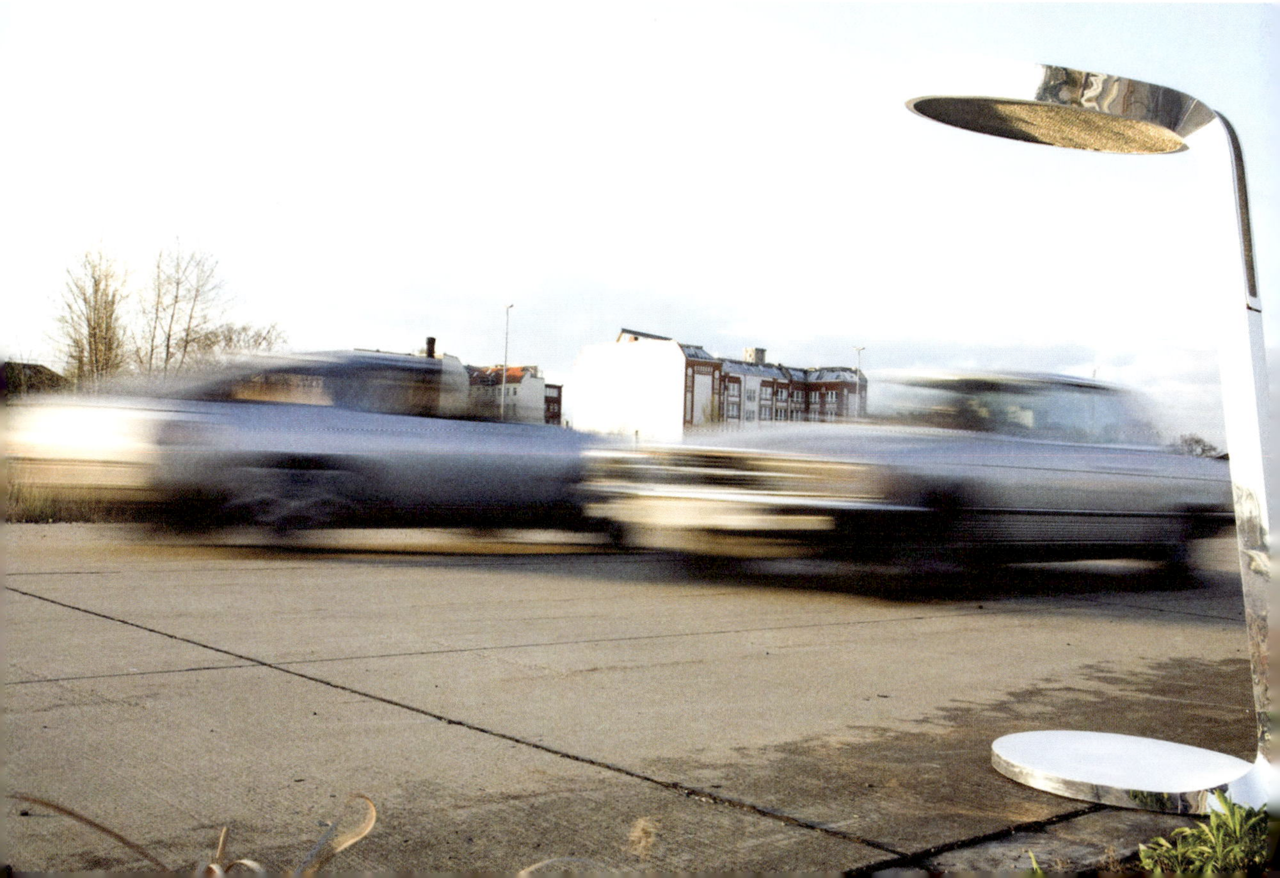

special thanks to Nicola Bramigk, Rolf & Renate Aisslinger, Achim Aisslinger, Julian & Florentin, Steffen Jänicke, James Irvine, Tina
thanks to Achim Gustavus, Ake Rudolf, Alexander Voigt, Alberto Perazza, Andreas Bracht, Andreas Brandolini, Andreas Radmer, Angela Schlicht, Angela Schönberger, Angeli Sachs, Anna Bernagozzi, Anna Bolletta, Anna Rojahn, Anne Havliza, Anne Urbauer, Antje Wewer, Arik Levy, Axel Kufus, Benita Braun Feldweg, Benjamin Hosbach, Bernard Petry, Bettina Schadow, Birgit Schmoltner, Branco Kecur, Camilla Peus, Carsten Kunze, Chantal Hamaide, Christian Friedrich, Christoph Fleckenstein, Claudio Greco, Claus Sendlinger, Daniele Greppi, David Abad, Detlef Bramigk, Detlef Mika, Dieter Eckert, Eberhard Laabs, Egon Bräuning, Egon Chemaitis, Eleonora Zanotta, Elke Trappschuh, Elmar Flötotto, Elmar Schüller, Eugenio Perazza, Felix Brandl, Filip Peers, Florian Hufnagl, Florian Kirchmeier, Florian Weitzer, Alessandro Vechiato, Francesca Martin, Frederik Flötotto, Friedhelm Laschütza, Gabriele Bramigk, Gabriele Gebert, Gavin Woo, Gilda Bojardi, Giulio Cappellini, Gregor Wöltje, Grit Seymour, Hans Jerg Maier Aichen, Harald Börsch, Hein Kleihues, Hermann Breitegger, Holger Boeven, Ingo Fast, Ingo Strobel, Jana Semeradova, Jasper Morrison, Jens Biegel, Jens Nordlohne, Jiri Zavadil, Joachim Kobuss, Joachim Sauter, Joana Breidenbach, Johann Tomforde, Johannes Wagner, Jörg Suhrmann, Josef Ackermann, Josef Innerhofer, Jovan Jelovac, Jürgen Plüss, Kai Hollmann, Karl Heinz Mohr, Kathinka Grelich, Katja Blomberg, Kerstin Reisch, Ken Koo, Kurt Weidemann, Leo Lübke, Helmut Lübke, Lorenzo Porro, Luca Fornasarig, Ludvika Kanicka, Manuel Vital, Marc Dubois, Marcel Wanders, Marianne van Dodewaard, Marion Godau, Mariusz Zac, Markus Jans, Markus Lobis, Markus Roessle, Marva Griffin, Mateo Kries, Matt Sindall, Matthias Dietz, Matthias Mai, Matthias Prast, Matti Matthes, Melanie Porcella, Michele de Lucchi, Mick Weidenmüller, Mike Meire, Mirko Van den Winkel, Moniek Bucquoye, Moritz Wilborn, Nicole Losos, Nic Bewick, Nic Hafermas, Nick Roericht, Nils Holger Moormann, Nils Jockel, Noreen Süsse, Norbert Ruf, Oliver Kraft, Patrick Chia, Patrick Draenert, Peter Fiell, Peter Pfeiffer, Peter Zec, Petra Kiedaisch, Rainer Mutsch, Ralph Anderl, Robert Birker, Rolf Fehlbaum, Ron Arad, Sabine Voggenreiter, Sevil Peach, Stefan & Anja Böwer, Stefan Koziol, Stefan Legner, Stefan Liske, Stefan Rothert, Stephan Schwarke, Stefano Barbazza, Stefano L´Abbate, Stephan Breidenbach, Steven Morgan, Susanne Schwenger, Teresa Carratero, Thomas Biswanger, Thomas Edelmann, Tim Brauns, Tina Bunyaprasit, Till Grosch, Tom Michelberger, Tory Lichterman, Ulrich Gerber, Volker Albus, Volker Domroes, Walter Wörner, Wolfgang Laubersheimer, Wolfgang Reul, Yann Grienenberger

photo credits

6, 8, 9, 14, 16, 24, 25, 28, 31, 34, 35, 38, 39, 44, 45, 48, 49, 54 55, 58, 59, 82, 83, 86, 87, 93, 103, 158, 159, 182, 183, 184, 185	**steffen jaenicke**
studio panorama, 18, 56, 57, 122, 123, 127, 163, 185	**markus roessle**
53, 62, 63, 65, 67, 88, 89, 94, 95, 96, 97, 110 111, 112(top), 120, 121, 148, 149	**rahel streiff**
7, 15, 72, 73, 76, 150, 151, 156 (right/top), 185, 187	**miro zagnoli for vitra**
90, 91	**tom nagy**
22, 23	**werner huthmacher for berker**
139 (part of)	**marc seelen**
32, 33, 36, 37	**dirk wilhelmy for loftcube**
109	**christian kerber**
17, 46, 47, 186	**hannes meraner for fincube**
166, 167	**lumas Courtesy www.lumas.com**
162 (left/top)	**dab**
5, 13, 183	**porro**
5, 14, 112 (fourth), 183	**cappellini**
64, 117, 119, 182	**magis**
112 (second, third)	**arte metropolis**
182, 183	**james pfaff for michelberger**
104,105	**roman raake**
182, 183	**idris kolodziej**
183	**albrecht kunkel**
182	**böwer**
182	**jonas&jonas**
184	**zanotta**
182	**view**
182	**zeritalia**
183, 184, 187	**interlübke**
182	**ideal form team**
187	**draehnert**
185	**biegel**
184	**weitzer group**
184	**behr**
184, 185	**piure**
184	**dab**
184	**fsb**
185	**school of governance**
184	**joquer**
186	**conmoto**
187	**more&more**
186	**berker**
186	**ic berlin!**
189 (middle)	**peter zizka**
studio aisslinger	**all other photos and plans**

imprint
Bibliographic information published by Die Deutsche Nationalbibliothek
Die Deutsche Nationalbibliothek lists this publication in the Deutsche Nationalbibliografie; detailed bibliographic data are available on the Internet at http://dnb.ddb.de.

Introduction/*Einleitung* Volker Albus
Project texts/*Projekttexte* Werner Aisslinger
Translations English-German/*Übersetzungen Englisch-Deutsch* Irene Eisenhut
Translations German-English/*Übersetzungen Deutsch-Englisch* Sean McLaughlin
(introduction, several project texts/*Einleitung, teilweise Projekttexte*)
Editing/*Lektorat* Petra Kiedaisch
Proof reading/*Korrektorat* Wiebke Ullmann
Layout/*Design* Nicole Losos, Rahel Streiff, Markus Becker
Printing/*Druck* Dr. Cantz'sche Druckerei, Ostfildern

ISBN 978-3-89986-139-6
Printed in Germany

avedition GmbH königsallee 57, 71638 ludwigsburg, germany
phone +49 7141 1477 391, fax +49 7141 1477 399, kontakt@avedition.de, www.avedition.com
studio aisslinger heidestraße 46-52, 10557 berlin, germany
phone +49 30 315 05 400, fax +49 03 315 05 401, www.aisslinger.de, studio@aisslinger.de

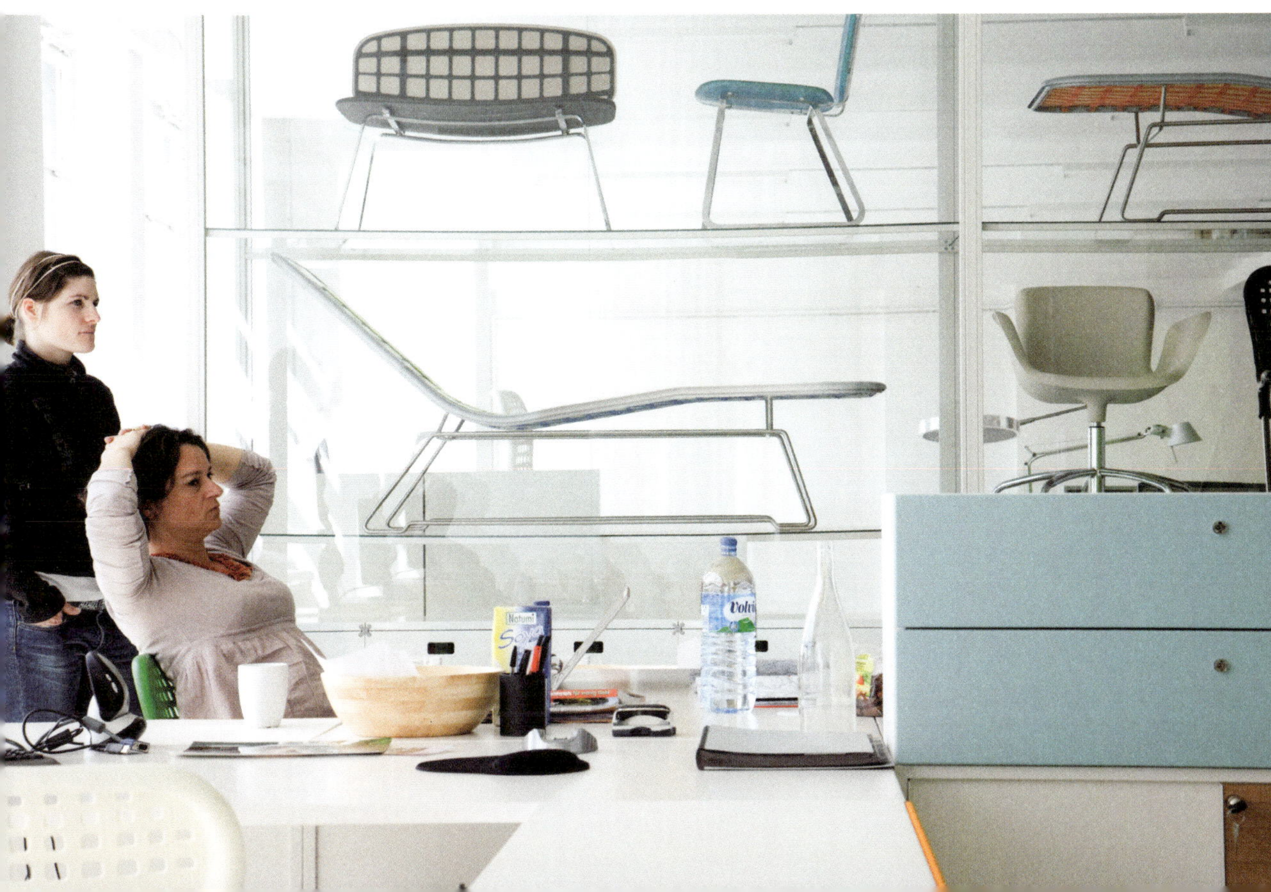

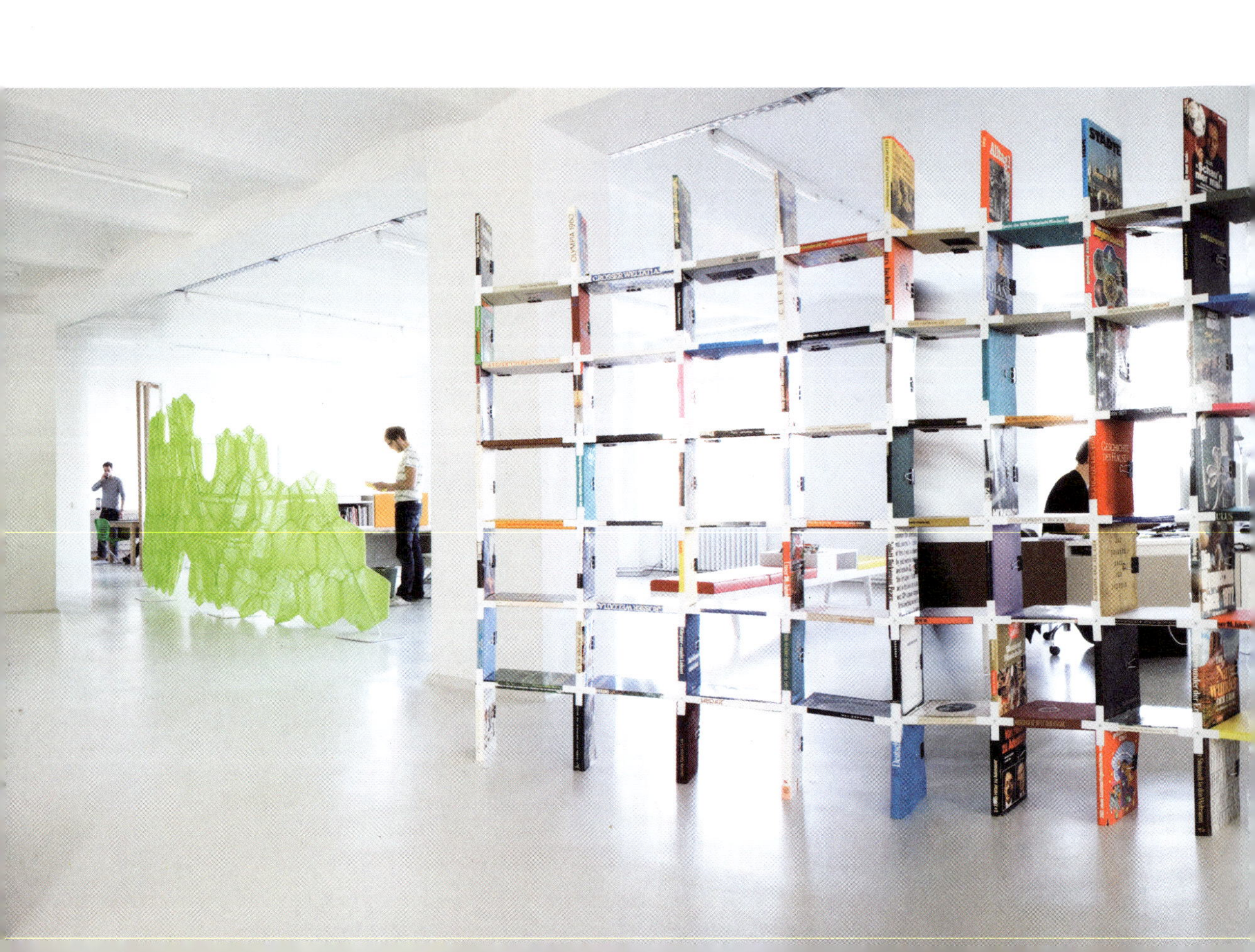
STÄDTE